Beer
FAQ

Beer FAQ

All That's Left to Know About the World's Most Celebrated Adult Beverage

Jeff Cioletti

Backbeat
Books

An Imprint of Hal Leonard Corporation

Published in 2016 by Backbeat Books
An Imprint of Hal Leonard Corporation
7777 West Bluemound Road
Milwaukee, WI 53213

Trade Book Division Editorial Offices
33 Plymouth St., Montclair, NJ 07042

All images are from the auathor's collection unless otherwise noted.

The FAQ series was conceived by Robert Rodriguez and developed with Stuart Shea.

Printed in the United States of America

Book design by Snow Creative

Library of Congress Cataloging-in-Publication Data

Names: Cioletti, Jeff, author.
Title: Beer FAQ : all that's left to know about the world's most popular adult
    beverage / Jeff Cioletti.
Description: Milwaukee, WI : Backbeat, an imprint of Hal Leonard Corporation,
    2016. | Includes bibliographical references and index.
Identifiers: LCCN 2016013887 | ISBN 9781617136115 (pbk.)
Subjects: LCSH: Beer—Miscellanea.
Classification: LCC TP577 .C526 2016 | DDC 641.2/3—dc23
LC record available at https://lccn.loc.gov/2016013887

www.backbeatbooks.com

To my wife, Craige,
who'll always be my No. 1 drinking buddy

Contents

Foreword

A few years back, I watched Jeff Cioletti cut a line of people to jump on the back of a mechanical bull. We were standing in the parking lot of the Karl Strauss Brewing Co. in San Diego after a long day of touring breweries and attending seminars as part of the annual Craft Brewers Conference.

I'm not saying beer was involved in his decision to get on the robotic beast, but in that moment I gained even more admiration for the man. You see, Jeff is a serious guy. He's a journalist. He cares about facts and getting the story right. He sweats the small details along with the big. He's a drinker who carefully examines every glass put in front of him and after a long career can offer accurate feedback to a brewer and helpful advice to a fellow drinker.

Jeff has traveled the world on a mission to uncover stories, to ask questions, and to chronicle one of the planet's most fascinating industries. What you hold now in your hand is his hard work and expert opinion.

Now, you've likely walked into a bar or bottle shop recently to check out the beer selection. It can be a daunting scene of color and styles and alphabet soup like IPA, ESB, IBU, ABV. Unless you've had a beer before, there's no telling what you'll get when you plunk down your hard-earned coin and bring a bottle home; it's rolling the dice.

The same might be true for when you're out at a restaurant and want to find the right beer to pair with dinner. Or when your social media feed is full of options for beer festivals both local and far flung, and you don't know which one or more to visit.

The beer world is full of questions, and Jeff is here to answer them. And in a time where the geeks have the loudest voice and increasingly, disappointingly look down on those just discovering the world's most popular beverage, having a thoughtful, intelligent, and yes, fun-loving journalist as your guide is a great thing.

Contained in the pages to come is all you need to be a better drinker (aside from an actual beer, so now's a good time to go get one). From the processes to the silly bits, to food, fun, and the people themselves, Jeff has brought us all with him to the front of the line, and now it's time to strap in.

John Holl, editor of *All About Beer Magazine*

Acknowledgments

Though I've evolved into more of a cross-drinker these days, beer will always be my first love. The process of writing this book has been akin to drafting a long-form love letter to this majestic beverage. And such an undertaking would not have been possible without the support and contributions of so many individuals.

First off, I'd like to thank my editor, Marybeth Keating, and the entire team at Hal Leonard for entrusting me with this massive project. Additionally, I'd like to give a hearty "prost!" to my agent, John Willig, who continues to help keep me sane throughout the insanity that is book publishing.

And speaking of Johns, a hearty "slainte!" to my friend, trusted advisor, and frequent writing-work-giver, John Holl. His position at the forefront of beer experts is well-earned. I include the rest of the All About Beer gang in that toast as well—especially Chris Rice, Jon Page, Daniel Hartis, Ken Weaver, and last but certainly not least, Daniel Bradford. Cheers to another one of the editors who continues to graciously allow my byline to appear in her magazine, Erika Rietz of Draft Magazine, as well as Draft's beer editor, Kate Bernot. It all comes full circle as those same publications appear quite frequently in my bibliography.

There are so many with whom I've crossed paths over the years who must be acknowledged. Those include, but are definitely not limited to, Brewers Association folk like Julia Herz, Charlie Papazian, Paul Gatza, Andy Sparhawk, Bob Pease, Nancy Johnson, and Barbara Fusco; the National Beer Wholesalers Association's Craig Purser, Rebecca Spicer, Kathleen Joyce, David Christman, Lester Jones, and Paul Pisano; and craft brewing icons like Jim Koch, Ken Grossman, Steve Hindy, Garrett Oliver, Gary Fish, Sam Calagione, Greg Koch, Kim Jordan, Dale Katechis, Irene Firmat, Jamie Emmerson, Jeremy Cowan, Augie Carton, Brock Wagner, Brett Joyce, and the late, truly great Jack Joyce.

And there have been so many people with whom I've shared a pint over the years: industry friends, fellow writers and editors, and generally folks with a similar passion for this frothy beverage (many with even more so): John Kleinchester, Natasha Bahrs, Don Tse, Chris O'Leary, Clare Goggin

Sivits, Adam Sivits, Christopher Shepard, Brian Yaeger, Jeff Alworth, Jay R. Brooks, Ruth Berman, Mary Izett, Chris Cuzme, Lisa Zimmer, Larry Bennett, Allison Capozza, Sarah and Giancarlo Annese, Josh Bernstein, Karen Auerbach, Jeff and Joanna Bauman, and Jim and Lisa Flynn. I'm probably absentmindedly leaving a few people out, but please know it wasn't intentional!

Finally, I want to give a shout-out to the best bar-crawling companion in the world, my wife, Craige Moore. It's fitting that our shared beer journey essentially started the same freezing weekend in Montreal when I proposed to you back in 2003. We fell in love with La Fin du Monde at a tiny (now defunct) TinTin-themed bar in the Vieux Port. It may have been called "La Fin" but it was really "Le début" of an amazing adventure together, in beer and in life.

Introduction
Sit Down, Stay a While, and Have a Beer

T here has never been, in the history of the world, a better time to drink a beer. That may seem a little too absolutist, not to mention hyperbolic, but it's 100 percent true. There has never been a single point throughout earth's existence when there was as much consumer choice as there is at this very moment.

If one were to make such a statement forty years ago, that person would have been laughed right out of the room. The number of American producers had sunk to the mere double digits. And as for the ones that were still producing, they all were pretty much making the same beer: pale, fizzy, industrial lager that was not only light in color but doubly light in flavor. To be sure, the handful that remained were doing quite well, having put small, regional brewers out of business or having absorbed them into their own snowballing operations. The big got bigger and the small . . . well, they just vanished.

But little did mainstream society know that a gargantuan tidal wave was bearing down on legal-drinking-age society. The DIY spirit of a handful of upstart American artisans was driving those enterprising individuals to mine the world's great flavor and style traditions—some still common in their local markets, others nearly extinct—and ultimately returning beer to its former glory.

And now, with more than 4,000 operating breweries in America—a number that's likely to double by 2025—and tens of billions of dollars added to the economy that hadn't been there previously, beer, to paraphrase legendary (albeit fictional) TV anchor Ron Burgundy, is kind of a big deal.

However, it's also a beverage that, more often than not, gets taken for granted by just about everyone who's ever drunk a bottle or pint or glanced at a beer ad or two. It's just . . . always been there.

But most rarely take a second to think about every little step—from the cultivation of ingredients to the design of a can or bottle's label—that goes into getting that drink to the store or bar and, ultimately, into the drinker's hand.

Beer is more than a beverage; it's the culmination of seven millennia of natural happenstance, technological innovation, political upheaval, and shifting social structures. It's the rare invention whose credit belongs equally to science and religion.

And the styles and brand imagery reflect that rather odd juxtaposition between those often contradictory forces. For most of beer's time on earth—remember, we're talking thousands of years here—its delicious, mildly intoxicating existence had been credited to divine forces. And as it survived through civilization after civilization, from the Sumerians to the Egyptians to the Romans and to the medieval citizens of the European feudal system, it ultimately was in the hands of the clergy where it evolved toward its contemporary iterations. Science perfected beer, made it replicable, and brought consistent quality into the equation, but it remains, at its core, art rooted in the spiritual.

Breweries continue to venerate beer's divine heritage by using names and imagery tied to ancient gods and goddesses credited with the beverage's invention, as well as the monastic tradition that formed its bridge to the modern era.

Beer
FAQ

The Birth of Beer

Ancient Traditions Evolve into a Modern Beverage

Beer is a lot older than you might realize. You think such fermented goodness got its start in medieval Europe? Think again. There's archaeological evidence placing the origin of beer—or what ultimately evolved into what we traditionally think of as beer—at around 4000 or 5000 BCE and the dawn of civilization (and why wouldn't such a civilized beverage be as old as civilization itself?). Molecular archaeologists are able to draw these conclusions because they've consistently found traces of ancient chemicals on pottery that would suggest beer's ancestor had been brewed in those clay vessels. There's "written" evidence, as well. Researchers discovered a six-millennia-old stone tablet in Mesopotamia—modern-day Iraq, Kuwait, and parts of Syria and Turkey—with carvings depicting what is believed to be ancient Sumerians drinking from a communal bowl through straws made from reeds.

Of course, there wasn't much science that went into making these crude precursors to what is now the largest alcohol beverage category in the world. The "magic" of fermentation was attributed to the work of the gods—specifically Ninkasi, the goddess of brewing. It wasn't until several millennia later that brewers realized there was no such sorcery involved—only the work of ambient microorganisms converting sugar to alcohol.

One of the Sumerians' earliest writings sings praises to the beer goddess in a poem known by modern scholars as the "Hymn to Ninkasi." Embedded in this lyrical work is what is, essentially, the earliest recorded beer recipe.

It's no accident that Ninkasi was a goddess rather than a god; women were the earliest brewers, a fact that can't be undone even by seven decades of gender-imbalanced advertising that has positioned beer as a "man's drink" by marginalizing and objectifying women. Even through the Middle Ages and the Renaissance period, women did the lion's share of the beer making.

So, what exactly is the deal with this Ninkasi? According to ancient Sumerian mythology, she was the daughter of the goddess of procreation at the temple of Ishtar. Sound familiar? No, it's got nothing to do with the legendary box-office bomb starring Dustin Hoffman and Warren Beatty, but instead it involves a certain holiday that Westerners observe each spring. Yes, Easter, many scholars believe (though it's a topic of much debate), actually derives from Ishtar, the celebration of all things coital and fertile. (Why else would the modern icon for the holiday be a bunny? What other mammalian species reproduces as heartily?)

The apple doesn't fall far from the tree in Ninkasi's case; not only does she provide the world with the secret of brewing, but she also has the more ambiguous power to satisfy human desire.

Ninkasi is such a popular figure in the fermentation world that an Oregon craft brewery named itself after her. (That would be Eugene, Oregon's Ninkasi Brewing Company. More on that brewery later.) The American Homebrewers Association even named one of its most prestigious awards after the goddess. The Ninkasi Award goes to the brewer who has accrued the most points in the final round of the National Homebrew Competition.

The Sumerians were also responsible for what was very likely the first brewing *industry*. After a couple-thousand years of homebrewing (okay, it was more like *village* brewing), they started to commercialize the product.

The Sumerians didn't horde all of this amazing brewing knowledge for themselves. It's believed that they shared it with the Babylonians, who also went commercial with it.

The Ancient Egyptians are often closely associated with wine, but they were pretty big on beer as well. The powers-that-be often paid workers with the beer-like beverage of the time, which historians believe was much thicker and sweeter than the beverage to which modern drinkers have grown accustomed (and many say it likely was more porridge-like).

Naturally, divine entities get most of the credit for this fermented-grain concoction. In this case, it was predominantly the god Osiris who supposedly taught Egyptians how to brew. And, like the Sumerians, the Egyptian women were the ones doing most of the heavy lifting when it came to brewing.

The base for Egyptian beer was very likely bread. It was baked, crumbled into dozens of small pieces, and then strained with water through a sieve. Since this was thousands of years before brewers started using hops, Egyptians probably used indigenous fruits like dates to flavor their beer.

Of course, not every ancient civilization was ready to enthusiastically throw its arms around beer. The Romans and the Greeks—two big-time grape growers—certainly had some beer in their cultures, but they considered it an inferior beverage. In a lot of ways, that's a misconception that the beer industry and its most devoted consumers have been trying trying to obliterate to this day.

While the Greeks certainly played a tremendous role in applying a mild stigma to beer, the Romans are probably mostly to blame for making it stick. After all, their ancient civilization lasted more than a millennium, from the emergence of its civilization in the eighth century BCE through the subsequent five-hundred-year Republic and the rise (27 BCE and fall (AD 476) of its Empire. Since the Italian peninsula was firmly in the wine camp, both climatologically and culturally, attitudes about the superiority of wine pervaded the Empire's territories. Beer, for both the Romans and ancient Greeks, was the beverage of barbarians. (It's no surprise, then, that much modern beer marketing often embraces the barbaric tendencies of its largely male target audience). Elitism most certainly is not a modern construct! Even after the fall of Roman Empire, beer typically was considered an underclass drink when compared with wine (of course, the underclasses far outnumbered the elite, so, arguably, more beer was being consumed).

Though barley ultimately became the dominant grain from which beer was fermented, it was one of many cereals that found their way into medieval beer recipes. Rye, wheat, and oats were among the other grains from which beer was derived. For most of the Middle Ages, however, beer had yet to be hopped. Instead, an herb combo known as *gruit* was the preferred method of flavoring beer before those bitter little flowers exploded onto the scene. There was no right way to make gruit; like the base grains, it really was a matter of what the locals could get their hands on and make at least semi-palatable to the beer-drinking masses. The most commonly used botanicals in medieval gruit included the resinous, eucalyptus-like sweet gale, also known as bog myrtle; the bitter-tasting yarrow; and wild rosemary, sometimes known as March rosemary. The rosemary typically imparted a spicy aroma to the brew and provided some additional bitterness for the palate. Among the other herbs used with varying levels of frequency were juniper—best known today as the core botanical in gin—mugwort, which remains popular in Eastern medicine; and wormwood, which is famous in modern times for its use in absinthe.

The first mention of hop cultivation in Europe dates back to the eighth century in the Hallertau region of what is now Germany, but historical documents place the first use of hops in beer there about a century later.

Hopped beer spread across other parts of Europe, particularly regions like Flanders, part of modern-day Belgium. However, hops took a bit longer to catch on off of the European mainland. The English were well aware of their use on the continent; that doesn't mean they liked it. In fact, English law banned hopped beer in 1471. Eventually, though, the English people warmed to hopped beer and grew to prefer it to the hop-less versions served throughout their land. By the end of the next century, the ban disappeared, and hopped ales dominated. One can't discuss the global history of brewing without detailing the church's role in its proliferation.

In the sixth century, Benedictine monasteries started popping up across Europe. As part of that monastic tradition, the brotherhood maintained self-sustaining abbeys, and brewing beer—a central form of sustenance in an age when you couldn't trust the water—was among the things the monks would be doing for themselves. They also provided it for folks just passing through, whether they were pilgrims seeking enlightenment from the brothers or those who needed lodging. (Remember, this was the Middle Ages and it took next to forever to get anywhere. When there wasn't any room at the inn, sometimes people were able to rest their heads in monasteries).

There was plenty of brewing going on among the lay population outside the monasteries during that period—some commercial, but most for at-home consumption—but what really made the monks' creations a breed apart was that they were very academic about how they developed recipes and replicated them. They, unlike their lay counterparts, had the luxury of time (what else were they doing all day, chanting?) and could, year after year and batch after batch, tweak and fine tune their recipes until they approached perfection. The monks also didn't cut corners on ingredients, much of which they grew on their own. No cheap adulterants for monastic brewers. It would be unholy!

And, as was the case in every other facet of their lives, they were fastidious about sanitation. They scrubbed and re-scrubbed vessels, well, religiously. They were among the first to take sanitation seriously. For non-abbey brewers, it was quite common to reuse the pot that produced today's batch for tomorrow's, as well. And the next day's. (And they may have very well been cooking dinner in it, too.)

In some instances, the Benedictines supplied beer to local villagers, especially when water supplies and overall brewing conditions were so poor outside the abbey's walls.

Historians also believe that monks were likely the first to brew with hops, as the first recorded appearance of hops in beer was at a German abbey in AD 822. Besides flavoring and bittering, hops also boasted a side benefit: preservation. The oils found in the hop flower are a natural preservative and have been invaluable in helping beer travel across long distances. However, it would take several centuries before the hop became one of the core ingredients in beer.

By the end of the Middle Ages, commercial brewing dominated, but the monks continued to do their thing and, save for a couple of blips during major conflicts across the continent and the world, many orders have carried on to this day.

The Industrial Revolution played the biggest role in modernizing beer and spreading it globally. And, while brewers had always known of the presence of "something" that eventually converted grains' sugars to alcohol, they weren't quite sure what that was until the nineteenth century (thank you, Louis Pasteur!). Prior to yeast cultivation, beer makers often would scrape off some of the foam that formed during the fermentation process to use it in the next batch—knowing it was crucial for making beer, but not really knowing why. (In earlier times, they'd also fall back on the old standby, divine intervention, to explain it.) Eventually, they figured out that microorganisms were responsible for the sorcery of fermentation, and they soon learned how to become yeast farmers of sorts.

The beverage has come a long way since Sumerians would sip the soupy stuff through a reed straw and praise Ninkasi for its wonders. But it will never lose its magic, no matter how much science gets involved.

Beverage Belts

If you look at a map of Europe, the continent can be viewed as a combination of belts, with the demarcation between beer cultures and wine cultures drawn largely on climatological lines.

It's a rather striking visual to look at a map of Europe divided into the wine, beer, and vodka belts. With red signifying wine, golden-brown representing beer, and blue standing in for vodka, countries like the United Kingdom, Germany, Belgium, the Netherlands, Luxembourg, Denmark, the Czech Republic, and Slovakia are almost entirely golden-brown. That's due to the fact that it's much easier to grow barley there than grapes. The wine belt is just as intuitive, with countries like Italy, Spain, Portugal, France, Greece, Macedonia, Moldova, Croatia, Georgia, Hungary, and Montenegro. Vodka belt nations, of course, are those northeastern spots most closely associated with the spirit: Russia, Poland, Belarus, Ukraine, and all of the Nordic countries, except for Denmark.

The notion of a "vodka belt" is more informal than the other two and dubbed such for the fact that (1) there's a cultural gravitation toward vodka-drinking, and (2) the more northerly regions tend to be devoid of hop growing (though there's plenty of grain being cultivated—predominantly wheat, which is a typical base for vodka distilling, as is the potato). Also, keep in mind that spirits distilling is a relatively recent development compared with fermentation. Where fermentation dates back several millennia, distillation is only about seven hundred to eight hundred years old.

Few countries are entirely rooted in one belt. Some are nearly evenly split between the wine belt and the beer belt. Switzerland is a perfect example of this, as it's predictably split along ethnic lines, with the German side being a center of beer proliferation and the French side a hotbed of wine production.

Others are multicolored, with little slivers of the other beverage cultures. A map of France isn't perfectly red, for instance. There's a little golden-brown slice in the northeast corner. It's no coincidence that the region borders Germany and Belgium, two of the biggest beer countries known to humanity. The section also includes Alsace, which, through the centuries, has alternated between being a part of Germany and France (France ultimately won, but German influences are palpable in everything from cuisine to town names and surnames). Alsace is the rare area in France known just as much for its beer as it is for its wine. It helps that it also happens to be the center of French hop growing.

The western third of Poland also bears a golden-rod hue, particularly the part that's nearest the German border. Austria's another country straddling two belts. It's hard to imagine a German-speaking nation not being part of the beer belt, but many maps actually depict it as part of the wine belt, as the country is quite famous for its wine-making heritage. Some more accurately portray it as goldenrod-red split, with a bit more real estate in the red zone.

A Few Notes on Terminology

Throughout the book there are some terms that will be kicked around quite liberally, and some deal with the peculiarities of beer volume measurement. Where virtually every other beverage category in the United States is measured in terms of gallons, beer retains its legacy system of volume measurement: barrels. A barrel is roughly equivalent to 31 gallons and change. To complicate things a bit further, non-US brewers—with the exception of the United Kingdom—typically express beer volume in hectoliters. A hectoliter is slightly smaller than a barrel—approximately 26.4 gallons. So it's frequently difficult to make an apples to apples comparison when dealing with both American and international brewers. As if the language barrier weren't enough of a hurdle!

There also will be a few acronyms that will come up from time to time. The most frequently mentioned one is ABV. That stands for "alcohol by volume." It's simply the alcohol content of a beer. Volume is the preferred method of measurement, though occasionally and mostly in relation to law and regulation, it's expressed as alcohol by weight (ABW). When measured by weight, the ABW will be a lower number than ABV. For instance, a beer with an ABV of 6 percent will have an ABW of about 4.7 percent.

The most common instance of ABW use has been with 3.2 percent beer. In 1933, beer got a bit of a head start over wine and spirits. On April 7 of that year, beers with a maximum ABW of 3.2 percent became legal nearly eight months before the rest of alcohol on Repeal Day, December 5, 1933. (3.2 percent ABW was the dividing line for what the government deemed "non-intoxicating beer.") The problem is that many states held on to that 3.2 percent ABW threshold (which translates to 4 percent ABV), and that's the ceiling for the types of beer that can be sold in grocery stores in those states.

2

What's In Beer?

Hops, Malt, Yeast, Water, and Magic

The short answer to that question is hops, malted barley (or other fermentable cereal), water, and yeast. Combine those four ingredients without any clue how to brew, leave them out, and one of an infinite number of random outcomes would be the inadvertent production of beer.

Life would be extremely boring if it were that simple. We wouldn't have the hundreds of styles we enjoy today without the exponential number of possible proportional combinations of those items, nor would we have the hundreds more that are possible when we let in a host of other ingredients. Everyone talks about hops and how they like their beers hoppy (or not), but the majority of people in America don't know or aren't quite sure what in the world hops are.

The hop might be the most popular component of beer these days, but among the four core ingredients, it was the last to join the group. Brewers started putting them in their products only about seven hundred or eight hundred years ago. Sounds like a long time ago, but, in the grand scheme of things, when a beverage is around 7,000 years old, it's like it just happened last week.

When people talk about hops, what they're really referring to is the flower of the hop plant, also known as humulus lupulus among scientists. These flowers look like tiny green pinecones. Within each one is a yellowish area that's home to the lupulin glands, which contain the alpha acids that impart the bitterness and essential oils responsible for beer's flavor and aroma. Hops have another benefit: they're a natural preservative and extend the beer's life.

More often than not, the hops used in modern beer production are in pellet form. The hop flowers are dried and compressed into tiny pellets that could pass for aquatic turtle food. The lupulin components are more concentrated in this form, meaning fewer are required to brew beer, although the processing does cause the hops to lose some of their aromatic quality. Brewers sometimes employ whole-leaf hops, which are dried hop flowers that have been baled together like hay. Since there's more of the actual plant left in whole-leaf form, brewers need to use a much greater quantity of them than they would if they were using pellet hops. Some producers may use a combination of pellet and whole-leaf forms.

Then there's the wet-hop phenomenon, which has become a popular way to amp up the complex flavor and aroma that the little flowers provide. Wet hopping entails adding fresh, whole hop cones, taken right off of the vine, into the brew. Pellets are still primarily used, but the fresh cones give beer an intensity it wouldn't otherwise have from pellets alone.

How about a little sugar to balance out this talk of bitterness? That's where the grain comes in. Malted barley is the grain of choice for beer, though plenty of other cereals are commonly used. The malt process is required to unlock the enzymes that convert starches into fermentable sugars.

To malt barley or other grains, the maltster must soak those cereals in water and allow them to germinate. When they begin to sprout, the maltster halts the germination process and then air-dries the grain. When that process is complete, drying continues in a kiln. The amount of time the malt spends in the kiln depends on the desired color and degree of flavor. On the light end of the spectrum, pale malts have very little roast character, while dark, chocolate malts have fresh-roasted coffee (and, of course, chocolate) characteristics.

Wheat has become one of the more popular non-barley grains to use in brewing. Hefeweizens, Belgian Witbier, Berliner Weisse, and other refreshing brews all use wheat in their mash bills, although the wheat is usually combined in varying proportions with barley malt. A classic hefeweizen may have a wheat-to-barley ratio somewhere between 50:50 and 70:30.

Malt plays just as crucial of a role in beer's flavor as hops do; the malt sweetness balances the hop bitterness. It also gives the brew a lot of its body.

But malt's most important job is to provide food for the yeast. And this is where beer comes alive. When malt and hops are boiled together in water, the resulting liquid is wort, which is an alcohol-free, uncarbonated precursor to beer that tastes vaguely like tea. It's only when the brewer adds yeast that the true magic happens.

In order to fulfill it's role in the beer-making process, yeast requires generous helpings of fermentable sugar. To put it simply, yeast "eats" sugar and excretes alcohol as a byproduct. When fermentation concludes, beer, for all intents and purposes, is the resulting liquid. However, it's going to be unpleasantly flat because it's yet to be carbonated. There are two ways to add carbonation: forced and natural. Forced is just as it sounds: CO_2 is added to the liquid, giving it its bubbles. It's the more economical method because it's much faster than naturally carbonating the brew. However, there really is no substitute for a naturally carbonated beer.

To go au natural, some sugar is added to the container holding the still beer—it goes right into the bottle if it's a bottle-conditioned brew—to activate the yeast. After about two weeks, here be bubbles!

And, voila! Beer has happened!

That's the Cliffnotes version. There are so many varieties of hops—with new species being cultivated seemingly every week—a vast array of malts, and a veritable kingdom of yeast species, that it's impossible to do little more than scratch the surface in these pages. But a brief snapshot certainly helps.

Hops

Cascade: When people talk about quintessentially American hop character, it's very likely they're referring to the Cascade type. Floral, spicy, and very citrusy, Cascade is a hop that screams out to be noticed.

Fuggle: The go-to English hop had its heyday in the nineteenth and early twentieth centuries. It initially grew wild in the hop mecca that is East Kent, until it was domesticated and commercialized in the 1870s by its namesake, Richard Fuggle. Today these faintly fruity flowers are used for aromatic purposes.

Golding: Another of the big English exports, Goldings also originated in Kent. The crème de la crème are East Kent Goldings; if they're grown anywhere else in Kent, they must be called simply Kent. Outside of Kent, they're just Goldings.

Hallertau: One of the noble German hop varieties, Hallertau has a mild, spicy, and floral aroma and therefore is ideal as an aroma hop. It's a bit of a Bavarian legend, as it was the predominant hop used in the region for some time.

Mosaic: Mosaic is the progeny of Simcoe (see below). This hop is characterized by its earthy, tropical, citrusy, and piney expressions and is relatively new to the party. It's primarily used as an aroma hop, most frequently in India pale ales.

Nugget: Nugget is an American hop variety first released in the early 1980s and has become one of the most widely grown hops in the state of Oregon. It boasts some fairly powerful bitterness thanks to its high alpha acidity. It has an herbal, earthy aroma and is used primarily for bittering purposes.

Saaz: Born in Bohemia (now part of the Czech Republic), this hop is the preferred variety for flavoring the classic Czech-style pilsner (the one by which all global variations on the style should be measured). This hop is more aromatic than it is bitter, and it's quite pleasing to the nose and the palate.

Simcoe: A popular component of hop-forward brews like pale ales and India pale ales, the Simcoe variety suggest pine forests and passionfruit.

Sorachi Ace: Japan's contribution to hops, Sorachi Ace has become a favorite of brewers worldwide for its intense bitterness, spice, and lemon-like qualities. It's such an iconoclastic hop that the Brooklyn Brewery named a saison after it.

Hop vines.

Tettnanger: Named for the Tettnang region of Germany from which it hails, Tettnangers are somewhat fruity and spicy and are, along with Hallertau, one of the German noble hop varieties. Alpha acids are on the low side in Tettnangers, and they are commonly used as aroma hops in a lot of the big, classic German beer styles like pilsners, Munich Helles and Kölsch.

Hops, of course, are only part of the story. Good beers require healthy malt backbones, and styles of barley malt are just as bountiful as hop varieties. However, malt character is more about the human interface, the level of kilning or roasting, rather than variations in species. To understand malts, it's important to distinguish between base malts and specialty malts. Base malts are going to contribute most of the starches that will be converted to fermentable sugars. Therefore, they're the ones that will be used in the largest quantity in the brew. On the other hand, specialty malts are used to impart certain desired elements—such as flavor, color, and mouthfeel—that the beer won't get from the base malts alone.

Base Malts

2-Row Malt and 6-Row Malt

Two-row and 6-row malt are so named for the way the barley grows on the stalk; with the former, the kernels are arranged in two rows, while the latter's kernals grow in six rows around the stalk. Because of the smaller number of rows, 2-row malt kernels are typically larger than 6-row kernels. Six-row tends to have more protein content, while 2-row has more carbohydrate composition. Two-row usually results in a maltier flavor, while six-row tilts toward a grainier flavor. Six-row grows only in the United States.

The two most commonly used 2-row malts are the British and US variations. The main difference between the two is that the former tends to be a bit darker and produces slightly fuller-bodied beer. The British variety also is known to impart "bready" elements to the finished brew.

It has the potential to get confusing when we talk about the further varieties within 2-row:

Maris Otter is on the darker, nuttier side of British 2-row malts.

Golden Promise, a less commonly used British 2-row, frequently produces a sweeter end product.

Pilsen or Pilsner Malt

Most standard lagers will use the very pale pilsner malt. In the world of base malts, they're kind of the wallflowers. They show up, but they stay in the background, letting the other malts get all the attention. That's especially beneficial if the brewer is trying to achieve a certain flavor, color, or body with specialty malts; pilsner malt won't stand in the way. There are, of course, many geographic variations of the standard pilsner malt—Belgian, German, and American, to name a few.

Pale Ale Malt

A touch darker than pilsner malts, pale ale malts are the typical base malts of English-style beers and their many descendants (American pales, IPAs, and the like).

Munich Malt

Taking its name from the Bavarian city, Munich malt imparts some sweet characteristics as well as a bit of an amberish hue.

Jars of malted barley.

Wheat Malt

As its name suggests, wheat malt is derived from a grain other than barley. It's the core element of wheat beers, whether they are Belgian wits, Bavarian hefeweizens, or the various other wheat-centric styles.

Vienna Malt

One of the more notable characteristics of the malt named for the Austrian city is that it gives beer a bit of an orangish complexion. Vienna malt is fairly biscuity in flavor and is frequently the base in Vienna lagers (naturally) and other amber-red brews like Märzen. It's somewhat similar in color to Munich malt but slightly less dark.

Specialty Malts

Speciality malts account for only about 10 to 20 percent of the overall grain bill, but that's enough for them to contribute various desired flavor and

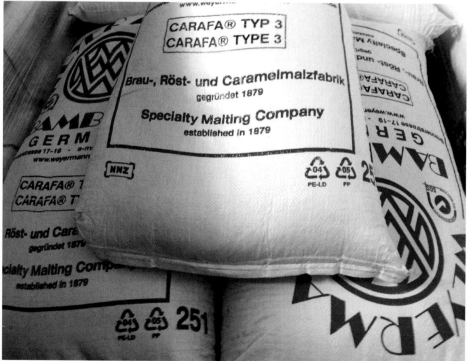

Sacks of malt from Bamberg, Germany's Weyermann.

aroma characteristics. Here's a snapshot of some of the most commonly use specialty malts.

Caramel and Crystal Malt

Caramel and crystal are terms that are often used interchangeably; the former is the more descriptive of the two, as it relates to the caramel-like flavor these types of grains impart to the beer. Maltsters achieve such characteristics by applying a much different process to the grains than they would to the common base malts. For standard malts, the maltsters heat the grain in a dry kiln, but for caramel and crystal malts, they stew what's called green malt in a very moist oven. Putting the malt in the water is akin to putting it in a mash tun, where the grain's starch is converted to fermentable sugar. But this process doesn't actually produce wort since one critical step is missing: the milling/crushing process. What actually happens is that the grain crystallizes when cooled, resembling sugar crystals. It's then dried with heat.

Like many other malt classifications, caramel malts have various sub-categories:

Cara-pils is light in color and adds a bit of sweetness to beer. It's typically used to foster better head retention.

Cara-Vienne is darker (as the beer style hinted at in the second part of the name suggests) and adds body to the brew.

Cara-Munich also adds body and a richer mouthfeel and is popular in a lot of more robust German styles like bocks and Oktoberfest/Märzens.

Biscuit Malt

The malted grain whose name sounds like a cookie is lightly roasted and notable for its toasted bread, cracker-like characteristics. It's a common malt in Belgium.

Chocolate Malt

Yes, chocolate malt is brown in color and, no, there's no actual chocolate involved. This malt's primarily roles are to darken beer and impart lots of roasty, chocolate-like notes. Stouts and porters get their defining hue and flavor characteristics from chocolate malt.

Black Patent Malt

Like chocolate malt, black patent malt is extremely dark, but it doesn't have many of the flavor characteristics of the former. Use of this malt is ideal when color, not flavor, is the objective.

Roasted Barley

What sets this dark brown grain apart from the previous two is that it's not malted before it's kilned—therefore it is not actually a malt. It's a very coffee-like component of stouts.

Other Grains/Cereals/Fermentable Bases

Oats

Oats are typically used sparingly and mostly in one particular style of beer: oatmeal stout. The inclusion of oats creates a remarkable smoothness plus a hint of sweetness. Oats account for between 5 and 10 percent of a typical oatmeal stout's grain bill, and usually they appear on the lower end of that range. Too much oat content could make the beer unpleasantly viscous.

Rye

Rye beers have become incredibly popular in recent years—and it's no coincidence that the demand for whiskeys based on the same grain has been surging, as well. Rye bestows some tart, spicy, and black peppery characteristics to beer, elevating it to a whole new level of complexity. Unlike whiskey, though, there aren't any 100 percent rye beers. Rye is more like a specialty malt used in conjunction with the main grains, usually barley. Grain bills with 10 to 20 percent rye tend to be the norm. India pale ales are particularly welcoming environments for rye because the spicy elements of the grain complement the floral, citrusy hop bitterness of that style. However, rye has been known to find its way into porters and stouts as well, offering a nice contrast with the roastier elements of those dark brews.

Corn

Corn is also frequently used as a fermentable base in beer and traditionally has gotten a bad rap among beer enthusiasts for its use to lighten flavor and body (thanks to its lower protein content) in industrial lagers. However, the tide is turning somewhat as folks are beginning to realize that it has a place in many quality recipes and, in some cases, actually enhances flavor. Yuengling has used corn in its famous lager since its creation nearly two hundred years ago; back in the nineteenth century brewers had to use whatever was readily available to them. The Pennsylvania brewer continues to use corn to this day, giving its lager a distinct sweetness. (Corn is actually sacred when it comes to bourbon, but it's been fighting to improve its reputation in beer. And, in a lot of ways, bourbon is just distilled and aged beer, so what's the problem?)

Rice

Rice is the second most common adjunct—any fermentable ingredient that supplements the main grain—used in American beer and had been maligned by beer geeks as much as rice had been. Rice doesn't impart the kind of sweetness that corn does. For that reason, it plays fairly well with others and doesn't detract from the dominant characteristics of the other malts in a particular recipe. (And just remember that it's the crucial component of the much-venerated Japanese beverage, saké. So it's all a matter of context.)

Candi Sugar

This sweet adjunct is a staple of strong Belgian and Belgian-inspired brews like Dubbels, Tripels, and Quadrupels. Its services most commonly are sought to boost the alcohol content of beer without adding any extra viscous body. It has a secondary use in bottle conditioning, as it's frequently added to a bottle to jumpstart the yeast and inaugurate the secondary fermentation/natural carbonation.

Sorghum

The use of this cereal is fairly common in parts of Africa, like Zimbabwe and Botswana (there's a lot of it there, versus other grains), but sorghum barely registered as a brewing option in the United States until more and more people were diagnosed with Celiac disease. Sorghum is gluten-free, so it's a workable barley alternative, if not the tastiest option. However, as the gluten-free movement grows, brewers have been getting more creative with their beers sans gluten and have developed flavorful alternatives with and without sorghum.

Sweet Potatoes

The use of sweet potatoes in brewing originated, for the most part, in Japan. And that's for two reasons: one, the starchy vegetables are immensely popular there, and two, taxes. Japanese brewers are taxed based on their creations' malt content, creating the necessity for a category of low-malt beers called happoshu. The sweet potato is just one of the fermentable sources that has been used to replace some of the malt content. American brewers have been experimenting with sweet potatoes, as well. One of those, Epic Brewing Company, did it to create a flavorful gluten-free beer. Sweet potatoes worked much better than sorghum.

Microflora (Yeast, Bacteria, and Their Ilk)

We've covered two of the four primary components of beer thus far. We won't get too much into water because most people have a general concept of what it is and its role in brewing. Any further description would veer too far into technical territory. So that just leaves the yeast.

Before anyone got savvy about cultivating different strains of these wee beasties to produce various desired flavor profiles, there basically were two types of yeast with fancy-sounding names: *Saccharomyces cerevisiae* and *Saccharomyces pastorianus*. The former is of the top-fermenting variety (ales), and the latter is of the bottom-fermenting sort (lager). But with those two very general names, we've barely scratched the surface.

There are a lot of variants under each, and sometimes pastorianus is referred to as *Saccharomyces carlsbergensis*. The origins of each can be found in their names. Pastorianus is named after Louis Pasteur, while carlsbergensis is a nod to the Danish brewery, Carlsberg. It was in Carlsberg's lab that fermentation scientist Emil Christian Hansen isolated and cultivated yeast back in the 1880s. The name carlbergensis has mostly fallen by the wayside in favor of pastorianus (Pasteur is much more of a household name).

"Cerevisiae," interestingly, is remarkably similar to the Latin word for beer, *cervisiam.*

There's also another lager yeast, *Saccharomyces uvarum*, which is sometimes used as an umbrella term for those bottom-fermenting species. However, uvarum is widely viewed as a lager contaminant.

And here's where things get really crazy. Brewers play around with all sorts of microscopic wildlife to impart strange and wonderful flavors to their products that wouldn't emerge through conventional yeast alone.

Brettanomyces

A microorganism genus that has drawn a near-religious devotion among makers and lovers of wild ales has been *Brettanomyces*, usually shortened to "Brett." (Everyone wants to be a friend of Brett!) And it's a rather counter-intuitive development, as the funkiness such yeast would impart, in most beer and other fermented beverages, would be considered off-notes. If Brett got anywhere near a batch of wine, that wine would be dumped. The same would be true for most beers as well, but leave it to the Belgians to intentionally enable such an unwelcome invader to propagate. There are many variations within the genus; the one most lovers of Belgian-style wild ales are likely to have encountered is *Brettanomyces bruxellensis.* The name should be the giveaway, as it has "Bruxelle"—as in the French spelling of Brussels—embedded right in it. It's this variety that does all the dirty work in lambics, gueuze, Flemish sours, et al. (We'll get into those in greater detail later.)

There's a reason the ales brewed with Brett are called "wild." There's usually no predicting just what the wee beasties might do, and that's part of the fun. The words that frequently come up to describe the typical notes for which Brett is responsible are horsey (more like the blanket one would put on a horse, not what, umm, comes out of a horse) and barnyardy. Not exactly appetizing in most contexts, but it is one of those acquired taste kind of things. American brewers have been experimenting with the stuff so much that you can't really call it "experimenting" anymore. However, that doesn't necessarily make it mainstream. Ninety-nine percent of whatever most people are likely to drink probably won't contain it.

Brettanomyces are not the most efficient little critters, either. Brewers need a great deal of patience when working with Brett. For a Brett beer to reach its prime, it often will take a year or two—a lifetime when compared with most styles.

Lactobacillus

Those who recall their high school biology class will recognize the root word *bacillus*. That puts it in the bacterial, rather than the yeast, domain. Bonus points for remembering that it's of the rod-shaped variety (versus the coccus, as in strep-throat causing *streptococcus*, which is more spherical in appearance).

Lactobacillus is the culprit (in a good way) responsible for the character of many types of sour beers—each with varying levels of funk, but typically not nearly as much funk as beers resulting from Brett's handiwork. It's part of the same group of bacteria that convert lactose, the sugar found in milk, into lactic acid (which is one of the active components of yogurt, cottage cheese, and even sourdough bread). It does the same thing with the sugars in beer (versus converting them to alcohol like other microorganisms do). Beer-wise, it's what gives the Berliner Weisse is signature tartness. It's also present in Belgian sours and another indigenous German style, gose. (More on those later.)

Pediococcus

Like *Lactobacillus*, *Pediococci* are bacteria. As noted, coccus bacteria are ball-like. Aside from the shape, the *Pedicoccus* (affectionately known as "Pedio") bacterium shares a lot in common with Lactobacillus; it, too, converts sugar to lactic acid, but it doesn't produce any carbon dioxide as a byproduct of the fermentation process. These bacteria frequently contaminate beer, giving it a kind of buttery flavor—the calling card of diacetyl, the compound that Pediococci produce—but, when controlled, they can be harnessed for certain desired sour components. They're usually used in partnership with Brett, as Brett tends to cancel out the diacetyl present in the wort.

We can devote an entire microbiology course to these crazy little creatures. But if you wanted a science lesson, you'd be reading another book.

3

A Brief Primer

Major Ale and Lager Styles

t this point in our journey, it's probably a good idea to get a primer on the major styles of beer produced at breweries worldwide. Let's start at an incredibly basic level and get more specific from there.

Ale vs. Lager

Ale and lager are two terms thrown around by brewers, advertisers, and anyone who's been within a mile of a beer. But few actually go out of their way to explain the difference between the two.

It's not uncommon for someone to ask what the difference is between "beer" and "ale." This confusion is primarily due to the lack of information in traditional beer advertising (read: least common denominator comedy and T&A print and broadcast spots).

First of all, ale is beer. And so is lager. Beer is the umbrella term. Ale and lager are the subsets.

So what's the difference? At the most fundamental level, ale is brewed with top-fermenting yeast, and lager is brewed with bottom-fermenting yeast. Okay, so exactly what the heck does that mean?

Ale yeast isn't doing all of its work at the top. It's performing its alcohol-making function throughout the liquid—the wort—and ultimately rises to the top toward the end of the fermentation process. When lager yeast has performed its task, it settles to the bottom (though, like ale yeast, it does its business throughout the volume of the wort).

Temperature has a great deal to do with how these two different types of yeast perform. Ales have a greater tolerance for higher temperatures and therefore ferment at those higher temperatures. Lagers, on the other hand, require cooler temperatures to perform. Ale yeast is typically most active at temperatures between 65 and 75 degrees Fahrenheit, but the yeast will become dormant if the temperature falls below 50 degrees Fahrenheit. However, below that threshold is where lager yeasts thrive.

Lager yeasts are more sensitive to alcohol than those for ale and therefore will stop converting sugar to alcohol when a certain degree of the latter is present. The fact that a disproportionate number of high-alcohol beers are ales is due the fact that the yeasts in such ales are still actively performing long after lager yeasts would have raised the white flag.

Top-fermenting yeasts also are known to produce esters that give ale a kind of fruity character. Ester production is pretty much nonexistent in lagers, which therefore tend to have a crisper, "cleaner" character.

Time is another key ingredient. Ales usually complete their primary fermentation phase after seven days. Lagers, however, take significantly longer. After primary fermentation, the temperature is lowered a bit during the "lagering" phase, which is absent from ale production.

"Lager" actually means "to store." The term emerged in relation to cold storage; in pre-refrigeration days, brewers would store beer in cool caves. Brewers discovered that the yeast continued to produce alcohol long after the beers were stored.

The entire lager fermentation process takes several weeks. This is a key reason why, at least initially, craft brewers predominantly produced ales. The longer turnaround meant more time that beer needed to sit in fermentation tanks. Not only is that real estate at a premium in most brewing facilities, but the more time beer spends in the brewery means the longer it will be before it's out on the market generating profits.

Boston Beer Company and the Brooklyn Brewery were two notable craft brewers marketing lagers as their flagships, both of which were amber in color and far more flavorful than than the mass-marketed macros available on the market back in the 1980s. They had a bit of an advantage early on, at least from a space standpoint, as their products were primarily contract-brewed; they didn't have to worry about allocating their own fermentation infrastructure for the lagering process, as they were having their products produced on the unused capacity in partner breweries.

Lagers have made a bit of a comeback in recent years, as craft brewers are pushing the boundaries on bottom-fermented beers and innovating in ways many didn't even think was possible.

In beer taxonomy, you can't get much broader than simply labeling something a lager or an ale. It's time to dive deeper into styles within both of those categories. At this point in time there are literally hundreds of beer styles, and it will be difficult to include all of them in a concise manner in these pages. So we're going to stick to just the A-list (and maybe a few styles from the B-list) without going too far into the weeds with substyles and sub-substyles. This list is not meant to be definitive. Think of it as a greatest hits album.

Lagers: Light to Dark

Pilsner

Pilsner is named for the city of Pilzn in Bohemia (now a part of the Czech Republic), where the style was first produced. Pilsner Urquell, originating in 1842, gets the credit for being the first iteration of the style, and it's still widely consumed today. (The brand had been a part of the portfolio of global beer conglomerate SABMiller for many years; it's now part of the even larger entity that formed after SABMiller merged with competitor Anheuser-Busch InBev.) Pilsner (sometimes spelled "pilsener") is characterized by its paleness. There are key distinctions between Bohemian-style and German-style pilsners. There's a slight sweetness to the original, Bohemian variety, and its hop bitterness is moderate. The dominant hop in the Czech pilsner is the herbal, aromatic Saaz. The Germans, on the other hand, tend to use noble hop varieties like Hallertauer and Tettnanger, which impart markedly more lingering bitterness on the finish. Most mass-produced American and global brands are based on the pilsner style, though many lack the flavor and complexity of their Czech and German ancestors.

Maibock/Helles Bock

Bock beers, by definition, are strong—compared with standard German lagers—and malty. Where traditional pilsners and helles lagers are between 4.5 and 5 percent ABV, bocks tend to start at 6 percent and can be as high as 8 or 9 percent (and sometimes as high as 11 or 12 percent if the brewer is really ambitious). Maibock, the pale bock, translates to "May bock" and is usually available in the spring. Maibocks usually have a bit more hop character than traditional bocks, which are darker in color and boast considerably more malt sweetness.

Amber Lager

This is another one of those umbrella categories under which there are many styles with their own unique nuances. One such style is Vienna lager, named for the Austrian city where it was born (but which is actually pretty hard to find these days; you're far more likely to encounter a wealth of first-rate pilsner brands). Usually Vienna-style lagers are copperish in color and malt tends to dominate the aroma and the flavor—hop bitterness is fairly restrained. Though Samuel Adams Boston Lager is loosely based on the Vienna style, it showcases considerably more hop character. Boston Lager is one of the reasons that the American-style amber lager stylistic category exists (Brooklyn Lager is another). The hops may be more assertive, but when done well, American ambers have a balance of malt sweetness and hop bitterness.

Märzen

The term "Märzen" is frequently used interchangeably with "Oktoberfest," even though "Märzen" means "March." Typically, the bready, malty, and red-dish/copperish beer had been available in the spring, but Bavarian brewers would roll out special versions for the fall festival in Munich.

Dunkel

The translation of this style's name, simply, is "dark." Dark malts are the headlining act here, imparting roasty, chocolaty notes, which are balanced by some mild hop bitterness. These brown-hued lagers are very reminiscent of darker biscuits and breads.

Doppelbock

"Doppel" means "double" and, as such, this style is a bigger and boozier affair and is considerably sweeter than helles bocks, with lots of toasted malt character. This beer is usually deep brown in color, and its alcohol content can range between the high 6s to about 9 percent ABV.

Schwarzbier

Another iconic style out of Deutschland, schwarzbier literally translates to "black beer." It's a bit darker and more opaque than dunkels; it can be dark or full-on black and noticeably drier than the traditional dunkel. There's a faint element of burnt toast in its flavor profile, as well.

Ales: Light to Dark

We started at the bottom (fermented); let's now move to the top.

Blonde Ale

Typically, blonde ales are designed to bridge folks who regularly drink mass-market lagers into more flavorful craft styles. Blonde ales typically are refreshing and easy drinking and have an ABV around 5 percent. They're usually well balanced; neither the hops nor the malt really assert themselves.

Pale Ale

Just like America itself, the style started as a British creation but then came into its own as an American original. American pale ales, along the lines of the flagship Sierra Nevada brew, have quite a pronounced hop character, usually from the assertive varieties grown on the US West Coast. Sometimes it's hard to distinguish pales from India pale ales; Oskar Blues Brewery's Dale's Pale Ale is one such brand that blurs the stylistic lines.

India Pale Ale (IPA)

As noted above (and at various other places throughout this book), IPAs are for hopheads. There's plenty of myth associated with the creation of the style, but most accounts agree that IPAs were aggressively hopped to survive the pre-canal ocean voyage from England to colonial India. The long journey would weaken the flavor, and the additional hops helped offset that. Hops are also a natural preservative and made the brews more seaworthy (though other styles were being exported, mostly unaltered). American IPAs are noticeably different than the original British versions, due, primarily, to the bold, citrusy nature of many American hop varieties. IPA continues, year after year, to be the reigning champ of popular craft beer styles. Recently, dark, roastier versions of IPA have emerged, though there has been a bit of controversy from an origin and nomenclature standpoint. For some, the rightful name is "black IPA," while, for others, the correct term is "Cascadian dark ale." IPA has also inspired a hoppy bottom-fermented style, India pale lager.

Amber Ale

Amber ales generally fall on the sessionable end of the spectrum, hovering around the 5 percent ABV range and moving up to about 6 percent. They're usually well-balanced, though some can tilt more toward the biscuity malt side, while others might have a bit more hop bitterness. The quintessential American amber is Full Sail Amber from Hood River, Oregon's Full Sail Brewing Co. The beer first appeared in 1989 and continues to be a go-to for folks in the Pacific Northwest and all points south and east.

Brown Ale

Another style of English ancestry that Americans have adopted and made their own, browns can be all over the map on the hop/malt spectrum, depending on who's making it. Original English browns typically have less pronounced hoppiness than many American iterations, but that is by no means a rule. There's plenty of roasty character, but markedly less so than in the even darker porters. There frequently are some nutty elements, as well as some mild chocolate notes. Across the pond, a good representation of the style is in the form of Samuel Smith's Nut Brown Ale from the venerable Samuel Smith Brewery in Tadcaster, North Yorkshire. The brewery's roots date back to the mid-eighteenth century, and Nut Brown Ale is, perhaps, its most visible style on these shores. For a world-class American version, try Ellie's Brown Ale from Boulder, Colorado's Avery Brewing Company. Named for founder Adam Avery's late chocolate lab, Ellie's has plenty of sweet maltiness with a bit of nuttiness.

Porter

Porter is a very close cousin to stout, and frequently some of the most beer-literate aficionados are hard-pressed to describe the exact differences between the two. Generally, porters are a bit lighter in body and a little less opaque than stouts. Within porter, there are several subgroupings that have their own unique nuances. There's the brown porter, which tends to be mildly roasty, medium-bodied, and light-to-dark brown in color. Robust porters have more pronounced roastiness and a fairly strong malt flavor. They're usually a bit darker than brown porters, as well. Then there's the Baltic porter, so named for the region in which they were most popular (there are some influences from Russian imperial stouts—which you'll learn a bit more about in the "extreme beer" section). Baltics are conspicuously sweeter than browns and robusts, sometimes with dark fruit qualities (raisins and their ilk). They're also decidedly fuller in body than the other two substyles.

The "porter" name is believed to have been a nod to the porters who worked in markets. It was the type of beer they would consume after a long, hard day of moving merchandise around for vendors and shoppers.

Stout

Stouts are very roast-forward and coffee-like and have even more variations than porters. These beers run from quite dry to quite sweet. The classic dry stout emerged in England as an outgrowth of the porter. It got its name because it was meant to be a more full-bodied and creamier—or, if you will, "stouter"—version of a porter (in fact, it was often called "stout porter"). Dry stouts also have a bit more hop bitterness than other versions. On the flip side of dry stouts are sweet stouts, which exhibit markedly lower hop bitterness than the former. Then there are oatmeal stouts, which incorporate a little bit of that particular cereal (rarely exceeding one-tenth of the grain bill) to give it a bit of a fuller, creamier body. On the far end of the style spectrum are imperial stouts (often called Russian imperial stouts), which we'll get into in a bit more detail in the "extreme" chapter.

Barleywine

These are typically big, bold, boozy brews, usually brownish-red in color and best served in small doses in snifter-type glasses. (Technically, barleywine also falls under the category of "extreme beer," which you'll read more about in the next chapter.) Like porters, stouts, pales, and IPAs, barleywines were born in Britain and then augmented in the United States and abroad. Flavor-wise, they can run the gamut from very malty to very hoppy (and are sometimes a combination of the two).

Niche and Emerging Styles

The styles detailed previously are old standbys. There are many others that are either synonymous with a certain season or were once oddities that have evolved to become a stylistic category unto themselves.

Pumpkin Beers

There are few styles more polarizing than pumpkin beers. You either love them or hate them, and there's very little middle ground. They've become a rite of fall (though they seem to come out earlier and earlier every year; sometimes you'll see them as early as July, which is nothing short of a crime!). As with any style, there are some standout offerings, as well as some not-so-great selections. For far too many brewers "pumpkin beer" has come to mean "any brew using spices that evoke the taste of pumpkin pie." These can go great after the turkey, but then again, so does actual pumpkin pie. The good ones actually challenge the palate with some of the more complex, squash-like elements of the flagship ingredient.

Chili Pepper Beers

Beers brewed with varying forms of hot peppers—be they chipotle, jalapeño, ghost, habanero, and what have you—could very well have devolved into gimmickry. But there are many that capture the spicy essence of those peppers without frying one's palate or overpowering the other important ingredients that make beer beer. It's difficult to drink multiple chili beers during a single sitting, but they definitely are worth checking out.

Flower Beers

These are really a niche within a niche within a niche (and so on), but some brewers have been experimenting with flower-enhanced beers. But isn't the hop a type of flower, you ask? Well, yes, but the ones we're talking about here are of the more perfumey kind. At one point, around 2011 to 2013, hibiscus beers seemed to be all the rage within some circles. So far, they've mostly been one-offs and limited releases. Chicago's Revolution Brewing, Brooklyn's Sixpoint, and even Sam Adams have played around with such floral ingredients. In fact, back in 2011, Sam Adams collaborated with Delaware's Dogfish Head to create Savor Flowers, the commemorative beer at that year's Savor craft beer and food festival in Washington, D.C. It was practically a bridal bouquet in a bottle, combining hibiscus with rosebuds, jasmine, and lavender. It's a trend that seems to already have peaked, but these types of things occur in cycles, and the next wave may be on the horizon.

Gose

The sour and salty German-born *gose* style (pronounced goh-zuh) has made a comeback worldwide in a big way. But we'll get a bit more into that in the chapter on Germany's beer culture.

A Beer for All Seasons

When the Brewers Association releases its annual list of the top craft beer styles, number two on the list (behind the ubiquitous India pale ale) is usually "seasonal." That, of course, is not a style, but a collection of many, many styles that are in and out of the market in the space of three months. (Unfortunately the Brewers Association's tally doesn't include how well each of the individual styles is performing, but that's difficult to do since they're only sold for a small slice of the year, and their volume is pretty small anyway.) While this writer is of the opinion that any beer can be enjoyed during any season of the year, the reality is you're likely to find them only in their respective seasons. (In some cases you'll find them months later, but be extremely wary; those are going to be far from fresh.)

So, let's take a guided tour across the calendar and sip the best of the seasonals.

Spring

Of course, you're thinking, "Why are you starting with spring, when spring doesn't even begin until late March?" The primary reason is that even though winter occupies only the last ten days of December, winter beers start showing up in November (sometimes even in October, which is known as "seasonal creep" in beer geek circles, and it's been known to enflame quite a few negative passions). And many have holiday season themes, so it's kind of a bummer to be starting with them in January.

It's with the spring beers that brewers shift away from the chewy, boozy brews that fill one's belly and warm one's soul in frigid months toward the crisper, snappier options with many floral and fruity elements that evoke the sensations of the pre-summer months.

Fort Collins, Colorado's New Belgium offers a seasonal it calls Spring Blonde, a Belgian-style blonde, whose sweetness from pale and Munich malt is balanced by some dry bitterness, thanks to the Nugget hops. It's lighter and breezier than the typical winter mainstays, but not quite as refreshing as the traditional summer fare (and that's spring in a nutshell).

Since Earth Day happens every spring, it's fitting that many spring releases are quite earthy in nature. Among those is Bell's Smitten Golden Rye Ale, whose floral and grapefruity hop elements complement the spicy rye malt.

Adding rye to hop-forward beers is quite alluring for spring-minded brewers. In 2012, Sierra Nevada launched its spring seasonal, Ruthless Rye, an IPA with a bit of the tartness one comes to expect from the alternative grain.

Boston Beer Company invented a sort of "fifth season" when it launched its limited-edition Cold Snap in 2014. The unfiltered spiced wheat ale (its own twist on a traditional Belgian witbier) was designed to bridge winter to spring—to parallel, in a sense, that post-Groundhog Day mix of despair and optimism.

Summer

If there's such a term as "refreshment-forward," it would describe summer seasonals to a T. These are the types of brews people will want to drink while they cook a few hot dogs and burgers on the grill or hang out by the pool. Wheat-based weissbiers used to be the quintessential summer drink. Walking down a city street, it was always a familiar site to see the tall, slender glasses with the bulbous mouth filled with the hazy, straw/golden-colored loveliness on many sidewalk restaurant tables. And that's still the case, but their popularity has made them a permanent part of many brewers' year-round portfolios. So they're hardly "seasonals" in the in-and-out sense. (A notable exception is Lakefront Brewery's Wisconsinite. It's a weissbier, but with a locally minded spin. All of its ingredients, including its yeast, are grown and cultivated in the Milwaukee operation's home state). That's okay, because entire new and limited-time-only genres have emerged to challenge the palates of refreshment-seeking beer lovers. And many of them wear their desired season on their sleeves, er, labels. There's Brooklyn Summer Ale, for instance; can't get any more direct than that. If anyone's brazenly stocking this stuff in December, it's best to just turn around and leave that store immediately. It's a balanced pale that goes down a bit more easily than most versions of the American pale ale style proper.

And though weissbiers have, for the most part, gone year-round, summer continues to be the preferred sales window for one type of wheat-based beer:

Berliner Weisse (though some—including your humble author—believe it's too good a style to be pigeonholed for one season and should be consumed year-round). A perennial favorite has been Dogfish Head's variation on the style, Festina Peche, which incorporates some peach (subtly) into the mix. At 4.5 percent ABV, it's a bit on the high side for a Berliner Weisse (they usually hover around 3 percent ABV) but very much on the low side for a Dogfish Head brew.

One of the more recent styles to emerge, session IPA—an easier-drinking, low-ABV India pale ale—has found quite a following in the warmer months. A great example of the style is one of Firestone Walker's seasonals, Easy Jack, which combines hops from across the globe in a surprisingly compact 4.5 percent ABV brew.

Fall

Fall is the season to beat in the beer world—part of this has to do with the fact that it's traditionally harvest time—and there's really no more flavorful part of the year. Thankfully, autumn seasonals are not limited to just the love-em-or-hate-em pumpkin beers. For one thing, fall is a big time for märzens because of their historical link with Oktoberfest. (Most of them, in fact, are called Oktoberfest beers; some, like the Sam Adams variant, choose the English spelling, Octoberfest.)

Regardless of how big Sierra Nevada Brewing Company may get, the company never gets lazy. Innovation is still a huge part of its business model, and when it innovates, it usually does so far better than most. The brewery had made an Oktoberfest offering for many years (it was one of the "Octoberfests" with a "c"), but in 2015 it decided to take things up a few notches and collaborate with a different German brewery each year for a series of märzens whose flavor profiles were as variable as snowflakes. For its inaugural foray, it teamed with Brauhaus Riegele, a family-run operation that's been going strong since 1386 (and is currently in the hands of its twenty-seventh generation).

When it comes to Oktoberfests, sometimes you've got to have the Münchner originals. Spaten and Hacker Pschorr still export solid versions of the classic style (and you're not likely to find it if you go to the actual Oktoberfest).

But if there's ever been a beer that just screams "fall," it's the one from a certain Maine brewery that puts the proper name of the season right on its label: Geary's Autumn Ale from Portland's D. L. Geary Brewing Company.

This brew is neither a pumpkin nor a märzen, but, instead, it draws its inspiration from English brown ales. In a glass, the stuff even looks like fall, with its reddish/amberish/brownish tint, and it even tastes like the season, if that's possible. Its nuttiness evokes chestnuts and other sundry squirrel bait that falls to the ground when the air starts to get crisp. Geary's Autumn Ale is best enjoyed in its home city or at least the surrounding region. No one does fall like New England, even if it only lasts a week before winter starts.

I'd hate to make this a Portland, Maine lovefest, but there's another consistently solid fall offering that deserves a mention. Gritty McDuff's is one of the most famous brewpubs in the United States (it also packages its beer for distribution), and when the leaves start departing from the trees, Gritty's has, without fail, impressed with the annual release of its Halloween Ale. Like Geary's Autumn, this beer's color evokes the October foliage. It also draws its inspiration from Great Britain—not a nut brown this time, but an Extra Special Bitter. The sturdy malt backbone tastes like the harvest.

Okay, I have to mention one pumpkin beer, but only because it has the most awesome name and label imaginable. It's from another New England brewery, New Haven, Connecticut's Two Roads. What's it called? Roadsmary's Baby. And even though it is a pumpkin beer, it doesn't phone things in. It's aged in rum barrels for a bit of added complexity, and its label has a baby carriage with a jack-o'-lantern's face carved into it. Two Roads wins Halloween!

Winter

At last, we've reached the point in the year where the beers often get as heavy as the blankets under which its drinkers disappear. Brewers frequently amp up the malt quotient of their cold-weather beers and add a little spice (literally) if they're targeting the more festive, less depressing part of the season.

One of the most venerable of the winter offerings is Jubelale from Bend, Oregon's Deschutes Brewery. This beer has many qualities—such as raisin, fig, and molasses notes—that essentially make it a Christmas cake in a bottle. Each year the brewery commissions a different artist from the greater Bend area to design a wintery scene for its label.

On the opposite coast, Northeasterners always eagerly await a certain holiday season product from Boston institution and sometime Deschutes collaborator Harpoon Brewery. Harpoon's Winter Warmer is the winter seasonal by which many other cold-weather beers should be measured and is more of a welcome arrival in New England than Santa Claus himself. Its cinnamon and nutmeg flavor and aroma are evocative of the types of cook-ies kids would leave out for the red-suited one.

Speaking of welcome arrivals, Britain's Samuel Smith Brewery's depend-able Winter Welcome is another long-time fixture of the chilly months. The malty, pruny, toffee-like concoction pairs well with a good Dickens book.

Bringing things back to the States—but with a very obvious English accent—is Old Man Winter from upstate New York's Southern Tier Brewing Company. The roasty, chocolaty, nutty, caramel-y symphony is reminiscent of drinking a cup of joe while eating a chocolate-caramel-nut "turtle."

Okay, one more icy-weather seasonal and we'll call it a night—in fact, we'll get ready for a long winter's nap—and what better way to do so than with a brew called Hibernation Ale, the classic seasonal from Colorado, a state that's been known, on occasion, to get snowed in. Denver's Great Divide Brewing Company first launched Hibernation in 1995, and it has since racked up plenty of awards at beer festivals worldwide. Like many winter brews, it's a malty, English-inspired old ale, but, with an ABV that approaches 9 percent, Hibernation has considerably more heft than some of the others. You're definitely in for the night with this one.

There are quite a few beers in Great Divide's portfolio that easily could be considered winter seasonals—except for the fact that they're avail-able year-round. The most noteworthy of those is the 9.5 percent ABV Yeti Imperial Stout, whose roasty malt character is tempered by a little more hoppiness than most are accustomed to within the style. Its IBU (International Bitterness Units) is 75, which more or less puts it in IPA ter-ritory as far as bitterness is concerned (anything over 100 barely registers on the human palate). The barrel-enhanced version, Oak-Aged Yeti, is also worth checking out.

4

German Brewing

Centuries of Tradition in the Most Iconic Beer Country

Furthermore, we wish to emphasize that in future in all cities, markets and in the country, the only ingredients used for the brewing of beer must be Barley, Hops and Water. Whosoever knowingly disregards or transgresses upon this ordinance, shall be punished by the Court authorities' confiscating such barrels of beer, without fail.

Few commerce-related statements made in the sixteenth century have had as much of an impact on modern business as those two sentences. That, of course, is one of the key tenets of the Reinheitsgebot, also known as the German Beer Purity Law. It's one of the reasons why Germany, in the eyes of the world, has been synonymous with brewing for centuries. To be sure, the Reinheitsgebot also can be fairly polarizing; many say its mandate that beer may only be made from barley, hops, and water (and later, yeast, when they discovered fermentation didn't occur via divine intervention) has stifled innovation. For instance, if Belgium had to comply with the law, the styles we have come to embrace as quintessentially Belgian would not exist. A lot of Belgian styles incorporate herbs and spices, such as coriander and orange peel, into their recipes, while others use cherries and candi sugar. By German definition, those ingredients are "impure." Coffee beers? Impure. Chili pepper beers? Ditto. The list goes on and on. But many argue that the great German styles likely wouldn't be so great if someone didn't put the reins on brewers that were running amok by the middle of the fifteenth century.

Technically, the law started as the Bavarian beer law. At the time, the Kingdom of Germany was part of the Holy Roman Empire. Duke Wilhelm IV of Bavaria enacted the law in 1516, and Bavarian beer became such a beacon of quality that the other German duchies eventually adopted it as well. To this day, German beer labels bear one of two statements: "Gebraut nach dem deutchen Reinheitsgebot" (brewed according to the Germany Purity

Law) or "Gebraut nach dem Bayerischen Reinheitsgebot von 1516" (brewed according to the Bavarian Purity Law of 1516).

Prior to 1516, beer makers were putting whatever they could get their hands on into their products, letting quality take a back seat to easy profit. Some of those ingredients, like wild roots and even animal byproducts, were potentially harmful.

The rest of the world should be a pretty good indication of how things could have played out in the German brewing industry had the law not been enacted. Before the rise of craft brewing, American beer was the laughing stock of the beverage world. That was partly due to the thinning of flavor that resulted from the use of such adjuncts as corn and rice. To be sure, some really tasty beers have been able to use corn and rice to great effect, but that wasn't the intention of the rapidly growing American macros. German brewers wouldn't have been allowed to use corn or rice if they wanted to. Reinheitsgebot forbade it.

So enduring was the law that, following World War I, it became part of the German tax code after the formation of the Weimar Republic. Bavaria threatened to forgo joining the new republic if its then four-hundred-year-old mandate was not enforced throughout the country. The law survived the dissolution of the Republic and the rise and fall of the Third Reich, only to be undermined by the European Court in 1987. The court found that it posed an importation conundrum. By barring non-Reinheitsgebot-compliant brews from entering Germany from other parts of Europe, it was stifling the free trade that the freshly integrated European market was trying to promote.

After the 1987 ruling, adjunct- and additive-laden brews were allowed to breach German borders and comingle with the home-grown products. However, despite the fact that Europe at large didn't have to adhere to the five-centuries-old law and that the Germans had to respect the products of its neighbors, most Deutschland brewers chose to continue to adhere to the Reinheitsgebot—European market be damned! And the vast majority of German beer drinkers wouldn't have it any other way.

Regional Styles

To refer to something as "German beer" is to not really know German beer at all. It's true, Germans are a proud bunch when it comes to their fermentables, but there's a far greater sense of local pride that trumps any national identity. Münchners (those who reside in Munich) are fiercely protective of their city's signature helles (pale); North-Rhine Westphalia neighbors Cologne and Düsseldorf have an ongoing rivalry over whose traditional brew is better, Cologne's Kölsch or Dusseldorf's Altbier; the resurgent gose style is what put Leipzig on the German beer map. Understanding German brewing is as much about understanding geography, but instead of a boring exam at the end of lesson, you get beer!

Munich

Munich is, hands down, the first city anyone thinks of, either consciously or unconsciously, when someone mentions German beer. And for good reason. It's the capital city of what is now the German state of Bavaria, it's been home to Oktoberfest for more than two hundred years, and it has one of the biggest beer tourist ~~traps~~ attractions in all of Europe and, perhaps, the world: the Hofbrau Haus. Going to the Hofbrau House is a bit like visiting Paris. You plan to see the Eiffel Tower the first time you're there, and you should. But you're not going to hang out there every day and then keep going back to it on subsequent visits to the City of Lights, are you? That's the Hofbrau Haus. You've got to sit down at a long, communal wooden table, marvel at the intricate old-world wooden architecture, order a gigantic, one-liter mug of the Helles or Dunkel ("bright" or "dark"), flag down the young woman in traditional Bavarian garb hawking pretzels the size of an adult human torso, clap along with the oompa band, buy a cheap tchotchke, and be on your way. It's not likely that your reaction will be: "wow, that placed changed my life, and we need to go back again tomorrow." It's a one-and-done type of scenario. (Those Bavarian pretzels, on the other hand, are not. You will happily make a meal out of those every breakfast, lunch, and dinner, and will stuff as many as you can into multiple gallon-size Ziploc bags so you can bring them home with you. Luckily, you can't walk twenty feet in most major Bavarian cities without encountering a pretzel vendor.)

The aforementioned Munich Helles is one of the city's greatest contributions to worldwide drinking. Its key distinguishing factor from the Bohemia-born pilsner style is that it balances the sharp hop bitterness with more of a malty backbone. In fact, its creation was a direct response to the encroaching popularity of the Czech innovation, which, to this day, is the dominant style in the world. Munich's Spaten Brewery gets the credit for producing the first Helles in early 1894. (Interestingly, it wasn't the Münchners, but the citizens of Hamburg, who were the first to wet their whistles with this brand new Bavarian invention. Spaten sent it to Hamburg for a trial run. Once enough Hamburgers enthusiastically embraced it, it was ready for prime time back at home. Münchners finally got to taste it in the summer of 1895.)

Septemberfest?

There's always an easy way to gauge the authenticity of an Oktoberfest celebration held anywhere in the world outside of Munich. (Of course, one could make a convincing argument that the Munich original is the *only* authentic Oktoberfest, but let's give the autumnal tribute celebrations throughout America the benefit of the doubt. Many do keep it real.) The dead giveaway would be if the venue stages the event in the middle of October. The thing is, most of Oktoberfest proper takes place in September. The sixteen-day event begins around the third week of September and ends the first weekend in October. If a restaurant, bar, brewery, church, or community organization is intent on holding it in October to avoid confusing people, it's advisable that they do so no later than that first weekend (no later than the 8th of the month). But for real Bavarian cred, why not schedule it when it's still September?

However, ultra-purists could assert that the original Oktoberfest was held in its namesake month and deeper into that month than it's held in modern times. The inaugural event celebrated the marriage of Crown Prince Ludwig— eventually King Ludwig—to Princess Therese von Sachsen-Hildburghausen. The actual nuptials took place on October 12, 1810, and the big party that became the annual observance happened five days later at Sendlinger Tor, the southern gate of the Old City. The nearly 10 million people who attend Oktoberfest today would never fit there now, especially since the city's expanded well beyond the quaint, fairy-tale-like center. It's since moved to much larger fairgrounds (with all of modern fairs' usual trappings: bumper cars, food stalls, games of chance, and more).

The festival shifted to an earlier point on the calendar primarily for meteorological reasons. Munich Septembers are much milder than Munich Octobers.

The event has become a traditional showcase for Munich's leading breweries, with each constructing a sprawling beer hall under its own branded tent. (Tent is the technical term, but they're more like pop-up convention centers.) Hofbräu and Spaten always have quite a presence on the grounds, as do Hacker-Pschorr, Augustiner, Lowenbrau, and Paulaner. Getting in the tents is a feat in itself. Some—mostly trading partners and customers the breweries are trying to wine and dine—are lucky enough to score tickets from the breweries themselves, while most just wait in line until communal seating spots open up. There's usually great Bavarian food and live music—just don't let the band members' traditional garb fool you. Much of the time you won't be hearing traditional folk songs; a good chunk of their set lists read like the by-the-number selections performed by American wedding bands (even ditties like "You're the One That I Want" from *Grease*.)

Now, about the beer being poured within those tents. Oktoberfest has become synonymous with the Märzen style of beer, copper in color with a robust maltiness. It's one of the main reasons that fall is arguably the best season for beer. American craft brewers from coast to coast start unveiling their Oktoberfest/ Märzen-style beers usually by mid-August. Importers also roll out the best the old country has to offer, many from those same breweries holding court in the tent-buildings. However, those expecting a mug full of the bready, reddish-tinted elixir they've come to associate with the festival are likely to be disappointed. Sure, Munich breweries all still produce special releases just for Oktoberfest, but they often bear a striking resemblance to Helles in both their color and less caramel-like flavor. They are a tad stronger than traditional Helles, however.

That stylistic shift reflects a market reality that began to take shape in the late twentieth century. As more foreign visitors descended upon Munich for the city's annual rite of early fall, the brewers had to adapt accordingly. The rest of the world had grown accustomed to drinking only pale beers, thanks mostly to global consolidation and subsequent commoditization. (That's not to say these aren't amazing brews in their own right, regardless of their color and flavor profile. Don't forget, these Munich-based producers really know their way around a brew house.)

Oktoberfest should be on every beer lover's bucket list. But it's definitely another one of those one-and-done experiences. Unless you really like bumper cars.

Dortmund

Munich definitely has an advantage on the overall name-recognition front. Hosting the world's most famous beer festival certainly doesn't hurt either. But when it comes to homegrown local beer styles, plenty of other cities give the Münchners a run for their money. Among those is Dortmund, located roughly four hundred miles to the northwest of Munich in the state of North Rhine-Westphalia. In a lot of ways, the Dortmunder style, when compared to the pilsner and Munich Helles styles, is a bit of the best of both worlds. It's got a bit more hop character than the Munich style, but not quite as much as the pils. And it has considerably more malt character than the latter. It emerged around the same time as the Helles and, like that Bavarian brew, it established itself as a golden alternative to the increasing dominance of the pils. As coal and steel were nineteenth and early twentieth century Dortmund's bread-and-butter industries, Dortmunder became a favorite among workers after a long day in the dark, dusty mines. Dortmunder is often described as more rough-around-the-edges than pils and Helles and is, therefore, the perfect metaphor for the people who loved it most.

The most visible version of the classic lager is DAB Dortmunder Export, the creation of Dortmunder Actien Brauerei (the DAB on the label). The brewery's history dates back to 1868 when it was founded as Herberz & Co Brewery, after the company's original brewmaster, Heinrich Herberz (it's now part of the larger German corporation, Oetker Group). The untrained palate (that is to say, the palates of 99.99 percent of the world's people) might struggle to distinguish a Dortmunder from a Helles from a pils. However, with a comparative tasting, some of the nuances become more apparent.

Düsseldorf

And now for something completely different. About forty-five miles from Dortmund is the much better-known city of Düsseldorf, also in North Rhine-Westphalia. But don't let the proximity fool you. The brewing tradition of Düsseldorf is a million miles away from that of Dortmund. For one thing, it's one of the few places in Germany whose liquid *raison d'être* is still rooted in top-fermented beers (aka ales, although "ale" is an English term and not traditionally used in Germany). Düsseldorf's signature style is Altbier, which literally translates to "old beer," a nod to pre-lager brewing history. And, unlike Munich Helles and Dortmunder, there's no particular date of origin to which it can be traced. Altbier is essentially the culmination of centuries upon centuries of evolution. The only thing about it that's relatively new is its name. Calling it "alt" was a direct response to the encroachment of bright, crisp lagers coming out of what's now the Czech Republic, as well as other parts of Germany.

One of the more remarkable aspects of Düsseldorf is that it has largely resisted the allure of the hugely successful lager styles and has kept Altbier as its official style. In many cities, a drinker frequently must hunt high and low for the indigenous brew, but in Düsseldorf, if they ask for "ein bier," there's a better than 50:50 chance that the wait staff will deliver an Altbier (probably closer to 75 percent in the central Altstadt—old town).

The beer that arrives at the table typically will be bronze in complexion and will have a moderate malt sweetness complemented by just enough hop bitterness. Given its top-fermented lineage, Altbier typically has hints of fruitiness, common in many ales.

However, an ale it may be, but it shares some elements in common with lagers. It's usually fermented and matured at cool temperatures, which top-fermented brews usually avoid. (The term "lager" actually derives from the term for "to rest" or "to keep," as in the period of time it spends resting before it's ready for consumption). Fermentation temperatures range between 55 and 67 degrees Fahrenheit. Most ales avoid dipping too far below 70 degrees.

Düsseldorf frequently gets overshadowed by nearby Cologne, mainly because tourists love visiting the latter city's towering, ornate cathedral. But Düsseldorf retains a bit of an edge on the trendiness factor, thanks to its prominence as a fashion center (think of it as the Milan of Germany). Its Königsallee (King's Avenue) is one of the world's great high-end shopping thoroughfares, a scaled-back version of Fifth Avenue in New York or the Champs Elysees in Paris.

Cologne

No disrespect to Cologne or its many cultural landmarks; it's truly a beautiful city, bisected by the mighty Rhine River—strolling along which is a great way to burn off an afternoon. That, along with visits to all of the art galleries and that immense house of worship (Köln Dom), gets tiring after a while. It's time to sit down and relax with a few drinks. And that means Kölsch.

As session beers (those with modest alcohol content between 3.5 and 5 percent) have come back into fashion among American craft beer drinkers, one particular style that's grown in popularity has been Cologne's signature style, Kölsch. This style is so linked with its home city—Kölsch actually means "local to Köln," the German name for Cologne—that it's a protected appellation. Any breweries making it that are not based in Cologne should be calling it Kölsch-*style* beer. And, like the Altbier of its nearby rival (Cologne and Düsseldorf are separated by a mere thirty miles), Kölsch is of the top-fermented persuasion and, much like that style, cool fermented and cold lagered. But it couldn't be more different in appearance, flavor, and mouthfeel from its neighbor's contribution to global brewing traditions. Where Altbier is copper-hued, Kölsch is a very pale straw color, thanks to the proliferation of pale malt in the 1800s. It's very easy for most people to mistake it as a continental lager for that very reason. But those top-fermenting yeasts suffuse it with fruity elements that place it firmly within ale territory.

As ubiquitous as stateside approximations of the style have become, there are virtually no beer bars—save for odd, authentic to the core German restaurants—that are serving Kölsch (sorry, Kölsch-style) in the proper vessel, the stange (see the section on glassware). The biggest treat associated with drinking in Cologne (and one of the biggest across all of Germany) is the way the Kölsch just keeps coming in most beer halls. Servers make the rounds through the crowd with their circular tray of stanges and don't stop replenishing until you tell them to stop. Don't worry, the practice doesn't undermine anyone's best intentions of a moderate evening. A stange is 20 centiliters, which translates to roughly 6.75 ounces, which is just a little more than half of a standard US bottle of beer. And, since Kölsch is usually just shy of 5 percent ABV, it would probably take about seven stanges before it's time for a drinker of average size to be cut off.

Part of the credit for Kölsch's continued survival at home, along with its emergence as one of the go-to styles in the warmer months on these shores, goes to the brewers of Cologne for their forward-thinking proactivity. In 1948, as the city and the country were still in the early throes of rebuilding after World War II, local brewers got together and formed the Kölsch Convention, an association that established standards for the style and its production methods. Much like Britain's consumer-based Campaign for Real Ale (CAMRA, more on that group in a bit), a critical component of the Kölsch Convention's mission has been to preserve and promote the indigenous style. Without it, Cologne very well could have been steamrolled by Big Pils (not really a thing, but it has a nice, imposing ring).

Leipzig

Here's where things get a little tricky. Most in-the-know beer enthusiasts have rhapsodized about Leipzig in one way or another, whether or not they've actually been—the vast majority haven't— and that's for one reason in particular: gose. The style has attracted a loyal following among American drinkers, especially as sour beers continue to become all the rage. And, even those who eschew sour beers find much to love about gose. The style's tartness is fairly subdued, especially when compared with more pucker-inducing Belgian options like Flemish browns and gueuzes. And there's a subtle salty element that makes the gose an especially able-bodied dining companion.

The gose, sometimes referred to as Leipziger Gose, is another of the dying breed of top-fermented brews in Germany. But, unlike Kölsch and Altbier, gose is anything but ubiquitous in the city with which it is most closely associated, for Leipzig wasn't its first home. The style, which incorporates a considerable degree of wheat into its grain bill, is something of a transplant, having originated about a millennium ago in the town of Goslar, located on the banks of the River Gose. Gose-making eventually shifted to Leipzig after Goslar declined as a medieval center of industry. Gose's trademark salinity likely derived from the salty aquifers native to Goslar, which Leipziger brewers later adapted.

As far as where one should drink gose? Well, you're best bet is an American beer bar. Beer pilgrims heading to Leipzig in search of the local style will have to a fair amount of sleuthing to find it. To be sure, Leipzig pubs are still serving it; there are just significantly fewer of them doing so. Many travelers spend an entire day barhopping before they can find a glass of the stuff. But when they do, it's well worth it. Bonus points if they find it served in the traditional, cylindrical glassware, which resembles a much taller stange with an extended, circular base (it would tip over otherwise).

Berlin

It would be a gross oversight on this little tour of Germany to skip the country's densely populated capital city. However, those seeking a unified beer tradition are likely to be a bit confused. Berlin absolutely has a beer culture, one of the most pronounced in the entire world. However, that culture is all over the map. Berlin is essentially New York City, in that many of its inhabitants originated in other places. And, being such a cosmopolitan center, influences from all over the world are apparent. When it comes to beer, though, German products obviously dominate. But locals and visitors are far more likely to quaff ubiquitous pilsners and dunkels (as well as global styles popularized by American craft brewers) than they are the native style, Berliner Weisse. The wheat-based style that originated in the German capital is known for its pleasant tartness and low ABV (around 3 percent). The minimal presence of alcohol is only matched by its scarcity at Berliner bars, although it's not quite the phantom that gose is in Leipzig (it's likely to pop up at about every fifth watering hole or so).

Berliner Weisse has a couple of other things in common with the Leipziger libation. It's wheat-based and known for its pleasant tartness. But apparently the sourness (hopefully not the alcohol content) was a bit too much for some drinkers, so it became common to order it *mit schüss*, with a shot of red or green syrup—usually raspberry or woodruff flavor—to make it more pleasing to the palate. (These days in Berlin, many servers quietly laugh at you for even ordering a beer that has become the province of people's grandparents. They'll often ask that you repeat your order to ensure that they heard you correctly and that what you really wanted wasn't lost in translation.) To add even more insult to injury, the wide, cylindrical glass that serves as the traditional serving vessel usually comes equipped with a straw. Oh, the indignity!

Fortunately for lovers of good beer everywhere, the style has had a bit of a renaissance, thanks to artisanal American brewers (many even serve it *mit schüss* in their tasting rooms, which will never cease to be a point of controversy). However, it's yet to make a return in any significant way to its homeland, at least not until the stigma of "old person's" or "girlie" beer fades from the collective consciousness of Berliners.

Bamberg: The Beeriest City in Germany

When people mention that they are going on a beer trip to Germany, others immediately assume they are headed to Munich for Oktoberfest or maybe to Berlin to sample a cross section of the country's brewing output. Certainly, Oktoberfest is a rite of passage for many beer lovers and should be on everyone's shortlist, at least to visit once. As iconic an annual event as it is, it's overrun with tourists, the lines are endless, and there isn't that much diversity in the types of beer available. Berlin, meanwhile, absolutely warrants multiple visits, but not necessarily for the beer. It's a veritable melting pot of styles, but a good example of its own locally specific style, Berliner Weisse, is often hard to come by. Local brands of Berliner Weisse have all but vanished from the German capital; you're more likely to find a decidedly non-German style, such as an IPA or a stout, than you are a genuine Berliner Weisse.

But the one city whose beer demands repeat visits is Bamberg. It's a small town; there aren't any international airports into which one can fly (though it is home to Bamberg-Breitenau Airfield, which is mostly for charter flights). The closest semi-major city is Nuremberg, which welcomes very few direct flights from the States. One likely would have to connect in Frankfurt or Munich, or in possibly a non-German hub like Paris, London, or Zurich. From Nuremberg, the train ride to Bamberg takes about forty-five minutes to an hour. It may seem a bit off the beaten path for American travelers, but the trek is well worth it.

Within the city limits, there are, at last count, nine breweries. This may not sound like a lot to many people, especially anyone who's ever been to Portland, Oregon, and this is Germany, so most people probably expect to find the streets awash in beer. But when one takes into account that Bamberg has a population of little more than 70,000, the number of breweries suddenly becomes a really big deal. For those keeping score, there is a brewery for every 8,000 people.

The city is also home to two malt houses—companies that supply malted barley to breweries in Germany and worldwide—the best known being Weyermann. Take a tour of any craft brewery and chances are you'll find sacks emblazoned with the Weyermann logo.

Bamberg is a picturesque little city in its own right, even for those with little or no interest in beer (when traveling in groups, more often than not there's at least one person who's not a fan). The medieval architecture and canals in the town, which was founded way back in the tenth century, are a big draw for anyone looking for a bit of old-world quaintness. If you walk through the stone archway that serves as the entrance to the old town atop the canal, you're immediately transported back about a half-dozen centuries. In that respect, Bamberg rivals places like Bruges, Belgium; Strasbourg, France; and, on the North American side of the pond, Quebec City.

The biggest non-beer-related draw for tourists is Bamberg Cathedral, constructed in 1237. It's the final resting place of an actual pope, Pope Clement II. And like any self-respecting medieval city, it has a castle to explore. Altenburg castle sits atop one of Bamberg's seven hills.

Now about those hills . . . Tourists traveling anywhere in the world are usually advised to wear comfortable shoes. But when venturing to Bamberg, one should think twice about not heeding this suggestion. Traversing its many paved slopes is often akin to mountaineering. The process of getting up and down seven hills—each with a church sitting atop it—is definitely enough to work up a thirst.

Fortunately, a visitor can sample multiple beer styles in Bamberg—which isn't always the case in other cities where pilsners and dunkels dominate—but the one with which the city is most synonymous is rauchbier. Rauchbier, which translates to "smoke beer," is distinguished by its strikingly smoky character. The flavor is often reminiscent of bacon or a smoked ham. Brewers achieve this flavor profile by drying the malt in kilns over an open flame.

The rauchbier with which most beer enthusiasts worldwide are familiar is Aecht Schlenkerla. The brewery, whose beer hall in the old part of town is often the most crowded attraction in the entire city, traces original production of its flagship brew to 1405. The pub—the very essence of "classic" with its wood-beamed low ceilings—still taps the traditional brew from wooden barrels.

Brauerei Spezial, situated closer to the railway station outside of the old town, is also quite adept at producing its rauchbier, but it's not as widely distributed as Schlenkerla. It's also not as much of a tourist magnet, which is definitely a good thing. However, being a non-German-speaking outsider can be a little disorienting at Spezial. The beer hall contains mostly long, communal wooden tables that seem inviting enough and of the sort you're likely to find in any German city, really. However, don't just sit down without express permission from the host. Often there will be small markers that read "reserviert," which is easy enough to decipher as "reserved." But it's hard to gauge just how much of a table is reserved when the marker is in front of just one seat. The servers will quickly let you know that you've got to leave by X o'clock because the group that reserved six seats at the table will be arriving then. Rule of thumb: regardless of how large a table is, if there's a "reserviert" marker anywhere on it, steer clear of sitting there. And if you do choose to sit there and have a half hour before the reserving party comes in, make sure you finish your entire half-liter glass of beer; an English-speaking local will waste no time in telling you it's considered rude to leave even 10 percent of the drink unfinished. That's especially difficult when you feel like you've hit your limit and things will get unpleasant if you reach the bottom of the glass. (Pro tip: If it really feels impossible to finish and you don't want to appear gauche leaving behind a half-drunk glass, smuggle it into the toilet with you and dump it out. Yes, it's wasteful. The sensible course of action, of course, would be to just know how many is too many before you order another one.)

Beyond the rauchbier breweries, there's so much to discover throughout Bamberg. Fässla, located directly across the street from Spezial, is another must-visit brewery; it actually has an attached hotel where weary beer travelers can rest their heads for the evening. When the weather cooperates—and even when it doesn't (the rain's never stopped anyone)—there's quite a sprawling courtyard beer garden with plenty of communal picnic tables and all sorts of little nooks and crannies with ledges on which drinkers can rest their beers. Fässla also doubles as a bit of a museum, as its walls are adorned with various ancient brewing tools.

Fässla usually seals off the outdoor area by November, but that shouldn't be a deterrent to dropping by in the colder months. For a truly local experience, hang out in the hallway/foyer. That's no joke. The long corridor—more of an oversized anteroom—offers some of the best local color the city has to offer. A server sells beer through a window that separates the hall from the dining area inside. On the opposite side across from that window is the entrance to the hotel. There are a few tables in the hall, but mostly folks sip and chat at ledges lining the room. It's particularly lively around 6 p.m. when most have just left work and are winding down with a couple of mugs before heading home.

Even if the place is empty, it's just as entertaining to lose yourself in the foyer's mural, which captures Bamberg circa the mid seventeenth century; Fässla reports an origin that dates back to 1649. Look closely and you'll notice that a gnome, Fässla's icon/mascot, is performing all of the brewing in the mural. He's visible on the glassware, the bottles, and the coasters, and is fairly ubiquitous throughout the brewery and all of its drinking areas.

Fässla's façade and communal areas have a very classic, old-world aesthetic, which contrasts starkly with the actual brewing facility in the back. Peeking through the brew house window, one half expects to see puffy-shirted horse-and-buggy-era artisans stirring the liquid in a wooden mash tun. But the operation is twenty-first century all the way with stainless steel kettles and fermenting vessels, all brand-spanking new from Krones, the leading equipment manufacturer in Europe and likely the world.

As for the beer itself, there isn't a bad one in the bunch. It wouldn't be a German brewery without a world-class pilsner, and Fässla Gold-Pils more than delivers. And lest we forget that this is Bavaria, the brewery offers Fässla Lagerbier, which adheres closely to a quintessentially Bavarian style, Munich Helles. Wheat beer aficionados will immediately fall in love with Fässla upon learning there are two hefeweizens available: Weizla Helles (pale) and Weizla Dunkel (dark). And speaking of dunkel, Zwergla is a nice, dark counterpoint to Lagerbier. Finally, those not driving will enjoy Bambergator, an 8.5 percent ABV doppelbock that's usually available in bottles only.

About two blocks from Spezial lies Bamberger Weissbierhaus (look for the bright yellow building), the beer hall for the Maisel brewery. Maisel actually ceased operations around 2008, but its brands, particularly its famous Maisel's Weisse, are still being produced under license. Weissbierhaus tends

A truck carries Fässla through Bamberg.

to be a little more low-key than the other two nearby beer halls, which is an attractive quality at dinner time, when one can either fill up before a pub crawl through the city or before capping off the evening. An epic option (for carnivores, that is) is the Weissbierplate featuring weisswurst (Bavarian veal-based white sausage), bratwurst, and kesselfleisch. The latter component, which translates to "kettle meat," is essentially boiled pork belly.

Back inside the walls of the old town, there are a few other breweries of note. Gasthausbrauerei Ambrausanium has the distinction of being based right next door to Bamberg's biggest beer destination, Schlenkerla. That's likely a boon on crowded evenings at the venerable neighbor (read: just about every evening). Schlenkerla is probably grateful to have and adjacent brewpub to shoulder some of the burden, especially in high tourist season.

Ambrausanium is decidedly more modern in its décor and overall vibe—it's actually a much younger operation, having opened in the current century. Visitors will sip its Hell, Dunkel, or Bernsteinweizen (hefeweizen) amidst the striking copper kettles sharing the space in the bar and dining area. The brewery will usually have one of its seasonals available as well: bock, doppelbock, or Sandkerwa-Festbier (a märzen-style brew).

Ambrausanium is definitely not hurting for business (thanks again, neighbor) and the twenty- and thirtysomething servers know it. They can be quite aloof at times.

Barely a five-minute walk from Ambrausanium—still in the Altstadt—is Klosterbrau, which, architecturally speaking, is much more in the traditional vein than Ambrausanium. And Klosterbrau has plenty of tradition from which to draw; it claims to be the oldest operating brewery in Bamberg, with a history that stretches back to 1533. It naturally has changed hands quite a bit throughout its five centuries of existence; the current owning family, the Brauns, took over the operation in the mid-nineteenth century and is now in its fifth generation.

The beer hall is significantly cozier than some of the others and is an ideal place to decompress, especially for those who've just visited Schlenkerla around the corner. All of the usual styles are represented—pilsner (Bamberger Gold) and hefeweizen (Braun's Weisse), in particular—and it's always a lucky evening when the schwarzbier (German black beer) is on tap. Seasonally speaking, there's Braunbier (an Oktoberfest/märzen style) and a Maibock at different times of the year.

But a true sampling of everything Bamberg and the rest of the Franconia region has to offer is found at Abseits, which is well outside the walls of the Altstadt and a good mile from Fässla and Spezial. Abseits isn't actually a brewery, it's a beer bar with an extensive list—between forty and fifty—that offers a cross section of brews you're unlikely to find in one place anywhere in the state of Bavaria. It's also as local as local gets in these parts.

Abseits is one of the very few places where visitors can sample experimental beers made by Weyermann's—yes, the malt house. The company has its own on-site brewery where it makes test batches to illustrate the complexity of the range of malt styles it offers. They're the beers Weyermann's serves at what is perhaps the liveliest and most hospitable booths at major European trade shows like Nuremberg's Brau Beviale and Munich's drinktec. And these beers are not limited to German styles. Weyermann often produces everything from pumpernickel porters to India pale ales.

5

Ale-narchy in the UK

The Beers of Britain and the Pubs That Love Them

The British have left such an indelible mark on brewing traditions throughout the world that they're often taken for granted. The American pale ale, which has become a reliable staple for craft breweries across the United States and other regions of the globe, would not even be a thing had it not been for its venerable English ancestor. The same goes for the India pale ale (IPA). American brewers adapted and reinvented the style in the late twentieth century and made international drinkers fall in love with the hop-forward brew, but had British brewers not overhopped the ale to survive the circuitous, nearly 20,000-mile ocean journey to satisfy thirsty soldiers and sailors stationed in South Asia, what's now the most popular craft beer style would never have been born—much less have such a household acronym. Also, the notion of the "session beer" that's sweeping the nation after an extensive period of high-ABV obsession? That's just "beer" to the Brits.

The next time you walk into a bar and hear someone ask "what's on cask?" remember that the term would never have even been used in reference to twenty-first century beer had it not been for the way English ale has been served and enjoyed for centuries.

Britain is one of those places in which where you drink is as important as what you drink. While it's perfectly fine to buy some pint bottles at the local Tesco or Marks and Spencer and bring them home to enjoy with dinner or in front of the telly, it is much more British to drink them at the pub. (And you'd better hurry up and do so because the classic British pub is a dying breed.)

For travelers touring the United Kingdon, drinking at a pub, whether it be in London, Manchester, Edinburgh, Glasgow, or Cardiff, is about as much of a cultural experience as visiting the plethora of history and art museums, watching a football match, and going to the theater. So it's

The UK's ubiquitous hand pumps, dispensing cask-conditioned ale.

important to include a pub crawl on the sightseeing portion of an itinerary rather than just relegating it to the "nightlife" elements. There's as much history contained inside the four walls of, say, Ye Olde Cheshire Cheese on London's Fleet Street as there is in the British Museum. It may not be as obvious and displayed behind a glass case, but it's there, and the bartender will be more than happy to discuss it with you over a pint or two.

There's a bit of etiquette for anyone who desires to order a pint at a British pub. Before you try to make eye contact with the barkeep—before you even approach the bar proper, for that matter—figure out what you want. If you're standing at the bar with a blank, indecisive look on your face, your bartender and the other pubgoers waiting to place their order will be visibly miffed. And, when it comes time to get the bartender's attention, do not wave money in his or her direction. That is truly bad form and is more likely to get you ignored than anything else.

Feeling peckish? If the pub serves food, don't sit down at a table and expect the waitstaff to come and take your order. Read the menu, make a decision, and order at the bar. Then go back to your seat. They'll bring it out to you. (This applies only to pubs, mind you. Don't try this is at a regular restaurant.)

If you're with a group, it's traditional for individual members of the group to each buy a round at some point—depending on how large the group is, of course. You definitely don't want to be the only one who hasn't bought a round. It's fairly bad form.

One of the sadder aspects of British drinking culture is that the same type of industrial macro lagers prevalent in the United States and other parts of the world have come to dominate the fridges and taps of even the most traditional of pubs. Preserving traditional British ales has been the *raison d'etre* of the Campaign for Real Ale (CAMRA), an organization that launched in the early '70s as those mass-produced, light lagers had already significantly encroached on the most British of drinking institutions.

The "real" ales to which CAMRA's proper name refers are essentially unfiltered, unpasteurized top-fermented beers served from special casks (originally wood, now predominantly metal) and containing live yeast cultures. There's no forced carbonation and the beverage is delivered via gravity or a hand pump that's part of an apparatus often known as a beer engine. Because the beer is a living thing, it has a very limited shelf life. It's pretty much past its prime after a full day or day and a half on the bar. Publicans must take great care to keep it at an optimal temperature to enable the yeast to continue to thrive. And, because all of the carbonation comes from the secondary fermentation in the cask, it's not always consistently carbonated.

For the most part, CAMRA has succeeded in its mission, as traditional, so-called "real ales" have survived and retained a loyal, albeit niche following. Such beers represent about 10 percent of the entire UK market, but without CAMRA, it's very likely that that number would be pretty close to zero.

British Breweries: Something Old, Something New

In most countries, including—well, especially—the United States, if a brewery claims a century-plus of history, usually that brewery (with a few notable exceptions) barely resembles that which it once was. And these breweries are often complaint magnets for beer drinkers, "The Man." Not so in some of the UK's more revered establishments. Fuller's is probably the best example of this dynamic. Founded in 1845, the company officially known as Fuller, Smith and Turner Plc is a respected London institution that continues to produce real ales of mostly unimpeachable quality. (That's not to say it doesn't have its detractors. Everyone needs something to complain about.)

The brewery, known for London Pride pale, Fuller's E.S.B. (Extra Special Bitter), and London Porter—the yardstick against which all other porters should be measured—has, since its founding, occupied its stately Griffin Brewery in the West London district of Chiswick. The brewery building itself is much older than the company that owns it, as it housed brewing operations for long-defunct proprietors as far back as the seventeenth century.

The Fullers tour offers a treasure trove of out-of-commission eye candy.

There are also plenty of London beer enthusiasts who resent Fuller's seeming ubiquity. It owns around four hundred pubs throughout southern England with a disproportionate number in the capital city itself. As for Chiswick, they might as well just rename the place "Fuller's."

But a drinker is unlikely to sample a better imperial pint of London Porter anywhere in the world other than the space within a two-mile radius of the Griffin Brewery. Even those in the "I don't like dark beers" crowd are likely to experience a near-religious conversion whilst in Fuller's orbit.

And then there's the brewery tour. All of the new upstarts are well worth touring. However, like most craft breweries, they're just unassuming industrial buildings with lots of stainless steel tanks inside. They get a little samey after a while (though there's no better place to sample their products, so by all means, old or young, don't avoid any of them.) Fuller's is living history. Sure, there's plenty of high-tech equipment there, but the powers that be didn't throw the baby out with the bath water. Much of the nineteenth century tech is still there for ornamental and educational purposes, and the fact that it was once in use at that very spot makes it so much more than a museum.

A rather *noir*ish look at the exterior of Fuller's Griffin Brewery in Chiswick.

Classic British Pubs

A new wave of beer bars has swept through the United Kingdom, offering stunningly long draft and bottle lists that feature selections not just from British breweries but from the Yanks and continental Europeans, as well. But we won't get into those bars quite yet; a couple of them will be featured later, in the section on the best international beer bars. Here, we're going

Real ale casks at Fullers.

Fuller's boasts a world-class barrel-aging program for some of its smaller-batch brews.

to cover the classic "locals," the pubs that have survived city-leveling fires, political upheaval, plague, and the Blitz.

Pubs typically fall into one of three categories: managed, tenanted, and free houses. Individuals in the employ of pub chains run locals of the managed variety. Meanwhile, pub corporations or breweries themselves own the building and all of its décor and equipment, which the pub's "landlord" rents from the owner. Free houses are just as the name suggests, free of ties to a larger corporation or brewery and owned by private individuals. The main difference between managed and tenanted pubs is that in the former, the parent companies and/or breweries exercise complete control over what's served at the bar (this is known as the "tied-house" system, which the Twenty-first Amendment prohibits in the United States), and with the latter, the owners have considerable, but not absolute, influence over what the drinking venue stocks. It's fairly common to enter a pub with six to eight cask hand pulls for different styles of beer, but, upon closer inspection, you'd see that they're all from the same brewery. And that's not necessarily a bad thing, considering the quality of some of those breweries, which include fine purveyors of real ale like Fuller's, Greene King, and Adnams.

As for free houses, since they're not completely beholden to corporate parents, they can usually carry whatever they choose (theoretically—at the end of the day it's up to what patrons ultimately buy, and, more cynically, whichever beer suppliers make the best sales pitch).

CAMRA's mission also extends to preserving real ale's optimal drinking environment: the classic British pub. In recent decades, generations-old drinking establishments have been closing fairly rapidly, but perhaps not as fast as they would have had CAMRA not been on the case.

The Mark of Quality

In-the-know drinkers are always on the lookout for the Cask Marque seal affixed to the door or a window of the pub. Cask Marque is a voluntary system of accreditation for pubs that do their best to present fine real ale in top form. It's run by an independent organization known as Cask Marque Trust. Since it was launched in 1997, Cask Marque has dispatched a certified team of forty-five assessors—similar to secret shoppers—to ensure that the cask programs at 20,000-plus pubs all over Great Britain (and even in the United States, since cask ales have become an increasingly popular option) are up to snuff. This process involves checking the temperature, appearance, aroma, and, of course, flavor of the ales. The assessors aren't just folks who want an excuse to drink a lot (sorry, aspiring assessors!);

rather, they're well trained individuals who are either brewers themselves or who have extensive sensory and technical training related to the handling of beer. Cask Marque Trust says its team of assessors represents a collective millennium of beer industry experience (an average of a little more than twenty-two years per assessor, so not too shabby).

The assessors use calibrated thermometers to ensure brews are within the range of 11 to 13 degrees Celsius (roughly between 52 and 55 degrees Fahrenheit to those of us on the non-metric side of the pond.) There's a degree's worth of wiggle room on either side. They're not monsters! It sounds warm, but remember, this is real ale, and it's best enjoyed at temperatures exceeding those to which most American lager consumers are accustomed. (Light lagers of the Coors Light and Bud Light ilk are usually served at around 38 degrees Fahrenheit.)

Next comes the visual test. If you're sitting in a pub and you notice someone holding the pint up to a light fixture and giving it a really intense stare, it's likely you're witnessing an assessment in action. If it's not a well-illuminated establishment, don't be surprised if the inspector starts shining a flashlight at it. (It's probably a little less obtrusive these days now that the vast majority of people have an adequate light built into their smartphones.)

Now it's time for the nosing. The assessor lets all of the aromatic complexity waft through his or her olfactory system. This is another instance where proper temperature is critical. If the beer is even a few degrees below 52 degrees Fahrenheit, the aromatics wouldn't be able to fully assert themselves.

Oh yes, and then they finally taste it.

While this may sound like a lot of trouble, it's all for a good cause. That Cask Marque logo on one's door is like its own currency.

And spotting a Cask Marque-accredited pub requires far less literal legwork. There's now an app, CaskFinder, which is loaded with nearly 10,000 certified establishments. When users actually reach one of the pubs, they can scan the QR code on the certificate and receive some charming swag (fridge magnets, bottle openers, and the like). The ones who scan one hundred barcodes are invited to become a Cask Marque Ambassador.

Ye Olde Cheshire Cheese (London)

Locals will tell you that Ye Olde Cheschire Cheese is mostly a tourist spot, and they'd be, for the most part, right. But that doesn't mean it' s not worth checking out, even for just a quick look-see. It's a bit of an institution; there's been a pub at its site since 1538. The round, illuminated sign dangling outside the pub reads "Rebuilt 1667." That, of course, is a year after the

Great Fire of London. The interior reveals quite a bit of old wood on the floors and paneling—it's not likely that most of it goes all the way back to the seventeenth century, but there's definitely some nineteenth-century carpentry going on there. It's nothing short of cavernous, with lots of nooks and crannies—some fairly intimate, others more partylike—on two levels. There aren't any windows, so absolutely no natural light makes its way inside. It adds a bit of spookiness to the experience, and it also helps sell the trip-back-in-time aspect. As is common with many of the classic pubs throughout the UK, it's operated by a single brewery—in this case, the Samuel Smith Brewery in Tadcaster, Yorkshire. Sam Smith brews are easy enough to find in the US, but there will probably be a couple on draft at Ye Olde Cheshire Cheese that don't make their way to these shores. And there's probably no better environment in which to try them. Unlike many of the generations-old brewing companies on the British Isles, most of Sam Smith's ales are not on cask; rather, they're on traditional draft.

London's Ye Olde Cheshire Cheese.

The George Inn (London)

This one has so much history embedded within its walls that an entire book has been written about it. Renowned British beer and cider writer Pete Brown's *Shakespeare's Local: A History of Britain Through One Pub* details the storied past of the George Inn, which is located in the Southwark neighborhood near London Bridge. Charles Dickens frequented the spot and, as the title suggests, William Shakespeare may very well have sipped at the location, as well. It's located fairly close to the original site of the Globe Theater, so there's a good chance (though no definitive proof) the Bard got his drink on at the George. The pub is quite spacious, as it's been built up over its six or so centuries of existence. There's a standard bar area, a roomy dining/drinking area in the back, and a function room upstairs with its own bar. There's also a fairly large courtyard outside with communal tables for those more temperate days (it's also the only place for smokers, as London has had an indoor ban for many years). Real ales on hand pump are mostly from Greene King brewery, but there are plenty of guest beers as well.

The Blackfriar (London)

Part of the Nicholsons chain, the Blackfriar has been at the space since about a decade before the outbreak of World War I. The establishment's monastic imagery is a nod to the Dominican friary that once stood at the site. It's one of handful of pubs throughout the British capital that's as much a sight to behold on the outside as it is on the inside. The pub is nestled inside a narrow wedge-shaped structure, not unlike Manhattan's famous Flatiron building, albeit considerably smaller. Blackfriar's aesthetic adheres to the Arts and Crafts movement, of which the building's designers—architect H. Fuller Clark and designer Henry Poole—were a part. It's impossible to get bored while sipping the freshest offerings from the likes of Greene King and Adnams and dousing your fish and chips with malt vinegar. The space is a veritable gallery of monk-centric sculptures, paintings, and mosaics. Even when the place gets jammed with people (especially during lunch and after work), there's still a laid-back, relaxing vibe. A bit of a religious experience, one might say.

A Not-So-Old Pub with a Classic Feel: The Knights Templar (London)

Though it's part of the Wetherspoon family of pubs, the Knights Templar on Chancery Lane in London is, visually, its own beast to behold. The interior

London's classic Blackfriar pub.

offers some gilded architectural eye candy, which is appropriate since it occupies the former site of the Union Bank. High, vaulted ceilings (up to twenty-five feet!), towering columns, chandeliers, and ornate trim make this a great spot to duck into after a hard day's work and get transported out of your own head and into another time. The pub takes its name from the Catholic Church-sanctioned twelfth-century military order. The Knights Templar is quite deceiving in its beauty. The antique décor makes it seem like the bar's been there forever. The building may have some history to it—the erstwhile financial institution set up shop in 1865—but the pub itself didn't open until the late 1990s.

The Kings Arms (Salford, Greater Manchester)

Manchester has long been famous for its music scene (Joy Division/New Order, the Smiths, the Stone Roses, Happy Mondays—too many to name), so it's fitting that one of its institutions of fine drink and socializing now belongs to the singer of '80s and '90s New Wave and Britpop bands. In 2011, Paul Heaton—famous as the front man of the Housemartins and, later, the Beautiful South—bought a storied pub in the greater Manchester borough of Salford (birthplace of the aforementioned Joy Division). The brick Victorian-era exterior of The Kings Arms resembles a small castle as it curves around its corner. Inside the double-story structure, some of its late-nineteenth-century woodworking and tile remains, and its six hand pumps (lots of local stuff that's hard to find outside of the north) make it a destination for cask ale seekers. But it's the modern touches that keep it relevant for an evolving clientele. Comedy and live music acts (what else would you expect from Heaton?) keep butts in the seats and beer flowing constantly.

The Blue Blazer (Edinburgh, Scotland)

One of the great things about drinking at a pub in Scotland is that you can get a fairly high-end single malt Scotch for what you'd normally pay for a latte at Starbucks. And, believe it or not, a good Scotch whiskey pairs remarkably well with a fine Scottish (or English, for that matter) ale. Whiskey is just distilled beer; both libations pretty much use the same malt. File the Blue Blazer under "Scottish institution." It's in the Old Town, so there will likely be a fair number of tourists there, but a goodly number of locals should offset the out-of-towner population. It's also an establishment that

Edinburgh's Blue Blazer is one of the better-known haunts in the Scottish city.

keeps its heart in tradition, while fully embracing the modern. In other words, there are plenty of hand-pulled Scottish 80-shilling real ales and such, along with selections from the new crop of craft brewers that have been popping up in Scotland and throughout the UK in the past decade. The pub manages to retain its classic feel with a bar made of dark wood and halved oak barrels mounted on the top shelf for added ornamental effect.

6

The Myth and the Monks

What's the Big Deal About Belgium?

There's a common trajectory among many enthusiasts' love affair with beer. The casual drinker—and this is a huge generality and is by no means meant to be a definitive rule—tends to equate brewing greatness with one country: Germany. And there's nothing wrong with that. As you've already read, Germany is one of the world's foremost beer cultures, and it's responsible for so much of what we're drinking today.

However, as the beer-curious get a little deeper into the subject, they begin to become fixated on another European country, one that had barely been on their radar, save for any thoughts related to waffles and chocolate. The moment many drinkers discover Belgian beer, their entire worldview shifts. A common first exclamation is along the lines of "Wow! I didn't know beer could taste like that." Even upon this revelation, they've barely just scratched the surface.

Entire books—series of books, even—have been written on the stylistic traditions that have emerged over the centuries in the tiny Western European country of Belgium, and even what these books cover is just the tip of the iceberg. On these pages, we'll hit on some of Belgium's regional traditions and how they shaped the styles we know today.

Trappist Ales

Trappist beers aren't a style per se but are more of a brewing tradition. To be designated Trappist, the brews must be produced by monks within the walls of a monastery that is certified to be a part of the Trappist order. Belgium used to lay claim to most of the beer-producing Trappist abbeys, but that's gradually changing. Just in the past few years, monasteries in Italy, the Netherlands, Austria, and the United States have been approved by the

International Trappist Association. There now are eleven operating Trappist breweries; six of those are in Belgium. Those six are Brasserie de Rochefort, Brouwerij der Trappisten van Westmalle, Brouwerij Westvleteren/St. Sixtus, Biéres de Chimay, Brasserie d'Orval, and Brouwerij der Stin-Benedictusabdij de Achelse Kluis (more commonly known as Achel).

Styles vary, but, for the most part, expect to find at least a Dubbel and a Tripel at most of them. Dubbels very often are malty and brownish with notes of dark fruit (figs, dates, raisins, you name it) and are usually around 7.5 percent alcohol by volume. Tripels can be dark, but the better-known

The elusive Westvleteren 12.

ones, particularly Westmalle Tripel, are more of a medium amber and are markedly dryer than the Dubbels. Expect them to be around 9 percent ABV.

The brothers' beer-making tradition reaches back centuries. Back in the day, the monks would often produce beer mostly for their own consumption (and for fundraising as well), and their brews were frequently their sole form of sustenance during heavy fasting periods. In the Middle Ages, it was a lot safer to drink beer than it was water (it was boiled, after all), so it was also the brotherhood's hydration substitute.

They are still brewing for their own consumption, but often those beers are a bit milder than the high-ABV stuff the public drinks (just over 6 percent is common). Proceeds from the commercially available brews support the abbeys and frequently fund infrastructure renovations and other improvements.

Abbey Ales

Abbeys and Belgian beer, well beyond just the Trappist offerings, are inextricably linked. Monks are very frequently part of the logos and general trade dress of brands that have no modern connection to abbeys. Often these brands' styles are similar to the Trappists' output, even if they're produced and marketed by laypeople.

That's not to say monks are completely out of the equation with all non-clergy-produced abbey-style beers. A commercial brewery might have an arrangement with a particular monastery.

That's the dynamic behind Maredsous, the name of which Duvel Moortgat licenses from the Maredsous Benedictine abbey. The Puurs, Belgium-based brewery first started making the brand in 1963 and today produces Maredsous Blonde, Brune, and Triple.

The St. Bernardus Brewery in the town of Watou used to have a similar deal with an actual Trappist monastery. Between 1946 and 1992, St. Bernardus was licensed by the monks at St. Sixtus to brew products under that abbey's name. When the order agreed in 1992 that Trappist beers may only be brewed inside an actual Trappist monastery, St. Bernardus continued to brew, but it now markets its products under its own name. The brewery's brands, which include St. Bernardus Tripel, St. Bernardus Pater 6, St. Bernardus Prior 8, and St. Bernardus Abt 12, are quite well known and respected in their own right. St. Sixtus, meanwhile, produces the often hard-to-find Westvelteren Trappist range, whose elusiveness (with a few exceptions, it's usually only available for purchase at the abbey) has led to all sorts of Westvleteren hoarding and horse-trading among beer geeks.

The Augustijn brand, whose labels feature a monk stirring wort with a large paddle, claims a heritage dating all the way back to 1295. That's when the brand's modern brewery, Brouwerij Van Steenberge, says the Augustinian friars commenced their beer-making activities at their monastery in the Flemish city of Ghent. In the late 1970s, the brotherhood hooked up with Van Steenberge, which has been brewing Augustijn in its current iteration since 1982. Today, Van Steenberge brews Augustijn Blond, Dark, and Grand Cru. In 2011, Van Steenberge's beers became available to an even wider audience as it signed a worldwide distribution agreement with global brewing behemoth SABMiller.

Speaking of gargantuan multinational beer marketers, the monk-free abbey-style ale that is perhaps best known among mainstream drinkers is Leffe, which is owned, in its twenty-first century form, by Anheuser-Busch InBev. The story Leffe's owners like to tell traces the brand's origins to about 1240. That's the year that the brothers at the Notre-Dame de Leffe abbey constructed their first brewery, whose products helped stave off all sorts

Brasserie Dupont.

Some eye-catching copper at Brouwerij Omer Vander Ghinste.

of nasty pestilences—particularly the Black Plague—transmitted through unsanitary water.

The abbey thrived for centuries before the French Revolution forced it to shutter, and it didn't reopen until nearly a century and a half later in 1929. It resumed its brewing operations about a quarter-century later and ultimately ended up in the hands of what would become AB InBev. Needless to say, the large industrial brewing conglomerate has no modern connection with an abbey of any kind.

Farmhouse Ales

As highly romanticized as monastic imagery has become, the monks aren't the only ones who have defined Belgian brewing. The farming community has played an equally important role, and the style most closely associated with the rural agricultural lifestyle is the saison, the name of which is based on the French word for "season." It's brewed in one *saison* and consumed in another.

The farmers had to do something to occupy their time and supplement their livelihood when the land was completely dead in winter, so they brewed beer with the grains they accumulated during the recent harvest. When summer came and it was time for the heavy field work, the farm workers had plenty to drink. Belgium has American craft brewers to thank for helping to keep the style alive because, much like an agricultural economy, saisons had become in danger of being relegated to the past. But there are many breweries in Belgium, particularly in the French-speaking Wallonia region, that have kept the style alive throughout the decades. The most famous of those is Brasserie Dupont, whose Saison Dupont has been brewed in one form or another since 1844. The 6.5 ABV beer—a typical strength for the style, but they have been known to be slightly higher or lower in alcohol—pours a deep straw-like blonde and boasts both a pronounced citrusy bitterness and a grainy breadiness, with a touch of wild, yeasty funk.

A much newer Wallonia brewery that produces a popular interpretation of the classic style is Brasserie Fantome, known for its flagship brew, Fantome Saison (look for the label with the rather impish-looking ghost on it). The brewery opened in 1988, a time when American craft beer was just in its infancy and most stateside producers had yet to fully discover the style.

Lambic Country

One can't discuss Belgian brewing without mentioning one of its most strikingly original styles, lambic. Produced in a region within about a forty-five minute drive of Brussels, lambic and its sister style, gueuze, have become something of a connoisseur's style. In their rawest form, they're not the most approachable of ales; their claim to fame is spontaneous fermentation, in which ambient microorganisms native to the region do all of the sugar-to-alcohol heavy lifting. The process results in a complex and intensely sour beer that's fairly off-putting for first-time drinkers (and for many seasoned ones as well). That's why the bulk of their commercial volume is from fruit-enhanced beers. One of the more popular producers is Lindemans, which is best known for Lindemans Framboise, a raspberry lambic. The fruit masks a lot of the style's funkier elements.

On the outskirts of Brussels lies the Cantillon brewery, which has become one of the biggest destinations for international beer pilgrims. (It's a wonder that any of them find it because it's so unassuming on a tight urban side street. Cantillon's legend makes it seem larger than life. One expects

The legendary Cantillon brewery.

to find a cross between a rustic farmhouse and the Parthenon, with Hollywood red-carpet-style spotlights swinging back and forth in front of it. The façade is deceptively unimpressive.)

The most appealing element of the Cantillon brewery, aside from getting to taste its very tart lambic and gueuze (a blend of young and old lambics) offerings, is the self-guided tour that lets visitors stroll through a portal into the past. Among the sights one can behold are ancient-looking fermentation tanks, along with dust and cobwebs strewn throughout the room. No, this isn't a poorly maintained museum; it's an actual, functioning brewery. The abandoned-attic motif attracts the type of ambient microbes that give lambic its wild character.

Stylistic Revival

The amazing aspect of many of the styles we traditionally think of as Belgian would be all but lost to history if it hadn't been for the encroachment of industrial lagers. When pilsener-style lagers were invented in the nineteenth century, they quickly swept Europe and became the world's dominant style. By the middle of the twentieth century, it became difficult for family-owned Belgian breweries to compete when the big guys were

Zwanze Day!

If you happen to follow any beer geeks or homebrewers on Facebook or Twitter, then you are no doubt familiar with Zwanze Day, the Cantillon Brewery's annual worldwide observance. It's a day that very likely floods your newsfeed each September and makes common folk (that is, 99.99 percent of the population) scratch their heads.

The word Zwanze loosely translates to "joker," or at least something related to joking, but Zwanze Day itself is no joke. Each year the Cantillon brewers experiment with styles that aren't part of their regular release schedule (as if lambics and gueuzes aren't the very definition of "experimental!").

For instance, the 2015 edition was a stout that incorporated the brewery's trademark spontaneous fermentation and spent more than two years maturing in casks. These were no ordinary casks, either. Some had previously contained lambic, others French wine, and the remaining were the maturation vessels for cognac.

The brewers produce a very limited batch of the stuff but generously share the wealth—what little of it there is—making it available at a very select group of locations worldwide. The number of US breweries and bars that get their hands on kegs is usually around twenty-five, coast to coast (and they're typically the crème de la crème of drinking establishments; many of them get shout-outs throughout this book). Worldwide, including the US, the number is fewer than sixty. You can imagine the scene outside of those places on Zwanze Day. Many sites make a party out of it, selling tickets (which sell out extremely quickly) or holding a lottery and giving the Zwanze brew away for free to a group of lucky winners. (Sometimes it's for legal or logistical reasons.)

making pils far more efficiently and on a much grander scale. It was around that time that many of those independent operations began reaching back into their respective pasts for styles that were very specific to their immediate regions but were all but extinct. (The Trappist and other abbey brewers, for the most part, have always been making their traditional styles because they didn't have to compete commercially with Big Beer; ditto with the core lambic producers.)

Pils is still the dominant style throughout Belgium; keep in mind that Stella Artois is Belgian, and it's a huge mass-market brand. It's easy to see that from Stella is where much of the pils volume is coming from, especially when you consider the fact that it's owned by the largest brewery in the world, Anheuser-Busch InBev.

It's the hovering presence of global behemoths like AB InBev that has made export a huge component of the independent breweries' business models. On average, the indies export about 60 percent of their output; some go as high as 80 percent.

Belgian beer has become so popular abroad that many breweries in the United States, Italy, Scandinavia, Japan, Korea, Hong Kong, and other parts of Asia are adapting the classic styles and developing products that, in a lot of ways, rival the originals. The independent brewers of Belgium saw that happening and, while they were honored that their traditions have inspired so many around the world (imitation is the sincerest form of flattery, after all), they became wary of the competition. In 2007, the owners of some of those breweries teamed up and created Belgian Family Brewers, a nonprofit federation of twenty-one producers from across Wallonia and Flanders—about 15 percent of all of the country's breweries—whose aim is to promote historic, independent family operations. The member breweries created a Belgian Family Brewers seal, which appears on their products and is designed to be a mark of artisanal quality. More importantly, it distinguishes the members' products from the thousands of imitations on the market worldwide.

Longevity is a prerequisite for membership; in order for a brewery to be eligible to join, it must have at least fifty years of continuous production under its belt. To put that into perspective, if American craft brewers had to meet the same criterion, there would be three members: Anchor, Yuengling, and August Schell.

Most of the members have far more brewing experience than that bare minimum. Collectively, the twenty-one members represent some 3,500 years of beer-making history. There are even a few that go back ten generations to about the fifteenth century.

What's most amazing about the organization is that it didn't launch until the latter part of the last decade. When dealing with centuries of familial pride, there are a lot of egos at play; some families don't always play well with others. That's what makes the fact that such an endeavor exists all the more remarkable.

Other Belgian Breweries of Note

It's a daunting task to narrow down Belgium's bounty to just a handful of breweries. Volumes upon volumes have been written about the inextricable link between the small country and its most prized beverage. But here are a few that are fairly renowned.

Duvel Moortgat

Duvel Moortgat is one of the largest of the family-owned breweries. Its annual output is around a half-million barrels (for some perspective, that's only about half the output of a US craft operation like New Belgium), and

The Duvel Moortgat brewery.

Vintage brand signage in Duvel Moortgat's tasting room.

in recent years much of its growth has come from acquisition. However, its acquisitions are not the same as those that have made the macros, well, macros. Duvel Moortgat hasn't been intent on driving the competition from the market but rather has attempted to preserve the heritage of some well-respected, classic Belgian brands that may have vanished or been absorbed by much larger companies in whose portfolios they wouldn't get the attention they deserve. Liefmans and Brasserie d'Achouffe are among those. But it was the brewery's purchase of iconic Antwerp brewery De Koninck (founded in 1833) in 2010 that best illustrated what Duvel's been doing—or rather how previous owner Modeste Van den Bogaert characterized the company's strategy: "The company wasn't in really good shape and Heineken was going to acquire it and, indeed, [Van den Bogaert] said 'I'm not even selling it, I'm lending it to you so you could continue the legacy of my brewery,'" noted Duvel Moortgat chief operating officer Daniel Krug, who reports to current CEO Michel Moortgat. (The Moortgat family still owns about two-thirds of the business; the remaining shares are publicly traded.)

There's a technique to pouring a good glass of Duvel.

While Duvel Moortgat has helped reinvigorate and grow many of the brands the company has acquired—it turned 20,000-barrel d'Achouffe into a 200,000-barrel business in the space of a decade—it's the home-grown brand that's now half of the parent company's name that really made Duvel Moortgat famous.

In 1871, Jan-Léonard Moortgat and his wife founded what was originally called the Moortgat Brewery. About a half-century later, Duvel strong golden ale debuted. (A tale the brewery likes to tell is that a local shoemaker in the company's home town of Breendonk tasted it and declared that the 8.5 percent brew was a real "duvel," meaning devil.)

The brand has attracted many imitators (many of which also have devilish names), but the strong golden ale—best enjoyed in a tulip glass that facilitates its huge, billowing head—approaches the century mark as the one to beat.

The Duvel Moortgat family of craft breweries extends to the United States as well. It now owns Cooperstown, New York's Brewery Ommegang (acquired in 2003), Kansas City's Boulevard (acquired in 2013), and Paso Robles, California's Firestone Walker (acquired in 2015).

Het Anker

Dutch for "The Anchor," Het Anker, which is located in the charming little city of Mechelen, is a destination in every sense of the word. For one thing, it has its own hotel attached to the brewery, which makes visiting (and drinking) that much easier. There's also a full-service restaurant where diners can enjoy fine Flemish and continental fare—its best during the fall and winter months when it's stew season! The first brewery at the site can be traced way back to 1471 and was founded by Beguines, a semi-monastic religious order of laypeople. Hit the fast-forward button to four hundred years later, and the Van Breedam family bought the brewery and modernized it (by late nineteenth-century standards). From the outside, the facility still resembles an industrial building of the period, with an Anker-branded smokestack piercing the sky, recalling its steampunk history (it's mostly ornamental now). Its most famous brand is Gouden Carolus Classic ("Golden Charles"), a dark copper-colored, malt-forward, warming 8.5 percent ale. It also brews Gouden Carolus Tripel, much paler in color but slightly higher in alcohol at 9 percent ABV. Recognizing worldwide beer lovers' gravitation toward all things hoppy, the brewery released Hopsinjoor, a brew that has five kinds of hops and is markedly more bitter than the types of beers Belgians have traditionally made.

Brouwerij Huyghe

History suggests that a brewery existed at the site of what is now the Brouwerij Huyghe since the mid-seventeenth century. But it was in 1906 that Léon Huyghe bought the brewery in the town of Melle and the site began to evolve into its current form. Two World Wars and economic ups and downs took their toll on Brouwerij Huyghe, as they did on most operations throughout the region, but the business persevered. What is perhaps the biggest milestone in the brewery's existence occurred in 1988 when it launched the beer for which it is world famous: Delirium Tremens. In fact, the brand is far better known than the name of the brewery itself. Mention Huyghe and you might get a blank stare. Mention Delirium Tremens and eyes are very likely to light up. The 8.5 percent ABV blond ale, easily identified by its pink elephant icon (and, when it's in packaged form, by its slightly speckled, opaque, off-white bottle with blue foil neck trim), has a great deal going on, flavor- and aroma-wise: a slight malt sweetness complements a veritable garden of spicy and floral notes.

The brewery itself represents Belgium in a nutshell. It's got all of the shiny, new high-tech equipment and automated systems required to run a truly modern operation, but, as a counterpoint, its old-school, 1930s-era tiled brew house with all sorts of coppery goodness remains. One foot in history and the other in the future. That's what Belgian brewing is all about.

Omer Vander Ghinste/Brouwerij Bockor

Brouwerij Omer Vander Ghinste, in the South West Flemish village of Bellegem, got its start in 1892 and launched its most widely consumed brand, Bockor Pils, in the 1930s (the brewery would take the name Brouwerij Bockor four decades later). Sure, it's a pilsner; most commercial Belgian brewers jumped on the pale lager train when it swept the continent. However, in the 1970s, Omer Vander Ghinste solidified its legend when it began producing its notable fruit beers in earnest under the Jacobins label. In 1970 the brewery launched Jacobins Gueuze, thirteen years later it unveiled Jacobins Kriek (a cherry beer) and, three years after that, it released its first batches of Jacobins Framboise (raspberry). But if there's ever been a white whale about which Belgophiles rhapsodize most heartily, it's Cuvée des Jacobins, a Flemish sour ale that's aged for at least eighteen months in large oak vats known as foeders. (That's the Dutch spelling in

An array of foeders (or foudres, if you prefer the French spelling).

Flanders; French speakers spell it 'foudre.') The foeder/foudre room at Bockor is a dimly lit wonderland of wild, sour, and fruity aromas from which visitors usually have to be dragged kicking and screaming. There's no experience that's comparable to drinking Cuvée des Jacobins fresh from the wood.

But there's plenty to love for those who don't like fruit beers, sours, or pilsners. In 2008 the brewery launced Omer, a blond ale that's a great entry point brew for those new to the Belgosphere.

Brouwerij Roman

Remember that brewery that's been around since the fifteenth century and is now in its fourteenth generation? That would be Brewery Roman, located in the village of Mater in the city of Oudenaarde. According to the brewery, Mater has been the home to the Roman family's brewing exploits since 1545. Buildings have come and gone, and the product lines have changed quite a bit in the subsequent four and three-quarters centuries. Its modern offerings include the Ename brand of abbey-style beers, featuring a blond, a dubbel, a tripel, and a rouge. The brand gets its name from the Abbey of Ename in the nearby town that bears its name. Historians place the abbey's origins in the nineth century AD; the Benedictines moved in a couple of centuries later in 1063. In the 1990s, the brewery sponsored the excavation of the site and began producing the Ename line at that time. Another one of its popular lines is Adriaen Brouwer, named after the painter who was born in Oudenaarde in 1605. Adriaen Brouwer proper is a sessionable 5 percent ABV brown ale, while Adriaen Brouwer Dark Gold is a much more potent 8.5 percent.

Brasserie Dubuisson

You can probably tell by the name of this one that we've moved out of Dutch-speaking Flanders and into French-speaking Wallonia. Age-wise, Dubuisson lies in the middle of the truly ancient Brouwerij Roman and the late nineteenth-century-born Bockor. Joseph Leroy, an ancestor of modern owner Hugues Dubuisson, opened the brewery in 1769. In the 1930s, the brewery unveiled what would become its flagship: Bush Beer. The management team chose an English name because English beers were in fashion at the time, and "buisson" is actually French for "bush" ("du" is a modifier). The line includes Bush Amber, Triple, and Noël, its Christmas seasonal.

Unless you're actually going to Belgium, don't expect to find a beer called "Bush." Oh, it's quite easy to find in the states, mostly at places that specialize in Belgian brews or, more generally, high-end imports. However, in these parts, it's a little challenging to try to sell a premium beer whose name sounds an awful lot like "Busch." (And, you know, lawyers.) When the beers are exported out of Belgium, they're marketed as Scaldis. Scaldis Amber has an incredibly assertive ABV of 12 percent. There have been some bars selling it that have marketed it as "the strongest beer in the world." That was true up until about the late 1970s, but they continued to do so well into the 2000s, and that's just dishonest. And, besides, it's an amazingly complex brew in its own right. The Dubuisson brewers would make a quality beer at any strength.

American Trappist

Think you have to travel to Belgium or the Netherlands to drink beer freshly brewed by Trappist monks? Think again. As of 2014, there's an operating Trappist monastery on American soil—in New England to be exact. The brotherhood at the St. Joseph's Abbey in Spencer, Massaschusetts, started brewing mostly out of necessity. For six decades the primary commercial enterprise in which the abbey was engaged was crafting and packing jams under the Trappist Preserves label. In an effort to step up their charitable endeavors and sustain their own community for generations to come, the monks found inspiration in the success of their European brethren's beer-making exploits. One of the brothers in particular had been bitten by the brewing bug and trained at a local brewery. Soon, a contingent of St. Joseph's brothers traveled across Belgium, dropping in on the storied Trappist breweries in the country and learning the trade from the likes of St. Sixtus (Westvleteren) and Westmalle. Today, the Masschusetts monks market the fruits of their labor under the deceivingly simple Spencer label.

7

Bohemian Rhapsody

The Czech Republic's Place in Brewing History

The modern use of the word "bohemian" has an odd sense of symmetry embedded within it. When we think of bohemia, we think of places like Berkley, California; Austin, Texas; or the hipster haven that is the Williamsburg neighborhood of Brooklyn, New York (despite the fact that Williamsburg stopped being "cool"—not to mention affordable—long ago). Bohemian locales are where folks walk to the beat of a different drummer and where tomorrow's trends are set before the rest of the world catches on.

So, the term "bohemian" is appropriate for a number of reasons. For one thing, the modern bohemias are, by and large, the places responsible for cultivating today's craft brewing phenomenon. However, more importantly, the real Bohemia is responsible for launching the greatest trend in beer's history: it's the birthplace of pilsner, which, nearly two centuries after its creation, remains the most popular and replicated style in the world.

We take pale, blond lagers for granted today; indeed, it wasn't too long ago that Americans couldn't even get their hands on another style. Pilsner is what the majority of consumers think of as "beer." It's become commoditized to the point that its reputation has been soiled and only now are people appreciating how good it really is when it's made well. But such a brew didn't exist before 1842.

It all started in the town of Plzen (internationally known as Pilsen) in Bohemia, a major region in what is now the Czech Republic.

It was typical, back in the day, for a beer's name to be derived from the town in which it was created. The Czechs named the beer Plzensky Prasdroj, which translates to "Pilsen's original source." But Czech was the local language. Bohemia, in those days, was but a cog in the giant machine that was the German-speaking Habsburg Empire. The beer, therefore, became better known by the German translation of its name:

Pilsner Urquell ("Ur" meaning "original" and "quell" meaning "source.") Its creator was a Bavarian transplant named Josef Groll, who took a brewing job in Plzen. Groll's invention exists to this day; the brewery claims to have retained its 1842 recipe through all modern iterations.

It didn't take long for the sparkly creation to catch fire and sweep across Europe. Breweries across the continent—especially in Germany—quickly replicated the style, putting their own local spins on it here and there. (The first German brewery to commercialize a pilsner was Aktienbrauerei Zum Bierkeller in the city of Radeberg. Today, the brewery is known as Radeberger, and it produces what is arguably *the* quintessential German pils—refreshing with just enough of a jolting, bitter, and hoppy bite.)

Since the word pilsner signifies that it is a product of Plzn, many brewers outside of the city and the country that adopted the enormously popular style use the term "pils" out of deference to the Czech creators.

The modern Czech market resembles that of just about every other industrialized nation. The multinationals run the show (SABMiller owns Pilsner Urquell, for instance), and the locals really haven't had the chance to experience styles other than mass-produced lagers. And why would they when they typically could buy two or three beers for the equivalent of one US dollar.

That is, until recently.

The Velvet Revolution of 1989 and the subsequent fall of communism made private business ownership possible, and many have gone into the brewing business. Today, there are some three hundred small breweries, with two or three opening each month and only two or three closing each year.

Most of their production is still geared toward light and dark lagers—about 75 percent or so—but, increasingly, they've been able to experiment with pale ales, IPAs, and other styles that have been sweeping the craft beer world.

Little by little, beer-loving Czechs have begun to appreciate handcrafted beers and are willing to part with five or six times what they would traditionally have paid for the beverage.

The Birth of Budweiser (No, Not That One)

The name Budweiser has always existed for those of us who are alive today. Its advertisements have been ubiquitous throughout our lives. We sang along with "Here Comes the King" when its TV spots aired in the '70s; bought the Spuds MacKenzie t-shirts in the '80s; chanted "Bud-weis-er" in our best froggy voices; and annoyed our family, friends, and coworkers with repeated exclamations of "Wassup?!" in the late '90s. And, we were more excited about the "Bud Bowl" ads on Super Bowl Sunday than we were for the actual game (the game whose ad prices were so high that only behemoths like Anheuser-Busch could afford to buy time). It's a household name, for sure, but most households wouldn't be able to answer a simple question: What is the origin of the name "Budweiser"?

It all started in a town called České Budějovice (the latter half, when spelled for German Speakers, is "Budweis"). And, since beers typically were associated with the towns in which they were brewed, the one created there was called Budweiser Burgerbrau. It was first brewed back in 1785 and exported to the United States in 1871.

In the States, the beer inspired copycats. Among those was Anheuser-Busch, which started marketing the Budweiser brand about five years after the original Czech brewer sent its first shipments across the Atlantic Ocean.

To complicate things a bit further, back home in České Budějovice, a second brewery set up shop in 1895, producing a beer called Budweiser. That company was Budejovicky Budvar, or the Budweiser Budvar Brewery. And, yes, it too was keen to reach the booming American beer market of the late nineteenth century and commenced exporting activities.

Predictably, trademark disputes ensued involving all three companies— the two Czech brewers and Anheuser-Busch—and in 1938 they reached an agreement that stated the St. Louis-based brewery was permitted to use the Budweiser name only in North America. But the legal wrangling was far from over (especially since the European map was about to get turned upside down when a little thing called World War II kicked off).

In the decades following the war, Budweiser grew to become a multinational giant with really good lawyers. Budvar, on the other hand, has remained state-owned. There have been plenty of battles throughout the 2000s, and the short version is that Budvar's exports to the United States must be marketed as Czechvar. Anheuser-Busch tried to register Budweiser as a trademark in the European Union, but in 2009 the EU trademark office rejected the American brewer's application on the grounds that Budvar had established a claim on the mark in 1871, whereas Anheuser-Busch had first commercialized its Budweiser product in 1876.

AB InBev, however, could trademark its products as "Bud," something that didn't make Budvar too happy. Budvar challenged the trademark, but, in 2013, the General Court of the European Union dismissed the challenge, clearing the way for Bud across the continent.

And the matter is far from settled. In 2013, a court in the United Kingdom ruled that both Budvar and Anheuser-Busch InBev had the right to market their respective Budweisers, stating that consumers can tell the difference. (To be fair, they do taste different, and it's hard to confuse the two brands' trade dresses. The logos, fonts, and even color schemes contrast significantly.)

Since then, though, decisions have mostly been made gradually, country by country. For instance, in 2014, a Portuguese appeals court upheld an earlier ruling that bars Anheuser-Busch InBev from registering its brand as Budweiser in Portugal.

That same year, AB InBev acquired a small Czech brewery, Pivovar Samson, which just happens to be located in the town of . . . drum roll please . . . České Budějovice/Budweis. AB InBev's rationale is that the purchase gives it more leverage in the ongoing disputes with Czechvar. It can now say it produces a legitimate Budweiser beer in the Czech Republic.

This sort of international legal ping-pong is likely to continue for many years, unless, of course, AB InBev ever decides to just up and buy Budvar. In 2013, the mega-multinational went on record stating it was abandoning any plans to buy its Czech rival, saying it no longer made commercial sense. But, as anyone who follows this (or any other) industry knows, there's no such thing as "definitive."

Besides, whenever the dust finally settles from the long, drawn-out AB InBev/SABMiller merger, AB InBev would perhaps get its hands on an even more iconic Czech brand: a little something called Pilsner Urquell.

8

Beer in the New World

Brewing Emigrates to America

There are myriad myths associated with the origins of beer in what would become the United States of America. One of the greatest tales that beer marketers and aficionados like to relay is that, if it weren't for beer, we'd never have Thanksgiving. As the story goes, the Pilgrims were headed for the Jamestown, Virginia colony, but they were several hundred miles off course when they first spotted land. They also happened to be out of beer. Back in those days, drinking water, especially on an ocean voyage, was fairly likely to kill a person. Beer was the safer option, primarily because it was boiled. Of course, this was before the discovery of microorganisms that were responsible for most food- and water-borne maladies. Pilgrim drinkers knew that beer was safer than water; they just weren't really sure why.

The Mayflower passengers were out of supplies to make that beer, so they got off the boat in what would soon be called New England to gather the necessary raw materials to make their beloved beverage.

There's some truth to that legend, but beer's importance to the mission has been overstated through the years. The thing is, folks with a vested interest, either commercially or emotionally, in more modern forms of beer seized on one particular quote that's been analyzed and overanalyzed throughout the course of the ensuing four centuries.

> "For we could not now take time for further search our victuals being pretty much spent especially our beer."

Author and beer historian Bob Skilnik (*Beer & Food: An American History*) has conducted exhaustive research on the topic and, through his work, has debunked some aspects of that popular myth.

The passage that has delighted beer enthusiasts for generations is actually quite incomplete. The Pilgrim myth is largely the result of a practice common among non-historians with a specific interest or agenda: cherry-picking. A more extensive version of the log entry, pulled from *Mourt's Relation: A Journal of the Pilgrims at Plymouth, 1622*, reads:

> "That night we returned again a-shipboard, with resolution the next morning to settle on some of those places; so in the morning, after we had called on God for direction, we came to this resolution: to go presently ashore again, and to take a better view of two places, which we thought most fitting for us, for we could not now take time for further search or consideration, our victuals being much spent, especially our beer, and it being now the 19th of December. After our landing and viewing of the places, so well as we could we came to a conclusion, by most voices, to set on the mainland, on the first place, on a high ground, where there is a great deal of land cleared, and hath been planted with corn three or four years ago, and there is a very sweet brook runs under the hillside, and many delicate springs of as good water as can be drunk . . ."

So, in short, beer was just one of the many reasons the Mayflower docked near the rock we call Plymouth. And some of the other reasons may have been far greater priorities.

The giants of the twentieth-century beer industry are really the ones to blame for overinflating beer's role in the formation of the New England colonies. It was all part of a post-Prohibition marketing campaign to boost beer's sales in a changing society. Prior to Prohibition, most of the beer was being consumed in taverns at all hours of the day. After Prohibition's repeal, however, it was more likely that consumers would be drinking at home. The problem was that they weren't accustomed to doing so. With the advent of the can in 1935, beer was primed to become a take-home beverage. In supporting ad materials, the major brewers played up beer's central role in American history and included all sorts of memorable quotes in the print advertisements, including the truncated text from the Mayflower log.

The pilgrim story became the centerpiece of Budweiser's Thanksgiving advertising well into the 1940s.

British colonists certainly introduced English brewing traditions to America, and many of them were aboard the Mayflower. However, they do not get the credit as the earliest American brewers. That distinction belongs to the Native American tribes that were concocting mostly corn-based beverages that are now considered to be early forms of beer.

Converting corn and other fermentable bases into modern beer's precursors was actually quite common throughout the Americas and was happening long before the Spanish, English, Dutch, and French landed on shores across the Northern and Southern Hemispheres. Throughout the Andean region, indigenous peoples developed what became known as chicha de jora, a drink made from fermented corn (a non-alcoholic version is known as chicha morada). Chicha traces its roots to the ancient Incas. Archaeologists have even managed to unearth some of the old drink-making apparatus at Machu Picchu. Scholars believe that chicha was quite a popular component of religious observances.

Chicha requires a specific enzyme—ptyalin, for the technically minded, which occurs naturally in spit—to kick-start the conversion of corn starches to fermentable sugars. For the Incas, chewing on corn and then spewing it into a vessel activated the process.

The chicha-making tradition has survived the millennium since the Incan Empire was at its peak, and it continues to have quite a following in not entirely licensed *chicherias*—often part of someone's home or a make-shift shack—around Cuzco and other parts of southern Peru. The beverage is likely similar to the types of drinks North American tribes were producing prior to colonization by the Europeans.

The ancient Aztecs contributed their own beer ancestor to the global beverage stage. Instead of corn, the ancient peoples of Mexico were fermenting with the nectar of the agave plant (a similar source contributes the base for tequila and mezcal distilling). The beverage survived Spanish colonization and ultimately evolved into what's known as pulque, a viscous, milky liquid that's around 5 percent alcohol by volume and is still widely consumed throughout Mexico.

The Dutch get some of the credit for bringing beer brewing to America, as well. In 1612, nearly a decade before the English Pilgrims landed at Plymouth Rock, Dutch colonists opened the first brewery in what was then New Amsterdam (soon to become New York). It wasn't long before the city and the outlying regions along the Hudson River became a hotbed of brewing activity.

Jump ahead to the next century and the era of No Taxation Without Representation and you'll find that the American Revolution is practically drenched in beer. For one thing, most of the planning and rallying for an independent America took place in taverns over countless tankards of the foamy fermentable. And many of the Founding Fathers were themselves brewers.

The obvious one, of course, was Boston's Samuel Adams—he didn't get a beer brand worth nearly a billion dollars named after him for nothing.

Ben Franklin and beer tend to get linked, perhaps, more often than they should, thanks to the romantic minds of brewing enthusiasts, but there's no disputing Philadelphia's most famous figure's connection with the beverage. Though for him, it was always his second fermented beverage of choice.

His most prominent association with the drink is through the oft-repeated quote, "Beer is proof that God loves us and wants us to be happy." The problem is that many scholars now assert that Franklin never actually said that—at least not in relation to beer. See, Franklin made no secret of the fact that he loved wine, and it was the grape-based drink about which he was speaking when he drew any sort of correlation between imbibing and God's good graces:

> "Behold the rain which descends from heaven upon our vineyards, and which incorporates itself with the grapes to be changed into wine; a constant proof that God loves us, and loves to see us happy!"

That was from a letter Franklin wrote to his friend, French philosopher, economist, and theologian André Morellet. And, it was written in French and later translated into English—which is at least partially to blame for the quote's erroneous association with beer.

There are even a few early presidents who brewed their own beer (or had it brewed for them). George Washington was known to be an avid beer drinker, and the stuff—some of it produced on-site—was served regularly at Mount Vernon dinners. In a letter Washington wrote to his farm manager, William Pearce, the first president noted that beer "may be brewed as usual as the occasion requires." Records indicate that hops were grown on the estate as well.

In the last years of his life, Washington turned his attention to whiskey, opening a commercial rye distillery in 1797. In 1799, the year of his death, the facility produced 11,000 gallons, making it the largest American whiskey distillery at the time.

More than two centuries later, the Distilled Spirits Council of the United States (DISCUS) partnered with Mount Vernon to excavate, restore, and reopen the distillery, which it did in 2006. Modern consumers can enjoy George Washington's rye whiskey once again.

From a beverage standpoint, Thomas Jefferson might be better known for the taste in wine he acquired during his time in Paris, but he actually spent a good chunk of whatever little free time he could carve out from his busy affairs to engage in homebrewing.

Historical records hint at his beer-making activities prior to his stint as vice president and then president (he even started planting hops as early as 1794), but it was during his retirement when he really got his hands dirty. By the fall of 1814, there was an operating brewhouse at Monticello. Always the scientific-minded one, Jefferson was fascinated by the science of brewing and, by all accounts, enthusiastically threw himself into the hobby.

If the colonial period through the early nineteenth century belonged to English traditions, the latter half of the nineteenth century was the domain of the waves of immigrants who settled in the young country. In the mid-1800s, large numbers of Germans arrived in America, many settling in Midwestern cities. Political unrest in the homeland has often been cited as the primary driver for the exodus. In her 2006 book, *Ambitious Brew*, historian Maureen Ogle noted that another reason many German brewers left their businesses in Germany was that the prices of coffee and tea were falling and many consumers were ditching beer for those caffeinated beverages (caffeine was a novelty at the time).

St. Louis was a major magnet for the new arrivals, among whom were two gentlemen by the name of Eberhard Anheuser and Adolphus Busch. Initially a soap manufacturer, Anheuser first settled in Cincinnati before relocating to St. Louis. He left the soap business and became part owner of what was the Bavarian Brewery, ultimately buying out his partners in 1860 and changing the brewery's name to E. Anheuser & Co.

Meanwhile, Busch had been a partner in a brewing supply business; it was, therefore, inevitable that the two would cross paths. In 1861, Busch married Anheuser's daughter, Lilly, and went to work for his father-in-law, eventually buying a 50 percent stake in the brewery. What would later become known as Anheuser-Busch Brewing Company was born.

Around the same time, not too far away in Milwaukee, Wisconsin, another dynasty of German-American entrepreneurship was taking shape. In 1844, Jacob Best formed the Empire Brewery (later renamed Best and Company), which, in its first year, produced only three hundred barrels. Fifteen years later, Best's son, Phillip, took over the business, which was now called Phillip Best Brewing Company, and Phillip's daughter, Maria, married steamship captain Frederick Pabst (born with the more Germanic moniker Johann Gottlieb Friedrich Pabst). Best's new son-in-law would soon leave the shipping business to become a partner in the brewery in 1863. Within the next decade, Phillip Best Brewing Company would become the second-largest beer producer in America, cranking out about 100,000 barrels a year. Frederick Pabst became president of the company in 1873, and, about a decade and a half later, the corporate name would change to Pabst Brewing Company.

It's usually pretty easy to find Pabst's booth at GABF.

The most famous product to come out of the company, of course, was Pabst Blue Ribbon, which had, prior to 1893, been called Best Select. Fred Pabst proved himself to be a master at brand promotion, playing up Best Select's many accolades—prizes of varying levels of significance from sundry beer judging competitions—by affixing a blue ribbon to bottles of the brew. After that, the history gets a little murkier.

You see, 1893 was the year of the iconic Chicago World's Fair. One of the aspects that made exhibiting at the fair so attractive to many purveyors of consumer products was the potential to leave the fairgrounds with awards of one sort or another. Pabst was among those that went home with a ribbon. In its subsequent marketing, Pabst Brewing Company declared what it was now calling Pabst Blue Ribbon the grand prize winner of the competition.

But, as Ogle asserts in *Ambitious Brew*, many brewers departed the World's Fair victorious. Brewers weren't necessarily in competition against each other; each was judged against certain common criteria, and those that scored above a certain level received an award.

Pabst's home city would become legendary as a hotbed for nineteenth century brewing activity. In 1855, another famous Frederick, whose surname was Miller, entered the American brewing history books. Armed with a proprietary yeast strain he brought with him from Germany, Miller bought Milwaukee's Plank Road Brewery (for somewhere between $2,300 and $8,000, depending on whose account you believe), creating Miller Brewing Company. A half century later, the company would launch Miller High Life, the oldest of Miller's brands that's still in existence.

Expatriate Germans' influence on the American beer industry was not limited to the Midwest. In 1868, a twenty-one-year-old man by the name of Adolph Kohrs boarded a New York-bound ship in Hamburg, Germany (company history states that he actually stowed away on said ocean liner), to find his fortunes in America. Upon arrival, the spelling of his name was changed to "Coors," and he moved to Chicago, where he worked odd jobs before landing a job at a brewery just outside the city. A few years later he headed west and, with partner Joseph Schueler, opened a brewery at the site of a former tannery in Golden, Colorado. In 1880, Coors bought out Schueler and re-christened the operation Adolph Coors Golden Brewery.

An ability to adapt to changing market dynamics and gamble on new technologies are what enabled brewers to break out of their local surroundings and introduce their products to far-flung regions of the country. The advent of pasteurization enabled the beer to survive long journeys, and the development of artificial refrigeration is what really brought the brewing industry into the modern world.

It's something we take for granted now, but there was a time, less than a century and a half ago, when most brewing activities had to be confined to the winter months. Brewers like Anheuser-Busch relied on cool, underground storage areas or ice houses to keep their raw materials as fresh as possible during the warmer parts of the year. As Anheuser-Busch's in-house historians tell it, it was a tremendous risk for Adolphus Busch to install newfangled refrigeration systems in the 1880s. But it was obviously a risk that paid off handsomely.

It was also around that time that refrigerated rail cars became a reality. For the first time, freight cars could be kept cool to carry brewers' products leagues beyond their geographic points of origin.

To maintain Anheuser-Busch's chilled freight system, Adolphus set up a network of rail-side ice houses ready to replenish the railcars' ice supply when it melted. How well a brewery was able to incorporate such logistical advances into one's business is one of the factors that determined which breweries survived the nineteenth century.

The immigrant success stories detailed above are familiar in the modern age because they speak of the companies that were able to remain relevant into the twentieth century. Those operations even managed to survive Prohibition mostly intact because of shrewd business decisions that allowed the companies to hit the ground running once alcohol became legal again in 1933.

Instead of completely shutting down (which was really the only option for a producer of a beverage that was outlawed as of 1920), Anheuser-Busch manufactured and sold everything from malt extract (the company certainly had access to malt), yeast (ditto), ice cream, and even truck parts. (Ice cream was also the product of choice for Pennsylvania's Yuengling, the oldest continuously operating brewery in America. The Yuengling ice cream brand was relaunched in 2014.) Anheuser-Busch also produced what was termed "near beer," a de-alcoholized version of its products.

Coors also made a near beer it called Manna, as well as malted milk, which it sold to confectioners like Mars. Under the banner of the Adolph Coors Brewing and Manufacturing Company, it also sold porcelain pottery, concrete, and real estate.

Being the true Wisconsinite it was, Pabst ditched beer in favor of cheese—a brand by the name of Pabst-ett to be precise. Pabst-ett was produced on an upstate Wisconsin farm and aged in Pabst's ice cellars.

According to Pabst Brewing Company, the cheese business was a raging success, with more than eight million pounds of Pabs-ett sold during those dry years. Soft drinks and malt extract were also part of Pabst's Prohibition portfolio. (Say that three times fast!)

Extracting the Truth

A funny thing about that malt extract that former brewers were so enthusiastically producing when its fermented form was now considered contraband: it was marketed as a healthy substance for nursing mothers. (A ban on alcohol may have been strictly enforced, but the same couldn't be said for the sort of advertising standards we have today.)

The ads recommending the use of malt extract practically winked at consumers because everyone secretly knew what the extract was really being used for: illegal homebrewing. It was no coincidence that the dormant breweries also happened to be selling yeast. Combine the two with a little rudimentary beer-making know-how (easy enough to obtain, even from some of the breweries themselves) and, voila! Beer!

Though a handful of those iconic nineteenth-century breweries have managed to survive into the twenty-first century, they've taken on dramatically different forms in the modern era. Since the mid-twentieth century, Miller Brewing has been the corporate equivalent of a football being passed around and intercepted by a variety of imposing players, a process that ultimately culminated in the acquisition of Miller Brewing by South African Breweries to form SABMiller. In 2005, Coors merged with Molson to form Molson Coors. Both multinationals formed a joint venture in 2007, combining their US operations to form MillerCoors. Anheuser-Busch managed to remain American-owned a little bit longer but was ultimately absorbed by InBev to form Anheuser-Busch InBev in 2008.

Pabst reached its peak in the late 1970s and then fell into a sharp downward spiral, closing brewery after brewery, culminating in the decommissioning of its iconic Milwaukee facility in 1996. It has contracted the brewing of all of its trademarks, including those it had acquired at the height of its power, such as Schlitz, Blatz, Old Style, Lone Star, and Ballentine, and about thirty others. Miller, in all of its late twentieth- and early twenty-first-century iterations, has produced most of Pabst's beers.

From an ownership standpoint, Pabst has been on a rather odd path for the better part of three and a half decades. In 1985, several years into the company's negative trajectory, millionaire Paul Kalmonovitz, through a holding company he called S&P, purchased Pabst in a hostile takeover. Kalmanovitz didn't live long enough to enjoy the spoils of his conquest; he died in 1987. But that's when things got really complicated. Kalmanovitz's S&P assets became part of the nonprofit Kalmanovitz Charitable Trust. Eighteen years later, the IRS gave the legal custodians of the trust an ultimatum: sell Pabst or forfeit the foundation's tax-exempt status. It took an unexpectedly long time for the sale to happen—about five years to be exact. That's when, in 2010, billionaire investor Dean Metropoulos purchased the company for a reported $250 million.

The Metropoulos era proved quite controversial, especially for the outgoing management team. Companies and brands change hands, executives resign (voluntarily or involuntarily), marketing strategies shift—these are facts of life in any industry and no less so in the beer business. However, regardless of whatever bad blood may exist between the old guard and the new, diplomacy usually prevails in the public aspects of such transactions. However, in 2011, the departing executive team bucked tradition and didn't mince words in their takedown of the Metropoulos regime in a *Chicago Tribune* article published in June of that year.

Among those quoted in the article were Kevin Kotecki, who served as chief executive officer of Pabst Brewing Company from 2005 to 2010, former vice president of marketing Bryan Clarke, and outgoing marketing director Kyle Wortham. The three were part of a mass exodus from shortly after the Metropoulos family took over, and they felt that Metropoulos and his two playboy sons—who would manage Pabst's new marketing trajectory—were undermining the work the company had done to revitalize the brand by appealing to certain consumers' niche desires, namely the desire for authenticity sought by hipsters.

Pabst enjoyed its hipster renaissance not through fancy promotions, lowest-common-denominator-skewing T&A ads, or celebrity endorsements, but through grassroots marketing that connected the brand with tattoo parlors, artists, bicycle messengers, skateboarders, and the like. Pabst initially focused on their targets' national habitats of Portland, Oregon; Seattle, Washington; Berkeley, California; and Williamsburg, Brooklyn.

The Metropouloses employed a markedly different philosophy, moving the corporate headquarters to Los Angeles (from San Antonio, Texas, itself a relocation from the Chicagoland area a few years prior) to better infuse the brand with the glitz, glamour, and celebrity focus that the outgoing team had prided itself on successfully eschewing.

The mindset shift was immediately apparent at industry trade shows like the Nightclub and Bar Show in Las Vegas. Scantily clad models in tight-fitting Pabst T-shirts drew nightlife professionals to the Pabst booth.

Clarke was the most blunt in the *Chicago Tribune* article. The article quoted him as saying, "I want it to fail."

Kotecki's quotes were a bit more measured. "Just about everything that I'd been working on or trying to accomplish ended up not being part of the plan going forward," he said in the article.

The Metropoulos family ultimately would sell Pabst Brewing Company in 2014 to Blue Ribbon Intermediate Holdings, LLC, a group formed by beer industry veteran Eugene Kashper and private equity firm TSG Consumer Partners.

Among the more recent developments was the company's announcement in July 2015 that it would resume brewing operations at the historic site of the original Pabst Brewery in Milwaukee. Brewing recommences in the summer of 2016, twenty years after production ceased at the facility. It's not expected to be a large-scale operation. At least initially, the location will serve as a small-batch pilot brewery, enabling Pabst Brewing to experiment in the craft realm and produce pre-Prohibition recipes for Old Tankard Ale, Kloster Beer, Bock, and Andeker. In a sense, operating a physical production brewery marks a classic, historic company's return to its roots and, in some small way, will help the company reclaim some of its authentic cred.

Marketing Timeline

The beer industry in post-Prohibition America is really a study of modern marketing milestones. When the ads work, they're highly entertaining and often funnier than most of the scripted shows on television. When they're not so great, they're at least a good sociological study, illuminating how the beer industry managed to throw gender balance out of whack by aggressively pandering to only male drinkers, often dumbing things down in the process.

Here are some key highlights (and, in some cases, lowlights) that helped define the business of brewing for most of the twentieth century.

Miss Rheingold

The New York brewery Rheingold, founded in 1883, made no secret of which gender it considered its target demographic. For a quarter of a century between 1940 and 1965, consumers would vote on a beauty queen that would be deemed Miss Rheingold for an entire year. She'd be featured in ads for the beer and would serve as an overall goodwill ambassador for the brand. Ultimately the Rheingold brewery succumbed to the competitive reality of the time, which pretty much sank most of the local and regional beer producers.

"You Didn't Burn the Beer"

In the early 1950s, Schlitz produced what is considered to be one of the most sexist print ads ever produced by the beer industry. The illustration features an aproned housewife holding a pan with black smoke emanating from it. As she weeps into a handkerchief, her business suit-clad husband—apparently just home from work—points to a pair of bottles on the table. In the most patronizing manner possible, he assures her, "Don't worry, darling, you didn't burn the beer!" The ad was, of course, a product of Eisenhower-era gender dynamics, but it reinforced the stereotype of beer as a "man's beverage." The mega brewers have done little to change that, but the more progressive craft beer segment has been working to balance the scales.

"That Man . . . He's Done It Again!"

Schlitz continued that theme in a magazine ad that depicts yet another housewife arriving home with a bag full of groceries (of course). The woman opens the refrigerator to discover there's no room for the provisions she's just procured because that rascal of a husband of hers has filled the fridge's every nook and cranny with bottles of "the beer that made Milwaukee famous." If the illustration didn't drive home who wears the pants in the family, the verbiage certainly does: "That man . . . he's done it again! It's very easy to understand a man's enthusiasm for Schlitz."

"This Will Soften the Blow"

Not to keep picking on Schlitz, but the company was quite prolific with its domestic bliss ads in the '50s and '60s. In this one from 1950, a woman holds her hands over her husband's eyes as they enter the living room. On the end table next to the man's easy chair (on the arm of which rests his pipe, waiting to be smoked) are three women's hat boxes. The wife obviously has returned from what women do best: shopping! Next to those boxes is a freshly poured glass of Schlitz (next to the bottle). "This will soften the blow!" the ad reads. "When a wife wants her husband to see things her way, a glass of Schlitz is always a welcome ally."

"Mabel, Black Label."

At first glance, the series of print ads for Carling Black Label with the catch-phrase "Mabel, Black Label" seems more innocuous than the "You Didn't Burn the Beer" Schlitz piece, but it turns out to be just as overtly sexist. In one we see a woman, presumably a housewife, holding in her left hand a bottle of Carling Black Label, which she just poured into a glass in her right hand. She beams brightly as she hands the glass up to her husband on a ladder. All we see of him is the lower part of his right leg and his right hand reaching down for the beer. Her doting eyes shine as she stares up at her manly man of a hubby. "Every day, more people say 'Mabel, Black Label.'" The wife's role in the ad is pure subservience.

"Where There's Life, There's Bud"

"Where there's life, there's Bud," was actually Budweiser's popular tagline for most of the '50s, and most of the print ads were fairly innocent. However, one in particular had a close kinship to the handy-husband aesthetic of the Carling Black Label ladder ad. It features a man holding a hammer over what appears to be a dismantled rotary telephone. (It's ambiguous as to whether he's trying to fix it or if its incessant ringing drove him to smash it in a fit of rage.) Meanwhile, his adoring wife pours him a glass of Bud.

A Touch of Class

Now, lest you think *every* beer ad made during the Eisenhower Administration and the "Mad Men" era that immediately followed was sexist, there were quite a few marketing pieces that were actually pretty classy. In fact, in some cases, they made a concerted effort to be inclusive of women.

"Put the Finest Label . . . On Your Table."

Miller was no stranger to efforts to class things up. The Milwaukee brewer is the one, after all, that promoted its flagship brew as "The Champagne of Beer." One such ad features a well-dressed man and woman enjoying a fancy steak dinner in front of a fire place. Each has a gorgeously poured, slender, inverted cone-shaped glass of Miller High Life. Beneath that illustration are two images that, in hindsight, seemed way ahead of their time. The first features the same glass of High Life next to a sliced (medium rare!) steak. The second features a bottle of High Life and a mug adjacent to a variety of cheeses.

If all brewers had applied the same aesthetic to their brands, wine would have never won the "What goes better with dinner?" wars that ultimately necessitated the paradigm-shifting beer-and-food-pairing movement that emerged in the early 2000s.

Hamm's: Land of Sky Blue Waters

The broadcast spot from the Hamm's brand's Land of Sky Blue Waters campaign appeared during the golden age of television in the 1950s has a bit of a split personality. On one hand, it features some truly romantic (black and white) imagery of a couple enjoying a meal on a riverside deck, clinking chalice-like glasses of Hamm's. There's even a close-up of said glass superimposed over the river that really emphasizes beer as a thing of beauty. But those shots are intercut with a cartoon featuring the Hamm's bear mascot dancing on a rolling log (freshly cut down by a cartoon beaver) that's floating down the river. The bear, of course, is dancing to the famous Hamm's jingle: "From the land of sky blue waters, from the land of pines, lofty balsams . . . comes the beer refreshing, Hamm's the beer refreshing." An ad like this would never get on the air today. The regulatory authorities have gotten pretty stringent about any imagery used to sell alcohol that might be construed as appealing to children (cartoon animals and such). Another ad featured the same cartoon bear in a boxing match with a live-action Rocky Marciano. Pretty groundbreaking stuff for its time. Imagine what sort of motion-capture wizardry commercial producers would be capable of producing today if they were still allowed to get cartoony.

Comic Masterpieces

Some of the most iconic beer commercials and series of commercials have been the ones that have been able to make audiences laugh for generations. Anheuser-Busch's ad agencies have had a particularly deft hand at tickling its target market's funny bone (and even the funny bones of those who can't legally be a part of that market).

Schaeffer Singing Bottle

No, it's not another animated ad. The 1950s spot features a (live-action) man opening a bottle of Schaefer beer. In popping the cap, the ad suddenly plays the übercatchy Schaefer theme song: "Schaefer . . . is the . . . one beer to have when you're . . . having more than one." The man, who wears a loosened tie around his neck—likely just home from work—is giddy with delight at the little orchestra that surely must be living at the bottom of his bottle (he even looks down the neck of the bottle to see if that is actually the case). When he puts his hand over the mouth of the bottle, the music ceases. After he pours the brew, he calls his wife over to share in the fun: "Hey, Agnes, come here, I have a bottle here that actually sings." To which Agnes replies: "Herbie, that's nothing but a bottle, a plain, ordinary, run-of-the-mill bottle. And you're telling me that it sings?" It's not hard to see where this is going. When he has her listen to it, not a single note is heard. After she walks away, the bottle, of course, starts to sing again. Herbie asks the bottle why it didn't sing for Agnes, to which the bottle replies, in a borderline demonic-sounding voice: "After what she said about me, I should sing for her?" This was high comedy for its time and is another example of an ad that would likely be banned in today's alcohol marketing climate, as hypersensitive regulators would claim that it hints at inebriation.

"Tastes Great, Less Filling"

The idea of a light beer, essentially a reduced-calorie "diet" brew, very well could have been a colossal failure had the ad agency behind Miller Lite's iconic "Tastes Great, Less Filling" failed to connect with its intended male audience. The spots, which ran for a staggering seventeen years between 1974 and 1991, aired during major sporting events and featured sports figures like Dick Butkus, George Steinbrenner, and Billy Martin, along with the odd comedian, most notably Rodney Dangerfield. The ads usually featured two factions arguing over whether the most appealing aspect of Miller Lite—originally called Lite Beer from Miller when it was introduced in the '70s—was that it tasted or great or that it was less filling.

Whassup?!

Say what you want about Anheuser-Busch, but the company really knows how to create a catchphrase. The iconic "Whassup" exclamation first appeared in a Budweiser commercial in 1999 and immediately invaded the cultural zeitgeist, running until 2002. Contrary to popular belief, the repeated exclamation did not originate in a Bud ad. It first appeared in a short film titled *True*, which had played at enough film festivals to catch the attention of the creative team from Chicago advertising agency DDB.

Real Men of Genius

In the ongoing effort to convince male consumers that it's okay to drink light beer, Anheuser-Busch in the late 1990s through early 2000s launched this celebration of the common man, originally titled "Real American Heroes." Against a soundtrack of '80s power pop, the tongue-in-cheek Real Men of Genius radio spots raise a glass to the unsung heroes of the everyday world—from "Mr. Portable Toilet Cleaner Outer" and "Mr. Beach Metal Detector Guy" to "Mr. Centerfold Picture Retoucher" and "Mr. Taco Salad Inventor."

Swear Jar

Perhaps one of the best and most hilarious TV beer ads was a spot that never actually ran on TV. The Bud Light spot was deemed too risqué for television, but fear not; it's available on YouTube. Set in a typical office, the ad begins with a man noticing a jar full of cash on the desk of one of his coworkers. She tells him it's a swear jar; every time someone at the office curses, that person must drop a quarter in the jar. The money, she says, goes to buy something for the whole office, say, a case of Bud Light. "F@#ing awesome!" the male colleague exclaims (bleeped out, of course). The rest of the ad features scenes from around the office with coworkers swearing profusely and usually for no good reason, with the obvious intent of filling up the jar as quickly as possible and shortening the time before they're able to enjoy their Bud Light. Since the ad was uploaded to YouTube in 2007, it has been viewed more than six million times.

The Most Interesting Man in the World

One of the most successful ad campaigns in the history of imported beer— Dos Equis's "The Most Interesting Man in the World" print and broadcast ads—features the titular suave, daring, and sagacious character whose badass exploits through the years are chronicled in a voice-over montage of mostly grainy, black-and-white travel films. Among the feats he's performed are freeing a bear from a trap, swimming in hot springs with snow monkeys, and splashing down in a space capsule. In various spots, the voice-over proclaims such hyperbolic attributes as "Sharks have a week dedicated to him," "Alien abductors have asked him to probe them," and "His beard alone has experienced more than a lesser man's entire body." When we meet the present-day version of the bearded, seventyish gentleman at the close of each TV spot, he's sitting in a booth at a nightclub, holding court among a bevy of attractive young women. "I don't always drink beer," he says, "but when I do, I prefer Dos Equis." He then punctuates each ad with his catchphrase: "Stay thirsty, my friends."

There's also a series of shorter spots that feature our hero doling out little nuggets of wisdom and life advice. In one such ad, he offers his insight on inspiring boredom: "Being boring is a choice. Those mild salsas and pleated khakis don't buy themselves." In another he advises on choosing a career: "Find out what it is in life that you do not do well and then don't do that thing."

"The Most Interesting Man in the World" first appeared in 2006, and ran continuously for a decade. The brand gave its revered pitch man a fitting sendoff in 2016 when he boarded a one-way rocket to Mars.

"Brewed the Hard Way"

The Budweiser ad that premiered during Super Bowl XLIX in February 2015 drew the immediate ire of the craft brewing community. True, just about everything the big brewers have done has irked the artisanal segment, but this time it was personal. The minute-long spot features a montage of Budweiser iconography, from the St. Louis brewery to the Clydesdales and an axe cutting beechwood, all set to some highly percussive electronic music. The narration is achieved only through bold, all-caps titles superimposed on the imagery:

> Budweiser: Proudly a macro beer. It's not brewed to be fussed over. (That last sentence is synched to an image of a twirly-mustached, bespectacled hipster nosing a snifter of a dark beer.) "It's brewed for a crisp, smooth finish. This is the only beer beechwood aged since 1876. There's only one Budweiser. It's brewed for drinking, not dissecting. The people who drink our beer are people who like to drink beer. Brewed the hard way. Let them sip their pumpkin peach ale. We'll be brewing us some golden suds. This is the famous Budweiser beer. This Bud's for you.

For the folks in craft brewing, the most incendiary aspect of the ad was the singling out of "pumpkin peach ale." Not only was that a direct dig at the types of seasonal brews commonly released by craft brewers, but it was a gut punch to one very specific brewery: Elysian Brewing Company in Seattle. Elysian had made a name for itself with its innovative pumpkin beers, including a peach variety. The brewery had also made headlines barely ten days before the Super Bowl when Anheuser-Busch announced it was acquiring Elysian. Many argued that even though A-B had bought a few craft breweries in the past several years (Goose Island, Blue Point, and Ten Barrel among them), its participation in the segment was driven more by opportunism than a belief in the quality products such brewers were producing. The shot of the stereotypical hipster sniffing and savoring a brew was a knock not only at such beers and brewers, but the drinkers of those beers.

Many also asserted that there was an underlying sexism to the spot in that "pumpkin peach ale" can be interpreted as code for "girly beer." Beer, after all, should be "manly." And there's no "manlier" beer than Budweiser.

Despite all of the flak A-B got for the ad, the company continued to run it on television and the Internet.

It's true that there sometimes can be a certain degree of pretension among a rather small percentage of folks who fancy themselves as beer connoisseurs. That element seems to be more pronounced among wine drinkers, but even among drinkers of that beverage, the perception of such snobbery is much greater than the reality; elitism is very much in the minority in that beverage category as well.

Beer marketers have used that perception, however inflated it may be, to hawk brands that appeal to a blue-collar mindset. But being mean-spirited about it and insulting other products isn't necessarily the right way to go about it.

Taking Back the High Life

On the other hand, having a good sense of humor about pretension, as well as one's own brand, is a more effective approach. In an effort to revitalize its venerable Miller High Life brand, SABMiller launched a fairly success-ful series of TV ads in 2007—eight years before Bud's "Brewed the Hard Way"—featuring a Miller delivery man who assertively confiscates cases of High Life from bars, restaurants, clubs, and other retail establishments that he deems unworthy of carrying the authentic, no-nonsense brand. The series is shot in a documentary/"Cops"-style, with a shaky camera following the deliveryman, who frequently breaks the fourth wall.

In one spot, he arrives at one of those velvet rope, bass-pounding nightclubs and sees that there's a rather exorbitant cover charge at that hot spot. "Here it is," he says, "home of the twenty-dollar cover charge. Twenty dollars, this is unbelieveable! See, this beer is about letting people live the High Life. It's a good, honest beer at a tasty price. That's it, it's simple. There's no cover charge for the High Life. . . . You just lost your right to sell Miller High Life, is what you did." In another he rolls up to a restaurant, grabs a menu from a waiter serving diners in the outdoor seating section, and discovers that the eatery is charging $11.50 for a hamburger. He storms inside and barges into the kitchen, reclaiming those High Life cases.

It's much more of a tongue-in-cheek social commentary than the straight-faced (some say arrogant) approach in Bud's "Brewed the Hard Way" ad. As a sad footnote, the star of the "Taking Back the High Life" spots, Windell Middlebrooks, passed away in 2015 at the tragically young age of thirty-six. He was an accomplished comedic actor, whose credits included multiple appearances on hit comedies like *It's Always Sunny in Philadelphia* and *Scrubs*.

Ales of the Revolution

An interesting footnote of sorts to the Founding Fathers' brewing exploits has been Yards Brewing Company's Ales of the Revolution series. The Philadelphia-based brewer released a variety pack of three beers based (approximately) on the likely recipes of George Washington, Thomas Jefferson, and Benjamin Franklin.

General Washington's Tavern Porter draws its inspiration from a letter the then military reader penned detailing his use of molasses to aid in fermentation. The addition of molasses complements the roasty notes from the dark malts and adds some caramel elements to the porter. Thomas Jefferson's Tavern Ale, meanwhile, is a replica of the types of beers the third president brewed at Monticello, and this strong golden ale incorporates honey, rye, and wheat into the recipe. Finally, Poor Richard's Tavern Spruce approximates Ben Franklin's amber ale recipe and combines barley with molasses and the essence of spruce.

Yards collaborated with Philadelphia landmark City Tavern, which has been a fixture of the City of Brotherly Love since 1773. When John Adams attended the First Continental Congress, he reportedly referred to the drinking spot as "the most genteel tavern in America." City Tavern—a museum of sorts—remains open to the public for dining and frequently features dishes specifically created to pair with the Ales of the Revolution.

9

The Renaissance Period

The Craft Brewing Movement in the United States

In the Beginning

The fact that the number of breweries in the United Sates is around 5,000 is nothing short of remarkable when one considers that, in the infant years of microbrewing, there were only about ninety total operations, micro or otherwise. The number peaked in 1873 at 4,131. In 1910, a decade prior to the enactment of Prohibition, that number had fallen just below 1,600. In the post-Prohibition, pre-craft-brewing years, the number topped out at 857 in 1941, just before the US got into World War II. The tally didn't get that high again until 1995, and now there are nearly five times that number. Let that sink in for a minute.

At the 2015 Craft Brewers Conference, Gary Fish—founder of Bend, Oregon's Deschutes Brewery and chair of the Brewers Association—spoke to some 11,000 attendees in Portland's Veterans Memorial Coliseum, saying, "We're living in the greatest age of beer in the history of the world." And it wasn't an overstatement.

The movement known as craft brewing owes its existence to the ragtag band of pioneers who defied conventional wisdom and got into an industry that was shrinking. Breweries were either going belly up or were being absorbed by a small number of players that grew larger and larger.

The pioneer among the pioneers, undoubtedly, is a man by the name of Frederick Louis "Fritz" Maytag III, who was the great-grandson of Frederick I, the founder of Maytag Corporation.

In 1965, rapid brewery closures had become a fact of life. Among those about to become a casualty that year was San Francisco's Anchor Brewing Company. The brewery's history was rooted in the California Gold Rush of the mid-nineteenth century. Among the 49ers was Gottlieb Brekle, who moved his family to San Francisco as he pursued his fortune there. In 1871, he opened a brewery. Twenty-five years later, another German brewer, Ernst F. Baruth, along with his son-in-law, Otto Schinkel Jr., bought the brewery, which they renamed "Anchor." The brewery became known for its brand of "Steam" beer, which it continued to produce up until Prohibition and then resumed after the law's repeal.

Over the years Anchor endured a number of setbacks (sudden owner deaths, the Big One of 1906, financial insolvency, the Noble Experiment, etc.) before it was ready to close its doors for good in 1965. Maytag learned of the imminent demise of the brewery that produced his favorite beer and decided to buy it.

It was a bumpy road for Maytag at first. Part of the reason Anchor was on the verge of folding was that the quality of Anchor Steam had declined over the years. Maytag and his team revamped the recipe, bringing modern quality control into the equation, and San Franciscans eventually rediscovered the local brand. By the early '70s, Anchor's product line had expanded to five, including, in addition to Anchor Steam, Anchor Porter, Anchor Liberty Ale, Old Foghorn barleywine, and its annual Christmas ale.

What would come to be known as microbrewing and, later, craft brewing, was born. Maytag ultimately sold the brewery in 2010 to Tony Foglio and Keith Greggor, who had managed the SKYY vodka brand.

The 1970s

A man who followed closely on Maytag's heels but whose status as a pioneer wasn't fully appreciated decades later was Jack McAuliffe, founder of New Albion Brewing Company, which is credited as the first microbrewery to be built from scratch (unlike Anchor, which was acquired and revitalized as a modern microbrewery). Like many other producers who came after him, McAuliffe started out as a homebrewer. During his time in the US Navy, he had been stationed in the United Kingdom, where he grew fond of the range of styles available there that one could not get in the US. In 1976, he opened New Albion in Sonoma County. Six years later, the brewery closed its doors, owing largely to a production issue that still plagues many craft brewers today: capacity. To be profitable, New Albion needed to scale up to make more beer. However, back in those days there was no investment capital available for such an insane venture as a brewery (the landscape is radically different today). It didn't help that the United States was in the middle of what was, perhaps, its worst economic downturn since the Great Depression, a plight that wouldn't be outdone until a quarter of a century later when the housing crash and subsequent financial crisis occurred.

Even though New Albion folded in 1982, McAuliffe demonstrated that it is possible to build a small brewery. Many followed suit, and the rest is history.

There are some happy footnotes to the New Albion story. When Sierra Nevada Brewing Company, the third-largest craft brewer in America—which had been the second-largest until the Brewers Association changed its definition and deemed Yuengling a craft operation—celebrated its thirtieth anniversary in 2010, founder Ken Grossman invited some of the other industry pioneers to brew collaborative beers at the company's Chico, California headquarters. McAuliffe, who had become something of a recluse in the preceding decades, was among those with whom Sierra joined forces that year. Others included Maytag, Brewers Association president; homebrewing trailblazer Charlie Papazian; and veteran beer writer Fred Eckhardt.

The biggest boost for McAuliffe's legacy occurred about two years later, with the help of another craft brewing icon, Boston Beer's Jim Koch. Boston Beer had earlier managed to acquire the New Albion trademark and assets, which it gave back to McAuliffe in 2012. Boston Beer actually did a full production run of New Albion's flagship pale ale, which it unveiled at a special reception at Marlowe's restaurant in Denver during the 2012 Great American Beer Festival. Koch donated profits from its sale to McAuliffe.

The now-retired McAuliffe has since transferred the trademark to his daughter, Renee DeLuca, who is running the relaunched New Albion, whose products are being contract-brewed by a Cleveland brewery.

The 1980s

If Jack McAuliffe was the one who made microbrewing happen, Ken Grossman was among those who rendered that word passé. The skilled homebrewer's first commercial foray into the beer world occurred the same year that McAuliffe opened New Albion. But Grossman's wasn't a brewery; it was a homebrew shop. A few years later he and partner Paul Camusi—whom Grossman eventually bought out in 1998—founded Sierra Nevada Brewing Company.

Given the current state of the craft brewing industry, it's hard to believe there was ever a time where it was difficult to get the necessary equipment and supplies for a small brewery. Walk the floor at any BrewExpo America—the trade show component of the annual Craft Brewers Conference—and you'll see no shortage of tanks, kettles, bottling and canning lines, and raw materials customized for even the smallest of operations.

But at the time when Sierra Nevada and its peers were launching, virtually nothing existed to suit a start-up facility. Overall handiness and an ability to improvise were invaluable skillsets in those days and the Sierra founders had those in spades. They built the brewery with whatever they could get their hands on, from old dairy equipment to a soft drink bottling line. And they didn't have much money to play with; they were able to come up with about $100,000 to get started. Even if you adjust that sum for inflation, it only amounts to about $280,000 in today's dollars—not nearly enough start-up funds for a new brewery to survive for even a month or two. But it was enough for Sierra Nevada to make its first batch by the fall of 1980 and create what ultimately would come to define the American pale ale style, now a reliable staple of craft brewers across the country and even around the world. Sierra's output now totals more than a 1 million barrels a

Sierra Nevada's East Coast brewery in Mills River, North Carolina, is like Willy Wonka's chocolate factory for grown-ups.

year. In 2014 it opened a second brewery on the opposite coast, in Asheville, North Carolina, to better meet demand in the Eastern part of the country. And recent reports have put Grossman's net worth at over $1 billion.

Grossman is not the only billionaire to come out of the craft brewing movement. Boston Beer Company founder Jim Koch is probably the most visible member of that extremely exclusive triple-comma club. He became something of a celebrity during the '90s with his string of Samuel Adams radio ads (the first time most Americans ever heard the term "Reinheitsgebot" was very likely in one of those broadcast spots). And, since Koch is such a folksy storyteller, many are well aware of at least part of the history and heritage of the Sam Adams brand.

Koch was the sixth-generation scion of German immigrant brewers who settled in St. Louis and founded the Louis Koch Brewery. His father would be the last generation to go into the family business. By that time American breweries were shuttering rapidly, and beer no longer seemed like a viable career path. Koch went on to get a joint MBA-law degree at Harvard; the combined degree program was a discipline relatively few completed. It's a pretty distinguished group who did; among Koch's classmates was Mitt Romney. He went on to start a lucrative career at Boston Consulting Group (BCG) but soon realized he'd rather be brewing. (Just when he thought he was out, beer pulled him back in!) He left BCG, took administrative assistant Rhonda Kallman with him, and, in 1984, the two of them launched Boston Beer Company. (Kallman cashed out in 2000 and went on to launch New Century Brewing Company and the brands Edison Light and Moonshot. Later, she got into the craft spirits game and founded Boston Harbor Distillery.)

The microbrewers of the time were mostly focused on making ales, mainly because of their shorter fermentation times—the faster the beer ferments, the faster it gets out to the market and starts generating revenue. But Koch was intent on brewing a lager—an amber, flavorful brew based on an old family recipe. That beer became Samuel Adams Boston Lager. Koch set the modest goal of selling 8,000 barrels annually by the end of the company's fifth year. Sam Adams caught fire much more quickly than he had anticipated, and the brand achieved that milestone by the end of its fifth *month*.

Part of what made the brand so successful so quickly—other than the fact that it was well made and looked and tasted like nothing else Bostonians had ever had—was that Boston Beer Company didn't have to worry about running an actual brewery. Initially, all of its volume was contract brewed.

Boston Beer Company founder Jim Koch.

That enabled the company to pour a great deal of its energy and resources into marketing and selling the brand, rather than the capital- and labor-intensive tasks of day-to-day brewery management. Boston Beer eventually bought its own breweries in Ohio and Pennsylvania, which produce most of its volume. Its only Boston-based facility is a relatively modest operation housed in the former home of the now-defunct nineteenth-century Haffenreffer Brewery in Jamaica Plain. The site serves a mostly R&D function; it also produces some of the very small-batch, limited-run products the company releases throughout the year. It also houses a fairly impressive barrel room, containing much of the cooperage in which its barrel-aged selections mature.

Few figures in the history of craft brewing have been as polarizing as Jim Koch, but there's no denying that more than thirty years on, the man is no less passionate about beer than he was when he was doing a test-brew of what would become Boston Lager in his kitchen. Contract-brewing still has its detractors—a few of them say you're not really a brewery if you don't actually own a brewery—but it's been a viable business model that has helped many of the most respected producers in the business survive and thrive. It's what helped Brooklyn Lager, the flagship brand from the Brooklyn Brewery, gain a loyal following in the New York market before Brooklyn Brewery had a production facility of its own (the flagship is still being produced under contract at F. X. Matt Brewery in Utica, New York.)

Brooklyn Brewery

Brooklyn Brewery, founded by former war correspondent Steve Hindy and banker Tom Potter about four years after Boston Beer, now sells around 250,000 barrels a year, and its products range from year-round offerings— like Brooklyn Brown, East India Pale Ale, and Brooklyn Blast! Double IPA—to its highly experimental Brewmaster's Reserve series. The brewmaster in question would be Garrett Oliver, who's become something of a celebrity in his own right. He penned the tome *The Brewmaster's Table*, a seminal work in the beer-and-food-pairing movement, and he also edited *The Oxford Companion to Beer.*

As American craft beer has attracted a following the world over, Brooklyn Brewery became the first to open a brewery on another continent. In 2014 it opened the New Carnegiebryggeriet (New Carnegie Brewery) in Stockholm, Sweden, through a joint venture with Carlsberg, the leading Danish brewer. A year later, Brooklyn Brewery announced a second partnership with Carlsberg to open E. C. Dahls Brewery in Trondheim, Norway.

Deschutes Brewery

Launched the same year as Brooklyn Brewery (1988), but on the opposite coast, was Deschutes Brewery, the brainchild of Gary Fish. Named for the river in Oregon, it began its life as Deschutes Brewery & Public House. With products such as Black Butte Porter, Mirror Pond Pale Ale, Obsidan Stout, the Abyss Imperial Stout, and its holiday seasonal Jubelale, Deschutes has, in the ensuing years, grown to become one of the top six craft breweries in the country, producing more than 300,000 barrels annually. The brewery has done so by staying true to its regional roots and by expanding ever so gradually eastward. It almost singlehandedly put Bend on the brewing map, and the city now boasts, at last count, nineteen breweries. Considering Bend is a city of roughly 80,000, there's a brewery for approximately every 4,200 people.

These days, though, Deschutes' operations aren't limited to Bend. In 2008 it opened a brewpub in Portland's trendy Pearl District, a stone's throw from the iconic Powell's Books, and in 2016 Deschutes announced its first East Coast operation in Roanoke, Virginia.

The 1990s

The success of craft brewing has been, by and large, the result of a group of highly passionate people making products of impeccable quality. But that's just part of the movement's success. The other key component of the story is . . . well . . . a story. The craft beer drinker has not only been gravitating toward great-tasting products using the best possible ingredients, but they've been attracted to the authentic tales the breweries have to tell about how they got started. And few such tales are as evocative as the origin story for a certain company based in Fort Collins, Colorado.

New Belgium

The year was 1989, and electrical engineer Jeff Lebesch took a bike ride across Belgium that would forever change brewing in America. The trip took him from brewery to brewery, and by the time he came home, he was ready to open one of his own. Working out of their basement, Lebesch and his then wife Kim Jordan (who served as CEO until 2015 and is now the company chair) produced their first commercial batch in 1991. They named the brewery New Belgium, after the country that inspired them, and their flagship product Fat Tire, after the type of bicycle that started the journey.

New Belgium has become as well known for its environmental and social stewardship as it has for products like Abbey, 1554 Black Lager, Ranger IPA, and its experimental Lips of Faith series. It's perennially voted one of the best places to work in America by various magazines and business organizations. The brewery has one of the most famous employee incentive programs in the industry.

When associates celebrate one year with the company, they get a limited-release Fat Tire Cruiser bike. Employees celebrating their fifth anniversary with New Belgium get an all-expenses-paid trip to old Belgium—the country, that is. At each of years ten, twenty, and thirty, associates get a four-week paid sabbatical. At year fifteen, they get a $1,000 travel voucher to take them wherever they want to go.

New Belgium is also one of a growing number of brewers to adopt an employee stock ownership program (ESOP) and has been 100 percent employee-owned since 2013. That same year it became a certified B Corporation, a designation bestowed upon companies that meet rigorous standards of social and environmental performance, accountability, and transparency.

Much like Sierra Nevada, New Belgium settled on Asheville, North Carolina, as the site of its second brewery, which opened in 2016.

The mid-'90s was a very bizarre time for the craft brewing industry. The period saw the birth of some of the most innovative players in the segment. Simultaneously, it was the point when craft beer's growth, which had been explosive up until then, ground to a halt. Many start-ups had gotten into what was still being called "microbrewing" for perhaps the wrong reasons. For every passionate producer like a New Belgium or a Sierra Nevada there were a handful that thought they could get rich quick by getting subpar product on the shelves as quickly as possible. It all came to a head when *Consumer Reports* published a rather unflattering piece on the burgeoning segment.

In 1990 there were 284 breweries. The number peaked ten years later at 1566—a net increase of nearly 500 percent. However, some of the less quality-focused breweries had already begun to rapidly leave the industry in the years immediately prior to 2000. But it was the following year when there was an actual net decline in the number of operating breweries.

The segment still managed to post modest growth in the low single digits even as it seemed to be hemorrhaging players. The success of the savvy ones that prioritized product quality—New Belgium, Sierra Nevada, Sam Adams, and others—were the proverbial rising tides lifting many of the boats that continued to sink.

There was a social Darwinian silver lining to what some have called the late '90s shakeout; only the strongest were surviving. In 2006 the number of US breweries started to grow again, and, since then, the number of breweries has nearly tripled. The fact that the mid-'90s additions to the industry are not merely footnotes in the brief history of a passing fad is a testament to their fortitude, marketing savvy, and brewing prowess.

Punk's Not Dead: Dogfish Head and Stone Brewing

Two of the most visible additions to the craft ranks were the punk rockers of the segment. In the town of Milton, Delaware, a twenty-five-year-old homebrewer with an English degree by the name of Sam Calagione

New Belgium's Fort Collins, Colorado headquarters.

launched Dogfish Head Craft Brewery. A year later, two refugees from the music business, Greg Koch and Steve Wagner, formed Stone Brewing Company in the Southern California town of San Marcos. (It has since moved to nearby Escondido.)

The flattening of craft volume would have scared away even the boldest of entrepreneurs, especially those just entering the game as things started to plateau. But Stone soldiered through those uncertain times, building a cult around such perennial favorite brands as Stone Pale Ale, Smoked Porter, and its colorfully monikered Arrogant Bastard Ale. One can easily argue that the name of the latter marketed itself. It grabbed the attention of many a festival-goer or pub patron in the early years. However, Koch was known to make those sampling it for the first time work up to it; they had to try some of the brewery's less assertive offerings before they "earned" a taste of Arrogant Bastard.

Dogfish Head, meanwhile, attracted its loyal fan base with 60- and 90-Minute IPA, as well as other "Off-Centered Ales for Off-Centered People," such as Palo Santo Marron, Indian Brown Ale, and Raison d'Etre.

With no budget for advertising of any kind, both operations relied primarily on guerilla marketing. (In a rather meta moment at the 2010 Craft Brewers Conference, Koch and his cohorts pulled a stunt that would make Banksy proud. During the general session, they disrupted Brewers Association director Paul Gatza's annual State of the Craft Beer Industry address and hijacked his Powerpoint presentation to briefly promote their panel on guerilla marketing. Gatza was in on it, but it speaks to the type of attention-grabbing stunts for which Stone was famous.)

In his book *Brewing Up a Business*, Calagione famously chronicles a promotional stunt that involved him rowing a wooden boat full of six-packs across the Delaware Bay to New Jersey, George Washington-style, to celebrate the brewery's first sale outside of its home state. The boat now hangs proudly from the ceiling of its Rehoboth Beach brewpub for all to behold.

Today, Stone and Dogfish Head each sells more than 200,000 barrels of beer annually, so they must be doing something right.

The 2000s and Beyond

By the middle of the first decade of the twenty-first century, the planets seemed to finally align for a more sustainable craft beer growth trajectory. The last of the subpar producers from the '90s surge had exited the business, and the ones that were left were passionate about what they were doing and religious about product quality. They also had the business sense to make it all work or hire the right people who could. And then there was the consumer factor; a new generation was starting to reach legal drinking age

By now, we're all tired of hearing about the millennials. Marketers tend to paint the age-group—born somewhere between 1982 and 2000—with extremely broad strokes. "They're entitled," many will say. "They're tech-savvy," others will assert. "They don't follow the herd; they're individualistic," more will claim.

Whether you buy into that or are skeptical about such focus-group and boardroom-born marketing mumbo jumbo, there's one fact that can't be disputed: There are a lot of them! And why wouldn't there be? For the most part, they're the offspring of the last colossal generation, the baby boomers. (Initially, demographic researchers and marketing analysts dubbed Generation Y as the "Echo Boomers," but the name didn't stick. Somehow, the term "millennials," for better or for worse, has stuck.)

The first wave of millennials could legally buy a six-pack around 2003. A couple of years after that, craft beer volume growth started to accelerate. By the end of the last decade, its percent increase was in the double digits.

There are a lot of theories as to why craft beer is connecting with the millennial market, but a common thread among them is the notion of "authenticity." The consensus (for what it's worth) is that millennials, more so than any demographic group before them, embrace authentic product and experiences that have a relatable story. Craft brewers easily fit that profile.

Further, millennials are supposed to be incredibly suspicious of any forms of marketing or advertising (at least overt forms, as, whether they realize it or not, they're being bombarded with stealthy marketing messages practically every second of every day, especially when they're on social media, which is pretty much always). Most craft brewers have neither the resources nor the desire to commit to traditional advertising. Before the advent of social media, they relied on word of mouth and guerilla marketing tactics to boost their presence among adults of legal drinking age. Then, Twitter, Facebook, Instagram, and their ilk completely leveled the playing field and became the promotional engine for the entire craft movement. And, of course, such platforms skew younger, specifically toward millenials.

The Millers and Budweisers of the world still pour most of their multi-million-dollar ad budgets into old standbys like TV commercials, and that's just fine with the millennials. They're not watching TV ads anyway.

Around the same time that millennials started to come of age, beer distributors began to embrace craft beer like never before, offering craft breweries fewer barriers to their routes to market. The number of new players getting into the craft segment has accelerated to the point that, statistically speaking, 1.7 American breweries open each day. More than six hundred opened in 2014 alone, and more than 2,000 were in some form of pre-operational planning at the end of that year. Overall craft volume has been growing in the double digits (sometimes as high as 18 percent) every year since 2010.

Such rapid growth has many pundits and media agencies kicking around the dreaded "b" word: bubble. And why wouldn't they? It makes a great story. Ever since the dot-com crash of the year 2000, analysts always seem to be waiting with bated breath for the next monumental bubble burst.

There are several arguments against the bubble narrative. For one thing, the US market can more than handle the speedy influx of new brewing operations. At the time of the publication of this book, there were nearly 5,000 operating breweries. This is still only about half the number of wineries, and there are plenty of wineries opening every year (not nearly the number that breweries are seeing, but it's still substantial). Another argument against the bubble is that the largest, longest-operating regional players are still the ones responsible for most of the segment's cumulative growth. If hundreds of the new start-ups were to disappear suddenly, the volume loss would barely put a dent in craft beer's total barrelage.

Those who require further evidence to silence bubble talk needn't look any further than some of the country's biggest beer cities. Portland, Oregon, arguably the center of the craft beer universe, is now home to about 60 breweries. And that number continues to grow at a remarkable clip. Most business-minded folk would argue that an entrepreneur would have to be insane to start a brewery in such a saturated beer market, but the city continues to support craft beer start-ups.

Colorado is another case study. Conventional wisdom would make most steer clear of the brewing mecca, but an unprecedented number of new start-ups in the state and its most beer-soaked cities—Denver and Fort Collins, in particular—continue to find success.

It's also a matter of Economics 101: supply and demand. Craft beer demand continues to outstrip supply. Most breweries can barely keep up with the demand. Bubble industries are those in which investors overestimate demand.

That's not to say there aren't real concerns with such a flood of new entrants. The word "quality" has come up quite a bit during the last several editions of the Craft Brewers Conference. It's been a particular rallying cry for Brewers Association director Paul Gatza, who has made it a centerpiece of his annual address.

When there are five hundred to six hundred new breweries opening each year and another 2,000 waiting in the wings, they all can't be winners. The simple rules of probability dictate otherwise. So, is there a danger that a handful of bad apples could potentially spoil the bunch? Not likely. But that's not stopping some media outlets from making mountains out of molehills. On more than one occasion, local news agencies have declared the supposed bubble on the verge of bursting when a single brewery goes belly up. Surely, they say, it must be a sign of things to come.

A mere two minutes of homework would prevent such shoddy journalism. According to the Brewers Association, a total of forty-six breweries shuttered in 2014—compared with the 615 that started up. That's a net gain of 569.

It's certainly easier for a new brewery to start up these days. Banks and investors are more than willing to commit start-up capital to such a booming industry. Private equity firms are keen to partner with existing breweries, if not buy them outright. That wasn't the case thirty, twenty, or even just fifteen years ago. It's also much easier to find equipment and supplies scaled to the small start-up brewery.

But most of the new operations to start up in the past few years may never truly know what it was like to rely on MacGyver-like DIY ingenuity to convert their dreams to reality. Part of the reason the Sierra Nevadas and New Belgiums of the world survived and thrived is that they were built by problem-solvers who knew how to think on their feet and improvise their way to success when they didn't have easy access to financial and mechanical resources. It's like learning to drive in the smartphone age. A whole generation will never know the experience of having to pull over to read a map or ask for directions. Their Google Maps app solves that problem for them.

Does this necessarily mean that new entrants lack survival skills to make it in today's market? Absolutely not, but there may be fewer opportunities for them to exercise their operationally creative muscles.

If a brewery that has started up in the past five years has aspirations of being the next Sierra Nevada, New Belgium, or Dogfish Head, they may be setting themselves up for disappointment. There's not much room left for the sort of large regional, semi-national, or national players that were born in the 1980s, 1990s, and early 2000s.

Flourishing beyond the second decade of the twenty-first century means embracing a hyper-local business plan. Breweries that establish a secure foothold in their home city, state, or immediate multi-state region and that focus primarily on winning over consumers in those areas are the ones most likely to be around ten or twenty years from now.

There are quite a few new brewers whose objectives are far more modest than that and are starting out so small that their existence has necessitated the creation of a whole new word: nanobrewery. In essence, a nano is a homebrewer who has gone pro, selling beer legally and commercially, but is still holding on to his or her day job. In many instances, nanos are completely self-financed operations, or their founders turn to crowdfunding platforms like Kickstarter or Indiegogo to finance their businesses. Once they cross the nano threshold into microbrewery territory, their expansion usually requires funding through more conventional channels. But much of the time, their ambitions do not extend beyond nano status. If a couple of local bars carry a few kegs of their product, they've succeeded. It's not unlike an indie rock band being thrilled to have a song played on a local college radio station and performing in front of club crowd of one hundred.

Whether a brewery is a fifty-barrel-a-year nano or a million-plus-barrel-a-year national, craft beer will continue to be an incredibly inclusive playground for experimentation and creativity for the next several decades to come. Will the segment continue to bask in the glow of 20 percent year-on-year growth? Probably not. The most likely scenario is that it will eventually settle somewhere in the mid-to-high single digits and maintain that trajectory for some time. But by then it will likely represent about a quarter of the nation's total beer volume and will be growing off of a massive base. The mega-multinationals still will be buying them, or will at least be trying to, but there will still be a staggering number of independents to carry craft beer toward the midpoint of the twenty-first century.

Defining "Craft"

Ask anyone what the most exciting segment of the modern beer market is and, invariably, the answer will be "craft beer." But what exactly defines "craft beer"?

That answer is a little complicated.

In the beginning, the purveyors of these hop, malt, yeast, and water concoctions were called microbrewers. The trouble was that the ones that were actually good at what they did grew to a point where "micro" didn't really work as a descriptor anymore. The movement needed a more all-encompassing label that could be affixed to the largest of their peers. The term "microbrewery" wasn't discarded all together; it's still used internally to describe a craft brewer whose annual volume is below 15,000 barrels.

Now, that's technically the definition that the Brewers Association uses, but let's just say that the task of defining "craft" has fallen more to Wikipedia than it has to *Webster's Dictionary*. The definition is a living thing that's constantly evolving; it's not etched in stone. Every couple of years it gets tweaked.

As of this writing there are three broad pillars of the Brewers Association's craft brewery definition. "An American craft brewer," the organization says, "is small, independent, and traditional." Pretty vague, right?

The association expounds further on each of those tenets.

By "small," the Brewers Association means that a brewery's annual production is 6 million barrels or less. And small is not as small as it used to be. Until 2011, the Association defined "small" as "2 million barrels or less." So, why the jump? The short answer: Samuel Adams. Boston Beer Company, known for the iconic Founding Father-inspired brand, was within spitting distance of that 2-million-barrel ceiling. Craft was at a crossroads. The Brewers Association could either bid farewell to its largest, most nationally visible member or raise the threshold. It chose the latter and tripled the limit. It should be at least a few years before Sam Adams sells enough beer in a year to render itself un-craft-worthy (or forces another change).

The decision to raise the limit proved to be somewhat controversial. Some of it was personal; Boston Beer and founder Jim Koch certainly have their detractors among the craft brewer ranks (though those folks will admit to a grudging admiration for the pioneer). The ceiling has been a bit of a sticking point politically, as well.

The Brewers Association's description of "independent," the second pillar of the craft brewer definition, is not without its own controversy. The organization states that "less than 25 percent of the craft brewery is owned or controlled (or equivalent economic interest) by an alcoholic beverage industry member that is not itself a craft brewer."

That line item is aimed squarely at certain small brewers that gave up a portion of equity to macro brewers, usually in exchange for space in the warehouses and on the trucks of wholesalers in those big producers' distribution networks. If the craft brewers sacrificed more than a quarter of their ownership to one of those huge multinational corporations, they no longer get to be part of the craft club.

There are plenty of significant precedents for such equity purchases. Back in 1994, Anheuser-Busch purchased 25 percent of Seattle-based

Redhook Brewery, which, coupled with an initial public offering (IPO) a year later, enabled Redhook to expand its operations and distribution. The brand is now available in nearly every US state and has a total annual volume of about 250,000 barrels. A few years later, in 1997, Anheuser-Busch made a larger investment in Portland, Oregon's Widmer Brothers Brewery, taking nearly 40 percent of the business in exchange for distribution access.

Ultimately, Redhook and Widmer, along with Hawaii's Kona Brewing Company—of which Anheuser-Busch also owns a piece—joined forces in 2010 to create Craft Brew Alliance. As of 2015, Anheuser-Busch—now part of AB InBev—owned 32.25 percent of that larger entity, which, collectively, produces more than 1 million barrels of beer a year.

Craft Brew Alliance also had a 42 percent stake in Chicago's Goose Island Beer Co., which it sold to AB InBev in 2011; AB InBev also bought the remaining 58 percent of that company.

Because the world's largest brewer, AB InBev, now owns nearly a third of Craft Brew Alliance and 100 percent of Goose Island, neither of those are considered "craft brewers" under the Brewers Association's definition. The creative forces behind the brands that form Craft Brew Alliance are none too pleased about being excluded from that definition, considering that they are some of the segment's pioneers. Redhook formed as far back as 1981—predating Sam Adams by three years—and Widmer Brothers, which played a huge role in popularizing wheat beers among American drinkers, formed in 1984. Both brands continue to thrive and innovate under the Craft Brew Alliance banner.

Things get even more interesting when one looks at Athens, Georgia's Terrapin Brewing Company. In 2011, the same year that AB InBev in one fell swoop erased Goose Island's "craft" status, MillerCoors—the US-based joint venture between second-largest global brewer SABMiller and Molson Coors—purchased a stake in Terrapin. However, Terrapin retained its Brewers Association-sanctioned "craft" designation, albeit by the skin of its teeth: the Georgia brewery agreed to sell just shy of 25 percent.

The "independent" provision of the Brewers Association's definition used to be considerably more rigid. It previously didn't allow a craft brewer to be foreign owned. At the time, that excluded a company like Brewery Ommegang, the Belgian-style brewery in Cooperstown, New York, known for such offerings as its flagship Ommegang dark abbey ale, Rare Vos amber, and Hennepin farmhouse-style ale. In 2003, Belgium's Duvel Moortgat Brewery—famous for its Duvel golden ale—acquired the then six-year-old brewery, establishing a footing in the US market. Ommegang doubled as Duvel Moortgat USA, the importing arm for its European owner's brands. Ommegang's reputation skyrocketed in 2012 when it signed a deal with HBO to produce a line of beers based on the überpopular series *Game of Thrones*.

The difference between a Duvel Moortgat and an AB InBev, aside from sheer size, is that the majority of the former's output, for all intents and purposes, would be deemed "craft beer" by even the strictest of definitions. Its flagship brew, Duvel, has become the gold standard (no pun intended) of its style, with many artisanal brewers trying to adapt and replicate its recipe for their own brands. Additionally, the brewery has gained a reputation for rescuing and preserving some classic, venerable Belgian brands that quite possibly would have vanished otherwise. Among those is De Koninck, the quintessential Belgian amber that's a source of extreme local pride for those who live in Antwerp.

Duvel Moortgat's portfolio has grown through further acquisitions to include La Chouffe, Maredsous, and Liefmans. Few could argue with the craft-cred of such brands. In 2013, it added to its US portfolio by purchasing Kansas City's Boulevard Brewing Company.

Duvel's US-based breweries are considered "craft" by the Brewers Association's revised definition. (For more on Duvel Moortgat, refer to this book's section on Belgium).

There has perhaps been no greater source of debate in the organization's definition than its "traditional" pillar. Prior to 2014, any brewery whose flagship product—the one responsible for most of its volume—contained adjuncts like corn or rice was excluded from the "craft" club. The definition was partial to all-malt beers, those that derive most of their fermentable sugars from barley malt.

The problem with the anti-adjunct bias was that it barred some of the nation's oldest and continuously operating family-owned breweries from being included under the craft umbrella.

Case in point: DG Yuengling & Sons. For those who live in the mid-Atlantic states, Pennsylvania's Yuengling brand is an institution. The Yuengling family founded the brewery in 1829, and, since then, its flagship lager has more or less retained its original recipe. But that recipe included corn. In the nineteenth century, folks had to use whatever they could get their hands on. There was an abundance of corn. Barley was a little harder to come by, so Yuengling had to use it more sparingly.

The same went for Minnesota's August Schell Brewing Company, which launched in 1860. Over its 150 years of existence, the brewery has expanded to include many German-inspired craft-staple styles like maibocks, hefe-weizens, and Oktoberfests, but its original lager is what kept it from entering the modern "craft" ranks—at least as it was defined by the Brewers Association—for so long.

Things came to a head in December 2012, when the Brewers Association issued its famous "Craft versus Crafty" manifesto, decrying the lack of transparency among mega brewers like AB InBev and MillerCoors when they marketed craft-like brands—particularly AB InBev's Shock Top and MillerCoors's Blue Moon. The association argued that the macros were promoting false provenance for their brands, hiding their true origins behind folksy, artisanal images.

The "Craft versus Crafty" campaign had the unintended side effect of stigmatizing companies like August Schell and Yuengling. The organization released a set of infographics separating breweries that met its definition of craft from a list of "domestic non-craft breweries."

Jace Marti, the sixth-generation of the family that owns August Schell, didn't appreciate his business being singled out as what amounted to a lesser brewery, so he issued a pointed missive taking the Brewers Association to task.

> "As a 152-year-old brewery, and the second oldest family-owned brewery in America, stating [sic] that we are not "traditional" is insulting. Their definition of what makes a traditional brewer, and thus a 'craft brewer,' comes down to the use of adjuncts. Big brewers often use adjuncts in excess amounts to cut down on brewing costs, and to lighten their beers—the opposite of what the craft beer movement is all about. While this is true for them, it is also a very shortsighted view of brewing in America, and most definitely not the case for in our brewery. When August Schell emigrated from Germany and founded this brewery in 1860, his only option to brew was to use what was available to him, as it was impossible to ship large quantities of raw ingredients from Europe at that time. The high-quality, two-row malting barley he could use back home wasn't native to North America. Instead, he had to use the locally grown, but much higher protein, six-row barley to brew his beer. When he decided that he wanted to produce a high-quality, clear, and stable golden lager, he had to cut down that protein content somehow. In order to accomplish this, he used a small portion of another locally grown ingredient he called "mais" as is hand written in our old brewing logs, better known as corn. He didn't use corn to cheapen or lighten his beer. He did it because it was the only way to brew a high-quality

lager beer in America at that point. . . . The question we have for the Brewers Association is why are we being punished for brewing with a locally grown ingredient, which started out of necessity and has continued out of tradition?"

At the time of the "Craft versus Crafty" initiative, the "traditional" component of the Brewers Association's definition read as such: "[A craft brewer is] a brewer who has either an all-malt flagship (the beer which represents the greatest volume among that brewer's brands) or has at least 50 percent of its volume in either all-malt beers or in beers which use adjuncts to enhance rather than lighten flavor."

The question of a brewer's intentions regarding adjunct use—again, the most common adjuncts used in American beer are corn and rice—opened a can of worms among many brewers. Who's to say what a brewer's particular motive was in using certain ingredients? A brewery that incorporates rice into its recipe might be trying to achieve a particular mouthfeel or "ricey" quality with the beer (saké, after all, is made with 100 percent rice, and it's a world-class beverage in its own right.) Conversely, any brewer that dumps in a load of corn might be doing it for corner-cutting, nefarious purposes but can easily invent a flavor-centric reason for doing so.

Another argument was that the old verbiage was discriminatory, as it related to lagers and lagers alone. Technically, anything that's not barley malt is, by definition, an adjunct. Therefore, fruit beers, spiced beers, coffee beers, and just about every Belgian style used non-malt ingredients of some sort. But those got a pass.

A little over a year after Marti's open letter, the Brewers Association tweaked its definition to be more inclusive of those legacy brewers that persevered through all of the ups and downs the American beer market faced between the nineteenth and twenty-first centuries (including a little something called Prohibition). Now the "traditional" component of the definition reads: "[A craft brewer is] a brewer that has a majority of its total beverage alcohol volume in beers whose flavor derives from traditional or innovative brewing ingredients and their fermentation. Flavored malt beverages (FMBs) are not considered beers."

Flavored malt beverages are products like Mike's Hard Lemonade and Smirnoff Ice that use fermented malt as a base but are flavored like cocktails. (It's a common misconception that products such as the Smirnoff line are actual cocktails that contain spirits, but they are not. The Smirnoff name is licensed to a beer brewer that produces the Ice range of products. The marketers don't really go out of their way to clarify that for consumers.

After all, Smirnoff is the top-selling vodka trademark in the world; why would the FMB producers go out of their way to let drinkers know there isn't any actual vodka in a beverage that bears the Smirnoff name?)

There's likely to be very little argument with the exclusion of FMBs—even from the largest craft brewer in the country that just happens to have an FMB in its portfolio. Boston Beer Company—remember, the brewer for which the "small" threshold was raised—produces Twisted Tea, a line of FMBs designed to taste like iced tea (the range has expanded to include lemonade-flavored products as well). If the Brewers Association's definition allowed FMBs to be counted as part of a craft brewer's volume, it would push Boston Beer closer to the 6 million barrel limit.

As inclusive or exclusive as the craft brewer definition may be, it still covers about 99 percent of the operating breweries in America. As of this

Thousands of barrels of beer quietly ferments.

writing the Brewers Association had counted a total of 4,011 breweries across the country. Of those, nearly 99 percent were considered "craft."

Succession

As many of the breweries that opened in the 1980s and 1990s are reaching maturity, the question becomes: what's next? Sometimes it's simple. In the case of a Sierra Nevada, the next generation is already running things. Founder Ken Grossman's kids, Brian and Sierra, have been immersed in the business for some time. Brian's the company's general manager and has been leading the operation at the company's Mills River, North Carolina brewery since it opened in 2014.

Other times, the succession plan isn't so cut-and-dried. Either the founders/owners lack progeny, or their kids aren't interested in going into the family business. Or, some larger corporate entity throws them a huge sack of cash and entices them to sell the company, rendering the next-generation question moot.

Often, the formation of an Employee Stock Ownership Program (ESOP) addresses the succession issue head on. The employees themselves become the stakeholders (the longer they've been there, the greater the stake). New Belgium and Full Sail Brewing were early adopters of the ESOP. Oregon's Deschutes Brewery, Colorado's Odell Brewing, and Boston's Harpoon Brewery integrated the concept in more recent years.

The ESOP is part of what has enabled New Belgium to remain independent, even after cofounder Kim Jordan passed the CEO torch to president and chief operating officer Christine Perich in 2015. Jordan has stuck around as the chair of the brewery's executive board. (Interestingly, the 2014–2015 timeframe saw a great number of the operations founded in 1980s and 1990s experience leadership changes. In late 2014, Brooklyn Brewery's Steve Hindy stepped down as CEO—like Jordan, he's still active as the brewery's full-time chairman—and transferred executive control to brothers Eric and Robin Ottoway. The Ottoways, years earlier, had bought Tom Potter's voting stock and ultimately purchased Hindy's. In September 2015, Stone Brewing's Greg Koch announced that he, too, would be stepping down as CEO. Meanwhile, Dogfish Head's Calagione promoted long-time chief operating officer Nick Benz to CEO. Calagione wasn't stepping aside or anything. There never actually was a CEO title at Dogfish—Calagione had been founder and president.)

And then there's the cashing-out option.

If the 2010s are remembered for anything, it's going to be as a period of rapid and dramatic change in the craft brewing segment. It was a time when the macros dug in and decided "if we can't beat 'em, join 'em" and began a long-term campaign to buy some of the best-regarded small breweries in the country. AB InBev followed up its acquisition of Goose Island in 2011 with a rather rapid succession of purchases between 2014 and 2016: Patchogue (Long Island), New York's Blue Point; Bend, Oregon's Ten Barrel; Seattle's Elysian; Los Angeles's Golden Road; Littleton, Colorado's Breckenridge Brewery; Tempe, Arizona's Four Peaks Brewery; and Lexington, Virginia's Devil's Backbone.

September 2015 was an especially busy month for such deals, with an unprecedented number of announcements from AB InBev and its principal competitors. On September 8, Heineken announced that it had purchased a 50 percent stake in Petaluma, California's Lagunitas. Two days later, MillerCoors revealed its own plans to scoop up San Diego start-up Saint Archer Brewery (which was barely two years old at that point). Less than two weeks later, the AB InBev/Golden Road deal happened (and, in the middle of all that, AB InBev announced that it wanted to buy the No. 2 player in the world, SABMiller).

Many times, though, the buying and selling isn't about succession but is about managing and financing growth. Most breweries, at one point or another, face capacity issues; the demand for their products races far ahead of their ability to supply it. So, they'll often sell a piece of their businesses or their entire companies to private equity, investor groups or other breweries to fund the necessary capacity expansion. (This was one of the factors in the Golden Road deal. Golden Road cofounder and president Meg Gill was thirty at the time of the sale and wasn't anywhere near retiring; she continues to lead the company under the new corporate parent.)

The continuing wave of acquisitions, primarily the ones involving mega-multinational corporations, has resurrected the "Craft versus Crafty" debate. It's even made some in the industry rethink their positions on the matter—and the word "craft" itself. Brock Wagner, cofounder of Houston's Saint Arnold Brewing Company, predicts that the term will likely disappear by the 2030s.

"Craft beer has been so successful that it's become just 'beer,'" Wagner explains. "And I think it's just going to continue to evolve. When we opened, we were 'microbrewing,' and you don't see that term anymore."

The word craft will likely become just as passé. And that's not necessarily a bad thing considering just how nebulous the term has become. John Holl, editor-in-chief of *All About Beer* raised a few eyebrows with the cover of the magazine's March 2015 edition. The cover line read: "Craft Beer is Dead, Long Live Craft Beer." In his editor's column that month, he pointed out that the simple, five-letter word has caused so much "confusion, blind passion, and confrontation." Holl also noted that the term has been co-opted; it's now as much about marketing as it is about beer.

"Most people silently agreed with me," Holl reveals. "It's a word that's been fraught with all kinds of baggage. It'll continue to change. Most brewers simply are just thinking of making beer of exceptional taste and quality."

Wagner—who played a significant role in, well, crafting the "craft" definition and who had previously taken a more hardline position on its application (he was among those who successfully rallied for the 25 percent threshold for ownership by a non-craft entity; it was originally supposed to be 49 percent)—admits that his own views on the matter have evolved over the years. He recalls a recent encounter with a consumer purchasing Blue Moon: "I was talking with him and he said, 'Yeah, I love craft beer, that's why I bought this.' I brought up that it was MillerCoors. He was like, 'Yeah, that's cool.' It's craft beer now . . . Ultimately we want to be educating the populace about what we do and why it's different, but at some point the populace just thinks that it's all beer. And [craft] has become such a significant part of the beer market that it's just *beer*. I don't know that that's necessarily a bad thing."

10

Pioneers and Rebels

A Shoutout to Some of the Key Players, Old and New, in the Craft Movement

Some Craft Breweries of Note

By the time you finish reading this sentence another brewery will have opened in the United States. Okay, that's a bit of an exaggeration, but in the time between the moment you started reading this book and the second that you turn the final page, it's likely that at least fifty new operations opened their doors (it could be twice as many or a half a dozen or so fewer, depending on how fast of a reader you are). In light of that, it's next to impossible to give every outstanding brewery its due. Let's subtract out the ones to which significant ink already has been committed up to this point (for those keeping score at home, that's Boston Beer/Sam Adams, Sierra Nevada, Dogfish Head, New Belgium, Brooklyn Brewery, Stone Brewing Company, Anchor, and Deschutes) and take a look at some other craft icons—both pioneers and newbies with incredible momentum.

F. X. Matt Brewing Company

The concept of "craft brewing" might be new, but for a handful of the breweries under that umbrella, the practice has deep historical roots. One of the most venerable among these breweries is F. X. Matt Brewing Company, which has been a Utica, New York institution since 1888 (talk about the Class of '88!). Much like most of the other breweries that emerged during the nineteenth century, it was the brainchild of a German immigrant—in this case Francis Xavier Matt, who worked for a time at Utica's Charles Biebauer Brewery before taking it over and reorganizing it into the West End Brewing Company, employing twelve, and producing about four thousand barrels a year. Then the dreaded Eighteenth Amendment happened, and Matt had to pivot to producing nonalcoholic beverages, such as Utica

Club brand soft drinks. When Prohibition ended, Utica Club had the chance to become a bit more famous as the name of the brewery's biggest beer brand. In the 1980s, as the third generation of Matts were running the business, the brewery launched its first foray into what would become the craft beer category: Saranac. With some of its available capacity it started contract-brewing products from start-ups like Brooklyn Brewery (the Utica facility still produces Brooklyn Lager to this day). By 1990, the management team had shifted its emphasis to Saranac, which runs the gamut of key craft styles, including Legacy IPA, Saranac Pale Ale, and Black Forest schwarzbier-style lager, tipping a hit to F. X. Matt I's home region in the old country. The brewery has also made its mark with seasonals, especially Saranac Pumpkin and Octoberfest in the fall and Caramel Porter in the winter. The brewery remains in the Matt family to this day, currently under the guidance of CEO Nick Matt.

Alaskan Brewery

It takes a rare form of fortitude to commit to starting a brewery in the coldest, most sparsely populated state in the country, as Alaska has a paltry 1.3 human beings per square mile, though quite a few more bears and wolves. Fortunately for the entire beer-drinking world, Geoff and Marcy Larson had just the right level of conviction, tenacity, and climate tolerance to launch Alaskan Brewery in 1986. When the state's 700,000 or so people are spread out across as many miles and the only transit options in much of that colossal expanse of largely untouched natural beauty are among the clouds, limiting one's business to a single state is not an option. Of course, the fact that the next closest state is nine hundred miles away (thanks, Canada!) doesn't help matters much. (The folks at Alaskan like to joke that their products are the only beers on the US market that are imported from America.) Alaskan's distribution footprint now stretches across seventeen mostly Western states.

Since its mid-'80s founding, Alaskan has helped define what have become some of the quintessential styles of the modern craft brewing era. Its amber ale—simply named Alaskan Amber—is considered the gold standard of American amber ale, especially those produced on the West Coast.

Alaska's salmon-rich waters get some of the credit for introducing most American drinkers to another style of beer. The Larsons enlisted the help of a local salmon smoker to smoke some of its malt, which ultimately went into the brewery's legendary 1988 creation, Smoked Porter. The German rauchbier style already had quite the cult following in Europe, but it was largely unknown at the time to stateside imbibers. Alaskan Smoked Porter changed all that.

Full Sail Brewing Company

There are so many breweries in the American craft movement that are known as much for their outsized personalities and bluster as they are for the delicious brews they produce (occasionally more for the former). Then

The barrel room at Hood River, Oregon's Full Sail Brewing Co.

there are those companies that are the quieter stalwarts, the ones that aren't about pulling marketing stunts, grabbing headlines, or giving their brews outrageous—sometimes punny, sometimes risqué—names. These breweries focus on a solid work ethic, a religious focus on consistent quality, and just good, old-fashioned, great-tasting beer. That about sums up Full Sail Brewing Company, founded in 1987 and located about an hour outside of Portland in Hood River, Oregon, a small town with a population of about 7,000 near the Columbia River Gorge. Under the leadership of founder Irene Firmat and executive brewmaster Jaime Emmerson—who was the company's earliest hire less than a year after its launch and who eventually married Firmat—the company mastered most of the classic styles, from Full Sail Amber to India pale ale, and has reinvented others, particularly lagers. In 2006 it launched the LTD Lager Series ("Live the Dream"), and each of the entries shows just how flavorful and complex bottom-fermented beers can be. Full Sail is also responsible for the much-celebrated Session line, including Session Lager, Session Black, and the holiday release Session Fest. Session brews are packaged in retro stubby bottles, capturing a bit of the beer category's and the Pacific Northwest region's blue collar roots.

Full Sail was also one of the pioneers of the employee-ownership concept (which served as the business model for New Belgium and, later, Deschutes and Odell). In 1999 the brewery transitioned to an employee stock ownership plan, making its staff partners in the operation. It turned out to be a shrewd move, as things came full circle for the plan in 2015 when an investment group calling itself Oregon Craft Brewers Co. approached Firmat and Emmerson about a potential merger. They put it to a vote among the employee owners, who overwhelmingly voted in favor of it, and everyone got to take home a bit of money from the transaction, thanks to the fact that they all owned stakes in the company (the ones who'd been with the company longest had particularly handsome deposits made into their bank accounts).

Fans of craft beer always get up an arms any time another individual or company—be it venture capitalists, a private equity firm, or (gasp!) a brewing behemoth like Anheuser-Busch—invest in or outright buy a craft brewery. But in most of those instances a couple of principals are usually the ones who make off with bags of money while their staff are left to wonder whether they're even going to get to keep their jobs. In this instance, not only did the employees remain employed, they also got a piece of the action.

Allagash

If you want to call your city Portland and don't want to be overshadowed by a bigger city about 2,800 miles away, you'd better have some good stuff to drink. Maine's coastal town of 70,000 or so people more than delivers. In 1995 founder Rob Tod set out to brew Belgian-style beers exclusively. Sure, it sounds de rigueur now, but in the '90s there wasn't a whole lot of the Benelux-inspired stuff coming out of American brewers. Sure, New Belgium had launched four years prior, but it was far from being a household name at that point, and the Fort Collins brewery's footprint didn't extend too far beyond Colorado's borders. Tod's decision turned out to be an incredibly smart move. Ask any beer geek to name the gold standard in American-brewed Belgian-style witbiers and the likely answer will be Allagash White. It was through the Maine brand that many had their first taste of a style that has since become ubiquitous (thanks in part to the marketing muscle of Coors and, later, MillerCoors, which has made a fortune convincing the public that its Blue Moon brand comes from a folksy little start-up brewery.)

Bell's Brewery

From an economic standpoint, Michigan may be best known for the automotive industry. But as the big American carmakers have become more famous for their contributions to the state's unemployment statistics, the brewing industry has been one of the Wolverine State's greatest job creators in the past few decades. And one of the most significant among Michigan breweries has been Bell's Brewery. Founder Larry Bell launched the business in 1983, initially as a homebrew supply shop, before he turned his attention to brewing his own stuff two years later. Since then, Bell's has grown to be one of the ten largest craft breweries in the country, producing some 300,000 barrels a year at last count.

Its most popular offering is Two-Hearted Ale—named for the Ernest Hemingway short story "Big Two-Hearted River" and the body of water that inspired it—the quintessential manifestation of an American India pale ale, with plenty of that grapefruity bitterness one expects from the style. It's also impressively balanced with a pronounced malt character.

Bell's has also done wonders with stouts. Its year-round brand, Kalamazoo Stout, complements its roastiness with a bit of brewer's licorice, for some faint herbal notes. Kalamazoo's joined by some limited-availability offerings like the chocolaty, 10.5 percent ABV Expedition Stout; the self-explanatory Rye Stout and Smoked Stout; Double Cream Stout, which gets its defining character from a blend of ten different malts, not any actual cream; and many others that pop up from time to time.

Between the summer of 2014 and the summer of 2015, Bell's undertook an ambitious project inspired by Gustav Holst's seven-movement orchestral suite *The Planets*. The brewery released its seven-part beer series of the same name, beginning with Mars, the Bringer of War, a double IPA. Venus, the Bringer of Peace—a blonde ale with honey, apricot, cardamom, and vanilla—followed two months later. Another two months after that came Mercury, the Winged Messenger, a pale Belgian "single." Then came Jupiter, the Bringer of Jollity, an imperial brown ale, with Saturn, the Bringer of Old Age, following closely behind. Appropriately enough, maturation was a key component of Saturn; it was a barleywine aged in bourbon barrels. Uranus, the Magician, a black double IPA, was the penultimate offering in the sequence. The experiment concluded with Neptune, the Mystic, a spiced (star anise, nutmeg and dandelion root, among others) imperial stout. Yes, Pluto got the shaft yet again.

Odell Brewing Company

Speaking of operations known for their consistent quality, Odell has managed to stand out in a city in which you can't throw a rock without hitting a brewery or two. That town is Fort Collins, Colorado, a beer lover's paradise in its own right. It's a city of about 150,000 people, but it has more breweries than most towns ten times its size. And one of those just happens to be New Belgium, one of the biggest in the country, producing some 1 million barrels a year. But Odell has been able to define itself on its own terms and hasn't been overshadowed by the larger, more recognizable neighbor (they're barely a mile away from each other). Doug, Wynne, and Corkie Odell kind of have dibs on Fort Collins anyway, since the brewery they founded predates New Belgium by two years. Most drinkers' first exposure with Odell is likely to have been through its flagship amber ale, 90 Shilling, a nod to Scotland's tax-based beer nomenclature. (The common brews were of the 80 shilling variety; those that were more special were 10 shillings more. One of Odell's more experimental brews is called 180 Shilling, which is a bold, oak-aged colossus of a beer, with boozy notes of toffee and vanilla and an ABV of 9.6 percent.) In fact, Odell does killer versions of many United Kingdom-inspired styles (Cutthroat Porter is another of its classic line). And then there's the Woodcut series of barrel-aged brews; enthusiasts

Odell Brewing Company is a standout among standouts in Fort Collins, Colorado.

eagerly anticipate the latest release in this ever-changing line. In 2015, Odell became one of the growing numbers to adopt the ESOP model; the Odells sold 19 percent of the brewery's stock to the employee ownership plan.

Rogue Ales

Rogue is part of the illustrious Class of '88, a distinguished group of breweries that started in 1988 and have grown to become iconic in their own right (others members include the aforementioned Brooklyn Brewery and Deschutes Brewery, as well as Fort Bragg, California-based North Coast Brewing Company; Cleveland, Ohio's Great Lakes Brewing Company; Chicago's Goose Island—which AB InBev acquired in 2011—and famous brewpubs like Portland, Maine's Gritty McDuff and Denver's Wynkoop).

Former Nike executive Jack Joyce (also an attorney) co-founded the company with two of his colleagues, Bob Woodell and Rob Strasser, in the fall of that seminal year in the sleepy little coastal town of Ashland, Oregon.

Less than a year later, they hired brewmaster John Maier, whose beer-making prowess really put Rogue on the map with the likes of Dead Guy Ale, Shakespeare Stout, and Hazelnut Brown. The Rogue team soon moved the operation to the slightly more bustling burgh of Newport, Oregon, and later opened public houses in Portland and San Francisco. Rogue quickly grew to have a presence in forty-nine US states, and the company also branched out into spirits distilling.

In 2006, Joyce's son, Brett—also a veteran of the sportswear business, at Adidas—joined the company as president and has been instrumental in making Rogue a true lifestyle brand.

Rogue never shies away from a good stunt—see the section on extreme beers for a bit on Rogue's "Beard Beer"—but it's also at the forefront of progressive brewing innovations, such as the farm-to-glass concept. It launched Rogue Farms, a line of brews featuring ingredients the brewery cultivated and harvested on its own farms.

Sadly, the craft brewing world lost a tremendous leader on May 27, 2014, when Jack Joyce passed away of a heart attack at the age of seventy-one. Ten days later, beer professionals and enthusiasts around the world honored Jack's memory in a simultaneous virtual toast at 5:42 Pacific Standard Time.

Brewery Ommegang

In 1997, husband-and-wife team Don Feinberg and Wendy Littlefield—who had brought many then obscure Belgian beers to the United States through their importation company, Vanberg & DeWulf—opened a brewery of their own in rural Cooperstown, New York, home of the Baseball Hall of Fame. They named the new company—a joint venture with some Belgian producers including Duvel Moortgat—Brewery Ommegang, after a popular festival in the Benelux countries. In 2003, Duvel Moortgat bought out its American partners and continues to run Ommegang as a wholly owned subsidiary making Belgian-style ales like the Abbey-style Ommegang proper, Hennepin saison, Witte witbier (white beer)-style ale, Rare Vos amber, BPA (Belgian pale ale), and Three Philosophers quadruple, as well as a host of seasonals and one-offs.

One of the biggest turning points for the small upstate New York farm-house brewery occurred in 2012 when it inked a licensing deal with HBO to brew a line of beers based on the most successful series in the premium cable network's history: *Game of Thrones*. Turns out that showrunners David

Benioff and D. B. Weiss were quite the Ommegang fans. The Ommegang *Game of Thrones* series has included Iron Throne Blonde Ale, Take the Black Stout, Fire and Blood Red Ale, Valar Morghulis Dubbel Ale, and Three-Eyed Raven Dark Saison Ale. The partnership has resulted in tens of millions of social media impressions for Ommegang.

Incidentally, Duvel Moortgat's US footprint does not stop at Cooperstown. In 2013, the European company acquired Kansas City's Boulevard Brewing, and, in 2015, Duvel added Paso Robles, California's Firestone Walker Brewing Company to its American portfolio. Speaking of which . . .

Firestone Walker Brewing Company

In 1996, British expat David Walker and his American brother-in-law Adam Firestone (great-grandson of the founder of the famous tire company) joined forces to create a brewery in the heart of California's Central Coast winemaking region (vineyards were among the Firestone family's many business interests).

In 2001, the brothers-in-law hired brewmaster Matt Brynildson, whose experience included a stint at Chicago's world-famous Goose Island brewery, completing the management triumvirate that helped grow the company to become one of the twenty biggest craft breweries in the country. Its flagship brew, Double Barrel Ale (DBA), quickly became a California classic. The beer blends stainless-steel-fermented batches of the British-style pale ale with those fermented in wooden barrels, imparting distinct oak and vanilla flavor notes.

Firestone Walker is among the breweries that have made drinking pilsner cool again; its Pivo Pils won the gold in that style's category at the 2015 Great American Beer Festival. The name is a nod to the pilsner's Bohemian heritage; "pivo" is Czech for "beer."

The Duvel Moortgat deal came at just the right time for the West Coast brewery. Firestone Walker's accelerated growth necessitated a capacity expansion. The Belgian brewery made that happen. "Sometimes those trains come along and you've got to jump on them, otherwise you miss the train," says Simon Thorpe, CEO and president of Duvel Moortgat's US-based unit. "So our job with Firestone Walker very simply is to help them with their very urgent capacity questions." The partnership resulted in an expanded Paso Robles brewhouse with plenty of breathing room.

New Glarus Brewing Company

Not expanding your distribution footprint beyond California is one thing, (although even Firestone Walker eventually breached its borders), but distributing in Wisconsin and *only* in Wisconsin is borderline lunacy. However, that's the business model that's made New Glarus Brewing Company a perennial fan favorite since its founding in 1993. It's one of the true entrepreneurial success stories of our time. Deborah Carey raised the capital for the brewery as a gift to her husband, Dan Carey, thus becoming the first woman to singlehandedly found a brewery in the country. Based in the Wisconsin city of the same name, New Glarus takes pride in the fact that if you want to taste its beers, you've got to head on over to the Badger State (or have some Wisconsin-based friends ship you some, though it's not legal to receive it in every state).

The brewery's most popular beer is Spotted Cow, an unfiltered farmouse-style ale. Those who like fruit beers are usually gaga over New Glarus's Raspberry Tart, which takes a cue from the framboise ales traditionally brewed in Belgium. Those lucky enough to be in Wisconsin during the warmer months should get their hands on New Glarus's epic interpretation of a classic Berliner Weisse, the tart, refreshing, low-ABV style that originated in Germany's capital city.

Lakefront Brewery

It would be unfair to discuss Wisconsin beer making without turning the conversation to the state's largest city and one of history's beeriest of metropolises, Milwaukee. While many mainstream consumers think about companies like Miller and Pabst (and perhaps the fictional Shotz Brewery) when they hear mention of Milwaukee, the city has made its fair share of contributions to the craft movement. Most notable among the modern crop is Lakefront. Native Milwaukeean brothers Russ and Jim Klisch started Lakefront in 1987, and it's since become a compulsory stop on any beer pilgrim's visit to the city. It's easy to see why; the chance to taste year-round brews like Fixed Gear IPA, Bridge Burner Imperial Amber Ale, and Fuel Café Coffee Stout at their point of origin is alluring enough. The brewery also has cracked the code on flavorful gluten-free beers with its New Grist Pilsner, brewed from rice syrup and sorghum. It also brews New Grist Ginger, with a spicy twist from that beloved root. Seasonally speaking, summer can't come soon enough, as it's the only time of year Lakefront brews Wisconsinite, a wheat beer using nothing but ingredients grown and

Milwaukee's Lakefront Brewery.

sourced in Wisconsin. And that doesn't just include the wheat, barley, and hops; it also extends to the yeast strain, which is indigenous to the state.

You haven't lived until you've attended the Lakefront Friday Fish Fry, which lets you pair your brew with tasty dishes like Milwaukee beer-battered cod and fried perch fillets. You can't leave the state of Wisconsin without trying the fried cheese curds, and Lakefront knows how to deliver with those. And there's a live polka combo playing to really give you that sense of place.

Fewer states seem to inspire so much home-field pride as Wisconsin, and it's heartening that breweries like Lakefront and New Glarus more than have beer drinkers' backs.

Anderson Valley Brewing Company

Northern California has been a veritable Garden of Eden of world-class brewers, and one of its more offbeat participants was born in a town known to very few outsiders. But Anderson Valley Brewing Company—founded by David Norfleet, Kim Allen, and Ken Allen in 1987—has certainly done its part in putting its native Boonville on the map. So remote is the Mendocino County town, which sits about 115 miles north of San Francisco, that it developed its own language of sorts, known as "Boontling." The lingo—a jargon, really—includes about 1,500 terms known only to its inhabitants and not to Brightlighters (the Boontling word for "outlander"). Other colorful terms include "cocked darley" (a man with a gun), "eesole" (an unsavory character—you can pretty much guess from what this derived), and "forbes" (fifty cents/a half dollar, short for four bits—double the two-bit status of a quarter).

Anderson Valley Brewing became an ambassador of sorts for the insular community of less than one thousand; some of its bottles feature a little bit of Boontling culture. One of its most popular brews—the caramelish, spicy, copper-hued Boont Amber—is considered one of the "bahlest" of its style. That's Boontling for best, by the way. Hop lovers have always held Hop Ottin', Anderson Valley's IPA, in high regard. And, you guessed it, "ottin'" is more Bootling. It's a form of "otto," which means to work or work hard. The hops are, indeed, working quite hard in this India pale ale. Much of the credit for the brewery's always-solid output goes to Fal Allen (no relation to the founder), who has worked for the brewery on and off since 2000. That's when he assumed the role of general manager before he went to Singapore to serve as brewmaster of Archipelago Brewing Company for five years. He returned to Anderson Valley in 2010, the same year that Ken Allen sold the brewery to the investment group HMB Holdings.

Saint Arnold

When people think of Texas beer towns, Austin tends to be more top of mind than the much larger Houston, but the latter city's craft brewing activity predates that of the more bohemian state capital. That's thanks to Saint Arnold Brewing, founded in the Astros' home city by Brock Wagner and Kevin Bartol in 1994.

"I tell people I started the brewery in 1994, and it turned out to be a brilliant idea in 2006," Wagner says, only half-jokingly.

The name Saint Arnold is the Anglicization of Saint Arnulf of Metz, the Old Frankish patron saint of brewing. The brew with which most non-Houstonians are most familiar is Fancy Lawnmower, a refreshing, Kölsch-style beer that's an ideal treat after cutting the grass on a typically muggy day in the Lone Star State. Lawnmower's counterpoint is Santo, which the brewery calls a black Kölsch—not actually a thing, but it's brewed like that Cologne, Germany-specific style, with the addition of black malt to give it its pitch-like hue. Santo is as famous for its flavor as it is for its label design;

it features a graffiti-like Day of the Dead skull, courtesy of Houston artist Carlos Hernandez, who's made a career out of a series of Day of the Dead rock star paintings.

In fact, Santo was a label before it was even a beer. The Saint Arnold team wanted to rename the brewery's brown ale, which people loved but didn't seem to want to buy. ("Don't call anything 'brown,'" Wagner advises. "That's my big marketing tip.")

When Hernandez designed the label for the beer formerly known as Brown, Wagner absolutely loved it. The problem was that it wasn't a good match for that particular brew.

The Saint Arnold tasting room in Houston, Texas.

"So now I had a label and no beer," Wagner recalls. "We always develop a beer and then it's 'What are we going to call it?' Having a label and then trying to create a beer is bass-ackwards of how we do everything."

After about four years and after taking trips "down a lot of rabbit holes," the concept finally dawned on Wagner. "I was at a Mexican restaurant one night and ordered one of those dark Mexican lagers. I got it and tasted it

"Saint Arnold" performs a "wedding" at GABF.

and didn't really like the flavor. That's what I wanted Santo to be: What I think a dark Mexican lager should taste like, but doesn't."

The Saint Arnold booth always attracts a crowd at the Great American Beer Festival. It's usually assembled to look like a medieval wedding chapel; the good saint himself is always on hand to perform fake weddings. At its shortest, the line is nearly an hour long.

Harpoon Brewing

New Yorkers can say what they want about one of their greatest rival cities—well, mostly its teams—but one thing they can't dispute is that is Boston's status as one the country's great drinking cities. The first brand that usually comes to mind is Samuel Adams, but for the longest time none of its beer was even being produced in the city. That's not the case for the second-largest Boston-based beer maker, Harpoon, which actually holds Brewing Permit No. 001 from the Commonwealth of Massachusetts, as it was the first to brew legally within the city for more than a quarter century. Founders Rich Doyle, Dan Kenary, and George Ligeti hired brewer Russ Heissner and, in the summer of 1987, rolled out their first batch of Harpoon Ale. In 1998, Harpoon launched UFO Hefeweizen (the "U" and the "F" stand for "unfiltered," which it is), which helped develop Northeasteners' thirst for wheat beers. The brewery eventually expanded the UFO line to include a white ale, a raspberry wheat beer, and a shandy. Those are all refreshing and sessionable, with each coming in under 5 percent ABV. But Harpoon is just as comfortable going big. Its Leviathan imperial IPA harnesses the citrusy power of American hops and plenty of malt to drive up the ABV to 10 percent. Its holiday seasonal Winter Warmer has a flavor reminiscent of Christmas cookies, and its annual arrival always makes the cold weather—especially in Boston—much more bearable.

Harpoon was ahead of the curve in the modern cider boom. It brewed its first cider in 2007, a few years before the category started surging well into the double digits and a full four years before Boston Beer launched its Angry Orchard line (now the No. 1 cider in the country). Doyle left as CEO in 2014 and went on to form Enjoy Beer LLC, a firm that partners with brewers and gives them the resources they need to avoid acquisitions by big corporate multinationals.

That same year, the company shifted to employee ownership by instituting an Employee Stock Ownership Program (ESOP). In 2015, it teamed up with another recent ESOP convert, Deschutes Brewery, for a collaborative beer, EHOP, which it debuted at the 2015 Great American Beer Festival in Denver.

Avery Brewing Company

The early-to-mid 1990s was quite a fertile period in the history of Colorado brewing—then again, when *wasn't* a fertile period in the state's beer scene—with the likes of New Belgium and Great Divide starting up. Another of the region's '90s-born icons is Avery Brewing Company, launched in the fall of 1993 by namesake president and brewmaster Adam Avery. The Boulder-based operation has become as famous for its extreme offerings as it has for its more conventional creations. Its best-known is Ellie's Brown Ale, a chocolaty brew named for Adam's beloved chocolate lab (who departed this world at the age of ten in 2002). Of the polar opposite hue is Avery's White Rascal, a faithful homage to the witbiers of Belgium. The brewery sometimes lets lunacy prevail, and that's a good thing. Without a healthy helping of crazy, Avery Brewing would never have brought the world its Dictator Series: Maharaja is an imperial India pale ale (get it? India? Maharaja?) that certainly doesn't skimp on the hops. Maharaja's got an IBU (International Bitterness Unit) of 102. For a little perspective, many sensory experts say the human palate can barely distinguish anything more biting than 100; it's sort of the sound barrier of bitter. Then there's the Kaiser, which Avery classifies

Avery Brewing Co. stands out in a state with no shortage of great breweries.

as an imperial Oktoberfest (a decidedly German beer requires a distinctly German dictator), a malt-forward übermärzen that measures somewhere between 9 and 10 percent ABV, nearly twice the alcohol content of a standard Oktoberfest. Finally, there's the Czar. In keeping with the ethnically appropriate theme, it's a Russian imperial stout that tops out at 12 percent ABV and has quite a bit of hop character to balance the roasty, mocha-like malt.

Left Hand Brewing

Not even ten miles from Avery in the town of Longmont is another of Colorado's most respected breweries, Left Hand, whose story actually begins under a different name. Founders Dick Doore and Eric Wallace incorporated the business in the fall of 1993 as Indian Peaks Brewing Company. However, it wasn't too long before they learned another brewery had named one of its beers Indian Peaks. The best course of action, the founders felt, was to simply change the brewery's name. It's remained Left Hand ever since.

The brewery got a boost in capacity and capability in 1998, when it merged with Denver's Tabernash Brewing Company, whose brands it ultimately phased out. The inaugural batch that Left Hand released in 1994 was Sawtooth Ale, a medium-bodied, well-balanced session amber that's still among the brewery's most popular today. However, it ultimately has attracted more attention for its famous Milk Stout, a sweet but balanced stout with pronounced coffee-like flavors. The sweetness comes from the addition of milk sugar. On draft, incorporating nitrogen in to the gas mix creates microbubbles that impart a creamy mouthfeel. In 2011, Left Hand figured out a way to give the brew a hit of nitrogen in the bottle, becoming the first craft brewer to bottle a nitrogen-enhanced beer (known as Milk Stout Nitro, which now accounts for a major chunk of Left Hand's volume). It's not the first time, however, that nitrogen was in a package. Diageo, the company that owns Guinness, developed a device called a "widget" that doses the stout with nitrogen when the drinker opens an aluminum can of the brand. Left Hand brought it to the bottle widget-free through a proprietary technology that it keeps pretty close to the vest.

Milk Stout and Nitro Milk Stout are only two examples of how Left Hand is a master of darkness. Deep espresso and dark chocolate-like flavors dominate its Black Jack Porter. On the boozier side, there's the ominously

It's easy to recognize Longmont, Colorado's Left Hand Brewing.

named Wake Up Dead, a pitch-black Russian imperial stout with a 10.2 percent ABV and some subtle raisin and licorice notes. On the limited-edition front, Left Hand's Fade to Black series is a comprehensive exploration of the dark arts. Entries range from a Baltic-style porter to a black rye ale.

But the brewery is just as adept at making brews on the lighter side. When Left Hand acquired Tabernash, among the beers it inherited was a pilsner. The brewers refined the recipe considerably with new hop and malt varieties. Ultimately that beer became Left Hand's famous Polestar Pilsner.

A trip to the brewery is always a treat, both inside and outside. It's on the banks of the idyllic St. Vrain Creek, which has a path alongside it for picturesque nature strolls. Inside, there's definitely a rough-and-tumble saloon vibe that fits in well with its Western setting.

21st Amendment Brewery

Extra points always go to the brewery that gives drinkers a little lesson in Constitutional history with every glass. The Twenty-first Amendment, of course, is the one that repealed the dreaded Eighteenth—Prohibition. The company began as a San Francisco brewpub—situated in a still popular spot that is now within a stone's throw of the ballpark that's home to the Giants—founded by Nico Freccia, who handles the business side, and Shaun O'Sullivan, the brewmaster. In 2008, 21st Amendment started distributing its beers in cans via a Minnesota contract brewer. Brew enthusiasts well beyond Northern California quickly gravitated to its range, most of which were rooted in some facet of American history. Back in Black, a black IPA, was inspired by Paul Revere's ride in the dead of night—an illustration of the famous Colonial silversmith appears on the can. Brew Free! or Die IPA borrows its name from New Hampshire's state motto and sports a can image that features Abe Lincoln, fist clenched, busting out of Mount Rushmore. The theme continues with its seasonals. Its baking spice-enhanced winter ale Fireside Chat is a malty warmer that lifts its name from Franklin Delano Roosevelt's series of radio speeches during the Great Depression. A drawing of the New Deal architect—complete with his trademark cigarette holder—graces the package. Hell or High Watermelon (a wheat beer brewed with fresh watermelon) may not sound like Americana, but the picture of Lady Liberty sitting on the Golden Gate Bridge (crown off, hair down, and torch resting on the bridge) is strikingly patriotic.

In 2015, 21st Amendment finally opened a packaging brewery of its own in nearby San Leandro, moving its distribution-bound production in-house.

Shmaltz Brewing Company

Had Shmaltz Brewing Company—maker of the He'Brew beer line—been born in anyone's hands other than Jeremy Cowan's, it would have been but a footnote among all of the failed brewery start-ups in the mid-'90s. Cowan's memoir *Craft Beer Bar Mitzvah* should be required reading in every business school. No, aspiring entrepreneurs won't glean any jargon-riddled management tips or eye-roll-worthy parables about mice and cheese, but they might learn whether they have the stomach to launch and run a company by following Cowan on his own adventure. It's a case study on tenacity and weathering all of the headwinds you encounter—including the ones you couldn't have anticipated in a million years—on your way to making your dream a reality.

"By far, our strongest skill has to be adaptability," Cowan reveals. "There's no possible way you can plan for everything that is guaranteed to happen every week. But if you can figure out a way to turn challenges into a chance to succeed, that's by far the most important skill."

The germ of the Shmaltz idea was a joke. Cowan was one of a small handful of Jewish kids growing up in a San Francisco Bay Area suburb. While riffing over a game of volleyball, he and his friends came up with the idea of launching a Jewish beer—it would be called He'Brew, naturally—and its tagline would be "The Chosen Beer." (That one actually stuck. Some of the other more facetious taglines—"Don't Pass Out, Passover," for instance—didn't make it on to bottles of the stuff.) For more than the first decade of its existence, Cowan barely had two nickels to rub together. But then things just started to click. Shmaltz, whose He'Brew line includes Messiah Nut Brown Ale, Bittersweet Lenny's R.I.P.A. (a rye IPA in honor of Lenny Bruce), and its annual Funky Jewbelation limited release, had also been the company behind the Coney Island Lager line. The company sold Coney Island in 2013. That was also the year Shmaltz opened its first actual brewery; for the first seventeen years of its existence, all of its volume was contract brew. It set up shop in the upstate New York town of Clifton Park and marked its new brick-and-mortar brewery status with the release of Death of a Contract Brewer, a 7 percent ABV black IPA made with seven malts and seven hops. (The brew has since been renamed Death Black IPA.)

Cowan and crew continue to roll with whatever punches the beer business throws at them.

"It's always something," Cowan concedes. "I hate clichés that also are true but are still clichés. It's true that it's always something. Thank God we can make really kick-ass beers to get us through all this insanity because it makes the whole thing worth it—being able to be super-creative, be our own bosses and miraculously find our opportunity to get to the marketplace. It's shocking that they let us do this for our jobs, but thankfully they do."

Two Roads Brewing Company

Most would be hesitant to include such a fledgling brewery among the more seasoned establishments with a couple of decades under their belts. But New Haven, Connecticut's Two Roads Brewing Company, founded oh so recently in December 2012 (good thing the Mayan calendar was wrong), forged such a connection with beer drinkers right out of the gate that it's become one of the bona fide rising stars of Northeastern United States brewing. The moniker was inspired by the literary stylings of one Robert Frost—in the classic poem "The Road Not Taken," of course ("Two roads diverged in a yellow wood . . . "). That's the company's philosophy in a nutshell: "We prefer the one less taken and having some fun along the way." The reference is fairly relevant to the brewery's backstory, as its founding quartet traveled more accessible routes before taking the one less traveled that led them all to their beer-soaked destiny. Brad Hittle's résumé reads like the script of an epic biopic; after college he went to work on an offshore drilling ship in Southeast Asia, eventually got his MBA, and worked in corporate America (including stints at Johnson & Johnson and Unilever) before he gravitated toward beer and became chief marketing officer of Pabst Brewing Company. Clem Pellani had a long and productive career in engineering—working in the F18 radar lab at McDonnell Douglas—before getting a brewing degree and working on the marketing of brands like Rolling Rock and Labatt. Peter Doering, meanwhile, was performing financial tasks for a Connecticut shipyard (after doing his time on an offshore drilling ship—spotting a pattern here?). Finally, Phil Markowski is a name that most avid beer geeks knew before the creation of Two Roads. He was a brewer's brewer, having won a treasure trove of awards while working at companies such as Southampton Publick House (famous for its Double White Ale) and New England Brewing Company. Now he's crafting Two Road standouts like Ol' Factory Pils (a hoppy little number if there ever was one, thanks to dry hopping, a rare technique among pilsners), Road to Ruin Double IPA (an 8 percent ABV brew with a piny, citrusy, and floral blast of four American hop varieties), and Lil' Heaven Session IPA. Here's a little-known fact about Lil' Heaven: according to some well-placed sources at Two Roads, it's named after a secret floor at the company's headquarters. See, long before it was a brewery, the then future site of Two Roads was the US Baird manufacturing plant. Lil' Heaven is where the amorous factory workers would steal away to engage in clandestine carnal activities.

Ninkasi Brewing Company

When a brewery names itself after the ancient Sumerian goddess of fermentation, you know it takes brewing pretty seriously, and this dedication shows in the much-revered product line from the Eugene, Oregon-based operation founded in 2006. The passion of founders Nikos Ridge and Jamie Floyd (and maybe a little bit of divine influence) shows through in brews like Tricerahops, an 8 percent double IPA that lives up to its name. Chinook, Cascade, Palisade, Summit, and Centennial hops create a citrusy, floral symphony of bitterness—with a triple-digit IBU to prove it! On the darker and maltier side, there's Vanilla Oatis Oatmeal Stout, which gets its vanilla notes not from a barrel but from whole vanilla beans. There's still plenty in Vanilla Oatis for hopheads to love, as the roasty, coffee-like malt character is balanced with a generous helping of Nugget hops and a moderate IBU of 50. There's quite a bit to write home about Ninkasi's special releases as well, including Ground Control Imperial Stout, which has an immense amount going on: Oregon-grown hazelnuts, star anise, and cocoa nibs (in addition to the usual dark roast malts), along with a yeast strain that's been to outer space and back (hence the name and the astronaut on the label). That big, boozy affair registers a hefty 10 percent ABV and an assertive 80 IBU.

Carton Brewing Company

Until recently, New Jersey had been, for the most part, a craft beer wasteland (your author should know, as he spent the first forty-two years of his life there), colossal Anheuser-Busch brewery across from Newark International Airport notwithstanding. (Flying Fish Brewery in Cherry Hill, New Jersey is definitely an early adopter, having opened its doors in 1995, but it's in a Philadelphia suburb, which makes it more a part of that city's legendary scene rather than the Garden State's nascent one.) But around 2010 things slowly but surely started to change, as a wave of new breweries began to open (Jersey's notoriously stifling laws started to loosen a bit around that time, so that helped a little). The one that quickly advanced to the head of the new class was Carton Brewing Company, based in the coastal town of Atlantic Highlands. In 2011, cousins Chris and Augie Carton (the latter is also the cohost of the weekly podcast *Steal This Beer*) turned a quaint old turn-of-the-twentieth-century red brick warehouse into a brewery. They almost immediately gained a rabid local following for their refreshing hop-enhanced, German Kölsch-inspired Boat Beer, 077XX East Coast Double IPA (the three digits are how many New Jersey zip codes begin), and B.D.G. (Brunch. Dinner. Grub.), a bready, herbal affair that's designed to be a flexible partner for many delightful dishes. Food has inspired some of Carton's one-offs and limited editions, as well. One summer it released Panzanella, whose recipe is meant to evoke the popular yet simple Tuscan salad that consists of day-old bread, tomatoes, cucumbers, onions, salt, and, frequently, garlic. Carton used actual cucumbers, dehydrated tomatoes, and salt, but approximated the other elements with certain hop and malt varieties. Carton is one of the twenty-first century breweries to watch.

Cigar City Brewing Company

Much like New Jersey, Florida wasn't actually on most people's short lists when they jotted down the top craft brewing regions, although the Tampa Bay area had a thriving industry for more than a half-century between the end of the nineteenth century until the 1960s (even during Prohibition, there was plenty going on behind closed doors). Tampa's Cigar City almost single-handedly put the Sunshine State back on the beer map when it opened in 2009, and it did so by fully embracing the heritage of the Tampa Bay region. It infuses each product in its portfolio with a unique sense of place—particularly as it relates to its stogie-making history. The malty Maduro Brown Ale, for instance, borrows its name from the famous cigars.

There are, of course, other components of Floridian culture that Cigar City incorporates into its brands. Its IPA is called Jai Alai, a sport (the one with the long curved mitts—remember the opening title sequence of *Miami Vice*?) that remained active and popular in Tampa into the 1990s (though it's vanished from the city, it's still played in other parts of the state). Cigar City taps into its local Latin heritage, as well. Its Cervezas Frescas series includes an ale that emulates a traditional horchata. It's brewed with ingredients common in a refreshing, nonalcohol horchata: rice, cinnamon, and vanilla. Then there's Cigar City's Cubano-Style Espresso, a brown ale with vanilla, cacao, and coffee beans.

The brewery's tasting room has become a top destination for locals and visitors alike.

Uinta Brewing Company

It's one thing to make fun of New Jersey and Florida for taking their sweet old time in developing world-class craft beer scenes, but Utah is in a class by itself. (Just putting "beer" and "Utah" in the same sentence is enough to make most people chuckle.) But despite itself, Utah has produced some of the finest breweries on the planet. The most notable of those is Salt Lake City's Uinta Brewing Company (named after a nearby mountain range), whose origins stretch all the way back to 1993. Many years and many high-profile awards later, Uinta has become known the world over for a diversity of well-crafted brews, like Bristlecone Brown Ale and Cuththroat Pale Ale (not to be confused with Odell's Cutthroat Porter, but they both use fish inconography—the cutthroat trout is the state fish of Utah, so Uinta wins this round). Others to emerge over the years have been Dubhe Imperial Black IPA (or, as others might call it, a "Cascadian dark ale") and Baba

Black Lager—a tasty, medal-winning riff on a German schwarzbier. In 2010, Uinta unveiled its Crooked Line, a range of bigger and boozy beers—some might fit under the "extreme" umbrella. Labyrinth Black Ale is a notable superstar within the Crooked Line. The style is somewhere between an imperial porter and a Belgian-style quadruple; the recipe includes black licorice, which complements the oak character that comes from aging in rye barrels. Take your time sipping and savoring this one, as it has a rather bold ABV of 13.2 percent. When the brewery turned twenty, it celebrated by crafting Birthday Suit Sour Brown, another in the Crooked stable. This one's not quite as potent on the alcohol front—7.4 percent ABV—but it delivers a healthy hit of tartness that should satisfy most drinkers with a sour tooth. (That should be a thing!)

When you open a brewery in a state so famous for its natural beauty, you kind of want to keep things that way. That's part of what drives Uinta to being one of the greenest operations around. In 2001 it became 100 percent wind-powered, and ten years later it installed a solar array on its roof. All the more reason to support a brewery like Uinta.

The Bruery

When your name is Patrick Rue and you have a career in beer making, of course you're going to open a company called The BRUEry. It's hard to believe that the Southern California operation has only been with us since 2008 because it's hard to remember a world without its innovative brews (or is it brues?). The Bruery is far from being an early adopter of barrel aging beer, but it has quickly become one of companies to master the process. And the types of barrels it uses are just as diverse as the beers that mature in the wood. The Bruery meticulously crafts beers to be aged in bourbon, new American oak, new French oak, tequila, rye, and rum cooperage. Most are limited-editions and one-offs—even its year-rounds aren't what one would consider conventional—but each is a tribute to the pioneering spirit that suffuses the craft-brewing sector. In 2013, for its fifth anniversary, the Bruery produced Bois, which is French for "wood." For those who follow tradition, something constructed of wood is supposed to be what's exchanged on the fifth wedding anniversary. But don't let the French part confuse you. Bois has quite an international pedigree. It's based on an English-style ale, although it uses a Belgian yeast strain (okay, so one could argue that's French—or at least half French). And it's blended through the solera method, which is a process that's more closely associated with Spanish sherry-making. (The short version of this method is that more mature beverages are married with younger ones, but it's a considerably more complicated process than that.) The Bruery saves a portion of each of its anniversary ales and blends them with future ones. When it turned six, The Bruery released Sucré, or "sugar" in French. (Candy is the preferred sixth-anniversary gift.) Sucré actually exists in several forms, and these forms are based on the different types of oak in which the brew is aged: bourbon, rye, rum, tequila, new American oak, and new French oak barrels, as well as port and Madeira casks. Admittedly many of those special releases are hard to find, given their very limited production. Easier to track down are the Bruery's year-rounds, like Humulus Lager, which is among the hoppier bottom-fermented brews. (The Bruery jokes that it's the closest it's come to breaking its promise to never brew an IPA.) Another portfolio highlight is its Loakal Red, an American red ale that's spent some time in oak (to which the vanilla notes can attest). Every beer's an event, and the fact that most of them come in wine bottles drives that point home. But each has a traditional metal crown closure to keep things real and remind everyone that it's still beer.

The Lost Abbey/Port Brewing Company

San Diegans never get bored, with all of the options available in the craft brewing mecca that it is. The scene is not lacking in personalities, either. Stone's Greg Koch has been one of Southern California's most vocal (not to mention eccentric) ambassadors. But, like Stone itself, Koch is far from being the only game in town. Tomme Arthur has become one of brewing's biggest celebrities, crafting some of the most revered offerings at Port Brewing Company and, especially, at its alter ego, The Lost Abbey. Both companies occupy the former San Marcos, California home of Stone, which eventually outgrew it and moved to the Willy Wonka-like wonder of the Stone Brewing World Bistro and Gardens in nearby Escondido.

Port Brewing is the more "California" of the two trademarks, with plenty of the types of hop-centric IPAs that made the West Coast famous (like Mongo Double IPA and Wipeout IPA), though the malt is no wallflower in chocolaty high-alcohol beers like the barrel-aged Old Viscosity Ale (10 percent ABV). But Arthur's freak flag really flies under the Lost Abbey label, which has a more European bent (particularly in the Belgo-French zone). Avant Garde Ale, which is an evolution of the biere de garde style of French farmhouse ales, alternates between fruity and biscuity and has a nice little hoppy snap. Much bigger and bolder is Judgment Day, which exudes all sorts of dark fruit character and boasts an assertive 10.5 percent ABV. Lost Abbey turns things up a notch or five with seasonals like Angel's Share, a reference to the small bit of alcohol that evaporates during whiskey's maturation process (and totally wasted on those winged celestial goody-two-shoes). And the name is not just a fleeting tribute; Angel's Share gets plenty of rest in oak barrels—a full year—before it's released to the world at 12.5 percent ABV.

Back in 2012, Lost Abbey unveiled its ambitious Box Set project. Each month for a year, it released an extremely limited brew. Each was deemed a "track" and was inspired by a particular piece of music (like Van Halen's "Runnin' With the Devil," for instance.) Lost Abbey created a special black, trunk-like box to house these beers and even tucked in some vinyl records to pair with them.

Boundary-pushing doesn't even begin to cover it.

Short's Brewing

If there's ever been a reason to attend the very first tasting session (the Thursday night edition) at the Great American Beer Festival, it's because one of Michigan's biggest innovators always seems to run out of at least one-third of the stuff it's tapping before the doors even open on Friday. (It's easy to find; it's usually the booth with the revolving statue of the lower half of a man's body—barefoot and, of course, wearing shorts). If there's ever been a brewery that embodies "something for everyone," it's Short's, founded in 2004 by its namesake, Joe Short. Its flagships are unassuming enough. There's Bellaire Brown, a robust brown ale created with enough of the elements that malty beer lovers enjoy: toasted malts, specialty grains, and notes of coffee and caramel. Those new to craft will find a lot to like about Local's, an American lager that bridges the gap between ubiquitous mass-produced brews and the more refined creations of Michigan's small brewers. It has a 4 percent ABV and only a 6 IBU, so there's not much bite in this brew. Things get a little hoppier with Space Rock American Pale Ale and a lot hopper with Huma Lupa Licious American IPA. Those all hold their own amongst the best within their specific styles. Things get a little weirder when you get into Short's specialty and imperial series. One of the first kegs to kick at GABF is its Bloody Beer, which is designed to emulate a classic bloody mary. Short's achieves this end by incorporating Roma tomatoes, black peppercorns, celery seeds, and dill—hair of the dog in its

Short's Brewing Co.'s innovations always draw a large crowd at GABF.

purest form! For those wanting to balance their savory with a little sweet, how about a taste of Strawberry Short's Cake? It's a golden ale brewed with fresh strawberries and milk sugar. And who doesn't like to share a variety of desserts when they go out to eat? Luckily, you can drink a glass of key lime pie, in the form of a beer of the same name. Short's brews the pie with fresh limes, milk sugar, graham crackers, and marshmallow fluff. Those put off by fruit, vegetable, and cake beers but wanting something bold might gravitate toward something like the Magician, a dark-red London-style ale that falls decidedly on the malty side and has notes of toffee, caramel, and dates.

It's hard to stand out in a great beer state like Michigan, but Short's never disappoints in its ability to do just that.

Funkwerks

Colorado is one of the most brewery-saturated states in the country. It takes a special kind of expertise and confidence to open a beer-making business in a place that's just soaked in the stuff. And it takes a special kind of crazy to open it in one of that state's most beer-dense cities, Fort Collins (home of New Belgium and Odell, which are just the tip of the iceberg). But in 2009, business partners Brad Lincoln and Gordon Schuck did just that

Fort Collins, Colorado's Funkwerks.

when they launched Funkwerks. What sets Funkwerks's portfolio apart is that it concentrates exclusively on Belgian styles. Back up a minute. A Belgian-style-only brewer in very close orbit of a million-barrel-a-year brewery that calls its New Belgium? For one thing, that venerable, employee-owned operation brews a variety of Belgian styles and in recent years has branched out beyond those traditions with session IPAs and the like. But Funkwerks cut its teeth on many iterations of a single style or family of styles: the saison. It started with a true-to-farmouse-style flagship, simply called Saison, and then experimented with different fruits (like apricots) and hop varieites for products like Aladdin Apricot Saison and Nelson Sauvin

Saison—named after the single New Zealand-born hop in its recipe. Funkwerks eventually expanded to other Belgian styles like tripels and quads, but it remains the only Belgian-style-only brewery in its zip code.

Golden Road Brewing

It's one of the world's great head-scratching paradoxes that, when it comes to good beer, an area like Greater San Diego can be a complete embarrassment of riches, but just two hours north, Los Angeles County's scene was sparse, at best. Of course, in the tradition of just about every part of the country that was lacking solid craft beer cred, things have turned around considerably and in a fairly short period of time. One of the breweries that can get some of the credit for pulling its home city out of the dark ages is Golden Road, founded in 2011 by entrepreneurs Meg Gill, a former sales rep for Oskar Blues Brewery and San Francisco's Speakeasy Ales & Lagers, and Tony Yanow, owner of a couple of beer bars in L.A. and Burbank.

The Golden Road mission was simple: become L.A.'s local brewery. And, why not? While the city had a couple of small operations, none had emerged to really be *the* hometown brewery for La-La Land. Golden Road did so by putting images of local cityscapes and natural beauty—in the form of urban oases like the region's hike-worthy hills—and by nurturing the city's famous day-drinking culture (lots of screenplays being written at bars and such) by focusing on sessionability. One of its inaugural flagships was Point the Way IPA, which has all of the requisite hop character to keep it true to style but is a tick or two below the ABV of an average IPA. Even beyond L.A.'s pervasive day drinking—or, what some of us like to call "drinking"—lower-alcohol beers are a godsend in a place where nobody walks and everybody drives. Golden Road's portfolio also includes sessionable delights like Get Up Offa That Brown (brown ale, 5.5 percent), Hefeweizen (4.6 percent), and 329 (Days of Sun) Lager (4.8 percent). But the brewery doesn't always walk on the mild side; it expanded its IPA offerings with Wolf Among Weeds, which delivers an 80 IBU and a not-so-sessionable 8 percent ABV (hey, that's what Uber's for).

Golden Road also gets philanthropic with its hops (philanHOPic?). It created its summer seasonal, Heal the Bay IPA, in partnership with Heal the Bay, a nonprofit that works to preserve Southern California's coastal waters.

It didn't take long for the big guys to notice. In September 2015, AB InBev announced that Golden Road would be the latest operation to enter its ever-growing portfolio of craft breweries.

Hill Farmstead Brewery

Few breweries have built a nationwide (and international) cult following as quickly as Hill Farmstead Brewery, born in rural North Greensboro, Vermont, in 2010. It's the passion project of Shaun Hill, who comes from a long line of dairy farmers who operated on the grounds surrounding what is now the brewhouse. Hill was garnering international acclaim in the brewing community years before he even launched the company. A stint at Copenhagen, Denmark's Nørrebro Bryghus was among his prior brewing gigs. (He made a name for himself quite quickly within Copenhagen's booming craft beer scene; during this writer's fall 2009 visit to the city's Øl Baren—a prime beer-drinking destination and pretty much the center of Copenhagen's craft universe—the bartender, a Swedish transplant, said, "You should meet Shaun Hill; he's actually coming here after his shift at Nørrebro." When Hill arrived he detailed plans for the Vermont brewing operation that would open a mere eight months later.) Three of the beers he brewed while there medaled at the World Beer Cup—two golds and one silver.

In 2010 the online beer community/review site Ratebeer.com named Shaun Hill the best new brewer, and a year later it named his start-up the best new brewery in the world. Hill Farmstead managed to garner these accolades without distributing too far beyond its home base. The best chance of getting any of its very limited output is to make the trek to North Greensboro. Otherwise there are twenty-odd bars, stores, and restaurants around Vermont that carry it. On sporadic occasions throughout the year, a tiny amount of the beer makes it to New York and Philadelphia. (Everything finds its way to Philadelphia, being the great beer city that it is—especially during Philly Beer Week.)

But this is no "white whale" scenario. The rarity of Hill Farmstead's brews isn't what's made them so sought-after; it's the quality.

Hill honors the two-plus centuries of farming heritage that came before him with the Ancestral Series: beers named after family members from past generations. Offerings include Biere de Norma, a French biere de garde-style ale named after Hill's maternal grandmother; Edward, a hoppy pale ale named for his grandfather; Abner, an imperial pale ale named after his great-grandfather; and Peleg, an oak-aged English-style old ale named after Peleg Hill Jr., Hill's great-great-great-great-grandfather, who was born in 1757, long before Vermont was a state and the United States was a country. Among the brewery's other lines is the Single Hop series, which showcases

Hill Farmstead Brewery has risen in the ranks as one of the most esteemed breweries in the US and the world.

in each offereing a different hop variety, including Citra, Amarillo, New Zealand's Nelson Sauvin, and everything in between.

It takes a lot to standout in Vermont—this is the state with the most breweries per capita, including legends like The Alchemist—and for Hill Farmstead to manage to do so is a testament to the talent of its team.

Top Beer States

Seventy-five percent of American consumers may live within ten miles of a brewery, but that doesn't mean brewing culture is spread out evenly across all fifty states. Some are more conducive to beer making than others, due to such factors as beer-friendly statutes, demographic makeup, how conducive climate and soil are to growing the proper raw materials, or any combination of the three. The Brewers Association continuously tabulates the number of brewery openings and closings in any given state and calculates each state's brewing density—the number of beer-making operations per capita. The top three states should come as no surprise to most readers, but number four and five may not be quite so obvious to most:

1. **Vermont:** The Green Mountain State might draw immediate correlations with skiing, but it also happens to have the greatest number of breweries per capita. (What better environment is there for sipping a barleywine,

an imperial porter, or a double IPA than in front of a raging fire at a ski lodge after an exhausting day on the slopes?) Some of the state's better-known producers include Hill Farmstead, Long Trail, and The Alchemist. According to the Brewers Association, there are 8.6 breweries for every 100,000 Vermonters of legal drinking age.

2. **Oregon:** You knew this had to be on the list somewhere. It must be noted that while there are far more breweries in Oregon than there are in Vermont, their concentration relative to population size is slightly lower. For every 100,000 consumers who are twenty-one and older, there are 6.7 breweries. Among those are legends like Deschutes, Rogue, Ninkasi, Hair of the Dog, and Boneyard. There are far too many to name to truly do the state justice.

3. **Colorado:** Another one that's not much of a shock. It is, after all, the state in which the Brewers Association calls home (when most other trade associations set up shop in the Washington, D.C. area). For every 100,000 legal Coloradoans, there are 6.1 breweries. Those include— where to begin? The list reads like a Rock and Roll Hall of Fame induction ceremony, if breweries were musicians. New Belgium, Avery, Left Hand, Oskar Blues, Ska, Odell, Great Divide, and Breckenridge are just the tip of the iceberg!

4. **Montana:** People may be hard to find across Montana's intimidating amount of open space, but in the places where human souls dwell, they're very likely to be dwelling in a brewery. The state only slightly trails Colorado in beer makers per capita—5.9 per 100,000 citizens of Big Sky Country. And wouldn't you know, that just happens to be the name of Montana's best-known brewing operation: Big Sky. The name of its top product is even better known: Moose Drool Brown Ale. None of the state's forty-plus breweries are what anyone would call large—Big Sky, the biggest, produces around 55,000 barrels a year—but they all have loyal followings in their own right. Other breweries include Great Northern, Outlaw, and the Bavarian-centric Bayern Brewing.

5. **Wyoming:** You'll notice a pattern here among the third, fourth, and fifth states in this list: They're all stacked on top of each other. Wyoming, which is sandwiched between Montana and Colorado, boasts 5.3 breweries per 100,000 adults of legal drinking age. Wyoming may not claim any world-renowned icons, but folks in the state are fiercely loyal to their local producers, which include Prairie Fire, Geyser, and Black Tooth.

Beyond Portland: Oregon's Other Gems

It's true: Portland, at last count, has about sixty operating breweries just within its city limits. A beer traveler could spend a month in the city and still only barely scratch the surface of all the fermented goodness that Oregon's biggest city has to offer. However, that doesn't mean every second of a Pacific Northwest beercation should be spent in Portlandia.

Rent a car, drive about 160 miles southeast, and spend a few days in Bend. (There's also an airport that's an easy connection from PDX, but "scenic" doesn't even begin to describe the drive. It's worth the extra time, and, with the way flights have been going these days, driving is probably the quickest way to get there). Calling Bend "Oregon's best kept secret" would be doing the city a disservice. The secret has been out for quite some time among the beer devout. It's just not the easiest place to get to from other parts of the country, so the vibe remains fairly low-key for a town with twenty-four operating breweries. The most recent tally puts Bend's population at just over 81,000; that's one brewery for every 3,300 people.

The number of souls inhabiting the thirty-three-square-mile city has increased nearly 60 percent since 2000. The natural beauty surrounding the region makes it an ideal place to retire. But it's an even better place to have a pint.

From a beer-making perspective, the company that put Bend on the map was Deschutes Brewery. Founded in 1988 by Gary Fish—who's still active in the business and also serves as the chairman of the Brewers Association—Deschutes has grown to become one of the top ten craft breweries in the country, producing around 350,000 barrels annually. (It also opened a brewpub in Portland's Pearl District, but Bend is where most of the volume is made.)

Bend is one of the growing number of cities to be dubbed "Beer Town, USA," and it's earned this nickname for many good reasons.

Top Craft Beer Styles

The Brewers Association keeps a running tally of the top trending styles (although some are more like umbrella segments than they are singular styles). Here are the top seven in descending order:

1. India Pale Ale (aka IPA)
2. Seasonal (again, not a style, but a group of styles)
3. Pale Ale (IPA's easier-drinking sibling)
4. Variety (a nebulous grouping, if ever there was one)
5. Amber Ale (think Full Sail and Alaskan Amber)
6. Amber Lager (Sam Adams Boston Lager, Brooklyn Lager)
7. Bock

Boneyard Beer

Don't let the sinister-looking skull and crossbones scare you off. Boneyard is quite the inviting establishment. It's also a testament to the DIY spirit that built craft beer. Founder Tony Lawrence launched the operation in an old auto shop in 2010. The name Lawrence chose for his brewery is a nod to the boneyard of secondhand (and possibly thirdhand) equipment he built from the spare parts of thirteen other breweries across America. As Boneyard has grown, some of those original pieces have been replaced with shiny new stainless steel, but the heart of this Frankenstein's monster of a company remains. The word "Bone" shows up quite a bit in many of its products, such as Bone-a-Fide, an American pale that balances Citra hops with a sturdy malt foundation. Then there's Backbone, a roast-a-licious stout that's the result of a collaboration with the local Backporch Coffee Roasters.

Crux Fermentation Project

Crux brings an impressive Bend-born pedigree to its operation. The founder is Larry Sidor, who had been Deschutes's brewmaster for eight years. Similar to Boneyard's origin story, Crux launched in what was once a transmission shop. It was no surprise when Crux quickly shot to the top of beer-lovers' must-visit destinations. Sidor makes full use of his Pacific Northwest terroir with products like Off Leash, a session IPA (4.5 ABV and a moderate 30 IBU). It's a brew that's more about the citrusy complexity of hops than their bitterness. Citra and Centennial whole flower hops from the region's lupulin epicenter—Yakima, Washington—do the heavy lifting here. Crux doesn't forego the IPA proper; Galaxy hops power its Outcast IPA. Those Australian-born hops also inspired the beer's name. Australia's original inhabitants, of course, were criminal "outcasts." This one falls into the traditional IPA range, having a 7.6 ABV and 60 IBU. Taking things up a notch is Crux's Half Hitch Imperial Mosaic IPA, which has a whopping 10 percent ABV 80 IBU and draws its floral, citrusy character from the namesake Mosaic hops. But it's not all about the hops at Crux. The brewing team has fun riffing on the wonders of Belgium with its 8.1 percent ABV Flanders Red Ale. Sour is supposedly the new hoppy, after all.

10 Barrel Brewing Company

Beer geeks will gasp at the inclusion of 10 Barrel because those who follow the Brewers Association's definition of "craft brewery" don't consider it one anymore. In late 2014, the alien mother ship known as AB InBev invaded Bend's airspace and didn't leave until 10 Barrel got caught in its tractor beam. In other words, it was just one of many craft brewer acquisitions the global behemoth has made to play in the exploding craft segment (and essentially dominate beer bars' taphandles). But, as we learned from AB InBev's 2011 purchase of Chicago's Goose Island, absorption by the macro of macros doesn't make a brewery any less a brewery. And the multi-billion-dollar multinational's interest in this rather folksy operation speaks to just how much global attention Bend has attracted as a beer destination. True to its Pacific Northwest roots, 10 Barrel dutifully provides plenty for hopheads, like its flagship, Apocalypse IPA, as well as Joe IPA. But it also covers many of the other flavor bases as well and gets a bit wild with the likes of Uberweiss Marionberry, a Berliner Weiss-style brew aged in Pinot Noir barrels and finished with Oregon's ubiquitous marionberries.

Hood River, Oregon

Hood River is considerably closer to Portland than Bend and is, therefore, doable as a day trip (but why would you want to rush?). Located a little over an hour from Portland, where the Columbia River meets its namesake body of water in the middle of the Columbia River Gorge, Hood River a great place to visit when the sun is shining (and even when it's not, but the town is so much better on the brighter days). Head down to the banks of the river and just absorb all of its visual splendor, both natural and man-made. In certain parts of town, you get a jaw-dropping view of the perennially snowcapped Mount Hood.

On any given day, the river's surface and the sky will be full of multicolored mayhem as kiteboarders and windsurfers strive to master the elements. The town's population isn't even a tenth that of Bend, but it's home to considerably more breweries per capita. Most notable among those is Full Sail Brewing, founded back in 1987. Speaking of sunnier days, Full Sail's back deck is the place to be in the summer. The brewery is up on a hill so visitors get a sprawling view of the river down below.

Over the years since Full Sail first opened its doors, many contenders have sprung up, distinguishing themselves from the others and coexisting in perfect harmony. Among those is Double Mountain, which comes from the same bloodline as Full Sail—its cofounders, Matt Swihart and Charlie Devereaux, are both former Full Sail employees, with the former rising in the ranks to assistant brewmaster. In 2007 they launched the brewery and never strayed far from their roots—physically, that is, since Double Mountain is about a block away from Full Sail. Year-round faves include Hop Lava, the type of citrusy, floral IPA that every dutiful Northwestern brewery must create; the full-bodied IRA, an "India Red Ale" that's a ruby-colored riff on an IPA; the Vaporizer, a dry-hopped pale ale; and Double Mountain Kölsch (pretty self-explanatory there).

When Dave Logsdon—another Full Sail veteran—opened Logsdon Farm Brewery, he had no interest in hitting all of the usual stylistic beats. He was intent on producing Belgian-inspired farmhouse ales, and he wanted to do so on an actual farm. Luckily, his family owns a ten-acre farm. Each of Logsdon's brews is packaged in an attractive 750-milliliter wine-style bottle with a painting of Mount Hood on the label. Among the innovations are Kili Wit, an unfiltered white ale brewed with African coriander; Seizoen (the Dutch/Flemish spelling of "saison"); and Seizoen Bretta, which includes that devilishly wild yeast strain, brettanomyces.

Another Hood River operation that's gained a cult following in a short period of time—it opened in 2012—is pFriem Family Brewers, founded by brewmaster Josh Pfriem (whose career also included time at, that's right, Full Sail—it's quite the talent incubator, is it not?) and business partners Ken Whiteman and Rudy Kellner. pFriem burst onto the scene with its own interpretations of tried-and-true styles like IPA, pilsner, and wit. Its more limited offerings include a single hop pale ale that uses only the Mosaic varietal (known for its mango-like qualities), a RyePA, and even a brew it calls Down Under IPA that celebrates the emerging hop varietals coming out of Australia.

BeerCity USA

In 2009, homebrewing pioneer Charlie Papazian, founder of the American Homebrewers Association and president of the Brewers Association, kicked off what ultimately was a five-year project to highlight the municipalities across the country—often small, relatively unsung cities—that exemplify craft beer culture. Through an online poll, beer enthusiasts would vote on the town that got to wear the crown of "BeerCity USA." Papazian pulled the plug on its poll when he declared that it had served its purpose.

Here's the list of winners, from 2009 to 2013, based on a cumulative vote count of 156,000 (be warned: the list gets a bit repetitive).

Kegs at the Lagunitas Chicago brewery.

2009: The first year's poll ended in a tie between Portland (big surprise there) and Asheville, North Carolina. The western North Carolina city in the Blue Ridge Mountains had long been a refuge for the artsy and bohemian sets. So it wasn't a huge stretch that it would evolve into quite the beer destination with a brewery for every 8,000 Ashevilleans. Wedge Brewing Company, Wicked Weed, Highland Brewing, and French Broad are just a few of the operations that have made a name for themselves in the town of 84,000. The greater Asheville area caught the attention of some very high-profile Western brewers looking to expand eastward. Lyons, Colorado's Oskar Blues chose Brevard, North Carolina—located about thirty miles outside of Asheville—as the site of its first East Coast brewery, which opened in December 2012. Then, Chico, California's Sierra Nevada opened a gargantuan, environmentally friendly second brewery, whose doors opened in 2014, in nearby Mills River. Finally, Fort Collins, Colorado's New Belgium chose Asheville proper for the site of its second brewery, which commenced operations in 2016.

2010: Asheville grabbed the brass ring again.

2011: Ditto

2012: Asheville, yet again, won the distinction; however, this time it had to share it with a newcomer: Grand Rapids, Michigan. The most famous of Grand Rapids breweries is Founders Brewing Company, known for Dirty Bastard, its malty, Scotch-style ale; All Day IPA; and the seasonal, coffee-infused Breakfast Stout (as well as the bourbon barrel aged version, KBS [Kentucky Breakfast Stout]). Grand Rapids is also home to one of the country's most popular brewpubs, Hopcat.

2013: Asheville finally let someone else have the spotlight. Grand Rapids flew solo in 2013, the final year of the poll.

Beyond the Known Universe

"Extreme" Brewing and Attention-Grabbing Stunts

T here are two distinct paths that drinkers may take to becoming a beer aficionado. One path may involve a mass-market lager drinker who never much liked the taste of beer but drank it because it was cheap and familiar. Then one day, at a friend's urging, that consumer tried a more flavorful brew, perhaps an amber lager or a pale ale, and the rest is history. The other path may involve a drinker who learns of a brand that has a 10 or 12 percent ABV and tastebud-obliterating hop content and is compelled to try it. "I want my beers to hurt" would not be an uncharacteristic statement for such an individual to utter. It's not unlike what motivates an elite athlete to complete an Ironman or a thrill-seeker to BASE jump off of a one-hundred-story skyscraper: a combination of masochism and an attraction to the extreme.

Perhaps it's fitting, then, that one of the key craft beer trends to emerge in the early 2000s was the concept of the "extreme beer." Usually an "extreme" offering is one whose alcohol content pushes the boundaries of convention, sometimes surpassing that of wine and even some spirits.

Of course, as more mainstream consumers experience craft beer, the goal post moves on what actually constitutes the extreme. At one time an IPA, with its outsized hop content and somewhat higher ABV—around 7 percent—would have been considered extreme, especially to a population reared on conventional flavor-restrained industrial lagers.

Jim Koch of Boston Beer Company (Samuel Adams) likes to point out that his brewery was, perhaps, the first to create an extreme beer. In 1994 the brewery unveiled Triple Bock, which, at 17.5 percent ABV, was the strongest beer on the market at the time.

While the term "extreme beer" is of American origin, the concept is most definitely European. Technically, many of the traditional Belgian styles could be deemed "extreme" in comparison with most other worldwide varieties, since a good number of them boast ABVs upwards of 9 percent.

However, the credit for the first extreme beer should go to a country not far from the Benelux region: Switzerland. A good decade and a half before Boston Beer made its first batch of Triple Bock, Swiss brewery Hürlimann released Samichlaus—"Santa Claus" in the local dialect—a 14 percent ABV lager rolled out only once a year. The release date is always December 6, Saint Nicholas Day, which is celebrated in many European countries. Hürlimann Brewery closed in 1997, but Samichlaus production resumed three years later through a collaboration with the brand's original brewers and Austria's Schloss Eggenberg. Those who know a few German words might know that "schloss" means "castle." Eggenberg is a medieval castle that's been brewing beer for nearly seven hundred years—commercially for the latter half of that time.

For a good part of the '80s and '90s, Samichclaus got to call itself the strongest beer in the world; at the very least it was the strongest lager, as there was a fair amount of envelope-pushing going on in the ale breweries of Benelux. It wasn't uncommon for a few bars to still be referring to it as such deep into the 2000s as well. A quick Google search would have been all that was needed to debunk the claim, but few who had tasted anything stronger were bothering to do so.

When Sam Adams unofficially ushered in the extreme era with Triple Bock, it initiated an arms race of sorts to see which breweries could push the limits the furthest.

Triple Bock was just the beginning for Boston Beer. In the early 2000s, the brewery launched the Samuel Adams Utopias series, a (mostly) annual release of a stave-enhanced concoction whose ABV typically hovered around 26 percent and whose flavor was a lot closer to that of a sherry or Madeira than a beer (it also lacked carbonation, which further prompted that comparison).

The very existence of Dogfish Head has been defined by high-ABV beers. For a while very few of its offerings dipped below 7 percent alcohol. (Later releases, like its Festina Peche fruit-infused Berliner Weisse-style beer, went in the opposite direction; the spring seasonal Festina is a modest 4.5 percent.) Founder Sam Calagione literally wrote the book on the subject; in 2006, his tome *Extreme Brewing* was first published.

Hopheads eagerly await the regular but limited release of Dogfish Head 120 Minute IPA, which cranks up just about every component that makes its

60 Minute and 90 Minute IPAs so appealing. Where the former brews boil and continuously add hops for a full hour and an hour and a half respectively, 120 Minute IPA does so for two whole hours. The brewers then dry hop it daily in the fermenter for a month before aging it for an additional month on whole-leaf hops.

But 120 Minute is not just a hophead's paradise; it's also quite strong from an alcohol-content standpoint. Depending on the particular release, it ranges from 15 to 20 percent ABV.

Another of Dogfish Head's special releases available on an infrequent basis is Raison d'Extra, a potent riff on its Raison d'Etre. Dogfish takes the the latter brew—a Belgian-style brown ale made with beet sugar, raisons and Belgian-style yeast—and amps it up to the nth degree, resulting in an incredibly malty beer that, at its most moderate, is 15 percent ABV and, at its strongest, is 18 percent ABV.

Meanwhile, with World Wide Stout, Dogfish Head does the same for the stout style, creating a dark, boozy concoction between 15 and 20 percent ABV—or about three times that of an average stout.

Imperialistic Tendencies

Stout is the style responsible for introducing a word that has become a prefix of sorts for just about every other beer classification: imperial. It was first applied to the dark, roasty English variety in the late eighteenth century when the Brits would export a stronger version that could survive the journey to Russia. As the story goes, Russian Empress Catherine the Great had grown quite fond of stout on her visits to England and requested that it be exported to her court. That's why the style that emerged is frequently referred to as Russian imperial stout. The stuff was not of Russian origin, as its name might imply, but merely of Russian consumption.

Today, "imperial" is affixed to any beer that's a cranked-up version of the traditional recipe for its respective style. However, when applied to anything other than stout, the moniker lacks historical significance.

Imperial IPAs are, perhaps, the most common. Dogfish Head's 90 Minute IPA certainly would fall into that category, as would 120 Minute IPA, for that matter (though most of the time they're a bit more modest in their alcohol content). The term double IPA (or sometimes triple IPA) can be used interchangeably with imperial IPA.

Three Floyds Dreadnaught Imperial IPA, is a solid example of the style, boasting all of the citrusy hop bite (100 IBUs!) one has come to expect from such a beer, as well as a significant malt expression. Though hop bitterness is the defining characteristic for IPAs, there's often the generous presence of malt sweetness to balance the even hoppier iterations. That's primarily due to the fact that it takes more malt to boost the ABV. The yeast need more sugar to convert to the additional alcohol.

Russian River's Pliny the Elder Double IPA has become nothing short of an icon among beer geeks. The 8 percent ABV, 100 IBU bottle of bitterness has won a treasure trove of awards and has, for seven consecutive years, topped the American Homebrewers Association's list of "Best Commercial Beers in America." It's also spawned the even bigger white whale, Pliny the Younger—an 11 percent ABV triple IPA.

But the Pliny family of Sonoma, California has been getting a run for its money from a certain brewery in Waterbury, Vermont. Heady Topper, brewed by The Alchemist, has become legendary. It ups the bitterness quotient considerably, registering a full 120 IBUs.

Imperial IPAs are just the tip of the iceberg. There have been imperial porters, imperial pilsners, imperial wheat beers, imperial saisons—you get the picture. The term is kicked around so frequently, you'd think brewers had licensing deals with Lucasfilm.

The pendulum does seem to be swinging in the opposite direction at the moment. There's a movement toward session ales; brewers are delighting in the low ABVs—usually 4 and 4.5 percent—of some of their newest offerings. There's a whole new category of "Session IPA" emerging, a style that's (relatively) light on alcohol but high on hop flavor.

It could very well be that moderation is the new extreme.

Jumping the Shark

The notion of taking things to the extreme is not limited to producing a beer with "a lot of something" in it, be it hops or alcohol. It frequently applies to those with ingredients that are . . . well . . . weird. This subset of extreme beers shall be deemed potential shark jumpers, a nod to that notorious 1977 episode of *Happy Days* when the Fonz did just that. "Jumping the shark" initially had been a term that was exclusive to the television realm, but, as the craft beer industry matures, it's become increasingly relevant in that space as well.

Oregon's Rogue Brewing Company has been known for some truly world-class beers that are icons in their own right—Dead Guy Ale comes to mind, as does its intensified version, Double Dead Guy. It's also been known for a few releases that many have called stunts. Among those was Beard Beer, which, tasted blindly, doesn't seem particularly intense. It has a relatively tame ABV of 4.8 percent, a modest 25 IBU, and some fairly standard Sterling hops and Munich and pilsner malts, all of which converge to form a flavorful session beer. Now, about what's converting those malts' starch into alcohol: It's not ordinary yeast; it was harvested from brewmaster John Maier's beard. I'm just going to leave that right there.

Another pair of Oregon brewers, Portland's Upright Brewing and Burnside Brewing, collaborated on a creation they called Captain Beefheart Beer. Their intent was to develop a brew that incorporated many savory elements from the kitchen, like Turkish bay leaf and long pepper. But those elements were fairly standard, compared with the main attraction: sixty pounds of charred beef hearts added to the kettle boil. It resulted in a salty little brew that's actually quite easy to drink at 5.85 percent ABV.

Some folks are more thinkers than feelers. Those who choose the mind over the heart will be happy to know that they can have their brains and drink them, too. Back in the spring of 2014, the *Walking Dead*-obsessed team at Philadelphia's Dock Street Brewery decided to produce a zombie-friendly beer to coincide with the season finale of the apocalyptic AMC series. The result: Dock Street Walker, brewed with cranberries and roasted goat brains. There's not much more to say about that one.

If livestock hearts and gray matter don't sound like your cup of tea, how about bones and heads? Smoked mangalitsa pig bones and heads are what give Right Brain Brewery's Mangalitsa Pig Porter its distinctive smoky pork flavor, which is complemented by a slightly chocolaty finish. The Traverse City, Michigan-based brewery releases Mangalitsa but once a year, and it's always a hit.

For a decidedly masculine beer, there's a little curiosity that came out of the brewhouse of Denver's Wynkoop Brewing Company: Rocky Mountain Oyster Stout. Oyster stouts have long been a popular style; the oyster shells bring a faint briny element to the roasty style, which makes a nice accompaniment when eating the little mollusks on the half shell. But the term "Rocky Mountain Oyster" might give most folks pause. Yes, they're bull testicles, and yes, their essence does find its way into the beer—each batch is brewed with twenty-five pounds of them!

The folks at Wynkoop knew how ridiculous a concept it was. In fact, it started out as an April Fools' joke. They posted a video on April 1, 2012, detailing the process of making the fictitious beer. Those who didn't get the joke were eager to try it. So, the Wynkoop team figured, why not? They made some very small eight-barrel batches of the beer and canned about 100 cases of it, as part of their Even Smaller Batch Series.

Wynkoop had a great deal of fun promoting the very limited release. The press release called it a "seminal moment" (pun intended), describing the beer as "an assertive, viscous stout with a rich brown/black color, a luscious mouthfeel, and deep flavors of chocolate, espresso, and *nuts*." (Pun intended again.) Wynkoop also notes that in addition to its 7.5 percent ABV, Rocky Mountain Oyster Stout contains 3 BPB—"balls per barrel."

Danish gypsy brewery Mikkeller, which pops up several times throughout this book, is no stranger to bizarre ingredients. One particularly noteworthy project was its Beer Geek Brunch Weasel, a variation on its coffee-infused oatmeal stout with an odd twist from the animal kingdom. No, it doesn't have actual weasels in it (though stranger rodent-related things have happened, such as BrewDog's End of History, which features a bottle packaged in a stuffed squirrel). What it does have is coffee beans harvested from the fecal matter of the nocturnal, weasel-like civet. See, these pesky little creatures have a taste for fine coffee beans. Their digestive tracts contain special enzymes that break down much of the bean, leaving them with richer, more concentrated coffee flavors. And then they end up in a brew kettle.

You've got to have a fairly strong constitution to consider that beer, much less drink it; but once you're able to get past the . . . ummm . . . unconventional concept, it's quite a flavorful creation.

The thought of this next innovation—Pastrami on Rye from Chicago's Pipeworks Brewing Company—might have certain gastrointestinal ramifications as well, but it's not as radical as it may sound. Unlike Captain Beefheart Beer, there aren't any actual cow bits in Pastrami on Rye. However, it contains just about everything else deli fans would come to expect from its namesake sandwich, from the condiments to the spices that give the classic cold cut its unmistakable flavor: black peppercorn, mustard seed, coriander, allspice, red pepper flakes, cinnamon stick, bay leaf, clove, caraway, and honey. Oh, and its grain bill, of course, includes rye.

There are those who love stunt beers and others (probably a greater number) who vehemently reject everything they're about, but there are very few who can ignore them. They create headlines and social media buzz for brewers that don't have the marketing resources of multibillion-dollar megas. They get people's attention when most wouldn't give them the time of day otherwise.

Craft Beer Abroad

An American Movement Becomes a Global Phenomenon

T he modern craft-brewing movement started in the United States, but it has since evolved into a global phenomenon. On nearly every populous continent, there are local markets where the beer game is changing. We're going to take a look at many of those across Asia, Europe, and South America.

Japan

When it comes to craft-brewing industry development, Japan is, hands-down, way ahead of the rest of Asia (and many other parts of the world as well).

Year zero for craft brewing in Japan, many would agree, is 1996. This was right after the Japanese government changed the law, loosening the restrictions on beer brewing in the country. Many of the country's top craft outfits started cranking out their products that year; a number of them had been producers of other alcoholic beverages that expanded their portfolios to include beer when it became economically feasible to do so.

The country's booming scene even spawned its own bilingual magazine, *Japan Beer Times*, inviting locals and travelers who don't speak the language to discover the wild and wonderful world of Japanese craft beer (as well as the far-flung international brewing traditions that inspire it).

The Breweries

Kiuchi

Kiuchi is the best-known Japanese producer, as it has a significant international presence—including in the US. The Ibaraki-based brewery might not

Japan boasts one of the most developed craft beer scenes outside of the US.

be a household name among craft beer aficionados, but its flagship product line is: Hitachino Nest.

Kiuchi's operation boasts more than 190 years of history, but only a fraction of that time has been devoted to beer making. The company began as a brewer of saké and a distiller of shochu, the native spirit of Japan, and continues to make those products to this day. But in 1996 it added craft beer to its repertoire. Its most visible product is Hitachino Nest White Ale, a Belgian-style witbier that has notes of coriander, orange peel, and nutmeg. Kiuchi also offers interpretations of other classic styles, like amber ale, stout, and India pale ale, as well as some decidedly homegrown innovations. Its Nipponia uses the Japanese breed of Kanego Golden barley, first developed in 1900, and combines that with a Japan-bred Sorachi Ace hop species. It's easy to recognize the Hitachino Nest range; just look for the label with the cartoon owl.

Coedo

Based in Kawagoe, one of Coedo's biggest claims to fame is its Beniaka beer, 75 percent of whose fermentable sugars are derived from sweet potatoes.

Beer Belly in Osaka serves as the tasting room for Minoh Beer.

Sweet potatoes are a hugely popular alcohol base throughout Japan. Sweet potato shochu is the top-selling variety of the spirit, far surpassing barley, rice, sugar cane, and buckwheat in popularity. Because most of its base comes from a source other than malt, it is classified as a happoshu—a low-malt beer. Beers in Japan are taxed based on their malt content, and many brewers produce lower-end beers with reduced malt content to minimize their tax burden and, therefore, their cost to consumers. Flavor, not cost-savings, was Coedo's aim with Beniaka. Coedo's beer portfolio also includes Kyara, an India pale lager, Ruri pilsner, Shiro wheat beer, and Shikkoku black lager.

Minoh

Minoh is the big local brewery for the Osaka area, located in its namesake town (more commonly known among locals as Mino-o) just outside the major city. In downtown Osaka, the brewery also runs a pair of bars known as Beer Belly, which serve as Minoh's urban tasting rooms and the place to try some of its rare one-offs and experimental creations. The brewery is known for its imperial stout, as well as its stout proper, and accessible styles like weizen, pilsner, and pale ale. Minoh's Cabernet ale marries the best of the wine and beer worlds—fermented grapes and malt.

Tamamura-Honten (Shiga Kogen)

Tamamura-Honten started brewing the Shiga Kogen range in 2004 in the city of Yamanouchi in Nagano Prefecture. It's quickly become a favorite of beer geeks worldwide, with a line that includes Miyama Blonde, House IPA, Shiga Kogen Pale Ale, and Shiga Kogen Porter.

Yo-Ho Brewing Company

Another of the Class of '96 brewers, Yo-Ho was launched as a subsidiary of Hoshino Resort Co., a hospitality management corporation. In the past two decades, the brewery has gained a following for such trademarks as Tokyo Black porter, Yona Yona pale ale, Sun Sun organic blond ale, and Indo no Aooni India pale ale. Like many American craft brewers, Yo-Ho has adopted the aluminum can as the package of choice, particularly for its eco-friendly and distribution-friendly (i.e., lightweight) characteristics.

South Korea

The country in the northern half of the Korean peninsula usually gets most of the international press, thanks to the antics of its totalitarian ruler. And it often overshadows some of the truly amazing things happening in South Korea. One of those is a burgeoning craft beer scene. The U.-based Brewers Association has had its eye on the country for some time. It's one of the fastest growing export markets for American craft, growing faster than nearby Japan (though, to be fair, Japan's market is much more mature and has a lot more of its own stuff to consume). In 2015, South Korea usurped Japan as the number five export market in the world for American craft beer. Though, for some perspective, it's still incredibly small. In revenue terms, US craft brewers collectively sold about $3.4 million worth of beer in South Korea (of a total $99.7 million in worldwide export revenue).

In the grand scheme of things, beer is relatively new to Korea. Its first brewery opened as recently as 1908. (Contrast that with the first commercial breweries in Europe and it seems like five minutes ago.) Today, it's pretty much a duopoly between Hite-Jinro (which also produces the top-selling brand of soju, South Korea's national spirit) and Oriental Breweries (OB). OB is probably familiar to anyone who's ever dined in a Korean restaurant in the States. It's ubiquitous.

It was under the long shadow of those two mega macros that South Korea's homegrown craft brewing industry emerged. The concept got a boost in the spring of 2014 when the country finally loosened brewing restrictions that made it nearly impossible for a small brewery to survive. (The macros are usually eager to protect the status quo; since they've got the deepest pockets, they can hire the best lawyers and the best lobbyists.)

The regulations were pretty ridiculous, and it's astonishing that the government was able to enact and enforce them with a straight face. South Korea had mandated, until 2011, that only brewers that could produce a million liters of beer a year could obtain licenses to make the stuff. That converts to a little more than 8,500 barrels, which is the annual production of a modest-size brewery in the United States. It's not a difficult level to achieve in a few years of operation, but it's an insurmountable task in most breweries' inaugural year. Most start-ups can't secure the kind of capital to have the capacity from day one to make that a reality, and that's before a drop of it has even been sold. In 2011, that threshold dropped to a more manageable 150,000 liters (just shy of 1,300 barrels). It gave new businesses a fighting chance, but it still excluded brewpubs. Most new brewpubs are lucky to produce a third of that in their early days. Finally, more rational heads prevailed and, in April 2014, the country lowered the minimum to 50,000 liters. Finally, cultivating a bona fide "scene" was no longer an impossibility.

It's going to take some time to see how things play out in the country. Imports still account for a significant portion of the meager 1 percent share craft commands of the overall South Korean beer business. But things are picking up. Seoul has its own semi-major beer event, the Great Korean Beer Festival, which is converting new drinkers to craft—not an easy task when recent laws and regulations were creating such an inhospitable environment for the concept to succeed. And start-ups have been generating sizeable buzz. Among those:

Magpie

Magpie hits most of the crowd-pleasing styles—pale ale, amber ale, and porter—that are typical in a country just getting its feet wet in the craft brewery scene. But it's also dabbling in more palate-challenging areas. For example, it produces a gose called Ghost (so whether you order it by name or style, there will be no mistakes).

Devil's Door

A popular spot in the posh Gangnam neighborhood—immortalized in that infectious song by K-Pop icon Psy—Devil's Door had the good fortune of deep pockets to get up and running. It's owned by Shinsegae, the leading department store franchise in the country. The ultra-high-ceilinged brewpub is as sprawling as the parent company's retail behemoths, but that doesn't make it easy to get a seat. There's almost always a thirty to forty-five minute wait to get in and try its products. Internationally accessible styles like IPA, stout, and standard American-inspired pale ale are usually what's on offer. The food's just as approachable. It's the typical international gastropub fare: pizzas, mussels, gourmet burgers, and some more Asian-inspired dishes like fried octopus.

Southeast Asia

Vietnam

Japan and Korea are not the only parts of Asia to get their craft on. Would you believe that Vietnam has a nascent scene of its own? (The operative word being *nascent*. Don't expect a beer geek's paradise quite yet.) There's been a massive learning curve for the country that's only been open to outside economic influences (post-Vietnam War) since the Clinton Administration. The preferred method of consumption in urban centers like Ho Chi Minh City and Hanoi is pouring beer over ice (refrigeration hasn't always been a given there, and it remains at a premium). The country has a couple of dominant national and regional brands, namely the ubiquitous 333 and Bia Saigon, but the normalization of relations with the West ultimately has opened the door for a local craft renaissance. European proprietorship is readily apparent in Ho Chi Minh City's brewpubs. For instance, there's Gammer, which concentrates on Czech styles. Bar staff even don traditional Bohemian-style garb. The selection is limited to one light and one dark lager, but both hold their own against their Central European inspirations. The copper-colored brewing equipment is proudly front and center in the beer hall, composing a key element of Gammer's décor.

Across town, the selection at the German-inspired Big Man Beer is equally limited, but both the pale and dark are worth a sip. The ambience is a bit more no-frills, but the quality of the beer elevates the experience. It's not uncommon to witness locals dropping a couple of frozen cubes in their glasses, even though the temperature of the beer is just fine. Old habits die hard.

Singapore

Singapore's a bit of an odd duck—as both a country/city (it's both!) and as a drinking destination.

The squeaky clean melting pot of Asian cultures—don't even think about spitting on the sidewalk; the US State Department will not bail you out for such tomfoolery—has some of the best food you're ever going to find in the world. The hawker centers are like food courts of awesomeness, with expertly crafted dishes inspired by cuisines from all over the continent. The food is dirt cheap, too, and taxis are quite reasonable for such a wealthy nation. A fairly lengthy ride likely will run you the equivalent of 10 to 20 US dollars.

But you know what traditionally hasn't been so cheap? Drinking. That's in thanks to exorbitant customs duties on alcohol. (Pro Tip: If you're visiting Singapore and staying in a hotel, the minibar is not your friend!) The average beer would cost around US$8 or $9, and if you're easily lured into tourist traps like the rooftop lounge at the Marina Bay Sands (the hotel that resembles a humongous surfboard resting on top of a trio of towers), you'll more likely spend closer to $15 or $16 for that same brew. A "cheap" cocktail is around $20.

The development of a craft beer scene had a couple of headwinds working against it. For one thing, that US$8 or $9 usually covered the local mass-marketed brand, Tiger. If you want a craft beer—say, something imported from Japan, the States, or Europe—you're likely to throw down $12 or $13 for it (not unlike one would in Scandinavia, but we'll get to that a bit later).

And then of course, there's the climate. Singapore is less than one hundred miles north of the equator and is, therefore, without discernible seasons. Temperatures above ninety degrees Fahrenheit, with about 85 percent humidity, are as common in January as they are in July. While there are plenty of craft styles perfect for such oppressively sultry days, dark, big, and boozy brews aren't likely to fare so well with the locals.

But despite all that, just as nature found a way in "Jurassic Park," craft beer found a way—albeit a bit more slowly than most—in Singapore.

Brewerkz

In 1997, American business partners Devin Otto Kimble and Daniel Flores tried their luck at bringing US-style artisanal beer to the tropical island city-state. They opened Brewerkz, a brewpub serving some of the usual bar fare paired with some of the more approachable beer styles likely to turn off neither the local population nor tourists and traveling business people. There's a little something for everyone in the lineup, which hits most of the beats you'd expect: Golden Ale, IPA, Pilsner, and Oatmeal Stout are a few of its perennials, along with Hopback Ale—what many would call a "session IPA"—and Iguana Lager, a light lager designed to hold up against the spicier dishes.

RedDot

RedDot's origins trail Brewerkz's by several years, but the brewpub likes to distinguish itself from the former by noting that it's Singapore's "first locally owned, independent commercial microbrewery."

Like many brewers in far-flung regions of the world, RedDot founder and brewmaster Ernest Ng encountered his brewing inspiration abroad. However, it wasn't the American craft beer scene or any old-world beer destinations like the United Kingdom, Belgium or Germany that sparked this inspiration. It was South Africa. Ng was on safari when he encountered a pair of South African soldiers, who offered Ng one of their cold beers. He was curious about the brand, but they told him it was no brand; it was home-brewed. That was Ng's first exposure to the concept, and he was an instant convert. The name "RedDot" actually stems from the first time he set foot in a homebrew shop. Some ingredients packages were marked with a red dot, while others were blank. He just, quite randomly and with no real agenda, chose one with a red dot. (There's almost a *Matrix*-like red-pill-or-blue-pill element to the origin story.)

After researching and pursuing practical education—including in the US—Ng opened RedDot. The brewery now has two locations serving food along with its beer, which includes quite a few refreshing styles—this is Singapore, after all—like a Czech Pilsner, a Kölsch-style brew, and a Summer Ale (which most probably would just call "ale," since it's always summer in Singapore). There's also a nod to the tropical bounty of the island in the form of RedDot Lime Wheat. Though Ng and his team tend to color within the lines with a lot of the styles on offer, they don't shy away from experimentation. RedDot's Monster Green Lager pours in the hue that its name promises, but it doesn't get that way from any silly St. Paddy's Day-like food coloring. It's actually infused with spirulina, the blue-green algae that's packed with all sorts of healthful components like proteins, vitamins, and antioxidants. Who says beer can't be good for you?

The Pump Room/Archipelago Brewing Company

Singapore's also home to the Pump Room, a rather incongruous place to house a brewery. The establishment markets itself as a "Gastrobar"—sure, it's a bar with plenty of decent food—but it has more of a nightclub vibe. In other words, it's more of a scene to see and be seen. It's also in the high-traffic entertainment district, Clarke Quay, which is a bit of a tourist magnet. The brewing operation is actually the result of a partnership between the club and Archipelago brewing, Singapore's first commercial brewery, founded in 1931 by German brewer Becks (now a part of AB InBev, but that's another story). Archipelago has a rather intriguing history, as far as twentieth-century beer making goes: When World War II broke out, the British—the colonial power in the island nation at that time—seized control of the brewery. This would not have been entirely unexpected, considering the fact that the brewery's founders were German.

Malaysian Breweries then acquired Archipelago, eventually became a part of the larger concern, Asia Pacific Breweries, and ultimately became a wholly owned subsidiary of Heineken International.

In the mid-2000s, Archipelago got a makeover as Asia Pacific Breweries' specialty arm under the guidance of American craft-brewing legend Fal Allen, who is best known for his work at California's Anderson Valley Brewing Company.

Hospoda

Being the cultural melting pot that it is, Singapore is a perfect place for a brewery based entirely on Czech-style brewing. In 2013, Hospoda set up shop in the Bencoolen neighborhood, brewing exclusively in the tradition of the birthplace of pilsner (much like Ho Chi Minh City's Gammer). As much as every beer enthusiast would love to transpose the 's' and the 'p' and make it Hop-soda (what a concept!), the word "hospoda" actually means "pub" in Czech (and it was also the chosen moniker of a now-defunct New York City bar). The brewpub keeps things simple with a choice between a light lager (a pilsner) and a dark lager, and there are plenty of food options—from the expected sausages to the less obvious grilled whole duck—to pair with the brews.

LeVel 33

Remember the three towers with the gargantuan surfboard? A five or six-minute walk from there is an upscale brewpub that promises an elevated experience. It's called LeVel 33 (for fairly obvious reasons), and it bills itself as the world's highest urban craft brewery (it's got a full eighteen stories on New York City's Birreria). And people definitely pay for the privilege of drinking at such great heights that showcase a billion-dollar view of the glorious Marina Bay and the illuminated downtown cityscape. Inside, copper brew kettles are prominently displayed for the requisite ambient brewery porn. The house beers are of the European, now global, tradition: 33.1 Blond Lager, 33.15 India Pale Ale, 33.3 Stout, 33.4 House Porter, and 33.9 Wheat. Food options veer a bit toward fine dining—steaks, braised short ribs, lamb, and the like—but they might as well; would you really want a steep upcharge on a hotdog?

Scandinavia

Few European regions outside of Germany, the United Kingdom, and Belgium have developed such a hardcore beer culture as Scandinavia. The country that's leading the charge among its fellow Nordics is Denmark, and, for the longest time, it was pretty much the only game in town.

Founded in 1847, Denmark's Carlsberg brewery has grown to become the dominant player across Scandinavia—and much of other regions of Europe, for that matter. It stands as the fourth-largest brewing company in the world, behind only, in descending order, AB InBev, SABMiller, and Heineken. It was hard to imagine any sort of craft beer scene popping up in any Nordic city—much less in Carlsberg's back yard of Copenhagen—but it has, and it's thriving.

"Around 2002 and 2003 there were only about twenty brewers in Denmark," reports Per Sten Nielsen, head of communications for the Danish Brewers Association, which represents about 98 percent of Denmark's industry. "Now there are 120, and we consider that a revolution."

For those who live in the United States, which has around 5,000 such operations, 120 may not sound like much. But when you take into account that the Danish population stands at just under 5.7 million—about 1/60th of the US tally—that number is pretty impressive. It's more than twice the number of breweries per capita that the United States boasts.

Craft volume also commands about 6 percent of the country's beer market, which, for a European country, is quite high. Revenue-wise, the percentage is considerably higher, at 16 percent share, thanks to the markedly higher price point on craft products.

For some comparison, the US market—the beacon for all things craft—had 6 percent craft share as recently as 2012. From that perspective, Denmark's craft share is not very far behind that of the US.

As macro as Carlsberg may be, it's one of the few global brewers that manages to dodge the "evil empire" label that many craft beer drinkers assign to the multinational mass producers. Sure, the Danish brewer's flagship lager is designed for crowd-pleasing mainstream consumption, but that's just what pays the bills. Carlsberg was the first of the world's largest beer makers to embrace the rise of craft beer. In 2005 it launched the Jacobsen Brewhouse, a specialty label, named for Carlsberg founder J. C. Jacobsen, designed to appeal to craft enthusiasts. Jacobsen hits all of the major styles, including IPA, weissbier, dark lager, brown ale, blond ale, and seasonal Christmas bock.

While American macro producers aren't allowed anywhere near the craft brewing trade association's (the Brewers Association) Boulder, Colorado headquarters, the Danish Brewers Association's board meetings actually include representatives from Carlsberg sitting alongside personnel from miniscule operations that employ two or three people. Carlsberg sees the value in collaborating with its craft brethren. Large American brewers mostly want to either buy them or bump them off the shelves or from the draft lines. The Danish relationship reflects a desire to combat the encroachment of wine and spirits into the beer space, a goal that the largest and smallest of brewers share. It's heartening that the crafts and macros were able to find common ground and work together. It's good PR for Carlsberg, too. They're still a Goliath, but they're perceived as a benevolent one that can sit down and have a couple of beers with all of the Davids.

Local Flavor

Initially, the Scandinavian movement was partly a revolt against traditional lager, much as it was in the United States and continues to be in other parts of the world. Most styles produced in Denmark and the other countries in the region reflect those popularized during the American craft surge, but some brewers are giving their products more of a sense of place. In many cases that means using indigenous botanicals that reflect the Scandinavian terroir.

The concept of the "Nordic kitchen" has been all the rage around the world ever since Copenhagen's famous, Michelin-starred restaurant Noma opened in 2003. But foodies really started to pay attention when *Restaurant* magazine ranked it as the Best Restaurant in the World four times in five years between 2010 and 2014. If eating in the Danish capital wasn't already expensive enough . . .

A less bankrupting way to get a taste of what Scandinavia has to offer would be through its beer, and brewers in the region are increasingly incorporating many components of Scandinavian cuisine into their brewed offerings.

Denmark

Mikkeller

One of the most famous of the Danish craft breweries on the world stage, without a doubt, is Mikkeller, which is interesting because for most of its existence it didn't operate a physical brewery. Mikkeller, founded in 2006 by high school teacher Mikkel Borg Bjergsø and journalist Kristian Klarup Keller (who left the business a year later), created the concept of the "gypsy brewery." The business model differs from that of a contract brewery in that the gypsy brewers don't outsource all of their brewing and packaging activities to an outside brewery or two. The owners of the gypsy outfit set up shop in a partner brewery, brew their batches, and move on to another one (sometimes they stick around for a while).

The practice has become a viable option in the States, as well, with producers like Maryland-based Stillwater Artisanal Ales, created by Brian Strumke, and the now-defunct Pretty Things Beer & Ale Project, founded by Dann and Martha Paquette.

The gypsy concept also caught on a lot closer to home for Bjergsø. His estranged brother, Jeppe Jarnit-Bjergsø, launched the appropriately named Evil Twin Brewing, which has become a cult favorite in its own right.

The brothers have taken their sibling rivalry beyond their home turf and have been fighting an East Coast-West Coast turf war of sorts. Mikkel opened a Mikkeller gastropub in San Francisco, while Jeppe partnered with New York chef Daniel Burns to launch Tørst, which has become the toast of the already robust Brooklyn beer scene.

(Though Mikkeller's nomadic founder spends a lot of time in the US these days, it's hard to characterize the brewery as anything other than Danish).

Oddly enough, despite its worldwide acclaim, Mikkeller was a late entry into the Danish Brewers Association. That's mainly because membership requirements are fairly stringent; a major prerequisite is operating a brewery. Mikkeller had been around for nearly a decade before it finally opened a brewpub in its home country.

Nørrebro Bryghus

When it comes to brewpubs, the Danes really know how to hit it out of the park. Nørrebro Bryghus, in Copenhagen's Nørrebro neighborhood, has a roomy, loft-like space in an industrial-chic brick building that almost makes the requisite Scandinavian sticker shock worth it. The diverse beer list wears its international influences on its sleeve. There's the dark golden New York Lager, modeled after pre-Prohibition Vienna-style lagers (not unlike a lager from a brewery named after a particular borough of New York City); the red ale Ravnsborg Rød, which has a distinctly Danish moniker, but its influences are largely British with some American overtones, thanks, mostly, to the Pacific Northwest Amarillo hop variety; Stuykman Hvede, which takes a cue from Belgian witbier; and Böhmer Pilsner, which, as one can easily surmise from its name, is a riff on a Bohemian (Czech)-style pilsner. Seasonally speaking, there's no beating winter, as that's the time to enjoy Nörrebros Julebryg ("Yule brew"). It's a close cousin to traditional winter warmers and is brewed with a proprietary blend of Christmas spices.

All can be paired with a host of Nordic and continental specialties on the lunch and dinner menus. And visitors can purchase bottles of most of Nørrebro Bryghus's regular beers. Though there's plenty of active brewing happening on-site, most of the stuff for packaged distribution comes out of its larger production brewery about half an hour outside the city in Hedehusene.

Norway

Over in Norway, the brewery that's made the biggest impact on the world scene has been Nøgne Ø (Norwegian for "Naked Isle"), founded in 2002 by Gunnar Wiig and Kjetil Jikun. Nøgne Ø's portfolio runs the gamut of European styles, from Belgian-inspired creations such as wit, saison, and tripel, to interpretations of English-born classics like pale ale, IPA, and brown ale. Nøgne Ø has a full calendar of seasonals as well; it's particularly busy during the holiday season with God Jul (Good Yule/Christmas), a dark ale, and Underlig Jul, a spiced ale whose name translates to "Peculiar Christmas." The brewery offers a third Christmas brew called Julesnadder, which is a direct result of Norway's strict alcohol laws—the most stringent of the Nordic region. In order for an alcohol beverage to be sold in supermarkets—where 98 percent of the country's beer is sold—it must be no higher than 4.75 percent ABV. Anything stronger than that must be sold through government-owned liquor stores. Julesnadder clocks in at 4.5 ABV so it can reach a broader market through the mainstream grocery channel. (God Jul and Underlig Jul are 8.5 percent and 6.5 percent ABV, respectively, and can't be sold in grocery stores.)

Sweden

Carlsberg has been spreading the craft love to other parts of Scandinavia, and that includes Sweden. Its most significant contribution to the furtherance of craft brewing occurred in 2014 when the doors of Nya Carnegiebryggeriet (New Carnegie Brewery) opened in the Hammerby neighborhood of Stockholm, Sweden. The brewery represented Brooklyn Brewery's first international operation—a partnership with none other than Carlsberg.

Nya Carnegie beers include Nya Carnegie Kellerbier, Nya Carnegie Amber, a session IPA known as J.A.C.K., Lumens in Tenebris Dark Saison, and Primus Lux Winter Warmer.

The collaboration proved to be just the beginning of a beautiful partnership; barely a year later, Brooklyn and Carlsberg announced a second venture, this time at the E. C. Dahls Brewery in Trondheim, Norway. Dahls was a classic Trondheim brewery founded in 1856, and the Brooklyn-Carlsberg partnership is keeping it alive by updating it for the twenty-first century. In addition to the flagship lager, which has been a local favorite for generations, Brooklyn brewmaster Garrett Oliver oversees a range of craft brews for evolving palates.

Nynashämns Angbryggeri

One of the early adopters of the Swedish craft craze was Nynashämns Angbryggeri, whose doors opened in 1996, just as American craft brewing's first wave was peaking. Its best-selling ale is Bedarö Bitter, an English-style bitter with an international pedigree of influences from the citrusy, piney, Pacific Northwest-born Chinook and Cascade hops to the pale ale, crystal, and wheat malts from English maltsters. It also happens to be the first beer the brewery based in seaside Nynashämn—about an hour's drive from the capital city—ever brewed. A bit on the maltier side is Nynashämns Angbryggeri's Brännskar Brown Ale, an American-style brown that includes chocolate and caramel and a mix of English and American hops.

Omnipollo

Founders Henok Fentie and Karl Grandin took a page out of the book that the founders of Denmark's Mikkeller wrote, embracing the itinerant/gypsy model that left them free to move about the world and work their magic in some of the globe's most renowned brewhouses. Their journey began in 2011, and they have left their indelible mark with products such as the pale ale Mazarin, which the team brewed at Belgium's De Proefbrouwerij. The brewers' residency at De Proefbrouwerij also resulted in Gone, its IPA with American Simcoe and Citra hops. Omnipollo produced it to celebrate the company's third anniversary. The label art features an American one-dollar bill. Fentie and Grandin journeyed to Spain's Cervesera del Montseny to concoct En El Bosque, a mind-blowingly complex mixture of specialty malts, rye, moscovado sugar, a variety of hops, and a bit of Spanish cranberries. They've ventured well beyond Europe as well; Omnipollo's oat-and-wheat-based imperial IPA Fatamorgana, for instance, was born at Maryland's Pub Dog Brewing.

Iceland

It's easy for most non-Europeans to forget that Iceland is among the Nordic countries, as it is so far removed geographically from the Scandinavian peninsula. (It's a good nine hundred miles from its closest Nordic neighbor, Norway.) And until the end of the first decade of the twenty-first century, the otherwise gorgeous, volcanic, and sparsely populated island was really beginning to look like the Land that Beer Forgot. It had its national macro lagers, of course, although for a country of a little over 300,000 people, how "macro" is macro? More people visit Iceland each year than actually live there full time. Viking and Egils were the most recognizable brands; locals and visitors were always sure to find those on draft or in bottles and cans at most corner bars in Reykjavik.

To be fair, we Americans can whine about Prohibition all we want, but most of us weren't even alive for it. In Iceland, however, it wasn't legal to brew conventional beer until 1989. The country fell victim to a temperance movement, not unlike the one that precipitated America's own Eighteenth Amendment, during the same late-nineteenth/early twentieth century time period that such campaigns were active in the United States. (It had the same moral underpinnings as the stateside Prohibitionist movement, but there was a political aspect to it as well; the movement to achieve independence from Denmark was picking up steam at this point, and the Icelandic population associated beer with the Danes.)

Icelandic voters approved, through referendum, a complete ban on alcohol, which went into effect in 1915. The public mood changed a bit, and Iceland lifted the ban in 1933 (the same year Prohibition ended in the United States, by the way), but it was hardly a full repeal. Beer could not exceed 2.25 percent ABV (kombucha usually has more alcohol!) for the next fifty-six years.

So, it's understandable why Iceland was a little late to the craft party; and the island nation has more than made up for it in such a short amount of time.

An early entry was Olvisholt Brugghus, based on an old dairy farm in the southern part of the country. Two farmers working the land in the area teamed up in 2007 to open the brewery. Skjálfti, which means "earthquake" in Icelandic, was the first exposure many Icelanders had to craft beer. The robust golden lager was closer in flavor to traditional Vienna lagers than the continental pilsners to which most were accustomed. It serves as a nice bridge beer into craft, and it came at a time when the country itself was just crossing that bridge.

The name refers to the fact that the farm brewery sits atop the point where the tectonic plates of the European and North American continents converge. A fairly destructive *skjálfti* hit in 2000, damaging the farm. The future brewers, a little more than a half-dozen years later, made lemonade (well, beer).

Nature's mighty power also inspired Olvisholt's imperial stout, Lava. The active volcano Hekla is visible from the brewhouse. The sweet, pitch-black beer is 9.4 percent ABV and was originally brewed to be sold in the Swedish market, but the brewery brought it home as Icelanders developed a taste for bigger beers. (Iceland relies a great deal on export revenue, as its home market is so small.) The line also now includes the balanced Móri red ale, with citrusy hop notes (thanks to the Cascade varietal) and a solid foundation of six types of barley malt and some wheat malt. Finally, there's Freyja, a Belgian-style witbier.

"Einstöck" means "distinctive" in Icelandic, and Einstöck Ölgerd ("ölgerd" being the word for "brewery") earns its name. Marketing-wise, the brewers like to use the hook that the production site is a mere sixty miles south of the Arctic Circle. And why shouldn't they? The water doesn't get much purer than it does there. The water from rain and prehistoric glaciers flows down a mountain and gets filtered through lava fields. But good beer is not just about what you've got, but what you're able to do with it. And Einstöck offers some solid Nordic interpretations of world styles, such as Icelandic Toasted Porter, a rich, robust affair with notes of toffee and dark chocolate and a hue that's as dark as the winter months that far north (it helps that the brew provides a fairly warming sensation). Its true winter seasonal, though, is Icelandic Doppelbock, which is malty, chocolaty, and bursting with flavor. At the time of year when the sun barely sets, Einstöck offers its seasonal Arctic Berry Ale, a witbier with indigenous bilberries picked near the Arctic Circle.

Iceland may historically have had a complicated relationship with Denmark, but those icy relations have thawed for the most part. Danish brewing's favorite son, Mikkel Borg Bjergsø, brought his Mikkeller empire to the island, opening another pub in his rapidly growing international portfolio.

Finland

Finland doesn't immediately come to mind in the context of great beer cultures, but the Finnish have more than a millennium's worth of brewing heritage that puts many other countries' brewing histories to shame.

That history wasn't lost on Dogfish Head founder Sam Calagione, who's made it his mission to resurrect ancient, long-dead styles of beer and pre-beer. In 2008, the Delaware brewery first produced Sahtea, a modern twist on the similarly spelled Sahti, a traditional Finnish beer rooted in the ninth century. Given its pre-hops lineage, brewers relied on a veritable potpourri of spices and herbs to give it a pleasing flavor. Cloves, ginger, cinnamon, and other flora were not off-limits, though juniper berries are usually the stars of the show (as they are in gin, by the way). But perhaps more noteworthy than its ingredients was its production method. The brewers used white-hot river rocks to caramelize the wort. Not one to cut corners, especially where tradition is concerned, Dogfish Head replicated that process when it first produced Sahtea. So distinct is Sahti that it enjoys protected status in Europe.

As for craft beer, Finland had a few hurdles to cross before it developed its own scene. For one thing, brewpubs weren't legal (not an uncommon tale). Many of today's most renowned American brewers had to get their states' laws changed before they could open their own brewpubs. Dogfish Head comes to mind. Sam Calagione had to lobby the Delaware state government to legalize such a business before he could open his pub in the seaside town of Rehoboth. And that was in 1995, the same year, coincidentally, that the Finnish government made it legal.

But that doesn't mean the floodgates opened for craft beer. The country, like the other Nordic nations save for Denmark, still has an uneasy relationship with alcohol. Similar to the situation in Norway, brewers may only sell beer stronger than 4.7 percent ABV in state-owned stores. In order to get their products in grocery stores, most brewers reluctantly play ball and keep their ABVs low.

To add insult to injury, the government has placed smothering restrictions on alcohol marketing. In 2015 Finland enacted sweeping regulations that banned any sort of alcohol advertising involving contests or giveaways. On top of that, the government no longer allowed beer marketers to talk about their products via social media, which has been the bread and butter for craft brewers worldwide. Many have argued that American craft brewing would not be growing nearly as quickly as it has without social media.

Some have found the environment so constricting that they produce primarily for export or they move their operations beyond the Finnish borders entirely. Sori Brewing is one such brewery. The founders Pyry Hurula and Heikki Uotila turned to crowdfunding for their start-up capital. Realizing that they never would grow as quickly as they needed to in order to become a profitable, self-sustaining operation, they decided to move their brewery to Estonia while maintaining their Finnish identity.

Sori does produce a couple of beers below that 4.7 percent ceiling— Out of Office Session IPA and Garden Wit—but the majority of the brewery's efforts are focused on pushing the boundaries of brewing. Sisu, for instance, is an 8 percent ABV double IPA, hopped to the stratosphere with five American varietals. Sisu, incidentally, is a Finnish term for "stoic determination, bravery, resilience, perseverance, and hardiness"—kind of what it takes to get to the bottom of such a big, hoppy brew.

South America

South America, like many other regions of the world, is a tough nut to crack as a beer market. The macro brands have the region in a colossal stranglehold. Each of the major countries on the continent has its own dominant brand to which the locals are extremely loyal. But most of those brands are owned by a single multinational brewing conglomerate. As tied as they may be to their respective homelands, there's still a gargantuan corporate parent that's pulling the strings.

Take Argentina, for instance. The dominant brand in the market is Quilmes, which was founded in 1888 and eventually, as the global market consolidated, became a part of the portfolio of Brazil's AmBev. AmBev and

Belgium's Interbrew merged in 2004 to form InBev, the same company that would go on to acquire Anheuser-Busch four years later to form AB InBev.

Despite a market that favors Goliaths, Davids have been able to emerge across Argentina and other parts of the continent.

Argentina

When anyone thinks of Argentina's great culinary contributions, the first two things to come to mind are steak and wine. Actually, those are usually the only two things to come to mind (okay, on the food side, maybe empanadas, as well). The country's reputation for fine wine is well earned. Malbec is the big varietal coming out of Mendoza—Argentina's Napa—but the region is no slouch when it comes to producing secondary wines like Tempranillo and Cabernet Sauvignon. Rarely, however, does anyone outside of South America think of Argentina as a hotbed of fine beer activity. As unlikely as that may seem, it's not half as unlikely as the part of the country responsible for an outsized chunk of its artisanal brewing. No, it's not cosmopolitan Buenos Aires—though there's plenty of great beer to be found there—but areas in and around Patagonia, the mountainous, snowy, and glacial area near the bottom of the world. It's actually quite logical considering how pure the water is there. There's already a substantial cottage industry of companies bottling its glacier water and just selling that.

Cerveza Beagle

We most likely didn't learn the name Ushuaia in our high school geography classes, but adventurous globetrotters who've stepped foot on Antarctica have more than likely passed through the Patagonian city in Tierra del Fuego at Argentina's southern tip (home to the seaport that's the most direct link to the world's southernmost and most barren continent). Ushuaia is home to Cerveza Beagle, named after the Beagle Channel, which is adjacent to the town. The channel itself was named for Charles Darwin's ship, the HMS Beagle, which spent quite a bit of time on those southern waters doing all kinds of sciency stuff. Cerveza Beagle features such maritime imagery on the labels of beers like Fuegian Red Ale (aka Rojo), Fuegian Cream Stout, and Fuegian Golden Ale (aka Rubia, Spanish for "blonde"). Incidentally, "Fuegian" refers to the inhabitants of Tierra del Fuego.

Cerveceria Blest

The city of Bariloche, in a more northerly region of Patagonia, has a booming artisanal beer scene. The best known among the breweries is Blest, which has operated a brewpub in Bariloche since 1997 and now hits all of the major stylistic notes with offerings such as Blest Bock, Blest Frambuesa (a raspberry-enhanced fruit beer), Blest Scotch Ale, La Cream Stout Blest, and Blest Pilsen (a pilsener). The brewery fully capitalizes on its locale, enticing visitors with its jaw-dropping vistas of the snow-capped Andes.

Chile

Let's not forget that Argentina doesn't have a claim on all of Patagonia; Chile also gets a piece of the region, as well. And, Chile's beer scene definitely gives the rest of South America a run for its money. The latest estimates put the number of Chilean craft breweries at somewhere between 150 and 200. (Some put the number at around 400, but most are so small that they barely register.) That's not a bad number for a country with a population of around 18 million. That's nearly the same number of breweries per capita as the United States.

In Chile, there isn't a trade association specific to craft brewers like there is in a lot of other countries, but a handful of the small players have been joining ACECHI (whose formal name is Asociacion de Productures de Cerveza de Chile), the trade association that used to represent only the large players. The craft producers saw the advantage in aligning with ACECHI as a means of getting laws updated to reflect the country's new brewing landscape, as well as to organize events to promote their industry.

The one thing about the country's small brewers is that they are truly small.

"In the US there tends to be confusion related to the larger breweries (some huge) that are still considered 'craft,' [while] in Chile we have a lot of homebrewers who have set up a 'brewery' as a small family business—they end up getting licensed, so I guess technically they are breweries," reveals Kevin Szot, founder of the Chilean brewery that bears his name. "But sizewise, many are smaller than many American homebrewers."

Homebrewers who go pro—even if only barely—and get licensed to sell beer are typically called nanobreweries. But many of these small family start-ups are more nano than nano.

Breweries of some scale that might fit the always debatable definition of "craft" that are driving the Chilean scene have been subsidiaries of large international breweries and wine makers (famous Chilean Concha y Toro winery bought a stake in the up-and-coming Kross brewery in 2011, for instance).

Still, the entrepreneurial producers have been making a name for themselves. And while Szot likes to say that it's still "1980" in Chile in terms of craft beer development, American breweries at that time were getting zero attention outside of their immediate areas. The world is already starting to notice some of the better brews Chile has to offer. Here are some of the breweries on the global radar.

Szot

The eponymous brewery of founder Kevin Szot—an expat from California who married a Chilean—has bottles that are as much fun to look at as what's inside them is to drink. Lining up its bottles next to one another on a bar is like setting up a mini art gallery. The label designs feature cartoonish illustrations of one-eyed red and yellow monsters (Negra Szot Stout), a horned individual in a tiny top hat and tie holding a mug of beer (Amber Ale), and a big-eyed human face that evokes a German expressionist painting (Barley Wine).

Cerveceria Mahina Rapa Nui

There's remote and then there's Easter Island remote. That's right, the island with the big stone faces—officially a part of Chile, though 2,300 miles of ocean separates it from the mainland—has its own brewery. Cerveceria Mahina Rapa Nui keeps things simple, both light and dark. Its limited offerings include Mahina Pale Ale, which adheres pretty closely to the English originals. Mahina Export Stout is the creamy, roasty counterpoint to the pale. Mahina's brews have taken on white whale status among some intrepid travelers, primarily because of its exotic, hard-to-reach birthplace. But provenance is only part of their appeal; they're good beers in their own right.

Cervecera Del Puerto

Seafaring iconography (pirates and such) dominates the trade dress of Cervecera Del Puerto, founded in 2003 in Valparaiso—a city that's enjoying a brewing boom unto itself. The label imagery reflects the history of the Pacific coastal city. Local stories tell of the very frequent attacks from maritime marauders, and the product names themselves celebrate those villainous characters. There's Barba Roja (Spanish for "Red Beard"), a reddish amber ale, and Barba Negra ("Black Beard"), a porter. (There's also Barba Negra Extra Fuerte ["Extra Strong"], which falls into the "robust porter" category.) There's no face on its Rubia ("Blond"), but the yellow label features a faint image of a seventeenth-century ship caught in some pretty rough waters.

Brazil

When the Brewers Association publishes the annual stats from its Export Development Program (EDP), Brazil is a perennial growth driver, frequently outstripping the growth rate for craft beer exports worldwide.

There's a good reason for that. Not only is Brazil a mega market for beer—it's the birthplace of AmBev, which became the dominant component of InBev and, later, AB InBev. But, like most beer-soaked countries, consumer tastes evolved, and they craved something more despite the best efforts of the dominant macros to make the beverage a commodity.

And, it's also a sign of the artisanal sector's maturity and staying power when the multinationals start taking an interest in its key players. On two separate occasions six months apart in 2015, AB InBev—under its local AmBev banner—acquired Brazilian craft brewers Cervejaria Colorado and Cervejaria Wäls.

Colorado was among the first movers in the local scene, setting up shop in 1995. And, while it's common for international craft brewers to emulate the North American brewers credited with starting the movement, Colorado went out of its way to make the concept its own and infuse its products with a distinct Brazilian-ness. Colorado does make a pilsner, for example, but Cauim, its interpretation of the world's most popular style, includes cassava (aka mandioca) in its recipe. The brewery's Appia is a traditional wheat beer with a not-so-traditional ingredient: Brazilian orange honey, or, as it's known locally, Mel de Laranjeira. Colorado brews its porter with Brazilian-grown coffee. Then there's Vixnu, a double IPA brewed with traditional Brazilian candy sugar.

Cervejaria Wäls, based in Belo Horizonte, Brazil, launched four years after Colorado and was equally intent on giving its brews local flavor. Aging in oak chips infused with Brazil's native spirit, cachaça (distilled from the juice of sugar cane), gives the brewery's Belô Ipê some earthy aromatics not traditionally found in the style. Belô Ipê impressed the judges of the 2014 World Beer Cup enough to earn it a silver medal. However, it was Belô São Francisco, Wäls's take on the Belgian dubbel style, that really wowed the judging panel; they gave it a gold that same year. São Francisco's little bit of Braziliana comes in the form of local raisins.

The innovations of Cervejarias Colorado and Wäls likely will benefit from enhanced visibility and broader distribution thanks to their acquisition by such a global giant. And they won't be the last, especially when you consider some of the other world class breweries operating in Brazil.

Cervejaria Bodebrown

Founded in 2009, Cervejaria Bodebrown is more than just a brewery garnering international acclaim; it also happens to be a brewing school—the first of its kind in its home country. Renowned industry pros teach courses on beer production, as well as tasting and food pairing. Among its award-winning offerings is Perigosa (literally "Dangerous," and for good reason), an überhoppy double IPA that's a bold 9.2 percent ABV. Bodebrown also attracted a fan from Escondido, California; in 2013 it collaborated with Stone Brewing Company on another creation within the India pale ale family. Cacau, as its name suggests, has quite a local twist: it was brewed with Brazilian cacao nibs. It was the toast of IPA Day. (Yes, that's a real international "holiday.")

Cervejaria Jupiter

The brewery with the godly name has most of the stylistic bases covered—IPA, pale ale, porter, Vienna lager—but it's particularly noteworthy for the limited releases that have quite the kick. Jupiter teamed up with De Cabron, a leading Brazilian hot sauce maker for Chipotle Porter. In addition to the usual dark chocolate notes common in porters, the use of smoked malt gives it the same smokiness for which the eponymous chili pepper is known. The Da Cabron partnership didn't end there. The relationship also produced Habanero Dubbel. Few breweries think to infuse a Belgian-style dubbel with habanero peppers (or any kind of spicy peppers, for that matter), but the pairing really works.

Cervejaria Seasons

No need to translate too many of the beer names here. Much like the brewery's moniker, Cervejaria Seasons prefers to use English words for its portfolio, which debuted in 2010, and those words make for some fairly offbeat labels. Green Cow is the name it chose for its IPA (partly because spent grain from the brewing process makes good cattle feed, and the cows return the favor by fertilizing the soil in which the hops and barley grow). The cow is the brewery's mascot appearing in its logo and on its various labels. Another of its creations is Basilicow, a witbier brewed with fresh basil leaves.

Like Bodebrown, Seasons has done its fair share of collaborating with California breweries. It teamed with Green Flash Brewery on Holy Cow, a West Coast-style IPA. Despite the cartoonish bovine's visual ubiquity, not all of Seasons' beers have the word "cow" in their name. There's Funhouse, a Belgian-style blond that was the first beer Seasons produced.

Cervejaria Landel

Landel is a Brazilian brewery that didn't just take a cue from the American craft brewing revolution; it seems to have the pulse of its *evolution* as well. As session beers have been all the rage in some sectors of US craft brewing, Landel adapted that concept for its home market. Its lower-ABV offerings include American Session IPA (4 percent ABV!), which has the requisite citrusy US-born hops, and Session Tripel, a style that rarely gets a session-able makeover (and when it does, it's often called a Single, at least in the States). The drinker gets all of the spicy, fruity aromatics they've come to expect from a tripel but experiences a much lower, 5 percent ABV. Landel also brews a dry-hopped German Pils that amps up the bitterness on the global style.

Given the size of Brazil's population—200 million plus—and Brazilians' unquenchable thirst for beer, Brazil hosts a craft culture that commands attention of the entire world. It's definitely one country to watch very closely.

The Brewmerang Effect

What Goes Around Comes Around for Old-World Brewing Traditions

Before the craft brewing movement reached its tipping point around the turn of the millennium, American beer, on the world stage, was considered a joke. Usually that joke went something like this: "Q: How is American beer like making love in a canoe? A: Because it's f*@king close to water."

The macro brewers not only had succeeded in growing their market share by either acquiring or eliminating weaker competitors outright, but they achieved a more dubious goal: total commoditization of US beer.

It wasn't all some nefarious scheme; part of it was responding to the realities of the market. Prohibition, unfortunately, did a number on American palates. After repeal of the law, consumers weren't looking for particularly flavor-forward beers. Whether they knew it or not, they were looking for something f*@king close to water, and the brewers were happy to oblige. In the process, their products became the laughing stock of the world, a reputation that would take generations to undo. There's only so much lack of flavor the public can stomach, and eventually consumers craved something more. And craft brewers answered the call.

Year zero for American craft beer was technically 1965, when Fritz Maytag, heir to the Maytag fortune, bought San Francisco's failing Anchor Brewery. After some fine-tuning, he reintroduced drinkers to a nineteenth-century style known as "steam beer," which was considerably more flavorful than the light lagers of the day. The style had originated in California and could, therefore, be considered quintessentially American.

However, in the next two decades, those who followed Maytag looked abroad for their inspiration. When Jack McAuliffe started New Albion brewing in the mid-'70s, he did so with an eye toward the English ales he had come to love during his military tenure overseas. A few years later when Ken Grossman launched Sierra Nevada Brewing Co., its flagship became the gold standard for the nascent American pale ale style, though its ancestry is decidedly British.

Other English styles, such as porters and stouts, soon became popular additions to many a brewer's portfolio.

Possibly the most significant tradition Americans inherited from the Brits involved a certain hop-forward ale originally brewed for soldiers and sailors stationed in one of the Empire's farthest-flung colonies: India pale ale.

Continental Europe has done its fair share for the late nineteenth-/ early twentieth-century American brewing scene. Beer geeks worldwide have exalted Belgium for its diversity of styles dating back generations. Belgian or Belgian-style ales are the ones that draw many drinkers into a world much larger than the one to which they've grown accustomed. Some are attracted to the high ABVs, others to the depth of flavors not typically associated with macro beer. The common reaction from those who know only mass-produced lager is, "Wow, I didn't know beer could taste like that."

Brewers themselves fell in love with the Western European nation, as well, and have built entire businesses around its traditions. In its two decades of existence, Portland, Maine's Allagash has produced Belgian styles almost exclusively. Its flagship product, Allagash White, is an award-winning American interpretation of the Belgian witbier; when it launched in 1995, few on this side of the Atlantic had encountered such a product.

Of course, one of the largest craft brewers in the country, New Belgium—which predates Allagash by about four years—took its name from the nation that influenced founders Kim Jordan and Jeff Lebesch. Its flagship, Fat Tire, draws its inspiration from Belgian amber ales along the lines of Antwerp's De Koninck. The Fort Collins, Colorado company also has ventured into Abbey-style, tripel, and Flemish sour territory, becoming one of the first to introduce American consumers to the breadth of flavors indigenous to the Benelux country. The brewery has since branched out to incorporate the likes of IPAs, pale ales, and pilsners into its repertoire, but its heart remains in Belgium.

But the first European country most think of when someone utters the word "beer" is Germany. Few countries have had as great an influence on global brewing cultures than good old Deutschland. Indeed, the Germans, for the most part, are responsible for globalizing pilsner, even though it's of Czech origin. (Out of deference to the Czechs, many brewers outside the Czech Republic label it as "pils," reserving the whole word for its creators—many, but not all).

Many craft beer newbies (drinkers, not brewers) dive head first into the big, bold styles like the überhoppy IPAs or the high-ABV Belgian tripels and quadrupels and frequently turn their noses up at the more nuanced creations coming out of Germany. (It's more out of insecurity than anything else; some believe the beers they drink have to hurt in order for the drinker to achieve true craft cred.) Fortunately, the pendulum seems to be swinging in the other direction. IPA is still the No. 1 craft style and not going anywhere any time soon, but the fact that such a thing as the "session IPA" now exists speaks to a broader trend toward less over-the-top offerings. The sessionability movement also has encouraged hardcore beer geeks to give classic German styles a second look; some craft brewers have even dedicated their portfolios exclusively to German-inspired brews.

The Germans—as well as the Brits, the Belgians, and the Czechs—seem to be returning the favor. Many of the classic styles born in Europe and adopted by US brewers have evolved into truly American iterations, using Pacific Northwestern hops known for their bold, brash, and citrusy character, versus the more nuanced nature of the bitter flowers grown across the pond. Additionally, US artisans have pushed the stylistic boundaries, experimenting well beyond the guidelines European brewers had established across generations. In the process, Americans have invented entirely new stylistic categories that have piqued the interest of even the most rigidly traditional beer producers.

If you had visited Belgium in, say, 2005, it would've been a pretty safe bet that everything in bottles or on tap from local producers—save for the macro-produced, mass-marketed lagers like Stella Artois or Jupiler—would have been a traditional Belgian style: witbier, amber, tripel, dubbel, Flemish sour, lambic, gueuze, saison, etc. If you were to travel there today you'd still be able to find all of those styles and more in great abundance, but you'd also encounter some curious new additions to a pub's beer list. More often than not those brews have a pronounced hop character, an attribute one wouldn't typically find in Belgium in years prior. That's not to say Belgian brewers didn't use hops. Of course they did. In fact they've been known to grow a few varieties. But there really wasn't a quintessentially Belgian style one would call *hoppy*. Poperings Hommel Bier ("hommel" means "hop" in the Flemish dialect) was really the only prominent brand with a pronounced hop profile pre-2005. And Brouwerij van Eecke, which produces the brand, is actually situated adjacent to a hop farm, so it was no surprise that, since its launch in the early '80s, it's contained a generous helping of the bitter little flowers.

The explosion of the US craft beer onto the global stage has given Flemish and Walloon brewers a taste for hops, especially those not-so-nuanced American varieties. As a result, hybrid styles have emerged; no one in a million years would have predicted a "Belgo IPA" would become a thing, but here we are.

Duvel Moortgat is one of the largest predominantly family-owned breweries in all of Belgium, known primarily for Duvel golden ale, which it launched back in the early 1920s. It's since acquired some of the most venerable brands throughout the country—DeKoninck and Liefmans among them—and in some cases rescued them from extinction. It also now owns three US craft breweries, including Ommegang, which it bought in 2003, and Boulevard, which it purchased a decade later. In 2015, it added Paso Robles, California's Firestone Walker to its portfolio.

In 2007 Duvel launched Duvel Triple Hop to appeal to palates that had grown fond of the hop-forward styles popularized by American brewers. Duvel proper's recipe includes two types of hops, but Triple Hop, as the name suggests, adds a third. But each year, the variety used changes, creating an annual vintage of sorts—no two years are exactly alike. Triple Hop also is higher in alcohol content with an ABV of 9.5 percent versus Duvel's 8.5 percent.

Not too far geographically from Duvel Moortgat is Het Anker, the Mechelen, Belgium-based brewery famous for its malty Gouden Carolus line that includes an original brown ale, an amber, and a tripel. In 2008, the company took a turn toward the bitter when it unveiled Hopsinjoor, a golden 8 percent-ABV brew that uses five different types of hops to achieve its signature bite.

You're probably noticing a trend here. Not only are classic Belgian brewers hopping up their ales, they're making sure everyone knows it by including some variation of the word "hop" in their beers' names.

Castle Brewery Van Honsebrouck, maker of the Kasteel range, kept things as simple as possible in 2013 when it released a brew it called . . . wait for it . . . Kasteel Hoppy. Strength-wise, it's on par with an average IPA at about 6.5 percent. And though the bitter flavor profile might draw its inspiration from the American movement, Kasteel Hoppy keeps things fairly local by using only Belgian-grown hops.

Now, brewers in the United Kingdom are the ones who created the IPA style in the first place. Surely there's nothing America has that the UK wants in the way of hop-forward beers, right? Wrong. In barely a half decade, a British craft brewing movement of its own has begun to bloom

and flourish. In the beginning, the few craft/micro brewers that were starting up adhered, for the most part, to classic English ale styles and methods.
They were traditional cask-conditioned "real" ales.

The Campaign for Real Ale (CAMRA) is still very aggressive in preserving real ale and the traditional British pub, but many of the newcomers to
the UK's craft scene since about 2010 have been breaking away from that
tradition. Their offerings frequently have more in common with the
American descendants of their country's signature styles than they do with
those styles themselves. Sample an IPA at one of their tasting rooms and it's
going to be a closer approximation of an American IPA than the one that
originated centuries earlier on their home turf.

One of those brewers, Camden Town, often goes out of its way to produce decidedly un-English beers. Its year-round products include Camden
Pils, which is more of an American riff on the lager style born in Bohemia.

Exterior tanks at Camden Town Brewery.

It's an unfiltered pilsner with "a good amount" of American hop varietals, including Zeus, Simcoe, and Centennial. Its pale ale has less in common with the pales conceived in Burton upon Trent than it has with those of Northern Californian extraction. The brewery, which was acquired by AB InBev in 2016, says it's "like the Queen wearing dirty sneakers"—even the word "sneakers" is an American one, as Brits are more likely to call them "trainers"—and is traditionally British with a "rock star twist of American hops," including Cascade, Columbus, Amarillo, and Citra.

Another is The Kernel Brewery in the south London district of Bermondsey. It brews different iterations of its pale ales and IPAs, including various combinations of American-grown Centennial, Amarillo, Mosaic, and Simcoe hops (as well as the Australian Galaxy variety, which exhibits a lot of the citrusy, passion-fruity characteristics of many American hops) for flavor notes more reminiscent of brews from West Coast producers in the US.

It's a phenomenon that's not limited to England. The best-known of the new breed of Scottish breweries that have sprung up in the past decade, BrewDog, thumbs its nose at tradition—particularly British tradition. Its founders, James Watt and Martin Dickie, launched the operation in 2007 as an alternative to not only the macro industrial lagers that had come to dominate Britain's (and the world's) market, but the "stuffy ales" of the sort that CAMRA has fought for nearly a half century to preserve. Don't expect to find BrewDog's portfolio at a real ale festival—it doesn't do the whole cask thing. What it does create are products that are very much in line with the brands that made American craft beer world famous in the first place. BrewDog fancies its flagship IPA as more of an act of rebellion than a beer. It even bears the name Punk IPA to drive that point home. In its own write-up on the brand, it describes Punk as a beverage that's "layered with New-World hops to create an explosion of tropical fruit and an all-out riot of grapefruit, pineapple, and lychee."

That "New World," of course, is predominantly North America, and the hops in question are the likes of Chinook, Ahtanum, Amarillo, Cascade, Simcoe, and the lone New Zealander of the bunch, Nelson Sauvin.

In the marketing materials for its Dead Pony Pale Ale, BrewDog pays its "hop-flecked homage to the glory of the Pacific Coast" with an "insane amount" of US hops.

As noted previously, another distinctly American concept is the "extreme" beer, those that turn up core components—malt, hop, and/or alcohol content—to eleven and throw subtlety and balance to the wind.

BrewDog's own foray into extreme territory wasn't so much an homage as it was a brazen act act of one-upmanship (or, more accurately, ten-upmanship).

The most famous of BrewDog's headline-grabbing stunts was what it called The End of History, a 55 percent ABV (!) brew that it packaged in a very limited number of bottles "swallowed" by taxidermied squirrels and stoats. It also released the (slightly) less potent Sink the Bismarck, a quadruple IPA (which wasn't actually a thing at the time) that contained four times the hops and was frozen four times to concentrate the alcohol to push the ABV to 41 percent. Those looking for a little more moderation in the extremity could instead drink Tactical Nuclear Penguin, a 32 percent ABV imperial stout. It's no exaggeration, therefore, to conclude that Belgium and the UK have wholeheartedly thrown their arms around the US beer scene that many of their own brewing traditions have inspired. Evolution is a good thing, and anything a particular country's industry can do to remain relevant among modern consumers and their ever-changing palates will only help ensure its longevity.

However, Germany—the first country that comes up in relation to "beer" in a game of word-association 999 out of 1,000 times—is probably pretty immune to any American influence, isn't it? After all, Germans are the ones who came up with the Reinheitsgebot, welcome tens of thousands of international pilgrims to Oktoberfest each fall, and ultimately globalized the one style that most people have come to identify as "beer."

Think again.

Since around the start of the second decade of the twenty-first century, Deutschland's brewing culture has begun to undergo a transformation— not among the macro producers who control most of the market share (not to mention most of the drinking establishments), but in the form of an emerging micro-tier. And they're not sticking to helles, pils, dunkels, and weiss biers, either.

Berlin in particular has become a hotbed of craft beer activity, from its fledgling producers offering their own interpretations of American-style pales and IPAs, along with other US-by-way-of-England standbys like porters and stouts, to the budding gastropub scene pairing culinary delights with local malt-and-hop concoctions that are unapologetically un-German.

Increasingly, the European Beer Star Awards—organized jointly by Privaten Brauereien Deutschland, Privaten Brauereien Bayern (Private breweries of Germany and the German state of Bavaria, respectively), and the association of small and independent breweries of Europe (SIB)—has become a showcase for America's might as a beer-making nation. And the event is held in Bavaria!

Exporting American craft beer to the rest of the world has become a collective $100 million business for the small US producers, and this business jumped 35.7 percent in 2014, according to the Brewers Association, the trade organization that represents the American craft segment. What's more, exports to Western Europe—which, as previously noted, has done just fine with its own beer—slightly outpaces overall export volume growth with a 37 percent gain. (Brazil has been the biggest growth market for those American products, surging 64 percent.)

And Germans have been perfectly happy to acknowledge the New-World influence on its younger generation of brewers. Visit the gastropub Das Meisterstück in Berlin and you'd immediately notice that the most prominent individual on its de facto wall of fame is not some venerable Bavarian beer maker, but Garrett Oliver, the vice president and brewmaster of the Brooklyn Brewery. Oliver has earned his place in the pantheon of worldwide beer industry personalities. His 2003 tome *The Brewmaster's Table* is largely credited with accelerating the beer/food pairing conversation in the United States and abroad.

What we're seeing is the *brewmerang* effect in its purest form: Old-world beer-producing nations that played a hugely significant role in the development of America's craft beer revolution are now finding inspiration in the same country they had inspired in the first place. It's the ultimate "Thank You/You're Welcome."

The Rise of Beer Tourism

Old-World and New-World beer cultures have plenty in common and one typically influences the other—and that's a two-way street. One particular attribute the classic and new wave beer countries share is that their brewing scenes have been quite the travel magnets. Many a hops-and-malt aficionado will opt for à la carte itineraries, identifying their favorite beer towns, breweries, and bars to visit and designing a complex map charting their circuitous course. As any avid traveler will tell you (this writer's hand is raised), things don't always go according to plan. Most cross-city, cross-country, and cross-continental crawls often prove too ambitious. And then there are always the unexpected twists and turns. Those are a huge part of the travel experience and add to the adventure.

Regardless of whether you're traveling alone, with friends, or a significant other, or as part of group, the planning aspect can be incredibly stressful, especially when it means having to find places that don't lend themselves to being found.

The rise in beercations has created an entire subindustry of companies and individuals that design and lead the ultimate tasting journeys—for travelers, not for tourists (there's a very big distinction).

It's easy enough to put together a list of all the hotspots to hit on a tour of Belgium. Cantillon? Check. 't Brugs Beertje? Check. Delirium Café? Ditto. But finding all of the beery nooks and crannies throughout the country takes practice and repeat visits. Not everyone has the time or money for that. That's when it's time to leave it to the experts.

One of the most prominent tour companies is Bon Beer Voyage, the creation of Boynton Beach, Florida-based beer-loving husband and wife (and long-time chiropractors) Ruth Berman and Mike Arra. Ruth's the CEO and BBB (Brains Beyond the Beer), and Mike's the CBO (Chief Beer Officer). Their CVs combine the best of both worlds: extensive beer experience (Mike's the beer guide and tasting instructor; Ruth's a Certified Beer Server through the Cicerone Program) and a couple of decades of travel industry expertise (they're both accredited travel agents).

"I was doing travel on the side for years," Berman reveals. "I was putting together trips for other doctors and friends, high-end cruises and hotels. Mike was way into craft beer and we had the idea that we were going to do something [with beer]. People were doing travel for wine all the time."

The couple were on a wine cruise on a barge through France, visiting a lot of hit-or-miss destinations, when they realized they could improve on the barge tour concept and apply it to beer. Thus their two signature excursions were born: an eight-day adventure through the canals and other connective bodies of water between Amsterdam and the picturesque Belgian city of Bruges/Brugge, and another journey of similar length through Belgium and France.

Attendees eat and sleep on the barge. There's always a highly skilled chef onboard to craft dishes based on the local cuisine. Brewers frequently come onboard to host beer pairing dinners.

One of the key selling points for traveling via barge versus bus is that the trip feels a little less whirlwind.

"When you get on the boat, you're unpacked and go play for a week," Berman points out. "Otherwise, you're packing and unpacking when you're going from place to place. We do that when we have to, but it's a lot nicer to walk downstairs to the breakfast area and not worry, 'Where am I going today? Is my battery charged on my camera?'"

And when the travelers disembark, they're not just hanging out in open-to-the-public brewery tasting rooms and visitors' centers. They're getting the full VIP treatment, enjoying access to experiences you won't find in any tourist book or brochure.

"We try to do something different," Berman notes. "A lot of times I have brewers or beer writers on my tours and they don't need to hear four times in one day how beer is made. Yeah, you can talk a little about the process, but realize a lot of people are doing this themselves. Tell us what's unique about your brewery."

At one of the breweries on the Netherlands itinerary, the group got to attend a master class with a chocolatier, pairing the fancy confections with the beer producer's best brews.

"We're very foodie-oriented," Berman says. "Aside from chefs onboard, we try to do at least one beer-paired meal off the ship."

One such dinner was the stuff of bucket lists. The Rodenbach brewery hosted the group for an unforgettable dinner in the cellar that houses all of the foeders—those large wooden vats in which Belgian sour beers mature. Candelabras illuminated the event.

"What's cool about it is we're going to make you go home and say, 'We tasted from the tanks,'" she says.

Sometimes the excursions are so off the beaten path that it's an adventure in itself trying to reach them by conventional land-based transportation. On one trip to a remote cheese farm, the access roads were so tight that the tour operators had to get off the shuttle bus and knock on a few doors to get people to move their cars out of the street so the bus could pass. But it was well worth the headache because the group got a one-of-a-kind tour and tasting with a small family farmer who made all of the cheese by hand.

"The people we visit are very passionate about what they do," Berman adds.

The expeditions aren't limited to Europe. Some of the greatest adventures are of a smaller scale and much closer to home. Bon Beer runs a series of "Beer Safaris"—weekend tours through cities like Asheville, Washington, D.C., Tampa, and St. Augustine (close to Berman's and Arra's neck of the woods).

Participants on a February 2010 Safari through Tampa got to be among the first to drink at Cigar City Brewing's just-completed tasting room.

The American trips aren't limited to the Safari weekends. One of Bon Beer's most recent creations is the weeklong Great California Beer Rush—an intense journey from San Diego all the way up to Santa Rosa, north of San Francisco—during which participants hit up twenty of the state's and the country's best breweries and brewpubs along the way. The stops along this route read like a who's who of modern American brewing: Stone, Lagunitas, Russian River, Ballast Point, Alesmith, and Green Flash, to name but a few.

Bon Beer also organizes custom beer tours for folks looking for an even more exclusive opportunity to explore and drink with family and friends with a specially tailored itinerary. Berman and Arra also have reached the point in their venture that other less beer-savvy travel companies are contracting them to develop tours.

All of the trips, from California to Florida to Belgium and beyond, come together as the result of some very exhaustive hands-on research from the Bon Beer team. Before they add any location to their tours, they always try them on for size.

"The trips have to be the trips I want to be on," Berman concludes. "If I can't wait to bring people here, it goes on the itinerary."

14

The Dynamics of Beer Distribution

The Three-Tier System, Franchise Laws, and the Sometimes Bumpy Route to Market

If there's one lesson we can all take away from Prohibition, it's this: with great power comes great irresponsibility. At the beginning of the twentieth century, the US alcohol industry was like one big party. The beer business in particular was at the top of its game, with thousands of breweries nationwide cranking out millions of barrels of the stuff. And it wasn't too hard to sell what they produced because they had ownership stakes in—or outright ownership of—the taverns that put their products the hands of consumers. This "tied-house" system is one of the elements that precipitated the industry's downfall. The landscape was so competitively cutthroat that the brewers would push their beers through by any means necessary, with little regard for the public's well-being or common decency. And the bars were beholden to them, so the proprietors of those establishments had no choice but to carry out the brewers' will.

These abuses only emboldened the dry movement, which, by the end of the century's second decade, finally got its way.

Flash forward fourteen years. The long national nightmare has ended and America is ready for legal alcohol once more. But wet advocates who fought long and hard to leave Prohibition in the rearview mirror were determined to ensure that it wouldn't happen again. That meant the now-legitimate industry needed to learn how to behave itself. One of the safeguards against the shenanigans of the past was a ban on tied houses.

The Twenty-first Amendment repealing "The Noble Experiment" gave the states the authority to regulate the sale and distribution of alcoholic beverages within their borders. It laid the groundwork for the modern three-tier system of alcohol distribution—the three tiers being (1) brewers/importers, (2) distributors, and (3) retailers/bars/restaurants. The structure has maintained the balance of power through a set of checks and balances ever since. In theory.

No regulatory framework is perfect, and the three-tier system definitely has its share of detractors. Not a day goes by when a small brewer isn't griping about the system. But some of their more seasoned peers grudgingly acknowledge it's a necessary, though considerably flawed, evil.

There's barely ever been a time when the system wasn't lopsided in favor of one of the tiers. In the years immediately following the repeal of the law, the main consideration was keeping the brewers at bay. It was their virtual omnipotence in the decades prior to the ratification of the Eighteenth Amendment (the one that established Prohibition) that got the nation into that nearly decade-and-a-half-long mess in the first place, and America certainly wasn't going to allow them to hold most of the cards.

Six decades later, the brewers really weren't the ones to be concerned about anymore. In the waning years of the twentieth century, retail became the dominant tier in the three-level equation—obviously not small mom-and-pop establishments, of which there were fewer and fewer, but the big box/club stores (Costco and its ilk) and the mega mass-merchandisers (Walmart, Target, and others—well, mostly Walmart). Their market hegemony afforded them unprecedented resources and lobbying muscle that essentially has enabled them to mold the marketplace to their liking.

As the bottom tier consolidated its power, another dynamic was playing out in tandem: top-tier consolidation. Medium-size breweries got scooped up by large ones or simply went out of business. By the 1990s, three companies dominated the US market, with one of them lording over the other two. Anheuser-Busch seized nearly half of the market by that point. Miller Brewing Company, then an operating unit of Phillip Morris (which acquired the Milwaukee-based brewer in 1969) was a distance second. Coors was the able-bodied No. 3. In 2002, Miller ceased to be an American-owned company when South African Breweries purchased it and formed SABMiller. Coors followed suit three years later when it merged with Canada's Molson Brewing Co., and two years after that SABMiller and Molson Coors combined their US businesses in a joint venture. For the next three years, Anheuser-Busch tried to exploit its competitors' foreign ownership as their Achilles' heels—that is, until it joined their ranks in 2008. InBev, the already massive conglomerate that emerged from the combination of Belgium's Interbrew and Brazil's AmBev, completed what was arguably the

Retail beer aisles showcase much more diversity than ever before.

most significant transaction of the modern beer age when it bought Budweiser's St. Louis parent for a cool $46 billion.

As this was happening, craft brewers were regaining their moment after a leveling off in the mid-'90s (when they were still, for the most part, called microbrewers). By 2003, craft volume was growing in the low to mid single digits and accounted for about 2 percent of the overall US beer market. By the end of that decade, that volume was in the double digits. By 2015, craft had achieved more than 12 percent beer share (and about 20 percent of the industry's total revenue). Craft brewers hope to reach 20 percent share by 2020 (provided that the AB InBevs of the world don't keep acquiring them, but that's another story entirely).

The small brewers and the big megas rarely have been on the same page about anything, and that includes distribution. The three-tier system prevents brewers and importers from owning distributors and retailers, but that doesn't mean they haven't found other ways to navigate around it. In the mid-'90s—not-so-coincidentally at the same moment the initial craft/micro-brewing movement was plateauing—Anheuser-Busch launched its notorious "100 percent share of mind" initiative, through which it demanded that distributors carrying its products carry ONLY its products. A-B was the only macro to impose such a mandate. It was actually fairly common for Miller and Coors products to be in the same distribution houses, which made it that much easier when they ultimately formed the MillerCoors JV in 2007.

Craft brewers whose brands were in A-B wholesale houses in the '90s were unceremoniously dumped thanks to August Busch IV's mandate. So, even though A-B technically didn't *own* its distributors, it proved that the word "ownership" can have many other shades of meaning.

Small brewers who struggled to gain or regain distribution had very little recourse beyond going out of business or self-distribution, and the latter was only a possibility in states that permitted self-distribution. As of this writing, thirty-four states allow small producers to distribute their own products. There's usually a cap on the volume eligible for self-distribution, otherwise it risks running afoul of the Twenty-first Amendment. That ceiling varies from state to state; in some states a brewer can distribute up to 25,000 barrels per year, while in others the number is 60,000, etc. For some perspective, Anheuser-Busch produces in the neighborhood of 100 *million*-plus barrels annually.

Some craft brewers have found considerable success launching separate distribution subsidiaries. Escondido, California's Stone Brewing, best known among mainstream consumers for its Arrogant Bastard brand, is a textbook case on how to run a craft distributorship. Not only does it distribute its own portfolio in its local market, but it's also a wholesaler for some thirty-five brands produced by other brewers. Like most craft operators that have self-distributed, it wasn't by design but by necessity that Stone Distributing Company came into being.

Stone Brewing launched in what was probably the worst year for the burgeoning craft segment: 1996, the year that A-B announced its share-of-mind scheme and *Consumer Reports* ran a pretty damning exposé of microbrewed beer (many say at the behest of A-B). Over the next couple of years more brewers were going out of business than were going into it. (But in a lot of ways, this was a blessing in disguise because the ones that folded, by and large, were those motivated by a misguided get-rich-quick mentality, making product of highly questionable quality.)

At that time it was next to impossible for a small brand to gain distribution at a house dominated by the large brewers. So Stone and many others took matters into their own hands.

On the opposite coast, Boston's Harpoon Brewery launched Harpoon Distributing Co. to move its own products in its home market. And, in 2015, it announced it was taking on brands from other producers, primarily those that were new to the greater Boston market.

The idea behind self-distribution is to build a presence in one's home market that is robust enough to attract the attention of distributors there and in other metro areas and states when it comes time to expand. But that doesn't mean a brewer's problems are over when it signs on the dotted line with a major wholesaler. If it happens to be in a state with ironclad franchise laws, its problems might just be beginning.

In states with strong franchise laws, it's extremely difficult—often impossible—for a brewer to end its relationship with a distributor. Let's say a brewer feels the distributor is not putting enough support behind its brand in the market and the brand is suffering for it. Meanwhile, here's another wholesaler down the road willing to more closely align its efforts with the brewer's expectations. If it's a franchise state, the brewer and its prospective new distribution partner are out of luck. The distributor currently carrying the brands pretty much owns them in its region until the end of time and doesn't have to let them go. Those brands could be doing little more than collecting dust in the distributor's warehouse, but the wholesaler still refuses to let them go. If it sounds fairly draconian, that's because it is.

Franchise laws are not a product of the repeal of Prohibition. Their existence in various states dates back only to the early '70s—a full four decades after ratification of the Twenty-first Amendment. At the time, distributors were on pretty shaky ground. There were only forty-odd breweries in the country at the time and around 5,000 distributors. These largely family-owned wholesale operations often depended on the brands of a single brewery for 100 percent of their business. To avoid the risk of overnight bankruptcy, distributors sought legal safeguards within their states to prevent brewers from suddenly pulling their products and moving them to another distribution house.

The landscape has changed considerably in the forty years since. There are now close to 5,000 breweries in the US—99 percent of those are defined as "craft brewers"—and the distribution tier has consolidated down to include barely one-fifth as many wholesalers as had been operating at the dawn of the franchise law era. Consolidation begets consolidation. As brewers on the top tier and retailers on the bottom tier M&A'd their way to greater power, so did the wholesalers on the middle tier. It was their only means of survival when they were being squeezed by their trading partners on either end.

One of the byproducts of consolidation has been an influx of an unprecedented number of new SKUs—"stock keeping units," which is distribution-speak for "individual brands or packaging formats that take up space in a warehouse and need to be delivered"—into a wholesaler's operation. (SKU is such an ugly acronym, one to be used sparingly.) Add that to the tidal wave of new products coming from those thousands (and counting) of new breweries. And those breweries' brands aren't finding it as hard to get distributors interested in their brands as they had in the late '90s/early 2000s. Between 2005 and 2007, distributors en masse started to find religion about craft. That's around the time macro beer volume started to flatten and decline and it became harder and harder for distributors to make a profit. And that contrasted immensely with the "good old days." Selling such iconic, large-scale brands during the first four or five decades after Prohibition had been a license to print money for distributors. Then it became an incredible struggle to squeeze a couple pennies' worth of margin out of a case of Budweiser or Miller Lite. It was all about pushing as much volume as possible and that meant massive capital investments in larger delivery fleets, warehouse expansion, and automation to move cases as quickly and efficiently as possible. Though craft brands account for significantly smaller volume than their mass-marketed counterparts, they're sold at a considerably higher price point, meaning greater profit potential for the distributors. They can make more money from products that take up a lot less space on their trucks, delivering to retailers to sell to consumers drinking less but drinking better (and willing to pay a couple of extra bucks on a six-pack).

During that period in the mid-aughts, the dynamic shifted to one where distributors were actively courting craft brewers. Larger wholesalers even launched specialty divisions to deal with the artisanal segment, as maintaining and selling craft beer requires a certain degree of TLC and a specially trained sales team.

For every distributor crossing every 't' and dotting every 'i' with its craft portfolio, there were a handful of "brand collectors"—those who wanted to see what "this craft thing is all about" and gain bragging rights that were more about the quantity than the quality of their craft brands. That created a scenario where there were more SKUs (there's that acronym again) than the distributor could credibly manage, setting such brands up for failure. The trouble is that if this situation happens in one of those franchise states, there's not a whole lot the brewer can do about it.

The Brewers Association has been confronting the franchise reform issue head on in its push for franchise law reform. Distributors who favor maintaining strong franchise laws have understandably pushed back, arguing that weakening such laws could be one step on a path back to Prohibition.

The Brewers Association has asserted that it has no interest in torpedoing the three-tier system. The fact that its most successful members got to be so successful, in part, thanks to its distribution partnerships is not lost on those breweries. In a one-two media punch in 2014, craft brewers made their case for franchise reform, shooting down distributors' assertion that such changes would destroy the three-level framework put in place by the Twenty-first Amendment. Steve Hindy—cofounder and president of the Brooklyn

Brewery, Brewers Association executive board member, and a former skilled journalist who worked as a foreign correspondent in the Middle East before getting into the beer business—authored a March 30, 2014 *New York Times* op-ed piece titled "Free Craft Beer." Hindy was on the Brewers Association's board of directors at the time and wrote it on behalf of that organization (and took some heat from distributors for doing so).

Meanwhile, Brewers Association president and godfather of American homebrewing Charlie Papazian published a piece a few months later in the organization's trade publication, *The New Brewer*, that sought to poke holes in the case distributors were making for business as usual.

With regard to the notion that reforming franchise laws in some states will compromise the three-tier system, Papazian contends that in states where such legislations are "more reasonable" (Papazian singles out Delaware, New York, and Washington as being among the reasonable ones) or non-existent (Alaska, California, and the District of Columbia), the three-tier system remains "vibrant and effective."

New York's wasn't always quite so "reasonable," as Hindy points out. He recalls the time he once tried to terminate a contract with an underperforming distributor in the state for selling products outside of his territory, as well as selling out-of-date beer. "I thought it would be straightforward," Hindy wrote, since my contract said I could leave 'with or without cause.'" However, the distributor took Brooklyn Brewery to court, and Hindy said that New York's franchise law, "which sets a high standard for showing cause, trumped whatever my contract said." Two New York State Supreme Courts upheld Brooklyn's position, but, fearing yet another costly, protracted appeal, Hindy settled out of court. Brooklyn was able to terminate the relationship, but only after paying more than $300,000 on legal fees for both appeals and the settlement—a huge burden for a small brewery.

It wasn't until 2012 that the state's franchise laws got a tad less insurmountable for brewers. That year, New York governor Andrew Cuomo and the state legislature agreed on a special dispensation for breweries that individually represent less than 3 percent of a distributor's business and produce under 300,000 barrels a year. Brewers of that size—which includes most craft breweries, save for the six or seven largest—may now change distributors by paying a "fair market value" of the distribution rights, as negotiated by brewer and the wholesaler. "Still an expensive proposition," Hindy wrote, "but easier than going to court."

Needless to say, many brewers have learned to tread extremely lightly as they approach new distributor contracts, but many of those same brewers are still dealing with the headaches of existing contracts in strong franchise states.

The National Beer Wholesalers Association (NBWA), the trade group that represents the nation's distributors, has been an advocate for preserving states' franchise laws as they are. NBWA's argument has been that such laws promote consumer choice and product diversity because they encourage distributors to make investments in small brands without fear of abrupt contract termination. When distributors are able to do that, they can stay independent, which, NBWA asserts, ultimately fosters greater consumer choice. NBWA also argues that there's a safety element. In a position piece on its website, the organization claims that franchise laws prohibit a brewer or importer from terminating a relationship "because the distributor refuses to violate federal or state alcohol regulations, such as selling to unlicensed retailers."

By and large, that last point is a rare occurrence and is very unlikely to apply to a small brewer. Craft brewers tend to have very limited resources, and they're not likely to risk what little they have by trying to force their distributors to do something illegal. That safeguard applies more to the macro brewers, but even they aren't willing to risk the bad PR and likely subsequent drop in share price that would result from anything so shady. (Mega brewers' shadiness usually manifests itself within the confines of the law.)

Efforts to keep every line of a franchise agreement intact in the name of public safety often come off as disingenuous and merely protectionist. It's hard to blame the distributors because they've got a good thing going, so why would they want to mess with it. But their critics accuse them of not fully recognizing how much market dynamics have changed. It really is an industry of small brewers and brands now, despite the fact that the macros—including domestics and mass-market imports—still account for nearly 90 percent of volume. But that share number is falling rapidly, and the macros can't acquire them fast enough to stem the tide (not for lack of trying—they've already absorbed plenty of once-fiercely independent breweries into their operations).

It's a tricky issue for the parties on either end of the debate. Craft brewers need distributors and they certainly don't want to alienate their route to market. Though many do self-distribute in their home markets, most don't want the headache of actually running a distributorship. Conversely, distributors have grown quite fond of the handsome margins their small suppliers' brands bring to the table, and they won't be giving up craft any time soon, especially since mega brand volume has flattened. And many distributors love working with craft brewers and all of their entrepreneurial (and often offbeat) personalities. A number have said selling craft has been the most fun they've had in the beer business in a very long time.

Though most of small brewers' criticism of the distribution tier targets franchise laws, many of their acolytes tend to be a bit knee-jerk and call for the complete dissolution of the three-tier system. As is the case with any form of fandom—be it sports, comic books, *Star Wars*, or *The Walking Dead*—passions flare and folks often make some impulsive comments (thanks, Facebook) based more on emotion than on actual facts. It's usually the less-informed consumers—or at least those who don't actually *work* in the industry—who make such blanket statements.

A number of other countries—many of which still have tied-house systems where it's immensely difficult for small brands to gain a footing—envy America's system. A disproportionate number of European countries are trying to curtail out-of-control binge drinking, a task that would be substantially less daunting with the checks and balances the US system affords, as flawed as it is.

On the business side, the industry that's been fairly vocal in its distaste for three-tier has been wine—small, independent wineries, to be precise. Much of that opposition stems from the issue of direct shipping. A significant number of states don't allow alcohol beverage marketers to sell their products on the Internet, and a lot of wine makers are pretty miffed about that. Rightly so, because they depend a great deal more on consumers outside their immediate area than brewers do.

Although the number of wineries in the country is about twice that of breweries, they're not as geographically dispersed as breweries. One of the Brewers Association's big talking points has been that 75 percent of Americans live within ten miles of a brewery. Wine producers can't really make the same claim about themselves, as their products, compared to beer, are more dependent on climate conditions. Obviously, there are exceptions; New York's Finger Lakes region isn't exactly known for its mild winters, but it does have a disproportionate number of wineries. Still, they depend on more temperate regions for a large percentage of their grapes, as their growing season is limited.

Most consumers can brag about their local breweries; most Californians, Washingtonians, and Oregonians can brag about their local wineries, but beyond those regions, things get pretty sparse (though urban wine making is a growing trend). Sure, there are burgeoning wine scenes in states like

Virginia, Texas, and the aforementioned New York, but one hardly could argue that most of those states' residents live within ten miles of a winery. If someone visits a winery, there's a good chance they're visiting from someplace else. If they want to buy a bottle of that Cabernet they tasted at that small mom-and-pop operation they visited outside of Sonoma, they'd better hope it's distributed in their state. If not, they'd better hope they live in a state that allows direct shipping.

The number of states that do permit direct shipping is growing, but legalizing the practice hasn't been without a fair amount of political and judicial maneuvering.

Perhaps the most frequently cited case related to in-state shipping was *Granholm v. Heald*, which went all the way to the US Supreme Court in 2005. The decision actually represented the convergence of separate lawsuits filed in the states of New York and Michigan. In the latter state, wine collector Eleanor Heald led a group of plaintiffs in challenging Michigan's Liquor Control Code, which allowed in-state wineries to ship directly to consumers but forbade out-of-state producers from doing so. The plaintiffs argued that preferential treatment to in-state winemakers violated the Dormant Commerce Clause of the US Constitution in that it discriminated against interstate commerce. The plaintiffs in the New York case, led by Virginia wine producer Juanita Swedenburg, argued a similar point.

After many rounds of appeals, the Supreme Court ultimately decided, in a 5-4 decision, that the Michigan and New York laws did, in fact, violate the Dormant Commerce Cause and were, therefore, unconstitutional. The states had two options: Either ban in-state direct shipping, as well as out-of-state direct shipping—forbidding it for both eliminates the possibility of discriminating against one in favor of the other—or legalize interstate shipping. Both states chose the latter.

The cases may have been specific to wine, but they applied to beer as well. And, as these cases played out in their respective states, the distributor lobby advocated against direct shipping every step of the way. Once again, distributors cited public safety concerns and their desire to prevent the three-tier system from being dismantled. Wholesalers argued that such commerce lacks gatekeepers; what would stop a minor from receiving alcohol through the mail and consuming it illegally? (In most states, however, a carrier won't deliver alcohol unless someone twenty-one or older signs for it.) The practice does, on a minute level, circumvent distributors and thus condenses the three tiers into two, but direct-shipping laws permit very small volumes to be sold that way. Distributors wouldn't be going out of business any time soon.

So, what is it that distributors actually *do*, besides getting beer from A to B, that is? First of all, beer (and all alcohol for that matter) is a highly taxed industry, and the distributors are the ones collecting the taxes.

Increasingly they're doing a fair amount of marketing as well. The brewers used to handle pretty much everything on that end, but now those suppliers from the top tier are focused primarily on national advertising. Anything local tends to fall on the distributors. It's not uncommon to walk into a distributor's warehouse and find a full-service print shop. That's because the distributor is tasked with producing items such as point-of-sale materials for local bars and retailers, as well as signs banners for community events.

Distributor in-house printing applies, for the most part, to the products supplied by the large macro breweries. Crafts tend to be regional operations and aren't really engaged in national marketing campaigns. Most of the time when a craft brewer's products enter a particular market, it hires local reps who work in tandem with their distributors to build their brands across the wholesaler's geographic footprint. When the relationship is solid, the brewery rep and the distributor rep co-host events like tap takeovers, beer dinners, and other promotional shindigs to boost the brand's profile in a particular region and make everyone—retailer/bar, brewer, and distributor—more money.

Additionally, the distribution tier has become a major source for market intelligence, something to which the companies have been able to adapt in the age of Big Data. Many have moved to virtually paperless operations with real-time information on product velocity, pricing fluctuations, retailer order history, inventory, and out-of-stocks at their fingertips. And they're able to share that data with their trading partners on either end of the supply chain to make the relationships (again, in theory) more profitable.

Still, there's no denying that distributors and brewers increasingly have been on divergent paths for the better part of a decade. And it's not just between the craft producers that have changed the dynamics of the beer industry and the distributors that aren't fans of change. The NBWA has been at odds with the large brewers on particular issues—namely, the question of whether breweries should be allowed to own distributorships.

Anheuser-Busch InBev has made no secret of its desire to control the middle tier any way it legally can. There was that aforementioned "share of mind" scheme, of course, but in some cases it has tried, and succeeded outright, in actually owning distributorships in some states (some states are bit more loosey goosey about the whole three-tier thing).

Back in 1978, thirty years before its acquisition by InBev, Anheuser-Busch successfully sued the state of Kentucky for the right to purchase a distributorship. After that, state regulators banned brewers from owning distributors, primarily to appease the latter. However, in 2014, AB InBev attempted to buy a second distributor in the Bluegrass State, suing the state once again to circumvent the regulation. And, yet again, the brewing behemoth was successful. However, state legislators stepped in to change the law, and, in the spring of 2015, the state senate voted to do so, requiring AB InBev to sell its distribution interests in Kentucky.

The divide between brewers of all sizes and the middle tier has played out on Capitol Hill, as well—or at least in the conference center of the Hyatt Regency at Capitol Hill. Each spring the Beer Institute, NBWA, and Brewers Association would convene there for a joint legislative conference. In addition to educating their respective memberships on the critical issues that affect all of them, they'd all get the chance to meet with their members of Congress. However, it ceased to be the NBWA/Brewers Joint Legislative Conference and became, simply, the NBWA Legislative Conference in 2010. Each tier had its own fish to fry and more and more those fish were at odds.

Perfection is never going to be in the cards for the three-tier system. If anyone expects that, they should probably consider getting into another business. On the continuum between "complete, unmitigated failure" and "perfect," the only place the three-tier system needs to reside is "functional/adequate"—somewhere close to the middle. For it to remain there depends on how willing to be flexible each of the stakeholders on the value chain is.

A group of legal experts at the 2015 Craft Brewers Conference in Portland, Oregon, wrestled with such issues in a panel discussion titled "Strength Through Flexibility: The Three-Tier System of the Future." It was a bit of a tug of war between small brewer interests (represented by a lawyer for equity funds that play in the space) and distributor interests (represented by a similar professional who advocates for the wholesaler tier). Though they predictably couldn't agree on much, they did find common ground on two fundamental realities.

Reality No. 1: With a new brewery essentially opening every twelve hours, there's unprecedented stress on the system of distribution as it exists today. Something's got to give. Business models will have to evolve in order to sustain the deluge of new players and products on the market.

Reality No. 2: Regardless of tier or financial interest, every business on the beer value chain works for the consumer. Brands aren't making TV ads for distributors or retailers, and they're certainly not fashioning their tweets to reach those trading partners. They're trying to reach the consumer. And ultimately, whether through introducing ballot initiatives, holding public demonstrations, calling legislators, or voting with one's wallet, it's ultimately the consumer who's going to decide what shape the future takes.

Taking It to the Hill

An intriguing sort of Cold War has played out in the legislative branch of the federal government between large and small brewers' interests. For several years, there were two competing excise-tax reduction bills circulating through the halls of Congress. The first of those was what's known as the Fair Brewers Excise and Economic Relief Act (aka the Fair BEER Act) of 2015, better known to public policy wonks as H.R. 767. That's the one that the Beer Institute, the trade group that represents the big brewers, and the National Beer Wholesalers Association (NBWA), the organization that represents distributors, supported. The small brewers, represented by the Brewers Association, had been lobbying for passage of what's known as the Small Brewer Reinvestment and Expanding Workforce Act (and, yes, in the spirit of catchy acronyms, it's more commonly referred to as the Small BREW Act), or, more formally, H.R. 494.

To the untrained eye, both bills were virtually identical. Both proposed a 50 percent cut in the tax per barrel on the first 60,000 barrels produced—from $7 to $3.50—and both create an intermediate level of $16 per barrel on those numbered 60,001 to 2 million. Brewers would continue to pay $18 per barrel on everything over 2 million barrels (currently everything over 60,000 is taxed at the 18 percent rate). The key difference is the Fair Beer Act proposed no tax on the first 7,143 barrels. This seems like a random number, but that's the threshold that defines a "small brewer," according to the federal Tax and Trade Bureau (TTB). Even though that element would benefit small brewers—90 percent of brewers in the US actually fall below that 7,143 line—the Brewers Association opposed it because the Fair BEER Act applied to *all* brewers; the Small BREW Act applied only to brewers whose total production is under 6 million barrels per year (i.e., craft brewers). Small brewers, the Brewers Association argues, are US-based and are creating US jobs, while cuts on macro-beer volume would just be lining the pockets of their foreign parent companies. (Remember, Miller was acquired by South African Breweries in 2002, forming SABMiller; Canadian Molson scooped up Coors to form Molson Coors in 2005; SABMiller and Molson

Coors formed the MillerCoors joint venture in 2007 for its US operations; and Budweiser's parent, Belgium-based InBev, acquired Anheuser-Busch in 2008 to form Anheuser-Busch InBev.)

The distributors and large beer companies had some serious problems with parts of the Small BREW Act—namely the 6-million-barrel ceiling. The FAIR Beer Act supporters don't think any brewery that produces between 2,000,001 and 6,000,000 barrels of beer annually have any business being considered "small."

Why should they care, you ask, when the Beer Institute's primary members and the distributors' biggest suppliers are multinational behemoths? The short answer: politics.

First, a bit of backstory. The biggest member of the Brewers Association is Boston Beer Company, better known by the name of its flagship brand, Samuel Adams. In a lot of ways, Sam Adams, particularly founder Jim Koch, has been the face of the craft beer concept for mainstream Americans.

Up until 2011, one of the key pillars of the Brewers Association's definition of "craft brewer" was a two-million-barrel ceiling. Once a brewer grew to surpass that threshold, they no longer would be considered "craft" in the Association's eyes. In 2011, Sam Adams was about to bust through that ceiling. That led to the organization's controversial decision to up the threshold to 6 million barrels.

In opposing the Small BREW Act, the Beer Institute and NBWA effectively were calling out that bill's congressional sponsors for including a provision that benefits two brewers (Boston Beer and Pennsylvania's D. G. Yuengling, which the Brewers Association didn't consider "craft" until it tweaked its definition yet again in 2014—but that's a tale for another day).

A more cynical view (to which some not-to-be-named industry insiders subscribe) was that Fair BEER Act supporters—again, these are the biggest of the big—don't want to give Boston Beer an inch. Koch's public history with the likes of Anheuser-Busch InBev has been spotty at best. There's a lot of bad blood there.

If all of this is confusing, think about how lawmakers must feel when there are two competing legislations coming across their desks. Congress already barely gets anything done. Confounding them with two nearly identical yet fundamentally different bills likely won't stoke the fires of legislative productivity.

But compromises do happen, and the summer of 2015 saw a very encouraging development. Congress introduced The Craft Beverage Modernization and Tax Reform Act, which actually covers all of the artisanal drinks segments: beer, wine, spirits, and cider. Like the Small BREW and Fair BEER Acts, the new piece of legislation (S.1562 in the Senate; its similarly named companion bill in the House of Representatives is H.R. 2903) cuts the federal excise tax to $3.50 on the first 60,000 barrels (again, cutting it in half) for domestic brewers. However, that would only apply to those producing fewer than 2 million barrels. The ones making up to 6 million barrels (Boston Beer, Yuengling, and others) still get a small break, but instead of paying $16 on every barrel between the 60,001 and 6 million, they'd be paying $16 on all of the first 6 million barrels. But it's not just those mid-size brewers getting the break. The first six million barrels of *every* brewer and beer importer gets to pay $16 up to that threshold. That part was a concession to the big brewers and the distributors.

The bill's introduction got the thumbs up from both the Small BREW and Fair BEER camps, which was a huge step in the right direction. The Beer Institute and the Brewers Association even issued a joint press release expressing their unity on the new bill. "The legislation is a big win for the brewing industry, bringing us together over the common goal of recalibrating federal excise tax," Bob Pease, CEO of the Brewers Association, said in that release. "The Craft Beverage Modernization and Tax Reform Act will greatly benefit America's small brewers and allow them to achieve their job creation and brewing capacity objectives."

Representing the macros, Beer Institute president and CEO Jim McGreevy called the introduction of the bill "yet another critical step forward in addressing beer excise tax reform in a way that benefits everyone. It's a great day when the entire brewing industry can support a solution to address an issue that has plagued us for too long."

Leave it to the media, however, to throw a great big wet blanket on this brief kumbaya moment. In a June 26, 2015 post on Dow Jones' MarketWatch website, columnist Jason Notte interpreted the bill as "an act of Congress to tell us what a craft beer brewer really is." Even the headline singled out Boston Beer: "Sam Adams is about to be kicked out of the 'craft beer' category." He was referring primarily to the various tax thresholds, of course.

It really isn't up to federal legislators to decide what company gets to call itself a craft brewer. It's a nebulous term with a smorgasbord of definitions ranging from the rigidly stringent to the liberally loose. The government really has no interest in enforcing semantics. Plus, if you recall the Brewers Association's definition—which iself is rarely free of critics—size is only one of three components of its definition (independent and traditional being the other two).

All that the bill's definition does is say a company the size of Boston Beer is not small, but mid-size.

Craft really is in the glass of the beholder, and its meaning will continue to be a source of great conflict for generations to come. And the debate will rage far from Capitol Hill.

15

Bottles, Cans, and Growlers

The Evolution of Modern Beer Packaging

The glass bottle, without a doubt, has been the beer package that has had the most staying power, especially when you consider how long it's been around and how pervasive it remains today.

For most of this country's formative years, beer was typically dispensed from wooden kegs at the bar. Bottling in glass was happening by the late eighteenth century, but it was still a tiny percentage of the overall packaging mix. The bottles of the time were made of very heavy black glass that was used to contain many other types of products, as well. By the late eighteenth century, brewers were using purpose-made beer bottles. The advent of pasteurization made it possible to ship bottled beer long distances.

In the early twentieth century and during the period just after Prohibition, draft beer still dominated, though bottles started to close the gap and ultimately shifted the dynamic in favor of bottled product.

Throughout the twentieth century and into the twenty-first, the glass bottle has taken many forms. Pre-Prohibition, bottles were commonly of the heavy glass variety, usually with the brewery's name embossed in the glass. Containers of this type are popular finds among beer enthusiasts and collectors who frequent antique shops.

The immediate post-Prohibition period was something of a creative pinnacle for glass bottle design. It was around 1935 when the public first drank beer out of a stubby (sometimes called the "steinie"), that squat, stout-bodied, short-necked container that always manages to tug at one's nostalgic heartstrings whenever a modern brewer releases a retro-inspired product in the stubby.

Bob and Doug McKenzie fans will recognize the bottle; it's the very essence of Canadiana, as far as its beer culture is concerned. For a good quarter-century or so, up until the mid-'80s, it was the dominant package in the Great White North. (Those who remember the Bob and Doug film *Strange Brew* will recall that it was in a stubby that the infamous mouse lived.)

In the late twentieth century and prior to their nostalgic renaissance, Jamaica's Red Stripe was one of the few mass-marketed brands to package its brews in stubbies.

In 2005, Hood River, Oregon's Full Sail Brewing Company sought to connect the Pacific Northwest's beer culture with its blue-collar roots when it launched Session Lager exclusively in stubbies. It continued the tradition when it expanded the line to include Session Black, Session Fest (winter seasonal), and Session Export.

Even more recently, MillerCoors got in on the act. Since the early 2000s—when the company was just Coors—the brewer had been trying to figure out just what to do with Coors Original. Coors Light had long surpassed it in sales. In 2007, the company reached back to the brand's origins when folks had referred to it as "the banquet beer," and the company rebranded it as Coors Banquet. However, as much of a throwback as it was trying to be, there was a certain retro aesthetic that was missing. In 2013, the nostalgic circle was complete when Banquet found its way into stubbies.

By the middle of the twentieth century, 12 ounces had become the standard bottle size for beer (11.2 ounces—330 milliliters—in Europe). That's not to say there wasn't any room for variation.

Those of us old enough to vaguely remember the '70s and very early '80s will remember that small, 7-ounce bottles were nearly as common as

Stubby bottles of Full Sail's Session Lager.

the ones nearly twice their size. These "pony" bottles started to disappear as quickly as breweries were vanishing during the period (though they did make a comeback, much like the stubby on a very small scale in the past decade).

By the '90s, longneck bottles had become the standard and remain so to this day. What's not so standard is the color of those bottles. And that's not really a good thing because the color of a bottle (or lack thereof) really can affect the quality of the beer.

The more opaque the bottle, the better chance it has of keeping light out. And light is one of beer's greatest enemies. Light negatively interacts with hops in beer, causing it to "skunk."

Clear bottles are the absolute worst, yet some very high-profile brands insist on packaging their product in those. Green bottles are nearly as bad and a disproportionate number of brewers bottle their brands in containers of that color, as well. It's very much the part of the trade dress of some brands—particularly certain well-known European imports.

As far as common bottle colors go, the dark amber/brown bottle really is the way to go because the depth of that color lets in far less light than bottles made of lighter green glass. Some glass manufactuers have even developed a black glass bottle, which turns the opacity factor up to eleven. Such bottles are a bit pricier and not widely available.

No glass tint is 100 percent impervious to light. But you know what is? Aluminum.

Yes They Can

Beer cans have been in circulation for more than eighty years. They first made their appearance on shelves in 1935 as the package of choice for the Newark, New Jersey-based Gottfried Krueger Company, producer of Krueger's Special Beer and Krueger's Cream Ale. The cans at that time, produced by American Can Company, were made of steel and required an opener—popularly known as a church key—to breach the flat metal top and deliver all of the sudsy goodness to a very eager drinker.

Around the same time that the world first beheld the steel flat-top container, a competing package came on scene: the cone-top. They were fairly bottle-like in appearance, at least as far as the top opening was concerned. They were sealed much like bottles, as well, with the metal crown closure that's still used on beer bottles today. The upside of the cone-top can was that the brewer didn't need to install an entirely new filling line to get its beer into the package. The cone-tops worked on the existing bottling machines of the day.

The late 1950s saw the introduction of the aluminum can; Coors usually gets the credit for being the first out of the gate with the newfangled container. MillerCoors celebrates January 22, 1959, as the day it says cans of its flagship brew revolutionized both beer and the overall consumer packaged goods industry.

Research began on the container in 1957 when William Coors, the president of what was at the time the Adolph Coors Company, tasked his staff of engineers with developing a solution that would cut down on packaging waste. The disposal of tin cans—by then, the standard packaging metal—created an environmental hazard.

Coors's directive was fairly visionary for the time period, considering that recycling was barely on the public's radar in the '50s.

The resulting aluminum container bested the tin package in recyclability, and it also eliminated a supposed aftertaste that many swore steel imparted on the liquid.

However, the aluminum can's adoption did not become widespread until the early 1960s when the pull-tab became the closure of the moment. It eliminated the need for the drinker to have a churchkey on hand; the opening mechanism was riveted into the top of the can and disposed of once removed.

Pittsburgh's Iron City brewery is widely credited as the pull-tab pioneer, first incorporating it into its package in 1962, but it was Schlitz that really took it national the following year. Others quickly followed.

Pull-tabs may have been all the rage, but they were anything but perfect. Their sharp edges often cut the people pulling them off, and folks were just tossing them everywhere, will-nilly, causing a bit of an environmental nightmare. Finally, in the 1970s, packaging manufacturers unveiled the stay-tab, the go-to closure that remains on the can once opened—still the widest used today.

The Can Comeback

In the early years of craft brewing, there were two containers in which these specialty beers were packaged: a keg and a glass bottle. The perception of the aluminum can was that of an inferior package, the province of the Bud Lights and Keystones of the world.

In 2002, Dale Katechis—owner of the then five-year-old Lyons, Colorado brewpub Oskar Blues—kept receiving sales flyers and calls from a Canadian company called Cask Systems, trying to entice him to buying a small canning line for his growing operation. Katechis's initially followed his instinct to ignore Cask's sales team. However, Cask's persistence paid off, and Katechis agreed to a meeting with them. By the end of the meeting, Katechis was sold and decided to do what seemed unthinkable—he put his flagship brew, Dale's Pale Ale, in cans.

It may have been unthinkable, but it wasn't unprecedented. In a 2013 cover story in *All About Beer Magazine*, beer historian and writer Tom Acitelli dispelled the myth that Oskar Blues was the first craft brewer to can. That distinction, he wrote, belonged to a much less celebrated company, Mid-Coast Brewing. In 1991, a full eleven years before Katechis first canned his eponymous pale ale, Mid-Coast released its aluminum-encased Chief Oshkosh Lager. Part of the reason the Chief Oshkosh story disappeared under a veil of obscurity was that the brand and the company folded a full eight years before Katechis became a metal head.

But, as Katechis proved, it doesn't always pay to be first. And the five hundred-plus craft outfits that now are happily packaging their brands in the lightweight containers are only doing it because Oskar Blues made it "okay."

It's a shame that there was such a perception barrier to shatter to make cans an acceptable package for these higher-end beers. The package makes sense from so many standpoints: cost, environmental impact, logistics, and general product quality.

Many of those are intertwined. Cans are lightweight, so that means the trucks carrying them expend less fuel—good for the pocketbook and good for the environment. (Aluminum cans are also 100 percent recyclable.) The lighter weight of cans also means that the labor involved in their movement is less intense.

Additionally, cans are welcome in far more places than bottles: concert venues, beaches, hiking trails, public pools, and water parks—you name it. And then, of course, there's the aforementioned opacity factor.

Canning Cottage Industry

Another key savings: Canning systems designed for small start-ups have been flooding the market in recent years, making it a fraction of the cost to package one's beer than it once was when bottles were the only option. Companies like Cask Systems and Wild Goose have been developing solutions tailored to the smallest of the small. Cask's entry-level machine was a manual, two-head filler that enabled brewers to fill and seal up to about twelve cans a minute. In an eight-hour shift, assuming a person does that one task all day or takes turns with others during that period, a brewery could fill a couple hundred cans shy of 6,000, which adds up to about 240 cases a day. If a brewery is operating five days a week, that's 1,200 cases a week. These breweries are definitely of the micro- or even nano-level ("nano" being a new designation for breweries that are smaller than micros). But they wouldn't be packaging otherwise. The only way their beer would be getting to the marketplace would be in kegs. A small system like Cask's 2-header levels the playing field in some minor way, enabling small breweries to get their products into retail stores without having to invest in expensive bottling lines or pay a contract brewer to package their brands.

Eventually, when an operation of that size outgrows its manual canner, it can sell it to a next-generation start-up and trade up to a five-head automated system, which can fill about thirty cans a minute when running optimally. There's also less manual labor involved, so a brewery staffer doesn't have to be manning it at all times.

As more craft brewers were bit by the aluminum bug, more equipment manufacturers started getting in the game to offer solutions designed for everyone from the nano-brewer who's just graduated from homebrewer, to the regional producers that require a machine that can fill and seam 280 to 300 cans per minute. Wild Goose Canning has become one of Cask's most significant direct competitors, catering from the tiniest of operators to intermediate-size players. Its basic piece of equipment is its WGC 50, which is similar to Cask's manual system and fills eight to twelve cans per minute. It increases from there, with a semi-automatic dual-head filler that can pack up to thirty-one a minute; a series of semi-automatic four-head fillers that can do up to forty-two cans per minute; and, finally, a system with two alternating four-head fillers, which, on a good day, can package up to ninety-five cans per minute.

When a brewery outgrows something of that size, it's time to move up to a filler from big European producers like KHS or Krones, which in the past decade have increasingly courted the US craft market. Previously, getting a canning system meant that a brewery needed to be producing the kind of volume that a multinational like SABMiller or AB InBev was moving. But recognizing that small stateside brewers were in a mass embrace with aluminum, they started to deliver for the regional players. Oskar Blues itself, now operating three production breweries—its flagship in Longmont, Colorado (it outgrew its original site in neighboring Lyons), another it unveiled in Austin, Texas in 2016, and one it opened at the end of 2012 in Brevard, North Carolina—outgrew its original Cask system a long time ago. It's now operating 280-cans-per-minute KHS solution.

Mobile Canning

These days, the micro players don't even have to invest in an entry-level system if they don't want to commit the capital or have the space to accommodate a canner. In the past half-decade, a new phenomenon has emerged that is taking budgetary and spatial constraints out of the equation: mobile canning. The concept is simple: A brewer makes its products, and when it's ready to package it, the company offering the mobile canning solution brings it to the facility.

The business model was inspired by something that was going on in the wine industry for some time. Many vineyards aren't large enough for bottling lines, so trucks loaded with bottlers would drive around, say, Napa, Sonoma, or Oregon, setting up camp at wineries in need of their services. Sometimes they'd stick around as long as a week until all of the necessary volume was packaged. Mobile canning works more or less the same way but with aluminum.

Two of the notable players in the mobile canning sphere have been California's The Can Van and Longmont, Colorado's aptly named Mobile Canning Systems (MCS, which partnered with Wild Goose to develop its solution). Yes, MCS's headquarters is in the same town that's home to Oskar Blues's flagship brewery. Coincidence?

Usually, the mobile canning purveyors will wheel their systems off of their trailers, roll them as close as they can get to a brewery's bright tank, and start filling.

Design Dynamics

The Can-aissance, or as Oskar Blues likes to call it, the "Canned Beer Apocalypse," has provided an attractive canvas for label designers, as they have more space to play with to tell their visual story versus the typical front label and back label of a bottle. Now, images occupy all of the available space on 12-ounce, 16-ounce, and sometimes even 19-ounce cylindrical aluminum containers.

Connecticut-based New England Brewing Company has had a field day with its irreverent aluminum can designs. For one thing, a product's name doesn't get more creative than "668: The Neighbor of the Beast." That's the moniker for the brewery's Belgian-style golden ale. (And it's not completely out of left-field, either. Satan had a hand in the creation of the style to begin with. After all, Duvel, the brand that pretty much started it all, was named after the devil. Many products within the style that followed have been named everything from Satan Gold to Lucifer.)

A drinker who reads that on the blackboard of his or her local beer bar is likely to try it on name alone. But if it's on draft only, they're being short changed. The can for this brew is a stroke of genius, and the drinker must rotate it 360 degrees to view the entire cartoonish image. There's an ominous, fiery glow emanating from house number 666. Next door, at 668, a rather meek, balding, middle-aged man in shirtsleeves is fetching his morning newspaper from the edge of his driveway. His look is one of put-upon resignation. The image would not be nearly as impactful if it were on a bottle.

San Francisco's 21st Amendment Brewery—named of course, after the constitutional amendment that repealed Prohibition—knows how to get fairly elaborate with its can designs. For instance, the front of its Brew Free or Die IPA container looks like a fine rendering of Mount Rushmore, but spin the can around and Abe Lincoln has broken away from the other presidential icons with fists raised, ready for a brawl. Its Marooned on Hog Island oyster stout requires a full rotation to read the story that inspired the product and to see what's happening on both sides of the island. Meanwhile, 21st Amendment's Fireside Chat spiced winter seasonal features an artist rendering of FDR, complete with protruding cigarette holder, sitting next to the White House mantel, calming an anxious nation.

The opposite of iconic presidential leadership is portrayed in the design of Anti-Hero, an IPA from Chicago's Revolution Brewing. The can design features a menacing military general whose head is a hop flower; behind him, other hop flowers are parachuting to the ground. The flip side of the can features Revolution's signature raised fist.

The entire notion of craft brewing exists today because some people broke the rules and defied convention. In the twenty-first century, that tradition continues as a new generation of rule breakers are redefining packaging and labeling aesthetics by reinventing a container that was once written off as inferior, and can manufacturers continue to devise ways to reinvent the aluminum package to keep it fresh and relevant for new generations of drinkers.

In 2013, Crown Holdings introduced the 360 End, which enables the consumer to pull the entire lid of the can off, essentially turning the container into a drinking cup. The rationale is that it lets the drinker experience the full flavor and aroma of the beer if they're not already pouring it into a glass. When consuming from a standard can, virtually none of the brew's aroma is making it to the drinker's nose, since the opening is too small.

Of course, it assumes that drinkers are being as fastidious about disposing of the tops as they are with the rest of the can (the lid has considerably more material in it than the mostly defunct pull-tab, which fell out of favor partially on environmental grounds).

Other suppliers, such as Ball Corp. and Rexam, have been marketing other solutions to make cans a bit more user-friendly. Normally, when a can is opened, there's no turning back. A person has to consume everything contained within or toss significant quantities of the liquid when they can't. But that could change if more brewers adopt resealable cans. Instead of popping the container open, consumers can slide it open and closed, much as they would with one of those revolving tops on a cardboard can of salt.

Then there are bottle/can hybrids that are just as reclosable. For all intents and purposes, they're bottles; they just happen to be made out of aluminum. Anheuser-Busch has deployed aluminum bottles of Bud Light in some venues—particularly nightclubs where there's a lot of human bouncing and gyrating, and beach and pool bars where glass is a no-no.

The crafts have also found a use for such containers. Even Oskar Blues abides. Back in 2012, the Colorado can evangelist teamed up with Indiana-based Sun King to produce the collaborative brew Chaka, a Belgian-style ale packed in Ball Corp.'s Alumi-Tek resealable aluminum pint bottle.

And, finally, an interesting little footnote to the whole modern canning revolution was the introduction of Churchkey pilsner, whose key point of differentiation was the fact that it's packaged in the classic flat-top can. And, yes, it requires a church key, which comes packaged with every six-pack, to open it. It definitely appeals to those who are nostaligic and to those who just want the experience of opening a can of beer in the way it was done before most of the target consumers were even born. Fans of the HBO series (and subsequent misfire of a movie) *Entourage* will be thrilled to know that Adrian Grenier—who plays movie star Vincent Chase on the series—is one of Churchkey's founders. Alas, not all celebrities can buy islands.

Growlers' First . . . Growl

The most ubiquitous form of packaging for craft brewers is neither the aluminum can nor the single-serve bottle; it's actually the growler. Not every brewery packages; many are draft only. And in the states that allow consumers to take beer home after their brewery or brewpub visits, the stuff's going home in a growler. A modern growler is usually a 64-ounce or 32-ounce refillable glass bottle branded with the brewer's logo and closed with a twist-off cap. Its contents are meant to be consumed within a day or two of the brewery visit. Its closure doesn't have the same gas-blocking properties of the crown cap, which keeps bottled beer fresh much longer. The growler is the best way to enjoy brewery-fresh, draft-quality ales in the comfort of your own home.

But freshness and great taste had nothing to do with the supposed humble origins of the growler. The first receptacles to be called "growlers," at least in the context of beer, were actually pails, not unlike the ones Jack and Jill carried up the hill on that ill-fated hydration-seeking expedition. Back in the nineteenth century it was common to use beer instead of water as a cooking base—a good hundred years before the beer cuisine revolution—mainly because beer was a purified product and less likely to kill you than the local water supply. And breweries of the time were happy to give away their less-than-marketable batches for free. There would be a tap reserved specifically for that purpose. And parents would usually send their kids to fetch a pail of beer (my, how the times have changed).

"It's part of Americana that not everyone knows about," says Connecticut-based beer history and breweriana expert Jeff Browning. "It was post-Civil War, pre-Prohibition—that's the general timeline."

Growler derives from an old slang term for "bucket." References to growlers full of beer popped up occasionally in early-twentieth-century blues songs (which often can be the best historical sources when there's no other physical documentation; people sang what they knew).

And though growler size has been standardized at half-gallon and quart sizes, there was no such delineation for the beer-fetching vessel.

"I've heard a lot of first-hand testimonies of people in their sixties and seventies whose mothers and grandmothers would recall going down to the brewery to get beer," Browning notes. "A lot of people said it was their job, to get a pail of lager and bring it back home. It speaks to the fact that the breweries themselves were pillars of the community."

The ManCan personal keg.

The ManCan

Admittedly, it's probably not the best product name, but it's worth mentioning in the context of beer receptacles. There has been a growing market for stainless steel growlers, versus the traditional glass ones, but the ManCan takes that concept a step further. It's a portable keg, available in 64-ounce and 128-ounce (one gallon) versions, complete with a CO_2 regulator and tap system. The rationale is it keeps take-home draft beer fresh longer than the standard growler, the cap of which allows carbon dioxide to escape pretty quickly.

16

Serving Beer

Finding the Right Glass

There really is no wrong way to consume a beer. It's all about personal enjoyment and whatever makes the individual drinker comfortable and happy. Like beauty, how one drinks a beer is in the eye of the beholder. Actually, it's in the hand of the beer holder. That's not to say there aren't ways to drink that are designed to enhance the beer experience and make the drinker even happier.

More often than not, you've probably been out at a bar, barbecue, or party where you've asked for a beer and—assuming it's one that's not available on draft—someone's handed you a bottle. Sometimes they might hand you a napkin to help insulate your body heat and not let the beverage get too warm. Again, drinking out of the bottle is not *wrong* per se. Certain types of beer—usually the mass-produced national brands—aren't particularly flavor-forward, so sipping from a longneck bottle neither detracts from nor enhances the moment.

When it comes to the hundreds of other craft beer and international specialty styles, the drinking vessel actually makes a huge difference. When most people taste something—be it food or beverage—they assume that most of the flavor sensations are all localized to the taste buds. That's not accurate. Most of what we taste—some 70 percent or so—is olfactory in nature. What we think we're tasting, we're actually smelling.

Think about the size of the opening at the top of a bottle. Is there anywhere to fit a nose? While you're sipping from the bottle, you're sniffing the air on the outside of it. None of the complex beer aroma is making it to your nose.

However, when you drink out of a glass, your nose dips in to the mouth of the glass, fully inhaling virtually every nuance of the complicated interplay of hops, malt, yeast, and other ingredients the brewer might use.

When the folks behind the Cicerone program (more on that in chapter 27) are promoting their certification system—be it at a beer festival or an industry trade show or conference—they distribute tiny packages containing a few red jellybeans. It's not meant as a snack to draw people to their table. It's an exercise that demonstrates just how important one's nose is in the tasting equation. People are directed to take a bite of a jellybean while holding their noses. They're then instructed to unclasp their noses while they're still chewing and note the difference in flavor. There's little to no flavor with closed nostrils. With open nostrils, the full berry taste is allowed to assert itself. It's not unlike having a cold. You can't taste well because your nasal passages are clogged, not because your taste buds are in some weakened state. So, when you're drinking a beer, wouldn't you want the tasty jellybean experience?

That's not to say all glasses are good for beer. In fact, the one that people are most likely to encounter on a daily basis is actually a lesser vessel, as far as the quality of the beverage in it is concerned. That would be the shaker pint, that sturdy, wide-mouthed glass with the straight sides that is fairly ubiquitous in any pub with draft lines. They were born as martini shakers and eventually became the default glass for beer.

They're extremely popular with bar owners for three main reasons. First, they're stackable. Real estate behind the bar is at a premium, and the more that bartenders can consolidate their glassware into columns that take up minimal shelf space, the happier they're going to be. Second, they don't break as easily as other glasses. Sure, shaker pints are not likely to survive a six-foot drop off of a shelf, but they're more than likely to remain intact if someone accidentally knocks one over on top of the bar. The third reason is of the least importance, but it's a reason nonetheless: shaker pints are extremely flexible as drinking glasses. A bar or restaurant is just as likely to put water, fountain soda, or iced tea in one of those vessels as it is likely to put beer.

The argument against shaker pints often comes from the brewers themselves and, increasingly, from the distributors who sell to those bars and restaurants. It's understandable as they want their brands presented in the best possible light. They want people to drink their beers more than once; if those people have a subpar experience, they're likely to blame the brand, not the bar.

So what exactly is wrong with the shaker pint? For starters, it fosters little head retention. The shape has been found to make the carbonation dissipate as quickly as possible. That's due, primarily, to the fact that the glass gets wider and wider the closer it gets to the top. As the bubbles push to the top, they get more area to spread out, therefore resulting in a thin, quickly disappearing head. (An ideal head, by the way, should be about as thick as two fingers—about an inch and a half.)

More importantly, the shaker pint is believed to adversely affect aroma and, therefore, flavor.

Not to get too scienc-y, but there are some thermodynamics at work (the folks at glass supplier Spiegelau are always happy to make such concepts as accessible as possible to the average consumer). The walls of the shaker pint are as thick as they are because there are certain impurities in the glass used to make them. The more impure the glass, the thicker the vessel needs to be, otherwise it would be unstable and would crumble in your hands. The problem is that thick glass absorbs temperature into it until it reaches equilibrium. There are two competing forces: the temperature of the liquid and the room-temperature glass. Therefore, to approach equilibrium, the thick glass could raise the temperature of the beer by 5 degrees in a very short period of time.

Vinnie and Natalie Cilurzo, the founders of Russian River Brewing Company in Sonoma, California, are part of a very vocal anti-shaker-pint contingent. (They've rallied their cause in a short YouTube video). They often recommend a side-by-side comparison between a particular beer served in a shaker pint and the same one poured into a wine glass. The wine glass better directs the aroma to the taster's nose and fosters a more robust flavor experience.

In his seminal beer-and-food-pairing tome *The Brewmaster's Table*, Garrett Oliver, vice president and brewmaster of Brooklyn Brewery, argues that it's okay for a drinker at a bar or restaurant that only stocks shaker pints for beer to insist on having the brew served in a wine glass. After all, he argues, the pub-goer is likely paying a little extra for a good beer, so he or she would be well within the realm of etiquette to ask politely for a wine vessel.

There are ideals and then there's reality. The reality is that the shaker pint is not going away any time soon. Even some of the most craft-centric bars predominantly stock shaker pints for most of their beers, regardless of style. Sometimes these bars will serve higher-ABV or rarer brews in a 10-ounce snifter because these beers are meant to be consumed in smaller volumes. However, for 75 percent of the brands written on a bar's blackboard on a given day, the barkeep will probably give you a shaker pint. And when it's draft-only, there are few other choices. You could ask that it be served in the smaller vessel, but you're short-changing yourself by losing several ounces of your beverage!

Brewers and distributors will continue to educate their accounts on proper glassware and encourage more style-appropriate vessels. But, at least for the foreseeable future, the ones that stock a variety of vessels will continue to be in the minority.

Belgian Glassware

If there's ever been a country that's led by example in the beer glassware realm, it's Belgium. Go into an authentic Belgian pub and you're likely to find not only glasses that are specific to style, but, in many cases, those that correspond with individual brands as well.

The default shape in Belgium is the tulip, kind of a cross between a brandy snifter and a wine glass. But even within the tulip style, there are many variations in shape and size. One of the most iconic is the proprietary vessel for the Duvel golden ale brand. The 33-centiliter glass—the volume of a full bottle of beer—features a short stem supporting a wide-bottomed reservoir that tapers inward toward the top before widening again ever so slightly near the mouth. The shape facilitates an outsized head when poured correctly. Belgian golden ale is the rare style that's meant to have a head that's larger than the liquid at the bottom. The foam takes up about two-thirds of the glass. It's the best way to appreciate the 8.5 percent ABV brew's flavor and aroma.

The glass also features an added bonus. Etched on the inside of its bulbous bottom is the letter "D" in the same font as the Duvel logo. It's more than just a cute little Easter egg. The fine grooves actually facilitate continuous carbonation. Look closely when the glass is full and you'll see a steady stream of tiny bubbles emanating from the etching, perpetually delivering aroma to the top of the glass.

Bosteels Brewery offers a different riff on the tulip concept for its Tripel Karmeliet brand (a Belgian tripel). The stem is considerably taller than that of the Duvel glass. The reservoir still has a bulbous base, but it narrows to a near-perfect cylinder toward the mouth. This brew also has a larger-than-average head, but, when poured correctly, the head is slightly smaller than the amber-colored liquid at the base.

Bosteels is also responsible for one of the oddest drinking vessels known to beer. At first glance, the apparatus for consuming its Kwak brand resembles equipment liberated from a chemistry lab. It's a tall, narrow glass with base that's somewhere between the shape of a teardrop and a perfect sphere. It narrows to a cylinder at the top of the round reservoir before gradually flaring out toward the mouth. Because of the ball-like nature of its base, the Kwak glass doesn't stand on its own. It comes with a wooden holder with a handle. The drinker grasps the handle while drinking, leaving the glass affixed to the holder. A little cumbersome and impractical, yes, but it's all part of the ceremony. Also, since you're never actually touching the glass, your body heat isn't raising the beer's temperature (that's also a big plus for stemmed glassware, but even with those, there's a good chance one's hand still will inadvertently make contact with vessel).

Trappist Goblets

Trappist ales, those produced by monks at Trappist monasteries and sold commercially, are usually served in stemmed, wide-mouthed goblets. But no two goblets are exactly alike—they vary from monastery to monastery. Chimay's and Orval's are slightly angular, while Westvleteren's and Westmalle's are rounded half-ovals. Rochefort's is rounded as well, but it slopes a bit inward toward the mouth. All are majestic in their presentation, befitting centuries of distinguished brewing tradition and European culture.

Weissbier

Among the taller vessels one is likely to encounter is the typical glass for weissbier. The German-style wheat-based brews benefit most from a curvy, hourglass-shaped container. When poured correctly, the top portion delivers a dense, white-to-off-white head reminiscent of whipped cream. The bubbles actually carry dissolved proteins to the surface, and since wheat contains more protein than barley, the head is usually more pronounced.

Pilsner Glass

There are appropriate vessels for the world's most popular beer style, even though about 99 percent of the time it's served in a shaker pint.

In some cases, a pilsner glass can resemble the one in which weissbier is served, though its contours are usually less pronounced and it doesn't slope slightly inward toward the mouth. On some, the sides are angular, forming a sort of upside-down arrowhead. It's also not uncommon for pilsner to be served in a chalice, à la Stella Artois's signature vessel. The key is for the mouth to be considerably smaller than that of the shaker pint to better concentrate the carbonation and aroma. In many German cities, pils is frequently served in a narrow mug.

Stange

When the pale, sometimes faintly fruity but always crisp Kölsch style is served in the United States, it's all too frequently served in the wrong glass—usually that dreaded shaker pint. At Cologne beer halls, servers glide through the crowd carrying circular trays holding a half-dozen perfectly cylindrical 6-inch-by-2-inch 20-cl glasses filled with the stuff. Locals refer to such a vessel as a stange, which means "stick" or "rod"—which the vessel very closely resembles. When poured correctly into a stange, Kölsch, with its flawless white head and straw-colored body, takes on the appearance of a giant cigarette in reverse. The stange is such a local icon that souvenir shops at Cologne's airport sell plush cushions shaped and colored like a glass of Kölsch.

Modern Developments

Glassware manufacturers take their research and development extremely seriously and are constantly refining designs to maximize beer presentation and flavor. In the mid-2000s, Boston Beer Company worked with renowned sensory experts TIAX and respected glassware maker Rastal (multiple manufacturers submitted proposals) to create the Samuel Adams Perfect Pint glass. The vessel, which it unveiled in 2007, is distinguished by its series of contours, starting at the bottom. Its narrow base widens a bit before sloping inward, creating a narrower grip, which the researches say minimizes heat transfer from one's palm.

Just above the gripping point, the glass slopes outward in an egg-like manner. The rounded shape of this section was designed to collect all of the beer's complex aromas—specifically those of Sam Adams's flagship, Boston Lager. It then narrows again as it approaches the top, mainly to help retain the hop aroma and sustain the head. Finally, it flares outward once more, tulip-style, to deliver the brew to the front of the tongue, where sweetness is detected—in beer's case, that sweetness comes from the malt. And, like the Duvel glass (and many others), there are laser etchings at the bottom for that continuous carbonation stream carrying aroma to the head.

The only imperfection with the Perfect Pint is that it can be quite top heavy. And the walls are thinner than those of typical pint glasses, so there's a good chance it's going to break if knocked over.

But Boston Beer founder Jim Koch insists the Perfect Pint presents Sam Adams—from flavor and aroma to color and mouthfeel—just as he originally had intended. So worrying about a little broken glass is a minor tradeoff when the drinker is getting the optimal Sam Adams experience.

Teku

Rastal, more recently, produced the Teku glass, which was designed to maximize the experience of drinking a broader cross-section of brands and styles. At first glance, it might be mistaken for a wine glass, but you'll immediately realize it's considerably more angular than the usually round wine vessels. It's technically a long-stemmed tulip glass, as it has a wide base that tapers inward in more of a triangular fashion before flaring outward slightly at the mouth. Its purpose, like the Perfect Pint, is to deliver a full sensory drinking experience. Its shape is supposed to capture and release all of a finer beer's range of aromas.

Also similar to the Perfect Pint, the Teku was the result of a collaboration with a well-regarded brewer and sensory analysis expert. In Teku's case, the brewer was Teo Musso, founder of Italy's Baladin Brewery, and the sensory consultant was Lorenzo Dabove, better known as Kuaska. Kuaska is widely considered to be one of the leading Italian authorities on Belgian beer (Baladin produces many Belgian-style ales). The name "Teku" is actually a combination of "Teo" and "Kuaska."

It's the glass of choice at New York City's Birreria, the rooftop brewery and pub that's part of Mario Batali and Joe Bastianich's Eataly, an Italian culinary market. The brewery was born as a joint effort among Musso, Leonardo Di Vincenzo of another leading Italian craft brewery, Birra Del Borgo, and Sam Calagione, founder of Dogfish Head Craft Brewery in Delaware.

The Teku caught on rapidly, and it's popping up in many eating and drinking establishments that take their beer programs seriously. Even the Brewers Association, the trade group that represents America's small brewers, distributed a logoed Teku to attendees at its 2015 Craft Brewers Conference in Portland, Oregon, and at its Savor craft beer and food event at Washington, D.C.'s National Building Museum. It's frequently used not just for drinking, but sensory analysis as well.

IPA Glass, Stout Glass, American Wheat Beer Glass

India pale ale remains the top craft beer style, and it doesn't look like it's going to relinquish that position any time soon. (People love their hops!) Oddly, it wasn't until 2013 that the style had its very own glass. Dogfish Head's Calagione, whose brewery is known for its 60-Minute, 90-Minute, and 120-Minute IPAs, had a hand in the development of the glass, as did Sierra Nevada Brewing Company founder Ken Grossman (who also knows his way around a good IPA). The two craft beer icons worked with five-hundred-year-old manufacturer Spiegelau—now a division of wine glass icon Riedel—to create the IPA glass. The vessel can best be described as a cross between a goblet and a chalice—with the notable exception that, instead of a stem, the glass is supported by slightly wider, grooved pillar that contains some of the beer volume. Those ridges are there for a reason; they're designed to aerate the beer. As a drinker lifts the glass, the bumps create resistance, unlocking more of the aromatics.

"It works like a washboard," explains Spiegelau sales VP Matthew Rutkowski. "If you're using a washboard, you want to get the bubbles going and this is exactly what a washboard does."

Those bubbles constantly carry the aroma to the bowl at the top, which is more of a truncated egg in appearance. The bowl narrows toward the top to focus the hoppy complexity toward the drinker's

Spiegelau's IPA glass.

nose. "With IPA," Rutkowski notes, "people want that injection in their nostrils; they want that dank, they want everything."

The dynamic's a bit different from the company's next creation: the stout glass.

This time, Spiegelau collaborated with Colorado's Left Hand Brewing Company and Oregon's Rogue Ales to develop a drinking vessel for the dark, roasty stout style. Both breweries are known for their world-class dark beers. Left Hand makes quite a few stouts, its best-known being Milk Stout. Rogue is quite prolific with the style as well, with such products as Shakespeare Stout and Chocolate Stout. The glass the team settled on resembled the IPA vessel a bit, though with a wider, more angular bowl and no ridges on the lower support. The design was best for concentrating all of those malty, roasty aromas.

Draft stouts frequently contain a fair amount of nitrogen in their gas mix, and this nitrogen makes for very tiny bubbles that generate a silky, creamy head and mouthfeel. The effusion of the CO_2 and nitrogen generates an effect not unlike the Columbia River Gorge where the Columbia and Hood River converge. The foam cascades down over itself. The ridged base of the IPA glass won't work here; there's no need for the washboard effect with such robust foam. Also you want to keep some of the aromas in check a bit.

Spiegelau's stout glass.

"Here you want to keep things a little more warhorse with a harness on it," Rutkowski says.

The stout glass decants and aerates the beer, offering the consistent delivery of rich aromas like coffee, mocha, and chocolate.

The company's third release in the style series was the American wheat glass, a bit of a reimagining and reinvention of the traditional German weissbier glass. It was the result of a collaboration with Michigan's Bell's Brewery, which knows a thing or two about wheat beers; its Oberon Ale is considered one of the greats. After many trials, the group settled on a glass with a shorter (non-ridged) base and larger bowl that narrows toward the mouth. It's designed to accentuate the notes imparted by the yeast, much as the IPA glass enhances the hop experience and the stout glass optimizes the malt-related components.

Spiegelau's American wheat beer glass.

Despite much of the shaker-pint hate circulating through the beer world, there's still a contingent of seasoned beer appreciators who say that drinkers shouldn't believe the hype around newfangled glassware and should instead drink out of whatever glass is available. It's impossible that any one bar—save for the most meticulous of international pubs—is going to have the perfect glass for everything that's on tap or in the fridge. As long as the manager is fastidious about cleaning the draft lines, maintaining proper temperature, and getting rid of products that are past their prime, a drinker is still very likely to have a positive beer experience, regardless of the shape, size, or overall aesthetics of the drinking vessel.

17

Bar-Hopping, American Style

The Best and Most Storied Beer Bars Across the US

When it comes to beer, *where* you drink is just as important as *what* you drink. It's great to have a stocked fridge and a vast craft beer selection to drink with dinner, while watching the big game, or while curled up with a good book, but there are times that you're just going to want to get out. And there's been no better time to leave the house because the number of bars and restaurants specializing in the better beers of the world is at a record high. The trouble is, it's hard to keep up with all of them. By the time you finish reading this chapter, ten more pubs with 25-plus taps will have opened up—and one or two will have closed.

But some have been around long enough to gain local, national, and international followings, and those are the ones that are definitely worth a look. It's impossible to list them all, but few beer geeks would disagree that the ones detailed here are anything short of iconic. So here they are, in no particular order, in every American time zone.

New York City, New York

Jimmy's No. 43 is a subterranean hideaway in Manhattan's East Village whose arched entryways evoke a cavernous Bavarian bierkeller with a bit of Czech-inspired flare thrown in for good measure. Proprietor Jimmy Carbone keeps things interesting by constantly updating the tap list, which gives special attention to New York State breweries, along with frequently hard-to-find selections from across America and the world. The menu usually features a couple of ciders as well, and Jimmy's recently secured a license to sell spirits (for most of its existence, the offerings were limited to beer and wine only), with a focus on those produced by small, artisanal distillers. The food menu is best described as "European rustic"; standouts include skillet-fried beer sausage; local cheese and pig-centric charcuterie plates; Brussels sprouts braised with olive oil, salt, and pepper; and house-made pickled veggies. The candlelit spot beneath E. 7th Street is versatile enough to be both a great first-date destination and an ideal spot for large groups of bar crawlers.

Carbone is actually an ambassador of sorts for not just his own bar, but the entire New York City beer scene. He's one of the driving forces behind the Good Beer Seal, an elite designation for independent pubs that further the city's beer community. He's also the host of the weekly "Beer Sessions Radio" on the Heritage Radio Network, as well as the promoter for several local artisanal food and drink events.

For those planning a splurge night, **Birreria** offers plenty of ways to spend money. It also boasts the highest-altitude full-on beer experience in all of New York. It's on the fifteenth floor, atop Eataly, Mario Batali and

Birreria sits atop Manhattan's Eataly.

Joe Bastianich's sprawling Italian gastronomy market (an elevator on the ground floor in the middle of Eataly takes drinkers straight to the top). Birreria stays true to the Old Country—it's a collaborative effort among Dogfish Head Brewery's Italian-American founder Sam Calagione and Italian craft beer pioneers Teo Musso of Baladin and Leonardo DiVincenzo of Birra Del Borgo. Those brewers' beers are always on tap, as are house-made selections that rotate seasonally. Yes, there's actually an operating brewery at Birreria, cranking out some innovative flavor sensations tied, in some way, to Italy. For instance, Gina is a pale ale brewed with thyme harvested from the hills of Borborose, Italy. It's got an aroma vaguely reminiscent of those old scratch-and-sniff pizza stickers.

The fare is largely rustic, with less of an emphasis on familiar pastas and more on items like beer-braised pork shoulder, grilled branzino, seared duck breast, sausages, and veal sweetbreads.

Birreria is actually an open-air rooftop affair, but there's a retractable roof so weather is never an issue.

Enough about Manhattan.

It's a shame that Brooklyn too often gets overshadowed by its prominent neighbor across the East River because when it comes to beer culture in New York, the Dodgers' former home leaves the more tourist- and movie-friendly borough in its dust. Brooklyn publicans don't just build bars there, they build concepts. What's becoming one of the more enduring and oft-replicated of those concepts is **Barcade**, a craft beer bar that doubles as a nostalgic arcade full of the video games that Gen-Xers grew up with in the '80s and early '90s. And the best part is, they still only cost a quarter. You also don't need to have someone guard your drink at the bar or your table because each game comes equipped with an adjacent wooden beer ledge. Barcade has since expanded to include locations in Jersey City, Manhattan, and Philadelphia. The twenty-five taps in each of the locations are reserved for American craft beer exclusively.

A relatively recent addition to the Brooklyn scene (launched in 2013) is **Tørst**, which, right out of the gate, achieved a cult status few establishments reach after years of existence. Located in the Greenpoint neighborhood, Tørst is a collaboration between Jeppe Jarnit-Bjergsø (Mikkeller Brewery co-founder Mikkel Borg-Bjergsø's estranged brother) and Daniel Burns, best known as the former head chef of the test kitchen for celebrity chef David Chang's Momofuku. The most striking elements of this fairly narrow space are the bar and the wall behind it, both fashioned out of white marble. Embedded in the wall are twenty-one taps, which rotate often, as the

The Jersey City location of Barcade, which combines great beer with classic video games.

frequently dry-erased glossy panel just above the draught lines will attest. Jarnit-Bjergsø is also the founder of the Evil Twin gypsy brewery, whose beer range is well represented at Tørst, as are plenty of other hand-crafted brews from across America and the world.

Denver, Colorado

It's difficult to single out a pub in Denver because the whole city often feels like a beer bar (especially in the fall during the Great American Beer Festival). But ask any local or frequent visitor for the first malt-and-hops-centric watering hole they can think of, and nine out of ten times they'll answer **"The Falling Rock Taphouse."** Seventy-five taps could be a reason to be wary of an establishment; for lesser bars, it often betrays an orientation of quantity over quality. Not the Falling Rock though. Those taps rotate extremely frequently; turn your head for a few minutes and, next thing you know, two or three kegs will have kicked and the bartender will be erasing those from the blackboard and replacing them with entirely new ones. The Falling Rock is a two-level affair with plenty of booths, tables, and bar stools on the main level and room downstairs to accommodate huge crowds. On busier nights you're more likely to be standing. There's also a street-level patio for when the weather's nice. It's spitting distance from Coors Field, so it's a popular spot before or after a Rockies game. Its food menu features the usual pub classics like burgers and Buffalo salads, as well as Southwestern fare like tacos and tamales.

Boston, Massachusetts

Boston has built a reputation as a classic drinking town, so it's no surprise that there's no shortage of great places to sip a couple of pints. Celebrated writer Charles Bukowski definitely knew his way around a watering hole and, therefore, it's fitting that there are not one but two bars named after him in the Massachusetts capital—one in the city's Back Bay area and the other in Cambridge near Harvard University. One of both locations' key quirks is that they're nurturing environments for the indecisive. Each features a multi-colored, beer-logo-adorned wheel of fortune that lets drinkers leave their beer selections completely up to chance.

Worcester, Massachusetts

Less than an hour's drive from Boston in Worcester is a hidden gem of a gastropub known as **Armsby Abbey**. There's nothing more inviting to a beer enthusiast than exposed brick interior walls, and Armsby more than delivers in that regard. Opened in 2008, Armsby Abbey offers twenty-two taps and about forty bottles full of carefully curated offerings from New England favorites like Allagash and Hill Farmstead Brewery, and quite a bit from beyond the region, including brews from California's Lost Abbey and Firestone Walker. And a bar can't call itself "Abbey" without having an outsized selection of Belgians; Armsby definitely earns its name. Most of its bottles are Belgian imports; many others are American interpretations of Belgian styles. Even a handful of its taps are reserved for the delights of Flanders and Wallonia. On the food menu, the biggest draw is its massive assortment of artisanal farmstead cheeses, available individually, in pairs or flights of three.

Philadelphia, Pennsylvania

Philly's another one of those cities where the streets are awash in beer. The City of Brotherly Love is also the City That Made Beer Weeks Cool. Philly Beer Week, since launching in 2008, remains the standard by which all other beer weeks must be measured. The concept caught fire and now there are location-specific beer weeks in every state across the country. Philadelphia would not be the beverage destination it is today if it hadn't been for Tom Peters and Fergus Carey, founders of **Monk's Café**. When it opened in the Rittenhouse Square neighborhood in 1997, it fired the first shot in Philly's world-class beer revolution. It also gets the credit for being many Philadelphians' first exposure to Belgian beer. Peters first visited Belgium in the early '80s and was floored by the diversity of styles available there; at the time when most thought of European brews, they thought of a certain brand in a green bottle whose name starts with "H." The bottle list reads like a novel, with a major focus on Belgians, but there are plenty of other options from the States and abroad. It's also one of only a handful of American bars that truly nail the Belgian aesthetic. Step into the back room and you'd swear you were in Brugge, Ghent, or Brussels. Its frites (fries) are also pretty legendary.

Being the beer town that it is, there are so many pubs just as deserving of shout-outs. As polarizing a subject as the hipsterfication of South Philly is, one of the upsides has been the emergence of so many great public houses serving fine libations. **Pub on Passyunk East** (affectionately known as the POPE), definitely falls into the "don't judge a book by its cover" category. On the outside, the corner bar resembles any old-towny dive bar from the days of yore, where you'd expect to find retirees bending the ear of anyone who'll listen as they hide from their spouses. Walk inside and, well, it still looks like a dive—and that's just the way its owners and regulars like it. But take a minute to read the blackboard of what's on tap and in bottles and you'll realize this neighborhood joint really knows what it's doing. And it's got it where it counts, food-wise. Cooked-to-order burgers, vegetarian options—like a Philly "cheesesteak" made out of seitan—and more healthful snacks

Philly's Pub on Passyunk East (PoPE).

like hummus and arugula salad round out the list. The jukebox ranges from classic rock to punk, and the staff couldn't be friendlier or more knowledgeable about what's going in your glass.

Barely a five-minute walk from POPE is a bit of an oddity of a watering hole known as **Garage**, which is, pretty much, what its name says it is. It's a very long and spacious room that's big enough for parking trucks. And there is actually a truck of sorts right in the middle of it—a food cart that features rotating cuisines. Additionally, it turns bar-based gaming on its ear; sure, it's got a pool table and a couple of pinball machines (retro!), but it also has skee ball! What sets Garage even further apart from its peers is its focus on canned craft beer. There are a handful of draught lines, to be sure, but the specialty here is aluminum packaging. The craft canning movement is soaring, and garage is a veritable shrine to that trend.

Chicago, Illinois

It's no secret that Chicagoans love their bars. When the craft beer revolution took hold, it fit the Windy City like a glove. And while the movement spawned many upscale "gastropubs," Chicago has proved that an establishment can offer a world-class artisanal selection while maintaining an unpretentious, blue-collar dive bar aesthetic. **Paddy Long's** is the epitome of that dynamic. It's also arguably one of the few places that successfully puts its beer and food on equal, 50:50 footing. (Most gastropubs will be more like a 70:30, food-beer split; then there are beer bars that just happen to serve food and it's usually an 80:20 beer-food divide.) Paddy's bills itself as a Bacon & Beer bar and it lives up to both; its logo is a pig wearing a barrel. Brew-wise, Paddy's boasts eighteen frequently rotating taps and around forty bottles and cans that highlight American craft brews, Belgian offerings, and a few rare specialties that drinkers would be hard-pressed to find anywhere else in Chicagoland. It offers beer and bacon tastings as well as some colossal pork-forward sandwiches that have gained a worldwide following. It's a popular destination for competitive eaters, particularly those brave enough to take The Bomb Challenge. The Bomb is a gargantuan affair: five pounds of ground sausage, pork, beef, mixed spices, and brown sugar bacon. It's then slow cooked in a pig roaster and served with a side of fries or potato salad. If it sounds like it can feed a family, that's because it does. Paddy's itself recommends it for six to eight hungry people. Then there are those who take the Challenge: One person has to eat the whole thing, including

Paddy Long's beer and bacon pub in Chicago.

a side of fries big enough to feed a T-Rex, in just forty-five minutes. Those who've succeeded are members of a very exclusive club.

For those who cannot live on beer and pig alone, Paddy's offers one of the most extensive whiskey selections in the city.

Chicago's best-known beer spot is perhaps the **Hopleaf** in the Andersonville neighborhood in the northern part of the city. It's definitely popular with the locals, but you're just as likely to find out of towners there as well, since it's one of those beer geek bucket list-type places. This is another one of those Belgian-accented bars with an extensive draught and bottle list of selections from the US and abroad. Spread out across two floors, the Hopleaf exhibits multiple personalities. The front entrance area resembles the type of no-nonsense, no-pretension pubs common across Western Europe (specifically in Benelux). Upstairs is more of a tony, exposed-brick, dining-room-type spot. When the weather cooperates (which is admittedly a tight window in Chicago), there's a back patio that's worth the extra wait (Hopleaf takes no reservations; it's all first come-first served here). Like all pubs of Belgian descent, Hopleaf serves a killer mussels and frites. Other tasty creations skew on the foodie side of the spectrum. The menu changes frequently, but you can expect items like apple-braised pork belly, organic grass-fed brisket, or a duck Reuben. Hopleaf also likes to subvert the peanut butter and jelly concept; its CB&J combines house-made cashew butter, fig jam, and raclette cheese on sourdough, served pan-fried with a side of stilton mac and cheese and house-made potato chips. It's as amazing as it sounds.

For a truly upscale dining experience, the **Publican** in the city's West Loop knows no peer. It's an airy hall with long, wooden communal tables that create more of a party atmosphere than an intimate affair. The food menu, like the space's architecture, is decidedly European, with a slant toward culinary roads less traveled. The term "nose-to-tail" comes up frequently in relation to the Publican. Options like beef heart tartare, sweetbreads, and potted rillettes give it that reputation. But there's also so much more for every taste: continental favorites like guinea hen aged ham and spring lamb often pop up on the ever-changing menu. There's also plenty of fish, some of which is served as sashimi. The beer list ranges from Chicagoland locals like Moody Tongue and Two Brothers Brewing Company to lambics and saisons from Flanders and Wallonia. Publican hosts a full calendar of beer tasting events and tap takeovers, as well.

No Chicago beer crawl would be complete without a stop in the Bucktown neighborhood's iconic **Map Room**, which accurately dubs itself "a beer lover's dream." The globetrotting-themed pub—whose logo features an overhead view of a retro-style traveler with a suitcase by his side and a map unfurled in both hands—displays an array of flags from around the world and has tables with historical maps embedded in them. It has the world of beer covered as well, with twenty-six taps and more than one hundred bottles. In the morning, the spot doubles as a café with fancy coffees and chai lattes, as well as bagels and freshly baked pastries from nearby Bennison's Bakery and sandwiches from the Goddess and Grocer.

Those in town for business or vacation will likely be staying close to the city center. There are plenty of options near there too, and they're not just for tourists. A bit of an institution in the River North neighborhood is the Clark Street Alehouse. At first glance it seems like a standard Chicago dive bar, but take a closer look at the taps (and the list of bottles on the blackboard) and you'll realize Clark Street takes its sipping pretty seriously. Bartenders often wear Prohibition-era vests as well, to drive home just how seriously they take it. It's a couple of blocks from Portillo's which is a great spot to pick up a Chicago dog, some Polish sausage, or an Italian beef sandwich to pair with your brews—Clark Street serves no food, aside from bountiful servings of pretzel rods.

Milwaukee, Wisconsin

It's a federal offense to write about beer bars across America and not mention a little town called Milwaukee. The city radiates beer culture and, despite all the changes that come with post-industrial modernization, gentrification, and hipsterfication, it still retains a lot of its hard-working mid-to-late-nineteenth-century aesthetic, especially in its architecture. Where most of today's major cities are barely distinguishable from one another—thanks to the scorched-earth tactics of condo developers and the like—when you're in Milwaukee, you know you're in Milwaukee. Another thing it's held on to is its distinct German-ness. And that bodes extremely well for beer. Plenty of cities are catching on to the craft beer movement, and many a gastropub is popping up to keep up with that trend. But a lot of times a trendy watering hole/eatery in New York looks no different than one in San Francisco or, say, Houston. For a place that's unmistakeably Wisconsin, a good place to start is **Über Tap Room**. The atmosphere at first seems like a no-frills dive bar. But look more closely and you'll discover that the place is quite classy without being elitist. The wood paneling around the spacious main dining/drinking area is of the sort found in a '70s rec room. The hardwood floors and high communal tables (though there are plenty of normal-height four-top tables, as well) definitely say beer hall. Über features thirty-six taps, all pouring local/regional stuff. It's a great place to try something from New Glarus Brewing, since it doesn't ship outside of Wisconsin. Oh, yes. One more thing. It's not just Über Tap Room, it's Über Tap Room *and Cheese Bar*. And yes, that means drinkers get to pair some of Wisconsin's finest artisanal cheeses with their brews. (Über is adjacent to Wisconsin Cheese Market, so that helps.) The best bet is the custom plate that lets you curate your own tasting with most of the key cheese styles—including cheddars that have been aged for as long as fifteen and eighteen years. Über's not shy about its local pride. Tin beer signs, from the vintage (Schlitz) to the modern (Lakefront) sides of Milwaukee brewing, adorn the walls, as do early photographs from the city's formative years.

Austin, Texas

Pray for warm weather (Austin is in central Texas, so it happens more often than not) because enjoying a pint or two in the wide-open beer garden is the best way to enjoy **Banger's** (though the indoor section has its virtues as well). And, this being Austin, the bar doubles as a live music venue and even hosts a Big Band Brunch every Sunday. As its name suggests, Banger's specialty, besides really good beer, is sausage. And there's an encased meat selection for all tastes—from a Turducken sausage and Jalapeño Cheddar Bratwurst to Andouille and a classic Bangers and Mash. Veggie versions are available (it's Austin, after all, the only place in Texas where vegetarians can dine without getting dirty looks). The bar stocks plenty of American crafts, as well as international specialty beers—a lot of Belgians, of course—and a sizeable selection of favorites from local breweries like 512 and Austin Beerworks.

San Francisco, California

If bikers and craft beer seem like an incongruity, you've never been to **Toronado**. In a nutshell, the now-iconic Lower Haight destination is a high-end beer pub trapped in the body of a biker bar. Appearance-wise, it's a first-class dive but in the best way possible (it's even been featured on one of Anthony Bourdain's travel shows). In the evening, you'll likely be greeted by a burly yet good-humored bouncer who definitely seems to know his way around a Harley. Inside, its most distinguishing element is the red neon sign high above the bar that reads "Garage Service." Just below the ceiling, tap handles of brands past and present line the perimeter. A sign on the wall reads "no crap on tap" and Toronado delivers in spades. A frequent tap offering is beer-geek Holy Grail Pliny the Elder from Sonoma, California's Russian River Brewing Company and sometimes the even Holier Grail, Pliny the Younger, like it's no big deal. Don't leave home without your ATM card because Toronado is cash-only.

San Francisco's dive bar cup may runneth over, but they certainly aren't the be-all and end-all of the beer experience in Fog City. For the international gastropub vibe, one of the newer spots that fits the bill is Mikkeller Bar. The spot is the brainchild of Mikkel Borg Bjergsø, cofounder of Mikkeller "Brewery" in Denmark. The quotation marks are intentional; Mikkeller singlehandedly launched the "gypsy brewer" concept whereby a brewer doesn't own a brick-and-mortar production space but, instead, moves from established brewery to established brewery and produces in those facilities. Mikkeller Bar set up shop in 2013 in an early-twentieth-century building in the city's revitalized Tenderloin district. The forty-plus taps have their fair share of Mikkeller brews, including some San Francisco exclusives, as well as plenty of American, Belgian, and German craft selections.

Artisanal sausages, charcuterie, sandwiches, and salads are the edible pairings in the eighty-seat pub.

Washington, D.C.

The District of Columbia has quickly become one of the prime beer-drinking cities in the country, and **Churchkey** has become the center of the better-beer universe in the nation's capital (especially after the legendary **Brickskeller** closed—more on that in a moment). Located upstairs from the beery eatery Birch & Barley, Churchkey features some 555 brews—fifty on draught, five hundred in bottles and cans, and five on cask—all curated by renowned beer director Greg Engert, whom *Food & Wine* magazine named among the best beer sommeliers in the country. Even though Birch & Barley offers more of a fine-dining experience, Churchkey does not lack for tasty bites—from burgers and sandwich innovations to off-the-beaten-path bar snacks like fire-roasted shishito peppers with spicy peanut sauce.

When Brickskeller ceased operations, it really was the end of an era. The bar had opened in 1957 and had more than fifty beers, which was unheard of at the time. By the time it ceased operations more than five decades later, its list numbered somewhere around two thousand. It was also a shrine for breweriana, as it featured a wall lined with vintage beer cans, mostly of brands that hadn't existed in decades. But its owners assured fans it was only selling the building in which it was housed, they weren't selling the business. In fact they held on to the name and continued with the Brickskeller tasting series at its sister establishment, **RFD** (which stands for Regional Food & Drink). RFD may lack some of the vintage ambiance of the Brickskeller—you don't get much of that, well, brick interior—but it isn't short on charm. Its black-and-white checkerboard tiled floor definitely looks like it'd be more at home in a diner, but that's part of its unassuming glory. Hidden behind the façade of a no-nonsense townie sports bar are thirty taps of the craft movement's finest and a bottle list that numbers somewhere in the three hundreds. The Brickskeller spirit.

The District's booming beer scene has spilled across the Potomac into Alexandria, Virginia, and the same restaurant group behind Churchkey and Birch & Barley runs a more upmarket gastropub called **Rustico**, famous for its innovative pizzas (one of which includes pulled pork, swiss chard, béchamel, white cheddar, caramelized onions, and North Carolina barbecue vinaigrette) but, more importantly, for its four hundred-plus beer selections from around the world (mostly bottles, but plenty of draft).

Los Angeles, California

As far as major US cities go, L.A. was a bit late to the party with the whole craft beer boom. (Maybe it's because it has such a driving culture and craft gained a lot of its traction with such road-unfriendly high-ABV brews.) But the City of Angels boasts a famous day-drinking culture (probably folks who are waiting tables at night between movie and TV auditions), and it was only a matter of time before it caught up with the other top brew towns. Among its attractions is the gastropub **Mohawk Bend** on Sunset Boulevard in the Echo Park district. The beer's always fresh, which is no mean feat because Mohawk maintains seventy-two taps, which is nearly as many the Falling Rock. It's quite a spacious venue, as it once housed an old vaudeville theater, so there's plenty of room to stretch out at the bar, in booths on high-boy and communal tables, or in its skylit atrium. It uses only California ingredients in its food, which ranges from thin-crust pizzas made with 100 percent organic herbs and tomatoes to grass-fed burgers. Mohawk Bend is the brainchild of Amy and Tony Yanow, the latter of whom is the namesake for another well-respected beer spot, Tony's Darts Away in Burbank. Tony also cofounded, with business partner Meg Gill, L.A.'s Golden Road Brewering Co., which they sold to Anheuser-Busch InBev in 2015, four years after the brewery first opened its doors.

But one can't talk about L.A. beer without mentioning the **Library Alehouse** in Santa Monica. The literature-inspired spot near the beach was craft long before craft was cool in LaLa Land. In 2010, the Library brought in executive chef Tom Hugenberger, who's turned bar food into high art. If you're wondering what that means, here are two words: Oxtail Poutine! If that's not convincing, here are a few more words: mac and cheese with truffle oil. The menu is designed to pair perfectly with any of the thirty or so draught selections and countless bottle options.

San Diego, California

L.A. may have had some catching up to do on the beer front, but its neighbor two hours south has always been way ahead of the rest of the country. At last count the greater San Diego area is home to some one hundred breweries, including nationally prominent producers like Stone Brewing, Ballast Point, and Port Brewing/The Lost Abbey. The greatest symbol of its craft cred has been Hamilton's Tavern. Like San Francisco's Toronado, Hamilton's is a nod to the city's blue-collar heritage with lots of great rotating draught options—twenty-six at any given time—and zero pretension.

Many of the best California breweries save some of their rarer kegs for Hamilton's. It's a perennial honoree as the best or one of the best bars in San Diego.

Its food menu is very vegan-friendly, with burgers and pork-forward pizza options to keep the carnivores happy.

If you're drinking alone or just plain bored, you can pass the time staring at the ceiling and counting all of the tap handles—present and long past—dangling from the rafters. It's way more visually pleasing than those glow-in-the-dark star stickers.

Hamilton's is a couple miles outside of the city center and requires a cab, Uber, or a rental car to access. If your time in San Diego is limited and you happen to be in the Gaslamp Quarter, Neighborhood is a safe bet. Twenty-six taps and around forty bottles should slake the thirst of most discerning beer lovers. Neighborhood offers some creative twists on traditional pub fare, from corn dogs and cooked-to-order burger innovations to seared albacore tuna sandwiches and steak tartare, all served on plates of varying sizes and levels of shareability.

Seattle, Washington

Seattle may be the bigger Pacific Northwestern city, but it's always been overshadowed by Portland in brewing circles. However, that doesn't mean Seattle lacks a beer scene. Quite the contrary, it boasts one that most other metro areas would kill for. (It is the city that birthed Elysian Brewing Co., after all, which was recently acquired by AB InBev.) It also has a bar that holds its own against the iconic pubs of the West Coast: **Brouwer's Cafe**. Diverse gastropub edibles complement an extensive roster of brews—three hundred-plus in bottles, sixty-four on tap—as well as sixty types of Scotch for those more in the mood for a whiskey. Lamb burgers, a traditional Belgian stew known as Stoofvlees, and beer Cioppino are just a few of the menu items. The very spacious establishment is as much fun to look at as it is to eat and drink in, with stone interior walls and a second level overlooking the downstairs main bar area, atrium-style.

Portland, Oregon

Determining the best beer bar in Portland is like a child trying to choose a single toy to bring with him on vacation. It's virtually impossible. At last count there were about sixty breweries within the city limits; many of those were bars unto themselves. We'll stick with the no beer-producing pubs to keep this list as equitable as possible.

Bars have come and gone over the past handful of decades, but few have been around long enough to witness the local brewing revolution in all of its phases. **Horse Brass Pub** occupies such rarified air. The SE Portland icon was bringing great beer to Portland before Portland was bringing great beer to Portland (and everywhere else, for that matter). Opening in 1976, Horse Brass modeled itself after the traditional pubs of Britain and served many UK brews (and classic edibles like fish and chips, meat pies, ploughman's lunch, and bangers) that were hard to get on the left side of the pond. As American beer evolved, so did Horse Brass's fifty-strong tap list, which incorporated many fine ales and lagers from the Oregon scene and well beyond. Horse Brass has always been a staunch proponent of serving beer in proper imperial pint glasses—the twenty-ounce ones that get a little bulbous two thirds of the way up the vessel before flattening out again near the mouth. With forty years of consistent quality, Horse Brass earns its right to boast: "If it were any more authentic, you'd need a passport."

It would be unfair to call **Belmont Station**—also in SE Portland—a beer bar, as it is so much more than that. For one thing, it's also a bottle shop, selling more than 1,200 beers of all kinds from all places. The "biercafe" component is an impressive setup in its own right, with more than twenty rotating taps and a hand-pull beer engine for cask selections. Not only is it a great spot to drink the beverage for which Portland is most famous, but its back patio is the home base for another concept with which the city has become synonymous: the food cart. The Italian Market, the independently operated mobile kitchen offers South Philly-style Italo-Americano comfort food; the meatballs are to die for and pair perfectly with just about anything Belmont Station might have on that day. The Italian Market is easily accessible through a door in Belmont Station's back room. The Station has been a fixture of the Portland Beer scene since 1997 and will likely remain so for decades to come.

Bailey's Taproom is a rather unassuming-looking spot in downtown Portland, close to the central business district, hotels, famous restaurants (like Jake's seafood), and the trendy Pearl district. Twenty-four always-changing taps and one hundred bottles touch on most of the country, but special attention is given to Pacific Northwestern creations. It's a popular after-work spot and can get quite crowded at happy hour; despite its proximity to tourist and business traveler lodging, the scene is very much local-centric. It's also a nice place to look at, with lots of exposed brick and a very well maintained wooden bar and tabletops. There's a constantly updating digital screen listing the draft selections and indicating how much of each remains. (It's one of the rare places where you don't have to worry about an out-of-date blackboard menu still featuring kegs that have long since kicked.) There's no food served, but you can bring food from plenty of nearby places into Bailey's.

Portland, Maine

Even though the much larger Left Coast Portland gets a lot more attention and is the premier beer destination, do not count out the much more modest New England city of the same name. For a town with a population just over 65,000—the largest city in the entire state, by the way—it has a colossal amount of beer activity going on. Not only is it home to great breweries like Allagash, Geary's, and Gritty McDuff's, it has pubs that folks travel to Portland just to visit. Chief among those is **Novare Res Bier Café**, a modest spot a few steps below street level in the city's revitalized Old Port district. Not so modest is the selection: more than five hundred bottles, twenty-five rotating taps, and two cask hand pumps. Though it's a local joint at heart, its soul belongs to the world. Its founders traveled the world to some of the premier drinking spots in places like Belgium, Japan, the UK, and Germany and drew upon all of those influences. The hand pumps, of course, are of British extraction, and the long wooden tables wouldn't be out of place in a sprawling German beer hall. The list is just as eclectic, with a bit of a tilt toward Belgians. The food's a few steps above the average bar bites, particularly with its à la carte cheese and charcuterie offerings. The name, Novare Res, is Latin for "to start a revolution," which is appropriate considering that's exactly what's been going on in the global beer business.

As amazing as Novare Res is, it owes its existence to a pub clear across town called the **Great Lost Bear**. It's in a far less touristy part of the city, outside of the downtown area, and it predates Novare Res by nearly three decades. When it opened in 1979, it didn't start out as a craft beer bar because, well, craft beer wasn't really a thing. But it was an early adopter. After the pioneering D.L. Geary Brewing Co. sold its first pint in 1986, solidifying Maine's position as a beer state, the Bear started adding more taps in anticipation of the nascent revolution. In its earliest days it had eight taps. That's tiny by today's standards, but still fairly impressive considering how few beer options there were in the '70s. That grew to twenty-four, then thirty-six, and finally seventy-eight. It's one of the best places in the

Northeast to sample New England's finest; the Bear dedicates fifty of those draught lines to regional brews and half of those to Maine-made offerings.

Being located two miles from the Old Port has its advantages. For one thing, there's plenty of room to move around. The bar area is set off from the multi-room dining space. Despite its extensive list, the Bear has a very unpretentious vibe that stays very true to Portland's blue-collar history. Deli sandwiches, barbecue, wings, and other bar fare dominate the menu, and there are plenty of selections for non-carnivores. Gourmet magazine has even named it one of 125 Places to Have a Beer Before You Die.

Charleston, South Carolina

After a slowish start, the craft beer movement has been accelerating considerably in the Southeast. South Carolina has been among the states to get in the game in a more pronounced way after a few arcane alcohol laws were updated, which created a more hospitable environment for brewing. And the best spot to soak in the burgeoning scene is the ironically named **Closed for Business**. The décor seems more Western/Frontier than Southern and includes rustic wooden walls and some taxidermy on and above a mantelpiece. However, its most striking visual element is the illuminated "453" mounted above the bar's glassware—not any deep significance, it's just the pub's address (453 King Street). The window to the kitchen features the

Charleston, South Carolina's Closed for Business.

equally large, equally lighted word "EAT." The food menu tries to focus as much as it can on fresh dishes made from locally source ingredients, and the forty-two taps give priority to brews from its home state. Spend some time in the bathroom. It's a shrine to beer literature; it's wallpapered with pages from guides and magazines on the subject.

Savannah, Georgia

Those who've read the book or seen the movie version of "Midnight in the Garden of Good and Evil" know that Savannah is an offbeat kind of place that defies convention and sometimes logic. That's why it's fitting that the town's best spot to sip some suds is a place with a rather incongruous moniker: **The Distillery Ale House**. To be fair, the site of this fine establishment was a working distillery generations before it was a beer bar. The owners began producing spirits at the site in 1904, just a scant decade and a half before the dreaded Eighteenth Amendment rendered such a business model illegal. The facility became a pharmacy—complete with the era-appropriate lunch counter and soda fountain—and remained so until 1940. (Local legend says the proprietors were making bathtub gin and illicit beer upstairs during the Prohbition years of 1920–1933.) Fast-forward nearly sixty years and Michael and Julia Volen brought legal alcohol back to the site when they opened the Distillery Ale House. The pub retains its turn-of-the-century industrial brick composition, with high ceilings that make the place feel massive. The Distillery lives up to its "No Crap, Just Craft" mantra, with twenty-one tap choices and nearly one hundred bottles from most of the US, including some nice selections from the burgeoning craft scene in the Southeast. And don't worry, "Distillery" isn't a total misnomer; there's a generous list of fine bourbons and other whiskeys, as well as world-class, handcrafted gin. It's just not made there.

Las Vegas, Nevada

I know what you're thinking. Vegas, really? Isn't that just a town of nightclubs serving overpriced glow-in-the-dark cocktails and scantily clad casino waitresses serving complimentary watered-down well drinks to compulsive gamblers? For the most part, yes, but finding good beer in Sin City isn't as hard as it used to be. Even Vegas isn't immune to the global craft beer boom. The best place to sample the bounty of American and international artisanal brewers is **Public House**, located in restaurant row inside the

Venetian. The gastropub carries more than one hundred bottles and offers twenty-four well-maintained taps pouring favorites from Western brewers like Deschutes and Ninkasi as well as brews from other parts of the country and the world. There's always a cask selection as well, served in impeccable form at just the right temperature. The menu carries the usual steaks, burgers, pastas, seafood and the like, with some less-common foodie fare like roasted bone marrow and potted duck rillettes. Don't throw your money away on the slot machines; an hour or two at the Public House is a much more rewarding experience.

18

Bar-Hopping, International Style

The Best and Most Storied Beer Bars Across the Globe

America has some truly iconic drinking establishments, but those are only a fraction of what the entire planet has to offer.

Toronto, Ontario, Canada

It's no surprise that Canada's largest, most cosmopolitan city has a fairly hopping (pun intended) craft beer scene. Mention beer to a local and the first response you're likely to get is, "Have you been to **Bar Volo**?" The venue became a fixture of central Toronto's Yonge Street in 1985, when it opened as an Italian restaurant. Talk about knowing how to evolve with a changing market: It eventually morphed into one of the most respected craft beer establishments throughout Canada, as well as a good place to eat, with lots of Southern Italian and Spanish-inspired small plates (mostly locally sourced), which go great with the more than fifty bottles of beer and cider, twenty-six taps, and six cask-conditioned offerings. Bar Volo was also home to House Ales project, its own small pilot brewery in its kitchen making English, American, and Belgian-style beers, often collaborating with some of Canada's finest production breweries. Dangling vines beckoned drinkers into the charming brick building, and rows of bottles serve as the primary décor inside; evening candlelight gives them an ethereal glow. If this is reading more as a eulogy than an endorsement, that's because in 2016 its landlord informed the Morana family, owners of the Yonge Street institution, that they would have to vacate the site by fall to make room for condos—sadly, an all-too-familiar scenario.

Vancouver, British Columbia, Canada

It's almost comical that one of Western Canada's best craft beer bars has the same name as the filthy den of liver-obliteration/sometime brothel on the Showtime series *Shameless*. But the **Alibi Room** in Vancouver couldn't be in starker contrast with the fictional Chicago dive. (To be fair, there are plenty of bars that have adopted the moniker.) The Vancouver spot is a sprawling two-story affair in a historical brick building constructed at the turn of the twentieth century along the side of the city's railyard—constructed for easy access to the city's still operational shipping port. Its twenty-first-century iteration is the center of British Columbian craft culture, and it has fifty taps (with flights of four tasters available) that heavily emphasize locals and regionals (the cask-conditioned offerings are almost always local). The food boasts equally artisanal and ethical origins, with locally sourced, free-range, naturally raised and/or ocean-friendly meats, fish, and vegetables. Those feeling sociable can sit at the long communal tables, but there are plenty of private spots to keep things intimate. The ample natural light makes it an ideal spot for day drinking—especially if you don't want to forget that it's

Vancouver's popular beer gastropub, Alibi Room.

the middle of the day—and for a hair-of-the-dog brunch. Tabletop candles set the mood after dark.

London, England

There's likely no better physical representation of the craft-inspired shift that's taking place in the United Kingdom than **Euston Tap**, which is located inside a small stone Victorian building that once served as a gatehouse near intercity railway terminus Euston Station. And it's also the perfect example of how to honor tradition while diving headlong into the future.

Like any good London pub, it has a healthy array of real ales on cask—eight at any given time and always rotating—nineteen standard draft lines, and 150 bottles. Up until recently, such numbers were unheard of in Britain, mainly due to the fact that brewers also control chains of pubs. Euston Tap is completely independent of that sort of arrangement. What's also unheard of is the fact that a pub near a train station has such a robust collection of drinking options.

The selection gives a nod to legends of the US craft-brewing scene, with some selections from other countries (Belgium among them, of course) as well. But you'll also get a showcase of the new wave of British brewers that are shaking up the country's centuries-old traditions. The street-level bar area with limited seating is fairly tight and gets crowded very quickly. (It almost seems like a dimension-defying feat getting all those brews in there.) There some more seating upstairs and a heated beer garden just outside so folks needn't feel like sardines.

Inverness, Scotland

In the northern Scottish Highlands, near the notorious Loch Ness, lies the great city of Inverness, which is just as famous for its legendary golf course as it is for the aquatic monster a handful of miles away. The best place to sample the pales, porters, IPAs, stouts, and lagers (on cask and in bottles) of one of the leaders of the new wave of Scottish craft brewers—nearby Black Isle Brewery—is at the festively named **Hootananny**. It didn't earn the moniker because of its raucous clientele—they tend to be much more laid back than that—but from the fact that it doubles as a live music venue. It's the best place to discover the up-and-coming acts of northern Scotland and beyond. On many nights, there are classic Celtic folk combos performing at a center table, allowing visitors to fully absorb the full Scottish experience.

Dublin, Ireland

For the longest time, Dublin has been a one-beer town. To be sure, Guinness is still ubiquitous and impossible to avoid when you're in the country, let alone the city in which it's brewed. But Irish pubs are getting more generous with their taps, as the global craft beer wave sweeps through the Emerald Isle. One of the best selections you'll find in the capital city is at **Against the Grain**. What it lacks in name originality, it more than makes up for in variety. It's owned by Galway Bay Brewery, which cranks out some favorable porters, IPAs, Irish reds, and, of course, stouts. But there's plenty more to discover at Against the Grain from breweries inside and outside the country. It's the best miscrocosmic snapshot a drinker can get of the grander Irish craft beer scene. There's plenty of space to spread out—lots of nooks and crannies, booths, and drinking ledges—and a tasty pub menu (burger meats include lamb). Lots to explore as far as taps and bottles go, as well.

Copenhagen, Denmark

If you're planning to visit Copenhagen, here are two pieces of advice: No. 1, consider winning the lottery or robbing a bank because everything there

Copenhagen's Øl Baren.

is ultra-expensive. It makes New York seem like a rural community in the heartland by comparison. No. 2, if you do go, you have to have a beer at **Øl Baren** (it's probably all you'll have money for anyway.) The space is fairly small, but the beer selection is far from it. Bottles from all over the beer-making planet line the top shelves behind the bar, creating a sort of beery little welcoming committee for all who enter. It's a popular spot among local industry folk. Local brewery and bar staff (yes, even other beer bars) often end up, post-shift, at Øl Baren and usually close the place.

A somewhat larger affair is Ørsted Ølbar, which is a bit more date friendly, with its evening candlelight (with empty beer bottles as makeshift candle holders), exposed brick walls, rustic wooden tables, and loungey couches and armchairs. The twenty taps serve a fresh, rotating selection of international artisanal brews. But the place knows how to let its hair down—there's a foosball table and plenty of European sporting events on the TV.

Stockholm, Sweden

For a sense of the beer scene in another Scandinavian country, **Akkurat** in Stockholm is a good place to start. The draft and bottle lists pull from the best brewing nations around the world and have a strong emphasis on Belgium. (Don't worry; there's plenty of Swedish stuff as well, including products from the Brooklyn Brewery/Carlsberg joint venture, Nya Carnegie Bryggeriet, and Skebo Bruksbryggeri.) Akkurat partners with the folks at the Belgian lambic brewery Cantillon, and there's always a surprising number of fresh Cantillon products for a bar that's not based anywhere near Brussels. A big chunk of the bottle list reads like a love letter to lambic and gueuze.

Tokyo, Japan

Japan's been a hotbed of craft-brewing activity of late, and the most vivid representation of that is a bar called **Popeye** in the Ryogoku district. The pub offers more than seventy beers on tap and has an international selection, but a lot of its focus is on the stuff produced on Japanese soil. It's a tough choice, so luckily you can order sampler trays to get a good cross-section of the local options.

It's also one of the few spots throughout the country where you can drink without inhaling secondhand smoke. Yes, there's still a robust indoor

Popeye, perhaps the most famous beer bar in all of Japan.

smoking culture in Japan, and it's all still legal. You could be sitting at a sushi bar, enjoying the fresh Chu-toro, and you could be bookended by two human chimneys. At Popeye, there is an outdoor terrace where smoking is permitted. So if you're a nonsmoker and the weather's nice, it's a bit of a tradeoff.

Inside, it gets noisy and crowded and the tables are very close together, but that's not a bad thing if you're in the mood. There's no better way to absorb the energy of the Japanese beer scene.

Brussels, Belgium

One can't speak about Brussels without mentioning three pubs in particular—two classics and one relative newcomer. Of the former sort, the one to which most folks passing through the Belgian capital often make a beeline is **Delirium Cafe**, if for no other reason than to experience a beer list whose extensiveness is nothing short of intimidating. In 2004, Delirium made the

Guinness Book of World Records for being the brewery with the most varieties of beer commercially available, which, perhaps not so coincidentally, was tallied at 2,004. At last count, it offered somewhere in the neighborhood of 3,000 different bottles. If you're lucky, you can get a peek inside the cellar in which they're all kept in tip-top shape.

About a seven-minute walk from Delirium, across the city's Grand Place, is another legendary Brussels staple, **Poechenellekelder**, which sits directly across from the famous Manneken Pis statue (the one of the boy urinating). There's a nice cross-section of Belgian ales, offering a tour through the country's wealth of styles. Aesthetically, the prime attractions of this two-story pub in the city's cobblestone quarter are the marionettes dangling from the walls and rafters. There's a romantic, medieval entertainment element to it, as well as a slightly creepy vibe.

The newer kid on the block, in the more modern part of the city, is **Chez Moeder Lambic**, which resembles more of a post-craft-beer-boom bar.

Brugge, Belgium

If Belgian beer is a religion, then **'t Brugs Beertje** is its cathedral. (The name means "the Brugge/Bruges Little Bear.") Metal signs from breweries from all over the country adorn the walls of its two rooms, and the list, which focuses only on styles of Belgian origin, features some three hundred bottles from across Wallonia and Flanders. Pilsner may be the most widely produced and consumed style in the country, but it's not quintessentially Belgian. Founder/owner Daisy Claes is a legend on the international beer scene. The menu features some light bar bites—cheeses, pickles, and charcuterie mostly. Claes and her staff are visibly passionate about what they do and are always happy to offer a suggestion or, when they're not slammed during peak times, just chat at length about beer. The bar is centrally located in Brugge's fairy-tale-like medieval old town of cobblestones and canals.

While we're in Brugge, we might as well stop in at **La Trappiste**, which has quite a robust list of Belgian ales, many of which you're likely to find over at 't Brugs Beertje. However, you don't' want to miss the chance to drink them in La Trappiste's setting; the place is a cavernous, partially subterranean pub with an interior almost entirely composed of brick. The arched ceilings and low lighting make it as close to drinking in a medieval castle as you're ever going to get.

Ghent, Belgium

Since we're already in the heart of Flanders, a quick jaunt to one of the region's other great cities, Ghent, is an absolute must (it's barely a thirty-minute train ride from Brugge). If there's ever been a drinking establishment that is inextricably linked with the city, it's **Het Waterhuis aan de Bierkant**, which translates to the rather playful moniker, "The Waterhouse on the Beerside." It's the owners' way of saying, "It may seem like our pub is adjacent to a canal, but it is really the canal that is adjacent to our pub." With close to two hundred of the best beers the smallish Western European country has to offer, it earns the right to have that name. Not to say the water is a mere supporting player. It's just as much a reason to spend an afternoon there sipping Trappist ales and Flemish sours paired with local delicassies and cheeses. There are plenty of views from indoors, but there's no comparison to sitting on a table on the patio, watching barges of sightseers drifting down the canal, and soaking in the Flemish architectural splendor of the

Het Waterhuis van de Bierkant sits on the edge of a canal in Ghent. Its name playfully translates to "Waterhouse on the Beerside."

waterside row houses and restaurants. Late spring and early autumn days are the best for that. It's also spitting distance from one of Ghent's biggest historical attractions, the medieval Gravensteen castle.

Sydney, Australia

Australia has had a bit of a craft brewing renaissance, not unlike America's, though it occurred a good fifteen or so years behind it. Around 2013 boutique beer bars started popping up in earnest, thanks to a change in the law that made the licensing for such startup craft-friendly operations much more affordable. Previously, it was next to impossible to turn a profit if a bar wasn't large and established and pushing high-volume macro-produced beer. Since the liberalization of such restrictions, local entrepreneurs wasted no time in fashioning a world-class beer bar scene. In Sydney's Darlinghurst district is **Bitter Phew**, which opened in 2014 and is something of a microcosm of the country's craft explosion. The upstairs climb reveals an airy, SoHo (New York) gallery-like space, complete with paintings and photos from local artists affixed to the walls. Bitter offers more than a *phew* selections. Twelve rapidly rotating taps and ninety-seven bottles put an emphasis on the global scale of the artisanal beer boom, with plenty of American, Belgian, and Scandinavian craft offerings to go around. The locals, of course, get their due with plenty of the draught lines dedicated to products from New South Wales and beyond. There's a definite hipster slant, but that's to be expected these days in craft beer bars. The music selections offer a little something for everyone, from big band to St. Vincent.

Keg & Brew (aka K&B), in the Surry Hills neighborhood offers an impressive cross-section of modern Australian craft beers as seen through the eyes of old Sydney. It was founded in 1936 and feels a bit like the love child of a traditional English pub and a rural American roadhouse. The walls are a shrine to taxidermy with the heads of stags, moose, and buffalo staring down into your pint glass. The food menu speaks with an American accent, with dishes like Kentucky Bourbon Black Angus Rump and Philly Cheese Steak (!). It takes pride in its whiskey list, which emphasizes American bourbon. K&B is the very model of a cross-cultural experience and worth every minute.

Bitter Phew is one of the more popular beer hangouts in Sydney, Australia.

Sydney's K&B.

Auckland, New Zealand

Kiwis have been riding the same artisanal wave that the Aussies have been enjoying, and the bar scene is all the better for it. And some of the best places to drink are popping up in some of the most unlikely of places. Case in point: **No. 1 Queen** in Auckland's central business district. At first glance, it appears to be nothing more than a coffee kiosk a stone's throw from the city's main mass transit hub—a place one would expect to grab a pre- or post-commute cup of joe and perhaps a doughnut. But on closer inspection, it reveals itself to be a full-on beer bar with some seating inside its walls but with more on picnic tables outside. In 2012 the spot made the wise business decision to become a showcase for the best brews the North and South Islands of New Zealand have to offer. The spot, named for its

Auckland, New Zealand's No. 1 Queen craft beer café.

address, also hosts a weekly craft beer market each Wednesday, when twenty or so brewery reps hawk their wares to the public. It's also reserved a full cooler for folks to share their homebrews.

Hong Kong

Hong Kong is a bit late to the party with the whole craft beer thing, but things are changing very quickly there. Since 2012 the city has hosted an enormously successful beer festival, and the local brewery activity has increased more than five-fold. The most vivid symbol of its burgeoning craft brew scene is a little pub called the **Roundhouse Taproom** in the Central district neighborhood of SoHo. Twenty-five taps as well as a generous selection of bottles await visitors. Everything from up-and-coming Hong Kong

Hong Kong's Roundhouse Taproom.

brewers like Young Master and Moonzen to international favorites like Evil Twin, Brooklyn Brewery, and Founders are well represented at this industrial-chic hideaway. It's definitely taken a cue from the United States; even its barbecue-centric food menu has an American bent. When it comes to beer, Hong Kong is on the cusp of greatness, and the place to witness the revolution—which, by the way, will not be televised—is the Roundhouse.

For a classic English pub feel (the Brits controlled Hong Kong until 1997, after all), there's the **Globe**, a stone's throw from the Roundhouse. And though it may have been founded by a British expat (Toby Cooper, who also happens to head the Hong Kong Craft Beer Association) and sport aesthetics and food menu of a UK local—it does have some real ale on cask—its beer list is beyond modern. One could even argue that it was ahead of its time for the city, offering the best of the best from the world's greatest craft brewers and showcasing the local upstarts that are redefining Hong Kong brewing.

19

Beer Cocktails?

Are They Ever a Good Idea?

In the early 2000s, the boardroom folk at the then Big Three beer companies (now Big Two), realized they were hemorrhaging alcohol market share as wine and spirits were gaining—more so for the latter category. The big question on every executive's mind was: How do we stop the bleeding? The big answer: Let's go after spirits drinking occasions. It would have been great if they had just stopped there. But "occasions," for many, meant "formats." And for spirits, that meant cocktails.

At the time it wasn't uncommon for a food and beverage journalist to get invited to luncheons hosted by Anheuser-Busch—in the days before InBev swooped in, cut every conceivable cost, and frowned upon its employees needlessly spending money on silly things like nutritional sustenance. One such event was designed to get media types to convince their readership to think differently about beer. And that event was a cocktail mixer.

Servers greeted attendees with champagne flutes garnished with sprigs of rosemary. In those flutes: Michelob Ultra. Of course, that's fairly basic and barely qualifies as a full-on cocktail, but it speaks volumes on how laughable a task it can be to try to turn beer into something it's not.

Many purists might cringe at the notion of mixing beer with anything. If it's good, it's good on its own. Period. But that doesn't mean using beer as the base of a cocktail is always ill-advised. For instance, look at the Mexican tradition of cervezas preparadas (prepared beers). The most basic of those is the michelada, which combines a brew with tomato juice—sometimes Clamato—some hot sauce, a rim full of spices, and usually a shot or two of lime. The more involved affair is the chavela, which incorporates a lot of those same elements but often throws in things like shrimp cocktail. It's not like anyone's using an imperial stout as the base. These are usually built on standard, refreshing Mexican lagers.

There are certain beer cocktails that always have seemed to get a pass from the beer-drinking public. Think about the Black-and-Tan, for instance.

The classic version involves mixing a stout—usually Guinness, because it's so damn ubiquitous—with a basic lager (often something like Harp, because of the whole Irish thing and the fact that they're both owned by Diageo.) Some bars have gotten creative and have updated the concept for the craft generation, even going so far as to mix an imperial stout with an IPA (though the lager, low-ABV dry Irish stout route is still the most popular—just with more artisanal brands). A lot of purists will deride the thought of adding anything to their beloved beer, but come March 17, they briefly change their tune.

And it's not just the Black and Tans. Many don't bat an eye when a bar dyes a lager green on St. Patrick's Day; nor do they seem to balk at the notion of an Irish Car Bomb: a Guinness base with shots of Jameson Irish Whiskey and Bailey's Irish Cream dropped in it. It's an ethnically specific—and, perhaps, mildly offensive—variation on the Boilermaker: a beer with a shot of whiskey in it. (Sometimes the shot is served separately and the beer is used to chase it. But why bother drinking a whiskey that's so bad it needs a chaser? Digression over.)

Another minor abomination in the face of all that is good and holy is the Saké Bomb. It's pretty much an Irish Car Bomb/Boilermaker, except it uses saké instead of a spirit. And that one's not just cringeworthy, it's actually kind of sad. Adding a 40-proof spirit to a beer is ridiculous, but it almost makes sense from a pure intoxication standpoint. If drunkenness is one's goal (and it rarely should be), at least a shot of Jameson is going to get the person there a bit faster than with beer alone. The Car Bomb wasn't invented for its flavor.

But among the many misconceptions about saké—admittedly a far less familiar beverage in the United States and therefore more prone to misinformation—is that it's a spirit. It is not. It is fermented like beer. And while it's considerably stronger than the average beer, "considerably stronger" means a total ABV of 15 percent (on rare occasions 18 or 19 percent). Trying to booze up one's brew with saké is about as effective as doing so with white wine and only slightly more so than doing so with unspiked Kool-Aid.

You can't blame the Japanese or the Irish for adulterating their respective beverages. Those are largely stateside inventions. (The conventional claim is that the Saké Bomb was invented by the occupying US forces in Japan after World War II, but there's really no documented proof to verify this.)

But you'll be surprised to learn that the citizens of a country that is synonymous with good beer in most people's minds are actually responsible for adulterating their most revered beverage.

Case in point: the Berliner Weisse and its red or green *schüss*. Doesn't that technically make it a cocktail? It certainly looks like one, especially when there's a straw involved.

It's not just the Berliner Weisse, though. Germany is also responsible for contributing the word "radler" to the liquid lexicon. Radler is usually a beer with a shot of (often carbonated) clear lemonade in it (Austrians are known for using cloudy lemonade with an orangeish hue). The concoction is very refreshing and very low-ABV (usually around 2.5 percent). It actually gets its name from the German word for "cyclist." After a long day pedaling on the pavement, riders would cool off with the sugar-and-citrus-enhanced brew.

Then, of course, there's the shandy, whose origins are British. It's not unlike the radler, except it can involve sweet kicks from things like carbonated soft drinks—often ginger ale and the like—and fruit juice.

The Brits also get the credit for creating the Snakebite, a refresher that's equal parts beer and (alcoholic) cider. The classic version involves lager and some sort of crowd-pleasing cider (usually of the sweet to slightly dry variety). But the cider renaissance that kicked into high gear around 2011 got the creative juices flowing, and bars have gotten more experimental with their Snakebites. Some will mix a stout with a very dry cider, or even something like a cyser—a cider/mead hybrid combining fermented apples with fermented honey. The Brooklyn BrewShop, purveyor of all things home-brewable, suggests topping it off with an optional shot of black currant syrup.

For the most part, many of those classics (well, semi-classics) in a lot of ways had the effect of weakening or masking the flavors of the beers being used. But are there any options out there in which all of the components enhance and complement each other?

Indeed there are. And some of them involve ice cream!

Drinkable Desserts

Among the best dessert-y concoctions involving our favorite fermented beverage is the stout float. Even better is the imperial stout float; imperials tend to have a lot of boozy complexity and more intense coffee and chocolate notes going on, and what says dessert more than those elements? Brooklyn Brewery brewmaster Garrett Oliver published a recipe using the brewery's Black Chocolate Stout:

- 2 bottles of Brooklyn Black Chocolate Stout (or comparable imperial stout)

- 1 pint of ice cream
- 1 spiced Mexican chocolate bar, such as Mast Brothers Serrano Chile, or dark chocolate
- glasses, teaspoons, straws

The first step is to pour the beer. It's tempting to pour the beer over the ice cream, like it's Hershey's syrup going on a sundae, but that's only going to make a huge mess. Once the contents of the beer bottle are emptied in to glass, you can carefully scoop the ice cream into it. To top it off, take a grater and grate some chocolate on top of the foam. Insert straw and enjoy before it melts.

Fruit beers are especially dessert-ready. Famous New York City chef David Burke has partnered with Boston Beer Company for many years on everything from pairing dinners to recipes including beer as an ingredient. Among those recipes was the Samuel Adams Cherry Wheat Milkshake:

- 1 cup of vanilla ice cream
- ½ cup of milk
- 2 tablespoons of sugar
- 1 tablespoon of malt powder
- 3 tablespoons of Samuel Adams Cherry Wheat.

Throw all of that into a blender and serve.

When you think about it, though, dessert beer is borderline food. When it comes to beer cocktails for cocktails' sake, things get a little trickier (and often incredibly creative). Anthony Burgess, the author of *A Clockwork Orange* (which Stanley Kubrick adapted into a movie), tends to get the credit for popularizing the Hangman's Blood, a drink that sounds about as deranged and chaotic as young Alex, the humble narrator of the classic work of fiction:

- 2 fingers of gin
- 2 fingers of whiskey
- 2 fingers of rum
- 2 fingers of port
- 2 fingers of brandy
- 1 bottle or can of stout
- 1 splash of champagne

Pour each of the spirits into pint glass. If that's not enough to sharpen someone up and get them ready for a bit of the old ultra-violence, then nothing is.

For a little less insanity involving Champagne (or sparkling white wine produced in another region that isn't allowed to use the Champagne appellation), another classic is the Black Velvet. It's also probably one of the quickest and easiest drinks to make:

- ½ flute of sparkling white wine (The dryer the better, but that's just one opinion.)
- ½ flute of stout (If it's disappointing having such a small quantity of a beer that's only 4 or 5 percent ABV, why not try using a Russian Imperial stout?)

The sparkling wine adds something of a refreshing element to a beer that's not conventionally thought of as "refreshing." But for something that is the very definition of refreshment, Chow.com touts a concoction called the Summer Hoedown. As the name suggests, it calls for Höegaarden Belgian witbier (white ale), but there are plenty of wits that would work just as well, if not better—see the aforementioned Allagash, Hitachino Nest white, or Ommegang Witte, for starters. Of course, that would render the name null and void, but really, what's in a name? (And Hitachino-down kind of has a nice ring to it, doesn't it?)

- 1 seedless watermelon, around six pounds, give or take, rind removed and diced into large pieces
- 2 tablespoons of granulated sugar
- ¼ cup of maraschino liqueur
- 4 12-ounce bottles of white ale

Begin by putting a fine-mesh strainer over a large bowl and set that aside for a moment. Put half of the watermelon into a blender and blend until liquefied. Pour through the strainer into the bowl, push the juice through with a rubber spatula or wooden spoon until there's only pulp left, and then get rid of the pulp. Repeat with the second half of the watermelon. Add the sugar to the juice, stir until dissolved, and refrigerate until chilled. When it's cold enough, transfer the juice to a three-quart container, add the maraschino liqueur and beer, and stir to combine. Instant summer refreshment!

For lovers of stronger beers and stronger spirits, there's the Green Devil, invented by esteemed Toronto-based beer writer Stephen Beaumont. First, a bit of backstory. When Duvel Moortgat Brewery's flagship beer (the core ingredient in the mixture—accept no substitutes!) was first brewed in 1923, the initial reaction was that it was like "the devil" because it packs quite a punch at 8.5 percent ABV. It was, therefore, named Duvel, which means "devil" in the local dialect spoken in the brewery's immediate area. (The traditional Dutch spelling is "duivel.")

And though many drinkers haven't had absinthe—it's only been legal in the United States since 2007 (long story)—most are probably at least vaguely aware that its most popular nickname is the "Green Fairy." So when a Satanic-sounding brew meets a sprightly spirit, the marriage produces the offspring known as the Green Devil. (There's also a botanical interloper known as gin.) And it all makes such logical sense, given the fact that Duvel's flavor profile can veer on the herbal, floral, and earthy side, much like gin's botanicals and the essential ingredients of absinthe (wormwood, et al.):

- 1 ounce of gin
- ½ teaspoon of absinthe
- 1 11.2-ounce bottle of Duvel

Handbasket for subterranean journeys not included.

Okay, one more spirit-based craft beer cocktail before we completely change the subject.

Gose is one of those esoteric German styles that had fallen under the radar when industrial pilsners took over. The style, which alternates between tart and slightly salty, became popular in the city of Leipzig, and it's the main reason international beer travelers make a beeline to that city when they find themselves in what was once East Germany.

American craft brewers have more than held their own with their interpretations of the style, which is climbing the charts of US drinkers' favorites. And it's spawned a cocktail that's a hybrid of sorts with the most popular mixed drink to come out of Mexico (well, at least Mexican-American restaurants). Its name, predictably enough, is the Goserita. This particular recipe comes courtesy of Anderson Valley Brewing Company:

- 1.5 ounces of tequila
- 4 ounces of gose beer (Anderson Valley recommends its own, Holy Gose.)
- 1 ounce of agave nectar (Tequila's distilled from the stuff, so it's more of an appropriate fit than white-sugar-derived simple syrup.)
- 1 ounce of lime juice
- Ice

Shake the tequila, agave, lime juice, and ice, and then strain. Pour in the gose. With Mexican, German, and American influences, this one's as international as they come.

Occasionally, beer cocktails are born out of necessity. Not every bar or restaurant gets a full alcohol license. Those that have only a beer and wine license might feel a bit left out as their regulars start singing the praises of the local mixology scene. Fritzl's Lunchbox in Brooklyn is one establishment that gives more spirited venues a run for their money with its innovative liquor-less concoctions. Its Morning Beer cocktail features house-made kombucha (the fermented tea beverage that's supposed to be quite good for the ol' gut) combined with an IPA from Grand Rapids, Michigan's Founders Brewing Company. It also reinvents the shandy with a combination of Sixpoint Brewery's The Crisp lager and brown sugar limeade.

No one who's really into beer is likely to fall in love with a cocktail made from it. And more likely than not, most will continue to turn their noses up at the idea, and that's okay. Good beer is always going to be better on its own. But there's no harm in observing, from time to time, whether it plays well with others.

20

Beer Festivals

Navigating the Great American Beer Festival and Beyond

S turgeon's law or Sturgeon's revelation, named for American science-fiction author Theodore Sturgeon, states that 90 percent of everything is crap. If Sturgeon had ever gone to a beer festival, he might have upped that percentage to at least 95 or 96.

Along with the explosion in the number of US craft brewers—around 5,000—there's been a corresponding proliferation of beer festivals. And, as expected, the vast majority aren't very good. Unfortunately, when an industry is hot, it tends to attract more opportunistic carpetbaggers than it does emotionally, as well as financially, invested organizers who put their hearts and souls into staging a world-class event.

The Anatomy of a Festival

No two beer festivals are exactly alike, but there are common elements one would expect to find at just about all of them:

Pouring tables: Individual tables or pouring stations representing a particular brewery, importer, or distributor, form a circuit across the floor of the host space, be it a convention or civic center, sports arena, hotel, abandoned armory, or outdoor park or field. Each station features a portable draught system, bottles, or a combination of the two.

Tasting glasses: Registered attendees receive a commemorative glass—most frequently with a 6-ounce capacity, but sometimes larger. More often than not, for various safety and liability issues, those "glasses" are actually plastic. However, it's not uncommon to find actual glass.

Long lines at "white whale" stations: The beer drinking community has its fair share of white whales, those hard-to-find one-offs or extremely limited releases, that many brewers roll out on special occasions. When such brands make appearances in a festival setting, beer geek Ahabs gravitate en masse to those particular brewers' tables, waiting sometimes an hour or more of the festival (and most festival's tasting session's only last three or four hours) for a one-ounce pour of their Moby Dick. And the brew usually runs out within that hour, rendering the quest fruitless. It's actually a very welcome development for those indifferent about chasing large sea mammals. While their peers are reenacting their least favorite Disney World memories, it's minimizing the wait at other tables.

Festival pricing procedures can vary. At some, attendees pay one price in advance, get a wristband and a tasting glass, and taste as many different beers as they can as many times as they want. Others sell drink tickets or tokens, limiting the number of tastes festival-goers can get. Some let drinkers re-up when they've run out; others will include, say, ten tickets or tokens with each admission and not allow any additional purchases. Once gone, the attendee may either leave or switch to water. The rationale is that festival organizers don't want the event they've worked many long hours to stage to devolve into one colossal drunk fest. Sadly, though, that's usually very difficult to prevent—which brings us to the No. 1 component of a truly awful beer festival.

Any time an event invites members of the public to drink as much they can in a four-hour period, it's going to attract an unsavory element to the premises: the binge drinker who's determined to get at least double his or her money's worth. To them, a beer festival is like a happy hour promotion on steroids. It's impossible to completely eliminate such behavior from a tasting session; but it's easy enough to ensure that inebriated bingers remain in the minority.

But, the thing is, the carpetbaggers don't seem to *care*. They're just trying to get bodies in the door and make a profit and, tragically, that means appealing to the lowest-common denominator.

The reputable festivals are reputable for a reason: because they earned it. For some of them it's taken years, even decades, of trial-and-error, ironing out the kinks and figuring out what works and jettisoning what doesn't.

The Great American Beer Festival

The Great American Beer Festival (GABF) got to be great by doing just that. The first edition was in 1982, when it occupied just 5,000 square feet. It has since grown about sixtyfold to take over most of Denver's Colorado Convention Center each fall, attracting some 60,000 attendees over its three days and selling out within about three minutes after tickets go on sale.

The same organization—or at least an evolved iteration of the original organization—has been running it for the thirty-odd years it's been operating.

Originally there were two trade associations representing the nation's craft brewers, Brewers' Association of America and the Association of Brewers. The two merged in 2005 to form the Brewers Association, which continues to manage the colossal event to this day.

The most striking aspect of the GABF is the wait time on the lines—or lack thereof. During the three-day event, Denver should change its nickname to the Mile-Long City because that's the length of the queue—no hyperbole—thirty minutes before a tasting session. Anyone arriving at 5:00 p.m. for the 5:30 session might get depressed, thinking that they'll be lucky to get in the door twenty minutes before last call. But they're pleasantly surprised to discover that the timespan from the moment the main door opens until the first beer is poured into their glasses is all of about fifteen minutes. Well-oiled machine is an understatement.

Despite its sprawling layout across the convention hall's floor, it's remarkably easy to navigate, even for a newbie. Each row of tasting tables is categorized by region of the country—West, Midwest, Southeast, etc.—and the attending breweries are arranged alphabetically within those sections.

Most of those doing the pouring are volunteers, which generally is a bad thing at lesser festivals. Try asking a volunteer about style or hop character at one of those events and you're likely to get a shrug or a deer-in-the-headlights look. That's not to say GABF volunteers are experts, but a majority of them are knowledgeable craft beer enthusiasts—most of them are from Colorado, after all—and are eager to talk about what they're pouring with folks who share their passion.

GABF is by no means the perfect festival. There are plenty of cringeworthy elements. There's a fair level of drunkenness and people behaving stupidly. There are four tasting sessions—one each on Thursday and Friday and two on Saturday—and knowing which one to attend is half the battle in avoiding such activity. Thursday night is usually a good bet; the crowd tends to be mellower. Saturday afternoon is optimal, but attendees must be

The famous lines at GABF.

members of either the Brewers Association or the American Homebrewers Association (AHA) to be admitted. (Annual membership is around $45, and it's well worth it, not just for access to the members-only Saturday session but for a host of other benefits and discounts across the country throughout the year.)

The other main attraction on Saturday afternoon is the presence of a larger number of actual brewers. The festival's awards ceremony immediately precedes—and often runs over and overlaps with—the session, and more brewery personnel—top brass, marketing and sales reps—will be hanging out at their booths (the bigger ones get these) or tables. So for those who really want to drill down into the stylistic nuances of the liquid being poured, Saturday's the day to try to make that happen.

Another plus? Since Saturday afternoon attracts, by and large, a more seasoned craft enthusiast, attendees are entrusted with tasting glasses made of actual glass; plastic is the only option during the other three. It's like getting to sit at the grown-up table at Thanksgiving dinner.

The one component that Saturday lacks, though, is the Farm to Table Pavilion, which has been a popular addition to GABF since 2009. It's an added charge for admission, but it's money well spent. It's an oasis amidst the madness of the tasting hall in its own separate room. Participating brewers pair select creations with culinary delights fashioned under the guidance of chef Adam Dulye. There's plenty of food to go around—everything from artisanal sausage to oysters—and no one leaves hungry. One would spend far more on dinner to get the same caliber of food that's sampled at Farm to Table.

It's a sort of mini-version of the Brewers Association's other signature pouring event, Savor.

Savor

If GABF is craft beer's Super Bowl, Savor is its Oscar night. People dress a bit better (sport jackets and dresses are the norm), pay a bit more, and enjoy more of a cocktail party vibe than GABF's Mardi Gras-like aesthetic. But included in the $135 admission price (as of 2016) is food—great food, at that, and lots of it. Dulye also leads the gastronomic efforts for Savor, cranking out choice bites to complement the wares of some seventy American breweries.

Its usual home is Washington, D.C.'s stately National Building Museum, though it made a brief detour in 2013 to New York's Metropolitan Pavilion. However, there really is no substitute for the museum in the US capital, with its towering marble columns and multistory atrium. It began as a single Saturday night event at a different venue—the Andrew Mellon Auditorium—but it has since settled on the Building Museum and has expanded to include a Friday evening session.

The District of Columbia works so well for the event because it serves a dual purpose. It's the one time of year that the nation's craft brewers can storm Capitol Hill en masse and tell their collective story to federal lawmakers. A goodly proportion of each night's 2,000 or so tickets are set aside for members of Congress and their staff (mostly the latter).

It's also quite a hot ticket for the brewers themselves. Since space is limited, any of the nearly 5,000 American craft operations must enter a lottery for a slot, unless they're among the "sponsoring" breweries—usually the likes of Dogfish Head, Brooklyn Brewery, Sierra Nevada, New Belgium, and other big craft players—that fork over significant cash for a guaranteed presence and a prime spot in the tasting hall. Those who win the lottery are required to send someone senior from the brewery to pour and expound on their offerings. And that's the element that makes it such a top-notch

Savor, the premier craft beer and food event, at the National Building Museum in Washington, D.C..

event. It's a rare chance for the public to interact with a veritable who's who of craft brewing entrepreneurs.

The absence of that A-list factor frequently is the major failing of most lesser festivals. Too often the tasting stations are manned by individuals who lack any knowledge of or emotional investment in the brands that they're repping at these events. Better brewers have local reps partnering with a region's distributors to not only sell the brands to retail customers, but educate those customers, who, in turn, can make more informed sales pitches to consumers. All the rest are beer producers who want to be everything to everyone; they want to boast about how many US states they're in without having any personnel in those states to make a credible impact. When there's a beer festival in an outlying area not core to their consumer base, those brewers are hard-pressed to get someone to staff their pouring stations. And most of the local/regional events possess neither the savvy nor the reputation of a GABF to attract or train capable volunteers to serve as well-informed proxies for the beers being served. In such instances, it's not entirely out of the ordinary for the organizers to recruit convention center or hotel staff to perform the serving duties. And the ones assigned to that duty tend not to be very enthusiastic about it. Sometimes they're downright rude, which, ultimately, is a horrible reflection on the brands. Not naming any names here to protect the not-so-innocent.

The Brewers Association, however, is far from being the only organization/company capable of staging a stellar beer festival.

World Beer Festival

The most notable among those not hosted by the Brewers Association is the **World Beer Festival**, which actually isn't a single event but a series of festivals throughout the year in multiple locations—many of them outdoors. It's organized by the folks who run *All About Beer* magazine, one of the oldest and most respected publications specifically for beer enthusiasts.

Columbia, South Carolina, is the host city for its January festival; Raleigh, North Carolina, is the backdrop for April; Cleveland, Ohio in June; and Raleigh's neighbor, Durham (the magazine's home city), in October. Most recently the team launched a Charlotte, North Carolina event, as well as one at northern New Jersey's Meadowlands Racetrack.

The Durham festival is the brand's oldest. Daniel Bradford, who bought *All About Beer* in 1991, launched it in 1996. Bradford was the head of the Brewers Association of America until it merged with the Association of Brewers to form the Brewers Association in 2005. Bradford knows a thing or two about running a beer festival; he was one of the founders of the GABF. Bradford ultimately sold *All About Beer* and its festivals to Christopher Rice in 2014.

The North Carolina events each draw between 7,000 and 10,000 visitors who are eager to sample products from some 100 breweries.

"Our events are started in places that did not have a core beer community," Rice notes. "There was no craft beer presence in Columbia [when it launched there] in 2008. There were no tap rooms, no retailers, and there are a number of people in the market [who] credit All About Beer for

The Oregon Brewers Festival.

showcasing the world of craft beer, creating demand and a real brewing community."

BeerAdvocate Presents . . .

Media companies seem to have a knack for organizing solid beer fests. BeerAdvocate, which had built an enormous web community years before it decided to launch a monthly print publication of the same name (in the

The Oregon Brewers Festival.

opposite order of how things normally work), stages a couple of annual gatherings in Boston (BeerAdvocate's original base), each focusing on a particular theme.

Boston is not at the top of most people's list of places to be in February, but BeerAdvocate keeps everyone plenty warm with the bold, boozy, high-ABV brews that are the centerpiece of its Extreme Beer Fest.

The publication/website also stages the American Craft Beer Festival, which BeerAdvocate hosts in conjunction with Boston's Harpoon Brewery. The event showcases between 600 and 700 beers from more than 140 American breweries. It's usually held in late spring, usually the end of May, and typically draws about 15,000 eager beer enthusiasts.

Oregon Brewers Festival

The most enduring summer beer festival has been the **Oregon Brewers Festival**, which is well into its third decade. When it comes to venues, few can claim to offer the precise mix of urban hipness and picturesque natural beauty that downtown Portland serves up in spades.

Some 85,000 beer lovers converge on the city's Waterfront Park in late July to sample some nintey brews as they gaze across the mighty Willamette River and its iconic bridges (thanks partly to *Portlandia*). When the sun's out—and it usually is that time of year—snowcapped, majestic Mount Hood looms just off in the distance.

It's one of the rare festival's that's not a ticketed event. Attendees can wander in for free if they just want to hang out. If they want to drink (and there's a 99.9 percent chance that they do), first they must purchase the 14-ounce souvenir plastic tasting mug. If they want anything poured in said mug, they've got to buy $1 wooden tokens—as many as they like. One token for a taste, four for a full pour (rare offerings fetch two tokens a taste).

Belgium Comes to Cooperstown

Twenty-eight hundred miles away, upstate New York's Adirondack Mountains provide the backdrop for one of the other world-class outdoor summer festivals, **Belgium Comes to Cooperstown** (BCTC). Hosted on the sprawling 140-acre grounds of Cooperstown's well-regarded, Belgian-inspired Brewery Ommegang, BCTC has become the Woodstock of craft beer, complete with sprawling tent city and live acts. Overnight camping is a key part of the experience; once the afternoon pouring session ends, bands play well into the night as revelers grill burgers and dogs on portable hibachis and propane-fueled stoves. The event has evolved beyond its Belgian roots; sure, Ommegang models itself after a Flemish farmhouse brewery and is owned by Belgium's Duvel Moortgat, but the growing roster of guest companies that pour at the festival offers selections that draw on a range of international and domestic influences.

Scoring tickets has gotten progressively more difficult; like GABF, BCTC passes disappear within minutes of the start of the public sale.

Other Fests of Note . . .

TAP New York

Upstate New York is also home to an annual festival that has gained quite a cult following in the region: TAP New York. The fest, held in the Hunter Mountain ski region at the start of the off-season in late April, launched in 1997 and bills itself as the longest-running event of its kind in the state. It also claims to be the largest single-state craft beer festival in the United States. Recent editions of TAP New York have welcomed more than 120 Empire State breweries, showcasing more than three hundred individual beers. TAP prides itself on being about not just imbibing, but education.

Denver Rare Beer Tasting

We're going to bring things back to where we started: the Mile High City. The Denver Rare Beer Tasting is a separate event that runs each year for an afternoon during the Great American Beer Festival (not during the main tasting sessions, mind you). The event, usually staged a few blocks away from the Colorado Convention Center at the McNichols Civic Center features the wares of about fifty brewers—mostly their harder to get stuff, hence the name—and it's all for a good cause. It's organized by Pints for Prostates, which raises prostate cancer awareness. Noted beer writer and prostate cancer survivor Rick Lyke founded the organization in 2008. It's a separate ticket price from GABF and it usually sells out nearly instantaneously. But not only is it the opportunity to sample some off-the-beaten path brews, it also offers the chance to rub elbows with the brewerati (and you're more likely to run into the likes of Sam Adams mastermind Jim Koch and Dogfish Head's Sam Calagione than in the gargantuan GABF tasting hall).

Big Beers Festival

Since we're already in Colorado, there's one more worth noting. The name says it all. Don't expect to find too many session ales and lagers at this event, which is staged each January—during peak ski season, of course—in Vail. Three hundred-plus bold brews pour throughout the festival, which also boasts one of the most extensive educational components found at a tasting festival. Most of the sessions are led by top brewers sharing their insights on their own beer-making experiences.

Holiday Ale Festival

There's no shortage of outdoor beer festivals in Portland, Oregon, regardless of the season. When things start to get considerably colder in December, it's time for the annual Holiday Ale Festival, a tradition dating back to the mid-'90s. It's staged at the city's Pioneer Courthouse Square under the shadow of an enormous Christmas tree. The more than 14,000 attendees that typically show up to try the big, boozy winter offerings from a host of mostly Western breweries needn't worry about freezing to death. The entire event takes place under a giant clear-roofed tent, complete with heaters. Holiday music is piped in to enhance the festive vibe.

Michigan Winter Beer Fest

And speaking of cold . . . it's February, and it's Michigan, which is not a place known exactly for mild winters. But, so what? Michiganders have more than made their peace with that reality. In fact, they embrace it and very bravely host Winter Beer Fest *outdoors*. It's definitely not a deterrent because the festival has upped its attendance tenfold since it first launched in 2006. Now, more than 10,000 people flock to a ballpark to sample a thousand beers from more than one hundred different breweries. And when there's snow on the ground, it only enhances the experience.

Festivals Outside the US

If you leave the country and you play your cards right, your trip just might coincide with some of the more renowned international beer festivals.

Great British Beer Festival

Denver has the GABF. London has the GBBF. This one's the brainchild of the Campaign for Real Ale (CAMRA)—you remember them; they're the saviors of traditional British ales and the pubs that serve them. The Great British Beer Festival predates pretty much every beer festival in the United States, including the aforementioned Great American Beer Festival. GBBF kicked off in 1977, a full five years before the inaugural GABF. The event has bounced between the city's Earl's Court and Olympia exhibition centers. The August festival attracts 55,000 thirsty attendees, who sip and savor nearly six-hundred brews on tap, as well as hundreds of bottles (including cider). GBBF is more than a festival, it's kind of one giant pub, complete with traditional pub games. Among those is Skittles, a sort of wooden, tabletop bowling game. Then there's Shut the Box, a game that involves twelve cards and a set of dice. There's even a bobbing for apples station. (Even Prince Harry has been known to show up at the GBBF and join in the fun.) The Brits know how to party!

A much smaller-scale child of the GBBF is the **Pig's Ear Festival**, which takes place at the beginning of December in what was once a rather large church in the Borough of Hackney. Visitors get to sample nearly 250 real ales, as well as ciders, perries (pear cider), and bottled beers (and damned good sausages, bacon rolls, and barbeque to boot). And many of the same pub games make an appearance on the Pig's Ear tasting floor, as well.

Zythos Bierfestival

Naturally, there must be an iconic beer festival in Belgium. The Zythos Bierfestival is the best known of the Benelux fests, and many would be surprised out how relatively new it is. The spring event started in 2004 in the town of St-Niklaas, but has since moved to Leuven (coincidentally the home base of what was Interbrew, the company that became InBev and that is now AB InBev). The two-day festival showcases around five hundred Belgian beers. It's impossible to hit every brewery in Belgium on a single trip, so the closest most will get to doing so would be sampling the cross-section of fine brews at Zythos.

Beervana

The development of the New Zealand craft beer scene has paralleled that of Australia, and the best representation of that phenomenon happens every August in Wellington. (Sometimes it overlaps with the GBBF; if it's an either/or scenario, you always could choose based on the weather. If you hate winter, you're better off hitting the British event, though Wellington winters are more like early spring). There are plenty of Kiwi beers to try at Beervana, along with a generous helping of brews from other craft cultures around the world.

Mondial de la Biére

Let's bring things back to North America for what has become one of the world's most epic tasting events. The five-day Montreal festival has been a fixture of the Quebecois beer scene since 1994 and has grown to attract more than 100,000 beer lovers to the city's Palais de Congres. Mondial de la Biére (World of Beer) also features a comprehensive educational component, with professional seminars throughout the fest. And, as it turns out, it got so huge that Montreal alone couldn't contain it. The organizers have gone on to launch festivals in Mulhouse, France, and Rio de Janeiro, Brazil. It's truly living up to its name.

21

City-Wide Sipping

The Rise of the Beer Week

A year after the Brewers' Association of America and the Association of Brewers merged to form the Brewers Association, the organization instituted what has become an annual rite of spring: American Craft Beer Week. Each year around the third week of May, breweries, restaurants, bars, homebrewers, and drinkers celebrate the nationwide community of craft beer. It evolved as a more compact version of American Beer Month (traditionally in July) and moved to May ahead of the start of the busiest beer season (and added the word "craft" to its name—macros need not apply . . . unless of course they're trying to buy another craft brewer.) It's not likely that American Beer Month had been on most people's radar at that point anyway (though it should be noted that the Good Beer Seal, the initiative that recognizes New York-area bars doing their best to further the better beer cause, celebrates July Good Beer Month).

The Brewers Association conducts an annual call for American Craft Beer Week events across the country and includes them in a centralized calendar. In 2015 it published an interactive map of the United States—composed entirely of beer bottles and cans—at CraftBeer.com called "Sweet Land of Li-beer-ty." Click on a container in any given region and you'll get a factoid about that state or city's contributions to craft culture. It's done wonders for publicity and has generally provided more fuel for the craft engine.

But American Craft Beer Week is but one week out of fifty-two. What is one to do for the remainder of the year? Drink good beer of course. But there's no need for the beer week festivities to end; just about every state in the country has at least one city with its own craft beer week. And, just as we owe Philadelphia a debt of gratitude for the Declaration of Independence, cheesesteaks, and Rocky Balboa, we have it to thank for the craft beer week tradition.

The beer week by which all other beer weeks must be judged always will be Philly Beer Week. Its first outing was in 2008, and it remains the largest and most revered of its kind. It's the reason that all that have come after it exist at all. And it's closer to "Philly Beer Week and a Half" because it begins on a Friday and ends nine days later. The ten-day celebration traditionally begins with the ceremonial Opening Tap, attended by none other than Benjamin Franklin himself (well, a pretty convincing look-alike and dress-alike anyway). The festivities commence with the opening of the bunghole on the first cask with the world-famous Hammer of Glory, a rather heavy sledgehammer emblazoned with the Philly Beer Week logo on its iron head. Over the next week-plus, the hammer gets relayed through the city by a succession of lucky souls attending the countless tap takeovers, festivals, meet-the-brewer events, beer dinners, tastings, and pub crawls taking place under the Philly Beer Week banner.

The first two editions of Philly Beer Week took place in March, but, in 2010, the organizers smartly moved it to June. The weather's a lot more pub-crawl-friendly.

Part of the reason for the success of the Philadelphia celebration is the fact that the city's history and culture had already been so steeped in beer. Philly was a beer town long before there were beer towns.

That's not to say those that followed aren't respectable in their own right. Many beer weeks across the country do more than just hold their own against Philly's example. We'll cover one for each month (minus December, which most cities avoid because of the holidays), but keep in mind that there are many more.

January

Alaska Beer Week

Yes, it's January. Yes, it's Alaska. Two things you can count on: It'll be cold, and it'll be dark. But Alaskans wouldn't have it any other way. It's not called Alaska Beer *Weak*, after all. Only the strong survive. And there's a strategic reason for scheduling it in the coldest month. Anchorage's Great Alaska Beer and Barleywine Festival predated the week by about a decade and a half. Now there's a whole week of events around it.

February

New York Craft Beer Week

The Big Apple has always had a complicated relationship with craft beer. It's home to quite a few famous producers—Brooklyn Brewery, of course, Sixpoint, and KelSo, along with newer arrivals like Bronx Brewery, SingleCut Beersmiths, and Big Alice—but it's also the most A.D.D. city that exists. There's so much else going on that folks don't traditionally think of New York as a beer town, even though it's got more beer bars and breweries within the city limits than most other municipal entities. The same applies during New York Craft Beer Week. There are plenty of fantastic events—the Brewers Choice festival is always a must-attend—but most of the folks in the city aren't aware the week is even happening (most of them would rather troll bass-pounding meat market bars, sipping $25 cosmos and gin and tonics). It's far different dynamic in Philadelphia. Philly Beer Week is just in the air when you're there. (The first thing the Philadelphia hotel registration attendant asks when you're checking in is, "Are you here for Beer Week?") To be fair, it's mostly Manhattan's fault. The borough of Brooklyn is very much a beer town. And the other outer boroughs are definitely catching up. But none of the cool people live in Manhattan anymore anyway, so it's probably just as well.

March

Tampa Bay Beer Week

March is also the month of Colorado Craft Beer Week, but Colorado's beer scene really doesn't need any help. Tampa's, on the other hand, still falls within the category of "burgeoning." But it's growing rapidly, thanks mostly to Cigar City Brewing, which put the entire state of Florida on the good beer map. The Tampa event started in 2012 and will be one to watch. And hey, there are worse places to be in March than the Sunshine State.

April

April is an extremely fertile month for beer weeks. Everywhere from Milwaukee, Wisconsin, to Tulsa, Oklahoma, to Reno, Nevada, has a week on the calendar for that month. Often bridging the month into May is Missoula Beer Week in Montana's second-largest city (with a whopping

70,000 people within the city limits—about 115,000 in the greater metro area). Missoula is home to no fewer than six (and counting) breweries—not a bad beer-to-people ratio. Founded in 2012, Missoula Beer Week is jointly organized by the creative forces behind the blogs Growler Fill and Montana Beer Finder.

May

Asheville Beer Week

Okay, this one's kind of a ringer. Isn't *every* week in Asheville a beer week? Maybe so, but the city didn't get that way by resting on its laurels and letting every other town in America eat its lunch. There are even more beer weeks on the books in May than in April (and some run concurrently during American Craft Beer Week). And there's one in virtually every time zone in the contiguous forty-eight states, including Albuquerque, New Mexico; Green Bay, Wisconsin; and both eastern (Spokane) and western (Seattle) Washington State.

June

Des Moines Craft Beer Week

It bears noting that June is also the month in which both Portlands have beer weeks. It's redundant to put the Oregon one next to the words "Beer Week." And the Maine one has a very developed craft beer scene of its own. But Iowa, like many of the Midwestern states around it, has been riding the craft wave quite nicely, and in 2014 its capital city kicked off a week to showcase that fact. The week culminates in the Iowa Craft Brew Festival, featuring forty-odd Iowa breweries, along with the best its neighboring states and the rest of the country have to offer.

July

Silicon Valley Craft Beer Week

Techies like their good brews, so it's fitting that the tech capital of the world has its own beer week. From Sunnyvale to Redwood City to San Jose, California, there are plenty of places for those in the Google set to get their drink on.

August

D.C. Beer Week

The nation's capital gets two major shots to show its stuff throughout the year. The first is the week leading up to the Savor craft beer and food pairing event, and the other is D.C. Beer Week proper, usually a couple of months later. D.C. has witnessed one of the more striking craft evolutions. The city previously had had a mostly transient population—one regime comes in, the other moves out—but as more people are sticking around, there's plenty of homegrown beery goodness happening. It helps that there are now multiple well-regarded breweries on either side of the Potomac, including DC Brau, Bluejacket, Atlas Brew Works and 3 Stars in the District, and Port City and Portner Brewhouse in Alexandria, Virginia.

September

Charleston Beer Week

The Southern brewing and beer-appreciating industry has come alive in recent years, and the historic South Carolina city of Charleston has been among the standard-bearers for the region. There's plenty of local flavor throughout the week, like beer-themed Low-Country boils and brunches—brunch is a sacred institution in old "Chucktown."

October

Baltimore Beer Week

As cities go, Baltimore frequently gets overshadowed by Washington, D.C., but the beer culture in Maryland's most populous city is far more developed than that in the nation's capital, thanks, mostly, to Baltimore's blue-collar industrial roots. Clipper City Brewing (Heavy Seas Beer) and Brewers Art are among the destinations that have drawn the attention of national beer geekdom. And there's a rumor that you can find some pretty mean crab cakes in town. And, during Baltimore Beer Week, you can also find ten days of tap takeovers, epic pub crawls, pancake breakfasts, and even a pumpkin carving party.

November

San Diego Beer Week

Here's another one to file under "redundant," but San Diego has really earned its mention here. Stone, Ballast Point, The Lost Abbey, Green Flash. Forget about the week. Just live there permanently!

December

Most cities have steered clear of December because there's so much else going on, what with office holiday parties and such taking over most of the available venues.

International Beer Weeks

It didn't take long for the rest of the world to catch on to the beer week phenomenon. You know the saying "It's five o'clock somewhere"? Well, the same applies to beer festivals. There's at least one on nearly every continent and in most time zones around the globe.

Toronto Beer Week

As close as it is, Ontario still qualifies as "international." (Americans' cell phone bills will remind them of that fact.) September is a busy enough month in Canada's largest city, but now there's another reason hotel rooms are impossible to come by on the cusp of autumn. The middle of the month is home to Toronto Beer Week, which spans seventy bars, pubs, and restaurants and involves thirty-five craft breweries and more than one hundred events over the course of nine days. It of course is a showcase of Canada's finest (east coast and west coast), but a few American breweries manage to cross the border for the event. Each year the Toronto Beer Week organizers partner with a local brewery to produce an official beer for the week. Offerings have included an imperial porter, a quadruple, a farmhouse ale, and a bourbon barrel-aged rye porter. The commemorative brews are quite the hot tickets; a little more than two thousand bottles are available throughout the city.

Montreal Beer Week

We can't talk about Toronto without at least a passing mention of another major city in eastern Canada (or, if some of the locals have their way, the Republic of Quebec). The most striking aspect of Montreal Beer Week is that it didn't start until 2015. The city has been home to one of the most successful and respected beer festivals in the world, Mondial de la Biere, since 1994. And, the city already had hosted such food-related observances like Poutine Week, Burger Week, Mac & Cheese Week, and Steamie Week (devoted to the Montreal hot dog, affectionately know as a Steamie or Steamy). May is the month for the first couple of editions of La Biére Week.

London Beer Week

London launched its beer week in 2015, which included more than one hundred official venues and seventy individual events. (The inaugural event kicked off with the city's first Beer Run, a 5k race for charity that finished at the beer week's central London hub.) Attendees wear wristbands that entitle them to specialty beers for a modest price of £3 (about US$4.75). London Beer Week grew out of the success of London Wine Week (launched the prior year) and London Cocktail Week; they're managed by the same umbrella organization, Drink Up.London.

Paris Beer Week

French beer is never going to be as world-famous as the country's wine, but the French have proved they have quite a few tricks up their sleeves to more than keep up with beerier neighbors like Germany and Belgium. Beer is food, after all, and who knows food better than the French? The ten days in May (Paris in spring!) are packed with more than one hundred events.

Berlin Beer Week

This is another one of those "isn't every week there beer week?" cities, but the brewing scene in the German capital has evolved tremendously. It's been letting in other cultural influences—porters and IPAs would have been unheard of in Germany not too long ago. To help celebrate the new face of German brewing, more than fifty breweries, pubs, bars, restaurants, artists, and tour groups united to stage the inaugural Berlin Beer Week in June 2015. The closing shindig in year one took place at the site of American brewery Stone's new Berlin location—which had yet to even open at that point.

HK Beer Week

Hong Kong was among the last major global cosmopolises to develop a bona fide craft beer scene. The tipping point was the launch of the inaugural edition of its local beer festival, Beertopia, and HK Beer Week has grown around that. (The October week culminates with the two-day festival at Hong Kong's Central Harbourfront; Beertopia has grown to attract nearly 20,000 beer lovers.) The week has been a great opportunity for local producers like Young Master, Moonzen, and Hong Kong Beer Co. to reach a broader audience and open locals' eyes to hundreds of craft offerings from Asia and the rest of the world.

Shanghai Beer Week

Mainland China's craft beer industry developed a bit before Hong Kong's (and, like Hong Kong's, most of it has been driven by expats from the US, Europe, and other parts of the world with developed brewing industries.) Shanghai Beer Week kicked off in 2012, and, much like the Hong Kong celebration, it finishes with a major beer festival. In Shanghai's case, it's the annual Sinan Mansions Beer Festival, which draws as many as 8,000 attendees over the course of the two-day event.

Tokyo Beer Week

In 2014, the Japanese capital launched its own specially designated ten-day period celebrating the craft beer culture that's been booming throughout Japan. The week typically kicks off at what's pretty much the center of the Japanese craft beer universe, the pub known as Popeye. Some eighty or so other bars, restaurants, cafes, and shops join in the fun. April has been the month of choice for the festivities.

Singapore Craft Beer Week

Southeast Asia finally got a week of its own when the island city-state launched Singapore Craft Beer Week in 2012. Dinners, demos, brewery tours, and tap takeovers abound during the eight-day event across the island.

Sydney Craft Beer Week

In the 2010s, Sydney has emerged as one of the world's great craft beer destinations. So, of course, it was only a matter of time before Australia's largest city had a week of its own to showcase local brewers like Young Henry, Batch, and 4 Pines, as well as the fine producers throughout the rest of the continent. The week launched in 2011 and offers nine days (usually in October) of events at more than seventy venues throughout greater Sydney.

Melbourne Good Beer Week

The other major southeastern Australian city would not be outdone by Sydney's shenanigans. Melbourne's beer week, like that of Sydney, launched in 2011 and now boasts more than two hundred events across Melbourne and the state of Victoria.

22

Perfect Couples

The Beer and Food Movement

How often have you arrived at a moderate- to-upscale restaurant, sat down at your table, and either found a wine list awaiting you at your seat or had it handed to you by an eager waitperson? And how often have you thumbed through it to find absolutely no mention of a liquid other than one produced from fermented grapes? Or, perhaps the server asked, "Would you like a cocktail while you decide?"

If the eatery serves alcohol, it will most certainly have beer. It may not have the most robust of selections, but there likely will be a least two or three taps and a small fridge below the bar stocked with brews. However, the onus has, more often than not, been on the customer to extract any beer-related information out of the restaurant staff.

And on more occasions than we'd care to admit, the conversation usually goes something like this:

"What kind of beer do you have?"

"The usual stuff."

"What's the usual stuff?"

"You know, Bud, Bud Light, Coors Light, Miller Lite, Guinness, Stella Artois."

"Do you have anything by a local brewer?"

"Ummmm . . . let me check."

One to two minutes later . . .

"We have a pale ale on tap from XYZ Brewery here in town. It's like Bass."

As much as diners love to kill the messenger (we've all been guilty of that from time to time), it's not the server's fault. It's the fault of the owners and managers for (A) not providing adequate beer training and (B) being unaware of just how well beer and food go together.

Fortunately, since about the mid 2000s, the above scenario has occurred less and less. But it's still happening a majority of the time.

One of the key movements among beer lovers, producers, and distributors has been the effort to reclaim beer's place at the dinner table (and the tables of any other meal for that matter).

If, not too long ago, one were to ponder what foods and dining occasions were beer-appropriate, the options one would come up with could be counted on a single hand: a hot dog at a baseball stadium, burgers and other meaty grillings at a cookout, or, that old standby, a pizza in the living room while watching whatever televised sporting event happened to be on that afternoon or evening.

And those are all delicious options, to be sure. Beer goes perfectly with all of those things. But it also goes perfectly with a heck of a lot more and in a heck of a lot more environments and levels of fanciness.

The brewing/culinary pairing concept reached a critical turning point in 2003. That was the year that *The Brewmaster's Table: Discovering the Pleasures of Real Beer with Real Food* saw its first publication. The tome—written by Garrett Oliver, the vice president and brewmaster of Brooklyn Brewery—has been adopted as the seminal piece of beer writing that inspired so many others to focus on that specific space. Though Oliver didn't exactly start the conversation, he most certainly amplified it to a level at which it could no longer be ignored.

From cover to cover he not only provides comprehensive suggestions on which foods—including what many consider "haute cuisine"—go with which beer styles, he also provides something of a travel log that details many of the European origins of such brews. In that respect, it serves as a wonderful introduction to the great beer styles of the world for those interested in learning a bit more about what they're drinking.

The book solidified Oliver's position as a foremost authority on beer and food pairing. Just over a decade after its initial publication, Oliver was honored as the "Outstanding Wine, Beer, or Spirits Professional" in the 2014 James Beard Foundation Awards, widely regarded as the Oscars of the food world. The following year, Brooklyn Brewery collaborated with the Culinary Institute of America to open an in-house brewery at the school's

Hyde Park, New York campus. Oliver and his team continue to help develop the curriculum to tie in with the brewing facility.

One of the biggest challenges of beer-and-food proponents has been to convince drinkers that beer is, in many respects, as good a match (and very often a better one) as wine.

Let's start with a very basic staple of many (non-vegan, non-lactose-intolerant) Americans' diets: cheese. We've all been to, or at least heard of, "wine and cheese parties." It was kind of a small crime that a "beer and cheese party" wasn't as much of a thing—if a thing at all. But, you know what? Ask ten chefs or sommeliers what goes better with cheese, wine or beer, and it's very likely that at least seven of them will waste no time in answering "beer."

There are a variety of reasons why this is the case, and a lot of them depend on the specific type of cheese and the particular style of beer. But the one factor that's common among most of the reasons is the fact that cheese's fat content coats the palate and beer's carbonation scrubs the palate clean, preparing it for the next course. (Yes, sparkling wines can do the same.)

Brooklyn Brewery's Garrett Oliver.   *Courtesy of Brooklyn Brewery*

But there are other elements as well. Take a fairly pungent cheese, for instance. The strong aromatics and flavor are going to overpower most wines. However, those same components are going to harmonize with bold, robustly flavored brews, creating a gustatory symphony like no other.

Now, consider a grassy, earthy farmhouse cheddar. You know where you get a lot of similar elements that match perfectly with that cheese? Hop-forward brews like pale ales and India pale ales. How about with aged, hard cheeses, like a three-year-old gouda? A nice English brown ale works well with the mature cheese's nuttier notes.

The American Cheese Society is quite hip to this trend. Every year at the Great American Beer Festival in Denver and at its companion event, Savor, in Washington, D.C., the not-for-profit dairy organization has a fairly sprawling set up (usually the longest, slowest lines to get through), offering all sorts of artisanal cheeses, from spreadable to hard and dense, with pitchers of the perfect liquid partners for each at the ready.

Garrett Oliver gets a lot of the props for opening the public's eyes to the gastronomic wonders of beer, but other noted brewing personalities have contributed a great deal to the ongoing dialogue, as well. In 2008, Dogfish Head Craft Brewery founder Sam Calagione teamed up with renowned wine sommelier Marnie Old to fashion *He Said Beer, She Said Wine*, a playful book that good-heartedly pits the two alcohol beverages against each other and that showcases each author making a case for which beverage pairs better with a particular dish. Well before it was even a book, the pair took the concept on the road, presenting a series of lunches and dinners where they let the diners decide which beverage was the winner. And usually the audiences were fairly impartial. Most even came with a little pro-wine bias because wine's culinary superiority had been so firmly ingrained up until that point. More often than not, though, beer was the overall winner, a result that surprised even those who found themselves voting in favor of good old malted barley and hops.

Spicy Sam

Never one to shy away from good media exposure, Boston Beer Company decided it wanted to get scientific about certain facets of the beer-cuisine marriage. In 2015, the brewer of Samuel Adams enlisted the help of no less than the Culinary Institute of America to figure out just how hops affect humans' perception of spicy food. (Thanks to Brooklyn Brewery, of course, there's a brewing facility on site now, so it made things that much easier.)

Jennifer Glanville, Sam Adams brewer and director of brewery programs, joined a panel of chefs and other food experts to get to the bottom of the hoppy/heat correlation.

Their lab tools of choice? Buffalo wings and Sam Adams's Rebel series of India pale ales: Rebel IPA, Rebel Rider Session IPA, and Rebel Rouser Double IPA.

Their conclusion? Yes, hops do affect how drinkers perceive spiciness. However, they also discovered that other factors are involved as well: malt and alcohol content were among the variables. Additionally, the hop varietals used also made a difference

The highest-ABV brew of the Rebels, Rebel Rouser Double IPA, resulted in the most pronounced spiciness perception. An 8.4 percent ABV and a relatively high IBU of 85, the team concluded, did their part in turning up the heat. The most balanced of the three turned out to be the 6.5 percent ABV Rebel IPA. That's primarily due to the fact that its hop content was more about other elements of hop character—citrus and pine components, in particular—than bitterness. Rebel IPA has a more moderate IBU of 45. It also has a sturdy malt foundation, which matches the sweeter characteristics of the wings and mitigates the heat a bit. Rebel Rider has a similar IBU but a lower ABV. However, its lower malt content and lighter body aren't sufficient enough to build a firewall against the spice. So there's more lingering perceived heat with the session IPA.

Tour de France

One of the more forward-thinking restaurant groups in the country has been New York City's Tour de France group. Among its popular eateries is Café d'Alsace, a purveyor of fine, rustic Alsatian cuisine on the Upper East Side. France's Alsace region is quite well known for its wine—mostly its whites, though many wineries produce a solid Pinot Noir—but what fewer people outside that area know is that it also happens to be a major center of French brewing activity. (It makes sense since the region, for centuries, had been kicked back and forth between French and German control.) Café d'Alsace was one of the first higher-end dining establishments to feature a well-stocked beer program. The Tour de France group was also one of the first to employ beer sommeliers. This was around 2005, when New York City hadn't quite arrived as the beer city it was destined to be. Cities like Philadelphia, Chicago, San Diego, and, of course, Portland were way ahead of it in their beery evolution. So it was a major vote of confidence in New

York's emerging beer scene to have fully trained and educated staffers at the ready to suggest ideal pairings for dishes like Baeckeoffe—an indulgent bit of deliciousness that combines chopped, marinated pieces of beef, pork, and mutton with onions and potatoes in a casserole—and Choucroutte—a paradise for lovers of encased and cured meats with three different types of sausages and various cuts of pork.

The American Craft Beer Cookbook

In 2013, Storey Publishing released *The American Craft Beer Cookbook* by noted beer author John Holl, who is also the editor of the enthusiast publication *All About Beer Magazine*. The book features 155 recipes covering every meal imaginable, all provided by breweries and brewpubs, as well as by other beer personalities from across the United States.

BA Schools Us

The Brewers Association (BA), the trade group that represents America's small brewers, has been beating the beer-and-food drum for some time. In 2008, the organization hosted its inaugural great-beer-great-food event, Savor, in Washington, D.C., and it has continued to do so every year since. The following year, at the Great American Beer Festival (GABF), it hosted its first Farm to Table Pavilion, an intimate—relative to the massive sprawl of the GABF proper—showcase of brews and bites. (In 2015, it rebranded "Farm to Table" as "Paired" to better reflect the direction in which the event was going.)

GABF's not-so-secret weapon on its culinary adventures has been chef Adam Dulye, a Culinary Institute of America graduate who has been on the forefront of the pairing revolution and who has contributed to such award-winning endeavors as The Abbot's Cellar and The Monk's Kettle in San Francisco. He has been the guiding force behind the menus for Savor and Farm to Table/Paired, leading a team of culinary professionals to concoct innovative dishes designed for maximum pairing potential with virtually every point on the beer style spectrum. In March of 2015, the BA formalized Dulye's role and named him the association's executive chef.

That came right on the heels of another major project on which Dulye and the organization collaborated, the CraftBeer.com Beer & Food Course. (CraftBeer.com is the BA's official consumer-targeted site.) Dulye and BA craft beer program director Julia Herz, a Certified Cicerone, divided the labor on the curriculum, a five-day, self-administered program that's free and downloadable at CraftBeer.com. It's designed as a crash course of sorts for all levels of culinary professionals wishing to expand their Beer IQ. Day One is intro day, offering an introduction to craft beer, including a historical overview, a rundown of current market trends, an ingredients primer, and information on style fundamentals. On Day Two, students learn how to taste, pour, and present beer to enhance food pros' understanding of how to better integrate beer with food. Day Three offers a more in-depth stylistic exploration, detailing how specific beer styles match with the flavor elements of different dishes. Students get their second tasting and pairing session, which helps them to attune their palates to nuances of style and train them to detect off-notes. On Day Four, participants learn how to pair craft beer with cheese and explore various techniques for cellaring and aging the beverage. There's also another tasting and pairing session featuring five common beer styles aligned with common food ingredients. This is also the day that they learn how to design the menu for a beer dinner.

On the final day, it's exam time! There's a fifty-question written test followed by a practical exam in which students will create a three-course menu matching dishes with flavor-appropriate beers.

There are plenty of downloadable resources at CraftBeer.com to help prospective students get ready for the comprehensive culinary curriculum.

Meal Time! A Few Sample Pairings

Building a meal around beer isn't an exact science. Sure, there's plenty of objective, scientific sensory stuff going on, but there's a comparable amount of subjectivity involved as well. Some pairings are going to press all the right emotional buttons with one diner and leave another completely unimpressed. It really depends on how much they like the food and/or the beer, and you can't please everyone.

But here are some fairly universal suggestions.

Pizza

What to pair with pizza really depends on what's on the pie. If it's a meat-lover's kind of situation, it wouldn't be a terrible thing to put a porter or a brown ale up against it. Sausage and meatballs, for instance, are going to get a little charred in the oven, and those qualities will be a good match for roastier ales. But if you're talking a no-nonsense cheese pie (or perhaps, extra cheese), you really need a no-nonsense beer. There's no substitute for a good, snappy unfiltered pilsner or a Kölsch-style offering. If you're the type of person who likes to coat your slice in a thick layer of crushed red pepper, crank up the hop quotient a little bit. Hops are known to enhance the spicy sensation. When you're trying to mitigate the heat a bit, hoppy beers are not the way to go. But if you're already trying to spice up your pie, mitigation doesn't appear to be on your immediate agenda. Therefore, an American pale ale or even an IPA is a good way to go. Even better is something from the new crop of "session IPAs"—the low-ABV yet still-hoppy-as-hell bunch. While it doesn't call itself a session IPA (it's more of a hopped-up Kölsch), Carton Brewing Company's 4.2 percent übersessionable Boat Beer is a terrific pizza partner.

Pasta with Red Sauce

The level of spice in a pasta dish's sauce is really going to determine what goes best with it. If it's an arrabiata we're talking about, get your hop on a bit. Pilsners are pretty flexible in this regard, but why not go for an imperial pilsner? Your tastebuds will thank you. If it's a less spicy sauce made with the crown jewel of the nightshade world, San Marzano tomatoes, an off-the-beaten-path pairing suggestion would be a beer that balances sweet with acidic, much like the tomatoes themselves. A mild Flanders red ale has many of those characteristics and works well with such Italian-inspired dishes—even more so if it's a meaty Sunday sauce or Bolognese. They're great with heavy meats.

Pasta with Cheese Sauces

If it's an Alfredo or a cacio y pepe scenario, your best bet would be something in the stout family. Since there's a pronounced black pepper component of the latter, why not seek out a dark beer with rye in its recipe. Rye often can impart some ground peppery elements to a brew, so it should harmonize well with cacio y pepe. Bell's Rye Stout would be an able candidate.

Burgers

The burger is a blank canvas. It's more about what you do to the burger than the burger itself. If you're just concerned with pairing a delicious beverage with the flame-grilled meat, drink something that's not going to overpower it. Ground beef is pretty sturdy and can hold up to a lot of things. But if you like your meat to be on the bloodier side of medium, tasting a burger in all of its juicy goodness is important to you. Pale ales are the usual go-tos here. But when you start adding things like grilled onions, you might consider going with something that has some caramel components. Märzens, Vienna lagers, and amber ales are nice companions here. Cheeseburger? Depends on the cheese. If it's a sharp cheddar, an IPA will work. If it's goat cheese, you might want to keep things on the delicate, wheat side. If the goat cheese has some tang to it, live a little and have a Berliner Weisse. If you're going crazy with sautéed mushrooms and jalapeños, go the earthy/spicy route. Farmhouse ales along the lines of Saison DuPont should be a good match. Pairing a beer with a burger really depends on what you want to be the star of the show. If it's the meat, pair for the meat. If it's the cheese, pair for the cheese. And so on.

Barbeque

Beer is a fantastic partner for barbeque. There are so many flavors and sensations going on with slow-cooked, smoky, spicy, and sweet meats that it's really hard to go wrong with any number of beers. In fact, you might want to work your way through a few different ones. (Cap it at three, though; moderation is your friend.)

If you've got a smoky slab of ribs, have a rauchbier (German smoked beer), for very obvious reasons. Smoked porter (like Alaskan's or Stone's) also goes well here. But don't stop there. What's your poison, as far as acoutrements? Are you into eastern Carolina-style sauce, the vinegar-based kind? Then have something on the sour/acidic side. How about a gose? Salinity balances sourness, and what says Carolina barbeque more than that? Of course, gose is not everyone's cup of tea. If you want to keep it simple, match some of the caramelized brown sugar qualities of the rub with an amber or a brown ale.

Sushi

If you're into eating raw fish, you're into tasting delicate things. So why would you want to obliterate it with a big, bold beer? Your brew of choice should be just as delicate. Belgian wits are the way to go here. So are most pale lagers—pilsners, helles, and such. You couldn't go wrong with a Kölsch for that matter. But don't be drinking an imperial stout. You'll only regret it, unless you're having some fresh, raw oysters with your nigiri and sashimi. Of course, not all fish are created equal. Some have more robust flavor. Mackerel and toro (fatty tuna) are among the oilier options. More acidic beers are always good to cut fat. But again, it's still raw fish and you might be a little crazy to try to pair something like Russian River's Supplication sour brown ale. (Toro usually runs about eight bucks for a single piece. It would be a big shame if you aren't able to even taste it. You'd be better off going out for hot dogs that night; you'd save a lot of money.) This is another area where those softer sours come into play: the Berliner Weisses and goses. (If you choose the later, you might not even need to dip the fish in soy sauce because it's got the salty part covered.)

Now, if it's sea urchin (uni) we're talking about, you can probably go nuts. No one's ever accused uni's flavor of being "delicate." Such intensity would probably hold up to an oyster stout. It may even harmonize with the funk in a wild ale, in which some assertive brettanomyces work their magic.

There's also a subgenre of beers that incorporate ginger into their recipes. Since you'd already be having some pickled ginger (gari) with your sushi, one of these ginger-infused beers might make an ideal alternative to the more common styles. And it will go with just about everything on your plate.

Seafood

We're talking the cooked variety here, not the raw swimmers that you're going to dip in soy. Similar to sushi, you're going to want to keep things on the delicate side, for the most part. However, there's plenty of leeway from species to species. And when it comes to shellfish, appropriate styles vary as wildly as the crustaceans themselves. It's been previously noted that stouts are a winning match for oysters. In fact, there's even a popular substyle, oyster stout, made with actual oysters. Lobster can be pretty versatile. Some moments a hefeweizen or a witbier may seem to be the right way to go—maybe at the beginning. But as you crack your way through the bug-like beast, you may suddenly crave something a bit on the more robust side. As you get closer to finishing and your palate is thoroughly coated in the melted dipping butter, a nice, acidic sour—something along the lines of Bockor's Cuvee des Jacobins—should cut right through that and still complement the dense meat of the lobster.

Spicier options should hold up to crab—especially if it's Maryland crab and there's Old Bay seasoning involved.

Stew

The fall and winter months are typically stew season, so it's no surprise that a lot of the brews that go best with rich, meaty single-pot meals are popular options during that period as well. But, as always, it really depends on what's in the stew. If you're talking about a hearty beef stew, you can rarely go wrong with something on the dark, malty, and roasty side. Porters and stouts are quite comfortable in this neighborhood. Now, if we're talking about something like beef Carbonnade, which usualy has a wine base, consider something on the sour side. An Oud Bruin (reddish brown Flanders sour) might be an appealing choice. Petrus Oud Bruin is a great match, for instance.

If you're leaving the farm and taking things up the notch with a wild game stew, the strong flavors should harmonize with something on the wilder side, perhaps a saison with brett.

23

At the Brewvies

Beer in Film and Television

Beer's role in modern popular entertainment has been, much like Hollywood's output over the years, uneven at best. Until the past few years, its depiction mirrored the general public's perception of the beverage: comical at best, low-class at worst. It's an interesting exercise to watch many of these films and TV series in chronological order, as it captures, in ways large and small, beer's place in the cultural zeitgeist of a particular moment.

In a lot of ways, television and cinema are still catching up to where beer is at the moment, but it's definitely getting there.

Cinema

What! No Beer? (1933)

Not only does this Buster Keaton-Jimmy Durante vehicle bear the distinction of being one of the first—if not *the* first—motion picture with beer as a major plot point, it's the rare film about the end of Prohibition that was actually made near the end of Prohibition. Elmer J. Butts (Keaton) is enamored, from afar, of a woman named Hortense. Elmer dreams of one day being incredibly wealthy so he can buy Hortense nice, worldly possessions and win her hand in marriage (this is the '30s after all). Elmer's buddy, Jimmy Potts (Durante) hatches a scheme to open a brewery just before what would be the Twenty-first Amendment repealing Prohibition. Master bootleggers they're not, and they manage to get raided by the police as they finish their first beer. I turns out they're even worse brewers than they are hoods, having inadvertently produced a beer with no alcohol. The upside is that they've broken no law, so the cops have to let them go. They ultimately partner with an actual bootlegger, as the two also have haplessly stumbled on a way to make a beer inexpensively. Hijinks ensue when they run afoul of the competition, another gangster, whose moll just happens to be the beloved Hortense.

Jaws (1975)

Okay, everyone knows that Steven Spielberg's classic, *Jaws*, is about a great white shark that eats a bunch of people in a rustic New England beach town at the height of the tourist season. However, it also turned out to be some of the best free product placement for one of the quintessential regional brands of the era, Narragansett. (It was the movie that single-handedly invented the concept of the summer blockbuster, after all.) Salty fisherman Quint (Robert Shaw) was quite the fan of the beer, and Rhode Island's Narragansett Brewing Company never forgot it. In 2012, the company reintroduced the '70s-era design of the can that Quint was so fond of throwing back and, most notably, crushing with a single hand in a display of machismo to put a little scare in Richard Dreyfuss's Hooper, the university-educated shark expert of upper-middle-class extraction. (Ultimately, the two got drunk and bonded together before Quint's untimely demise in the belly of Bruce, the Great White.)

Smokey and the Bandit (1977)

Sure, beer's really just the MacGuffin in the Burt Reynolds/Jackie Gleason truckers-and-Trans-Ams '70s stuntfest, but it's a great illustration of how certain beer brands become white whales of sorts to those who don't have immediate access to them. It's hard to believe there was ever a time when Coors wasn't ubiquitous, but that's exactly the market reality that set the film's action in motion. Father and son gazillionaires Big Enos and Little Enos Burdett (Pat McCormick and Paul Williams) are planning a party in Georgia and need four hundred cases of the Rocky Mountain original. The trouble is that Coors wasn't legally available east of Texas in those days. The duo offer trucker Bo "The Bandit" Darville (Reynolds) $80,000 to pick up the beer in Texarkana and transport it to Atlanta in twenty-eight hours (a minute later and he forfeits the purse). Bandit enlists his buddy Cledus "Snowman" Snow to aid him in the scheme. Cledus (Jerry Reed) would drive the tractor trailer full of Coors, while Bandit acts as a decoy in a black Trans Am, drawing law enforcement's attention away from their real target, the big rig full of sudsy contraband. They didn't count on one particular lawman—Sheriff Bufort T. Justice (Gleason), the titular "Smokey"—being so tenacious in his pursuit of the smuggling team. It was actually quite common back in the '70s for Eastern folks visiting the Western US to be tasked with fitting as much Coors in their trunks as they could to appease their thirsty friends back home. It was a precursor to modern beer tourism; many of the best craft beers today have either local or regional distribution and very few are available in all fifty states. That's part of the reason for modern white-whale-ism.

Midnight Madness (1980)

The film focuses on an elaborate all-night scavenger hunt through Los Angeles, pitting five teams of college students against each other. Each team's a different stereotype. There's the jock team, the nerd team, the nice guys and gals team (the heroes of the story), etc. They're tasked with solving clues at each stop to get to the next destination, all ultimately leading to the finish line.

The most noteworthy aspect of this generally forgotten madcap comedy is that it features a young Michael J. Fox in a supporting role. It also features something that is now an ancient relic: a Pabst brewery. See, despite the fact that Pabst Blue Ribbon is so popular among the skinny-pants-and-twirly-mustache set these days, Pabst Brewing Co. hasn't owned an actual working brewery in decades. It's essentially a holding company that owns a lot of trademarks—including Lone Star and Schlitz—but outsources all of the production to MillerCoors. One of the secret locations throughout the night is a Pabst brewery, much to the delight of the fratboy jock team.

Take This Job and Shove It (1981)

There's never been a better portrait of the state of the beer industry at the end of the 1970s and beginning of the 1980s. The film is mostly one of those "you can go home again" type comedies about a successful yuppie who returns to his rural hometown. In this case said yuppie, Frank Macklin (Robert Hays, riding high after the success of "Airplane"), works for a conglomerate that just acquired a handful of failing breweries, one of which is based in that Frank's hometown. It's Frank's job to turn the brewery around. One of the great tragedies of the twentieth century was the deindustrialization of America, which was especially felt with the rapid consolidation and closure of breweries nationwide prior to the craft beer revolution. Though *Take This Job and Shove It* preferred to focus on romance and monster trucks, it still managed to capture the very dark mood of the time within America's dying beer market.

Strange Brew (1983)

The 1983 Bob and Doug Mackenzie romp is an unqualified classic, there's no doubt about it. Even though it centered on these two bumbling, beer-swilling oafs, it was very smartly written. It was loosely based on Shakespeare, for crying out loud—*Hamlet*, to be precise. The main setting was the Elsinore Brewery, and one of the primary antagonists was named Claude, who married the heroine's mother, Gertrude. (The name of the heroine in question was Pamela—not quite Hamlet, but close enough.)

This was the early '80s, a very dark time for brewing in North America. So don't expect the classiest representation of beer. That doesn't mean it's not laugh-out-loud funny. The Mackenzie Brothers (Rick Moranis and Dave Thomas) set the wheels in motion with a harmless little scam to extort a bit of free beer out of Elsinore. They showed up at the brewery holding a bottle with a live mouse in it. They claimed to have found it in the bottle (a classic stubby!) while they were drinking it, but in reality they planted a baby mouse in it and waited for it to grow up. The scheme actually got them hired on the bottling line to scope out any infiltrating vermin.

Beer itself was a character in the film, mostly utilized for comic effect. There's a scene where Bob has to drink an entire vat of the stuff—probably in the neighborhood of 10,000 gallons—before he and Pamela drowned inside it. After accomplishing that, he put his bladder to good use by putting out a fire with his stream.

Blue Velvet (1986)

Three years after *Strange Brew*, David Lynch unleashed his seminal work of suburban depravity on an unsuspecting public, and to this day it remains not only his most quotable work but one of the most quotable films of all mid-'80s cinema. It's not about beer per se, but one of its most iconic lines focuses on two beer brands that targeted wildly disparate demographics. It occurs when villainous psychopath Frank Booth (Dennis Hopper) terrorizes our young hero, Jeffrey Beaumont (Kyle MacLachlan).

Frank: What kind of beer do you like?

Jeffrey: Heineken

Frank: Heineken?! Fuck that shit! Pabst! Blue Ribbon!

Even those who never have seen the film are familiar with that line. What's most interesting about the juxtaposition of those two brews? At the time, Heineken was considered the highest of the high end. It was the fancy import in the green bottle, the one to which a clean-cut college boy like Jeffrey would gravitate to for its badge value (an earlier scene has him singing the Dutch brand's praises). To him, it was a sophisticated affair. Now Pabst, at the time, was the rough-and-tumble working man's drink.

The Saddest Music in the World (2003)

Twenty years after Bob and Doug Mackenzie drank their Strange Brew, the indie film-going public was treated to a much different look at the Canadian beer industry.

It's 1933 and the Great Depression that started in America is very much felt the world over. In the film, Winnipeg, Manitoba has had the dubious distinction of being named the sorrow capital the world by the *London Times* for four consecutive years. It's there that Lady Helen Port Huntley (Isabella Rossellini), owner of Port-Huntley Beer, announces a competition to find the saddest music in the world and offers a purse of $25,000 (big bucks in those days) to the victorious performer. The contest is basically a promotional effort for her brewery—Prohibition is about to end south of the Canadian border, opening up a new market of thirsty Americans. The film, directed by Canadian auteur Guy Madden, is shot in grainy black in white—much of it on Super 8 cameras—giving it a true Depression-era feel. It's basically a campy, melodramatic, and sometimes soapy comedy. It's also got some fairly bizarre twists; Lady Port-Huntly lost her legs in an accident, and among her artificial limbs are a pair of glass legs filled with beer. It's definitely not a film for everyone, but it's worthy of a spot in the pantheon of brew-themed entertainment.

Beerfest (2006)

Craft beer was in the midst of its second (and more sustainable) upswing by 2006, but it took a while for Hollywood to catch up. With *Beerfest*, the Broken Lizard comedy troupe—whose previous cinematic efforts included *Super Troopers* and *Club Dread*—delivered a fraternity brother's fantasy of a beer-centric film that was more about binging and inebriation than it was about actually appreciating the fine beverage its characters were consuming. The film centered on a pair of brothers, Jan and Todd Wolfhouse (Broken Lizard's Paul Soter and Eric Stolhanske), tasked with transporting their late German-immigrant grandfather's ashes to Oktoberfest. While there they stumble upon a secret Olympics of sorts, with a series of events related mostly to college-style drinking games—beer pong, hardcore chugging, and more. They're forced into a future edition of the event by some distant relations with decades-old scores to settle against their family, and they return to the states to form a ragtag team of old drinking acquaintances (the rest of the Broken Lizard crew: Jay Chandrasekhar [who also directed], Steve Lemme, and Kevin Heffernan). The movie does have its share of laughs, but it does little to advance the perception of beer in the United States.

Beer Wars (2009)

Most of the entries on this list have been narrative films. This one's a full-on documentary. The overarching theme that filmmaker Anat Baron presented was David vs. Goliath. She followed a handful of small brewers as they dealt with the day-to-day trials and tribulations of making and selling beer in a market dominated by multinational players. The most interesting facet of the film actually happened offscreen. At the time *Beer Wars* was being edited, the market was undergoing a bit of a sea change. Large distributors, once hostile to small craft brands, had seen the light and realized the margins they could reap with craft were substantial. It became less of a struggle for brewers to find distribution. At that point, distributors were actively courting crafts, as they realized such brands were the future. Right around then, the segment started to achieve double-digit year-on-year growth and hasn't looked back since.

Drinking Buddies (2013)

At long last, an indie romantic dramedy firmly rooted in the world of craft beer. Filmmaker Joe Swanberg has carved out a niche for himself as the king of "mumblecore," characterized by low-budget production values and naturalist—often improvised—dialogue among its cast of characters. *Drinking Buddies* adapts that concept to a brewing milieu. The lead characters, Kate (Olivia Wilde) and Luke (Jake Johnson), work at Chicago's Revolution Brewing Co., an actual Windy City craft brewery. They're best buds, but there's obviously more of a connection there. The only trouble is that both are involved with other people. Things get a bit out of balance when Kate's boyfriend, Chris, breaks it off with her after kissing Luke's fiancée, Jill (the incomparable Anna Kendrick). (Jill and Luke don't break up.)

The film is wall-to-wall sexual tension. Sounds fairly trite on paper, but the improvised dialogue and the brewery setting make it all seem fresh. It's also one of the few films to actual get the modern craft brewing scene *right*. That's thanks, in part, to the fact that Swanberg is a homebrewer himself. He even insisted that his two leads learn to brew as soon as they arrived on location in Chicago (Swanberg's home, which put him doubly in his element). The opening montage features some of the best brewery porn—a term for gorgeous equipment and supplies, nothing more—ever caught on camera.

The World's End (2013)

Yes, it's ultimately about an alien intelligence infiltrating earth and replacing most of the population with synthetic replicas, but at its heart it's a love letter to the English pub. Gary King (Simon Pegg, who also scripted) has seen better days since the epic early-'90s pub crawl that he sees as the defining moment in his life. Twenty years after that crawl, he's chronically unemployed and in group therapy. He actually considers the original crawl a bit of a failure because he and his four friends didn't make it to the final destination, The World's End, on the twelve-pub journey. He reconnects with his buddies, who've all moved on and have found various forms of success, and manipulates them into reluctantly joining him on a repeat of the two-decades-old bar-hopping adventure—this time with the intention of finishing. Eventually, science fiction intervenes and things get progressively more ridiculous. But the nostalgia theme has another bittersweet layer. Britain's pubs continue to close at an alarming rate and are, therefore, a dying breed. Gary's wistfulness isn't just for a part of his life that no longer exists; it's actually for a major component of British life that's in danger of extinction.

Television

Laverne & Shirley (1976–1983)

Forget the years after the dynamic duo moved to California (and eventually ceased to be a duo). The golden age of the show was the Milwaukee era. (It was a spinoff of *Happy Days*, after all.) Since it took place about two decades before it was produced, it's not a snapshot of its times per se. But, with the titular team spending their days on the bottling line at the fictional Schotz Brewery, it captures the Wisconsin city in its prime as one of the great beer cities of the world. Milwaukee has become a hotbed for the craft renaissance as well, and the city's Lakefront Brewery invites its tour groups to sing along to the *Laverne & Shirley* theme song. Lakefront owns the actual bottling line used in the opening title sequence—and yes, there's a glove on one of bottles.

Cheers (1982–1993)

Of course a sitcom about a bar deserves a mention here. *Cheers'* relationship with beer is complicated at best. Bar owner Sam Malone (Ted Danson) is a recovering alcoholic so he's never really drinking any—except for a dark time in his life at the beginning of season 3, when he fell off the wagon following his (first) breakup with Diane Chambers (Shelley Long). Beer is most closely associated with barfly Norm Peterson (George Wendt), who was very likely a functioning alcoholic himself. On one hand, the show was supposed to be about unwinding after a rough day and going to a place "where everybody knows your name," but it played more like a cautionary tale centering on a lot of very broken people.

Breaking Bad (2008–2013)

Okay, this one's a bit of a stretch, but one of the things that made Hank Schrader—Walter "Heisenberg" White's DEA-agent brother-in-law and eventual arch nemesis—relatable was the fact that he was a homebrewer. (When he's first seen brewing in his garage, it's a major turning point for the character; it's about the time he becomes likeable and some audience members actually start to root for him.) He even named the stuff; Schraderbrau could very well have been the name of a legitimate brand. Unfortunately,

Hank inadvertently over-carbonated his bottles, which exploded in his garage, emitting a series of loud bangs that made Hank and his wife, Marie, think they were victims of a drive-by shooting.

Brew Masters (2010)

This one-season reality show chronicled the everyday challenges of running Delaware's Dogfish Head Craft Brewery. Dogfish Head founder Sam Calagione was the star and narrator of the program, which showcased some of the crazier concoctions the self-described "off-centered" brewery would cook up. One of those involved a tie-in with a surfboard company that resulted in a brew in which Dogfish Head incorporated pieces of those surfboards. It also followed Calagione as he traversed the globe in search of ancient inspiration. One such trip to Peru prompted him to create a brew based on Peruvian chicha, among whose ingredients is an enzyme found in human saliva.

Shameless (2011–)

The remake of the British series of the same name hasn't done beer—especially the Pabst-owned Old Style brand—any favors. To call Frank Gallagher (William H. Macy) a drunk would be offensive to drunks. It amazes me that Pabst authorizes the product placement for Old Style, which is a bit of an institution in the Midwest, especially blue-collar and hipster Chicago. (The brand actually got a more positive shout-out in the aforementioned *Drinking Buddies*, in which the lead character, Luke, wore an Old Style trucker cap throughout).

Brew Dogs (2013–)

Much like *Brew Masters*, *Brew Dogs* focuses on the antics of the founders of an against-the-grain craft brewery. In this case, the brewery is Scotland's BrewDog, which drew much of its inspiration from the more radical American brewers, including Dogfish Head. *Brew Dogs*, which has airs in the US on the Esquire Network, follows founders Martin Dickie and James Watt as they travel across America (and sometimes Europe) going from beer town to beer town and celebrating the local brews and culture.

Dinner and a Movie (Oh, and Beer!)

Tired of the fizzy sugar water and brain-freeze-inducing slushies available at multiplex concession stands? Afraid that you might get caught sneaking alcohol into the theater? Don't want to have to keep getting up during the movie for refills? The best advice: move to a town that has an Alamo Drafthouse.

The Alamo Drafthouse was born in Austin, Texas, in 1997 when rabid film buffs Tim and Karrie League opened the first location as a second-run theater. In addition to establishing itself as a corporate multiplex alternative—a destination run by movie lovers for movie lovers—it pioneered the concept of serving full meals, as well as alcoholic beverages (hence Drafthouse), with the entertainment. Each auditorium features long bar-like tables between the rows (so no fumbling with food and glassware). Audience members choose their selections from the menu and write it on a slip of paper, and quiet-as-mice waiters and waitresses collect the orders and deliver the bounty. The Drafthouse quickly evolved into a first-run theater (with multiple locations throughout Austin, some offering mainstream blockbusters, others focusing on artier fare) and has since expanded within Texas and beyond, with sites in Kalamazoo, Michigan; Kansas City, Missouri; Yonkers, New York; and San Francisco, California.

The Drafthouse takes the cinema experience very seriously. It has a world-famous zero-tolerance anti-talking/anti-texting policy and has been known to unapologetically eject transgressors (but there's always a warning first). It's also publicly shamed some of them. One Texas woman who had been removed from the theater for chatting on her mobile phone subsequently left a very vitriolic message on the Alamo's voicemail system complaining about her treatment. The message was played in its entirety in the Drafthouse's PSA on proper movie theater etiquette.

You know what else Alamo takes pretty seriously? Good beer. "Our obsession for movies is paralleled only by our obsession for beer," the theater chain proudly states on its website. "We pride ourselves in serving only the finest craft beers and supporting the best microbreweries. In every theater you'll find over 30 beers on tap in addition to a full selection of handcrafted cocktails . . . "

The beer's always fresh, and local breweries get special attention, though there are plenty of options from other parts of the country.

24

Cans, Church Keys, and Vintage Signage

The Wonderful World of Breweriana

For anyone passionate about beer, there's no better gift than a bottle, can, or growler of their favorite beverage. However, such gratification is fleeting; it remains in one's possession for only as long as it takes the possessor to drink it (unless it's a style that benefits from aging and can be cellared).

That's part of the reason why there's an entire subculture of memorabilia collectors who focus exclusively on beer-related artifacts, items known throughout the beer world as "breweriana."

Beer marketing tchotchkes were considerably more playful back in the day.

The largest collector collective in the breweriana realm is the Brewery Collectibles Club of America (BCCA), which boasts a history spanning more than four decades. There are now official chapters in thirty-six US states and four Canadian provinces. Overseas, Australia is home to two chapters, and Europe and Brazil each have one. If that doesn't sound like a vast enough network, there also are twenty-nine "at-large" chapters, which are based around members who share a specific collecting interest.

The organization launched in 1972, and in 1975 it produced a first-of-its-kind comprehensive compendium of beer can history, the *Guide to United States Beer Cans*. Today, BCCA prints a bimonthly magazine called

The gallon-size flat-top keg can was a short-lived format in the mid- to late '60s, but cans in good condition fetch hundreds of dollars among collectors.

Beer Cans & Brewery Collectibles, a full-color glossy magazine that packs its typical forty-eight pages with features on brewery histories, specific cans, and niches within the broader breweriana collecting world.

According to BCCA, among the original collectibles were the metal crown caps, which first showed up on the tops of bottles in the late nineteenth century. The majority of these caps were branded with their particular brewery, most of which don't even exist anymore.

The enactment of Prohibition in 1920 spurred a surge in collecting, as pretty much anything associated with the production, sale, and distribution of beer (and other alcoholic beverages) was rendered a relic.

Immediately after the repeal of Prohibition, before the newly legal beer was even cold, the next wave of collecting began in earnest.

While conducting research for a book on the subject, noted Connecticut-based breweriana and brewing history expert Jeff Browning got his hands on some old letters consumers had sent to breweries in 1934 asking for beer labels from their new products. Those likely came right from the presses, as the Twenty-first Amendment had just been enacted mere weeks prior. "The collecting gene seems to be prevalent in most of America, so I can't imagine that people weren't collecting prior to that," notes Browning, whose own collection includes about 40,000 items.

Then, in 1935—barely two years into legalized brewing—another facet of breweriana collecting was born, though most didn't even realize it at the time: beer cans and openers. (Beer was very likely finding its way into cans prior to Prohibition, as evidenced by the mention of both jars and cans of beer in old turn-of-the-twentieth-century blues songs. See the section on growlers for more on that blues connection.)

Browning has been an avid collector since the early to mid-'70s, a time when the hobby was expanding rapidly. Breweries, at the time, had really begun to forge significant marketing tie-in deals with sports teams, whose stars often appeared on cans—a novelty in those days. Artwork related to the approaching Bicentennial also found its way onto aluminum containers during that era.

It was also around that time that BCCA launched its annual collectors' summit, CANvention, which continues today, offering three days of wall-to-wall memorabilia. The most recent edition was in one of the all-time classic beer cities, Milwaukee, which practically invented breweriana.

The rest of the year, collectors often spend their time going through antique shops with a fine-toothed comb, seeking hard-to-find, tucked-away items to feed their obsession. And, then, of course, there's the Internet. One of the most significant buying/selling sites to help breweriana aficionados support their hobby is Breweriana.com, established in 1996 by lawyer Dan Morean. At the time, Breweriana.com was one of only two sites devoted

This vintage cone-top for the Weber brand has seen better days.

to the hobby; the other has since folded, but many others emerged over the years.

So successful was Breweriana.com that Morean was able to leave his law career behind and focus full time on the site. In 2000, he opened a 5,000-square-foot brick-and-mortar operation in Brimfield, Massachusetts, housing four rooms jam-packed with cans and other memorabilia. Each well-appointed room of this veritable museum is arranged around a particular theme. The first is its flat-top showroom, which displays, as the name suggests, mostly flat-top beer cans and post-Prohibition ads. Then there's the cone-top display room, which houses 500-square feet of those bottle-like aluminum cans. Next is its pre-Prohibition tavern room, which reproduces a late-nineteenth-century watering hole, complete with hickory floors, dark cherry molding, an antique mahogany bar and backbar, an 1880s pool table, and walls decked out in pre-Prohibition beer ads. Finally there's the crowntainer/bottle showroom, which displays mostly glass packaging, as well as a few other types of containers. Visiting is by appointment only, but beer lovers living in or visiting New England (it's about sixty-five miles outside of Boston) wouldn't want to miss the opportunity to stroll through a century and a half of beer history.

Like most antique collectibles, breweriana can be an extremely expensive hobby, depending on how serious the collector wants to get about it. The old flat-top, church key-opened cans vary wildly in value, depending on the brewer, the age, the rarity, and just how sought-after an item they are in the collecting world. Breweriana.com's online shop features modestly priced flat-tops, like an early 1950s-era Ballantine's Export lager can that fetches about $20. On the opposite extreme, the site recently showcased a Rheingold Pale Double Bock can produced circa 1937 that was listed for a cool $7,000. Vintage signage, beer ad lithographs also can change hands for the mid-to-high four figures and low five figures.

But, in many cases, that's chump change. Browning has seen single beer cans selling for as much as $30,000.

There's a certain allure with late-nineteenth-century printed marketing materials. Back in those days, the uneducated and illiterate made up a much more significant percentage of the American population than it does today (hard to believe in this era of the Kardashians and their sort). Brewers needed to sell a lot of beer, regardless of how many of their prospective drinkers couldn't even read or write. And they reached those consumers with very colorful ads; many couldn't read the name of the brand, but they were able to identify its logo. "Little kids can't read the name 'Heinz,' but they recognize the ketchup," Browning explains.

"It's basically pop art," says Browning.

An Unconventional Lot

There are few scenes that are more of a feast for the eyes for those who fancy ancient packaging and marketing materials than the Beer Collectibles Club of America's annual CANvention. The convention hall is a swap meet, a museum and Antiques Road Show rolled into one. It's a sea of church key-opened flat-top, cone-top, and pull-tab cans, as well as ceramic brand statues, tin signs, clocks, bottle caps, wooden signs, and just about anything on which a brewery could imprint its label. Some of it dates back to the nineteenth century, but the surprising part is that some of it is remarkably new. For every dinged up cone-top of long-gone brands like Koller's Topaz or Hanley's Extra Pale, there are fresh-off-the-seamer aluminum containers of more recent entries into brewing's hallowed halls, such as Abita, Sixpoint, and Oskar Blues. They're empty but completely sealed, with their tabs completely untouched and intact. They may not be worth a ton now, but as any collector knows, today's functional containers are tomorrow's treasures. It helps to be a bit ahead of the curve.

Interestingly, some flat-top pull-tab cans from the mid-twentieth century—from brands that are virtually extinct, like Huber and Piels, to surviving and thriving ones like Budweiser and Miller—were priced at only a buck a can in some circles. Some were even going for five for a dollar. Rarity is only part of their valuation. Condition is a huge component. Collectors kept the cans in pretty good shape for forty-odd years, but they're missing their pull tabs. (They were open and used at one point, obviously. Beer drinkers weren't hanging on to those pull-off opening mechanisms. Back in those days, they were a major source of pollution).

The cone-tops are the Holy Grails for many collectors, but it's really difficult to find any in a condition that's anywhere approaching mint. More likely they're dirty and rusted, with holes corroded into the sides and bottoms. But avid collectors are willing to part with five bucks for those.

Strolling table to table through the convention hall, one almost can piece together a visual timeline of nearly a century's worth of packaging evolution. And while most containers evolve, some outright fail. There's been a lot of trial-and-error involved in creating a format for multi-serve,

Fairly well preserved flat-top and cone-top cans.

take-home, draft-style beer, beyond purchasing a full- or half-size keg's worth of beer, of course. In the mid- to late '60s, brewers marketed tap-able gallon-size keg cans that looked like a much larger version of the classic flat-tops. After about four years on the market, packaging makers discontinued the gallons due to lack of interest. But there's no shortage of interest in these now-rare receptacles at Canvention. It's not uncommon to see some priced at $500 or $600.

Buyers and sellers frequently get asked what motivates them. For many, it's not necessarily about acquisition. A lot of times it's about the hunt. And hunt they will—through antique shops, rummage sales, and even landfills. That latter activity is known as "dumping." Armed with metal detectors, they'll often uncover breweriana that's been buried for decades.

Many continue with the hobby because of a strong emotional connection with the past, and usually it's personal. A common story told at the Canvention among mid-to-late-middle-age collectors is how their parents would take them along on hunts and even to collectors' conferences back in the '70s. Years later their fond memories would lure them back into the hobby.

That's what pulled Milwaukee collector Mark Navarre back into the breweriana world. He started orbiting rummage sales to find any cans he could. Eventually someone gave him a tip on a collection. He paid $700 for those three-thousand cans and never looked back.

"That's how you make these connections," he says. "One thing leads to another. You buy a big collection, keep ten percent of it for your own collection, and sell the rest."

Now he regularly books a table at BCCA to do just that.

25

Getting Schooled

Professional Beer Education

You've probably surmised by now that beer brewing is a magical convergence of art and science whose secrets have been passed down from generation to generation, thereby evolving and advancing for millennia. The art part, as in most other creative endeavors, is fairly difficult to learn. A brewer either has it or not. But the art doesn't really see the light of day without the solid practical and scientific foundation. Fortunately for aspiring and practicing brewers there has been a proliferation of educational programs designed to help beer-making professionals at any level of expertise develop and hone their craft.

One of the best regarded institutions by which many in the industry swear is the Siebel Institute of Technology, based in Chicago. Breweries large and small in about sixty different countries worldwide employ Siebel alumni.

The Siebel story began in 1868 when John Ewald Siebel, a recent émigré from Germany, opened John E. Siebel's Chemical Laboratory, which evolved into a research facility and school for brewing sciences. By the turn of the twentieth century, the institute was incorporated—it adopted its current name in 1910—and it offered a steady curriculum of brewing courses in both German and English. The earliest classes included a six-month brewer's course, a two-month post-graduate program, and a three-month engineering module, as well as classes in malting and bottling.

Of course, by that time, the specter of the Eighteenth Amendment loomed, so Siebel proactively diversified to survive. Its revamped curriculum didn't veer too far afield; educational tracks included baking—they had to do something with all of those grains—refrigeration, engineering, milling, carbonated beverages, and other related disciplines.

When Siebel passed away, it was almost as though he died of a broken heart; the date of his death was December 20, 1919, just shy of a month before Prohibition took effect.

In 1933, when the Twenty-first Amendment erased the scourge of the Eighteenth, the next generation of Siebels resumed the brewing curriculum.

Eighty years after Prohibition's repeal, Siebel moved to facilities within Chicago's culinary institute, Kendall College. (It had most recently been operating out of one of Goose Island Brewery's locations in the city.) Strolling through Siebel's new digs, it's impossible not to get overcome with emotion as you absorb a century and a half of brewing history and heritage. Photos of every class from every year adorn the walls of such hallowed halls. Not only do the latter-day class photos feature a veritable who's who of modern craft brewing, but walk back a couple of decades and you'll find generations of folks with surnames like Busch and Stroh.

Today's courses range from the entry-level to the advanced. Those toying with entering the brewing industry or those preparing themselves for the more rigorous education levels are advised to take the Concise Course in Brewing Technology. No prior brewing knowledge is required, but it helps.

Beyond those looking to one day work in an actual brew house, it's an ideal class for those working on the back-office side of the business—sales, marketing, administration, etc.—who want to expand their knowledge of the practical process.

Those serious about working in a production facility may want to follow that up with the Advanced Brewing Theory program, designed to give participants a detailed understanding of the major technical issues associated with brewing. This one does assume prior knowledge, and students must have completed the Concise Course as a prerequisite or get an online assessment to determine their existing skill set and knowledge base.

Those from outside the Chicagoland area needn't travel to the Windy City (especially during those treacherous winters). Siebel offers many of its courses online.

Those who want the actual classroom experience but in a much more temperate climate can head to California wine country. The West Coast state has quite the educational infrastructure for the fermentation sciences, given how much money the Golden State has made from grapes. Though wine was California's claim to fame long before the modern beer industry developed there, it is the state that can claim to be the one where craft brewing started—the Anchor reinvention, New Albion, and Sierra Nevada all happened in Northern California, after all.

And eventually, schools that traditionally catered to vintners began expanding their curricula to capitalize on the brewing renaissance. One of the best-regarded universities to accommodate the new beverage in town is the University of California at Davis. It makes a lot of logical sense, as it's also gained a reputation as the go-to academy for anyone who has considered working within a five-mile radius of a vineyard.

UC Davis wasn't just jumping on the bandwagon, either. It has offered courses in brewing science and brewery engineering since the late '50s, nearly a decade before Fritz Maytag had the insane notion to rescue Anchor from extinction. Most of its brewing curricula are available through the UC Davis Extension, the university's continuing and professional education arm.

Like Siebel, UC Davis tailors its academic offerings to the full spectrum of experience levels, though its entry-level course is even more concise than the former's "Concise Course." The class, titled "Brewing Basics: Going Beyond the Kit," has been designed with the homebrewer in mind. Its aim is to move those amateur beer makers away from the training wheels that all-inclusive homebrew kits provide and get them to understand the process in a slightly more professional manner. And, since it's not necessarily for the professional-minded, there's no time away from one's day job required. The entire time commitment for "Brewing Basics" is confined to a single weekend, and one gets to work with the equipment of a local brewery.

Closer to the "Concise Course" format, but still a more modest time commitment (five days), is UC Davis's "Introduction to Practical Brewing." The university describes the target audience as "advanced homebrewers and early career professional brewers."

The Davis faculty incinerates the kid gloves for the next level, "Intensive Brewing Science for Practical Brewing." The five-day course is an ideal follow-up to "Introduction to Practical Brewing."

If, after making it through the introductory courses, a student still harbors professional aspirations, it's time to graduate to the university's expanded programs. The first of those is the intensive "Professional Brewers Certificate Program," in which students meet six hours a day, five days a week, for a full ten weeks to learn everything from raw materials handling and analysis (grain basics, malting, hops, yeast, etc.) to the mechanics, sterilization practices, and scientific theory of brewing the perfect batch from start to finish. Those who complete the program get the university's Professional Brewers Certificate.

There are some serious math, biology, chemistry, and physics prerequisites for the certificate program, and transcripts are a must.

For those who really want to take things up a notch, there's the school's Master Brewers Program. This one's an 18-week affair designed to prepare students for the prestigious London Institute of Distilling and Brewing's Diploma in Brewing Examination (known around the campfire as the IBD DBE). That cumbersome acronym is one of the foremost designations in the world for those working professionally in the global brewing industry.

Passing the Master Brewers Program is one thing. Completing the IBD examination is another matter entirely. It's a nine-hour (!) test divided into three parts. And we're not talking multiple choice. Candidates must complete two papers in brewing science and one in brewery engineering. It's graded by a panel of brewing professors, scientists, and engineers.

Those interested in taking that rigorous test might consider studying right at the source as well. The IDB offers a number of tracks for all levels of brewing (and distilling) industry professionals. The London-based organization offers the "General Certificate in Brewing," which it considers an entry-level discipline for anyone working on a brewery's production team. Like the UC Davis's introductory courses, it takes up a full work week in various locations around the United Kingdom and Ireland.

IDB also offers a separate course for those seeking a certificate in beer packaging, as well.

There are plenty of other opportunities the world over to learn brewing at any level of competence. Here are a few more worth noting:

Brewlab

Those who fancy spending some time in Scotland (and who wouldn't?) will find plenty of educational opportunities at the University of Sunderland's Brewlab. The program boasts its own 3.5-barrel brewery, as well as kegging and bottling facilities. Curricula range from individual one-day workshops on topics such as microbiology and quality assurance to a comprehensive nine-week course that offers a diploma in British Brewing Technology. Multiday courses on start-up brewing, brewing skills development, and intensive practical brewing skills are also on offer.

Beer curricula aren't limited to those who want to work in a brew house. There are plenty of programs that address the marketing and general business side of the industry. It's an area that's generally been overlooked until recently. The commercial brewing world is full of one-time homebrewers who went pro and built enduring businesses. However, many of the craft pioneers had to make things up as they went along since they really were creating an industry from scratch. Today there is an exponentially greater number of brewing hobbyists with professional aspirations. But just because they can make a decent batch of beer and all of their friends tell them they should start a brewery, most don't have any experience with the actual, well, *business* side of the business.

The Scandinavian School of Brewing

Perhaps the Nordic countries have a bit more allure for a prospective brewer. The Scandinavian School of Brewing (SSB)—founded jointly by the Danish Brewers' Association, the Norwegian Brewers Association, and the Swedish Brewers' Association (and joined in 1993 by the Finnish Brewers' Association)—has been training beer professionals for more than ninety years. The school is conveniently located near Copenhagen, Denmark's Carlsberg Brewery. SSB offers diploma courses for craft brewers and master brewers, as well as curricula rooted in skills such as brewing business and supply chain management, among others.

Portland State University

Those interested in beer rarely need an excuse to spend some time in Portland, but, alas, PSU's "The Business of Craft Brewing" course is completely online. The curriculum consists of a series of four, five-week courses that must be completed within three years or in as little as two terms. Core requirements are "Basic Business for Craft Beverages" and "Craft Beverage Business management." Remaining courses include "Strategic Craft Beverage Marketing," "Finance and Accounting for the Craft Brewery," and "Craft Beverage Distribution," of which candidates must select two.

It's encouraging that such a program exists. Virtually every homebrewer daydreams about one day going commercial, but more often than not they lack the proper business chops to truly make a go of it. Before candidates complete the program, they will have put together an investor-ready business plan.

San Diego State University: Professional Certificate in the Business of Craft Beer

Another West Coast university—though one in a much more consistently sunny and warm part of the country—offers another program for the business-minded. San Diego State presents two levels certification levels: Level 1 involves six classes that students can complete in a single academic year. Its expanded Level 2 certificate requires the completion of nine classes over the course of one and a half academic years. The program is hands-on and interactive, with participants splitting their time between the SDSU campus and breweries throughout San Diego (and there are a lot of them).

The College of DuPage Business of Craft Beer Certificate

Chicago has become something of an epicenter for all facets of beer education; Siebel's there, of course, and it's also the birthplace of the Cicerone program (more on that in a bit). And that's no surprise because some of the most revered breweries have emerged from the Chicagoland scene. (Goose Island, Revolution Two Brothers, and Half Acre are notable home-grown operations; Northern California's Lagunitas picked the city as the base of its second gargantuan brewery as it expanded eastward; and 3 Floyds is a mere hour away in Munster, Indiana.) The College of DuPage was quick to recognize its region's contributions to better brewing—not to mention all of the employment that goes along with it—and launched the Business of Craft Beer certificate. Courses begin with the core prerequisite, "Foundations of the Craft Beer Industry," which includes all of the usual historical topics, along with a focus on beer styles. Once students complete that one, they get down to the real brass tacks of the industry. "The Real Business of Craft Beer" details the often-arcane intracacies of the three-tier system, and "Marketing Craft Beer" deals with branding-related concepts.

University of Vermont Certificate Program in the Business of Craft Brewing

The University of Vermont's program is the relative newcomer among the professional certificate programs focusing on the business of beer; the program's first classes were in February 2016. This one's a full twelve-week program—the length of an average college semester, give or take—covering everything from overall industry trends and dynamics to beer styles, branding, marketing, sales, and the legal landscape for craft beer. The University partnered with the Vermont Brewers Association to develop the curriculum, targeted primarily to college graduates with one to five years of experience in related areas such as sales, marketing, or business operations. An optional three-month internship at a commercial brewery or distributor follows.

Many individuals with a keen interest in beer might get scared off by some of the more involved curricula for working in the industry. But that's okay because there are many ways to work in the beer world without necessarily working in an operating brewery. Most of the major brewing schools offer classes for those who want to learn the basics of style, tasting, ingredients, and proper serving without brewing so much as a single batch on their kitchen stoves. And then there are certification programs outside of academia . . .

Cicerone and BJCP

Server certification has been a huge part of the wine world for about as long as there has been a wine world—in the modern sense, anyway. With hundreds of diverse styles coming onto the scene during the craft beer explosion, it's only logical that some sort of professional standards emerged to create the beery equivalent of sommeliers.

Cicerone

The most prominent and respected beer certification program is Cicerone, the brainchild of Ray Daniels, a well-known beer author, homebrewer, and festival organizer. He spent nine years working for the Brewers Association (and its precursor) as its director of craft beer marketing (a torch he ultimately passed to the talented, passionate beer-vangelist, Julia Herz).

Daniels sums up his motivation for launching the program in two simple words: "Bad beer."

"I was traveling all over the country and promoting American craft beer—this was still the early 2000s and things were starting to perk up again but they still weren't going full steam," Daniels recalls. "In an awful lot of places I'd go, the servers didn't know anything about [beer]. The pours looked like crap and the beer oftentimes didn't taste very good. I thought, 'My goodness, there are all these people jumping onto the craft beer bandwagon who don't know anything about the proper service of beer.'"

By 2007, Daniels was actively developing the program. On January 3, 2008, the program conducted its first exam.

However, it wasn't an overnight success. At the time of its launch, the economy was on the precipice of a global meltdown. So, it was slow-going at first, and Cicerone's widespread adoption wasn't a sure thing. But the tipping point occurred at the tail end of 2009, and by the beginning of

2010, it was a self-sustaining success. That was also the year that it received the endorsement of the largest craft brewery in the country, Boston Beer. After that, it really took off.

The word "Cicerone" refers to "one who conducts visitors and sightseers to museums and explains matters of archaeological, antiquarian, historic, or artistic interest."

To achieve Cicerone certification, candidates must be well-versed in five areas: beer storage, sales, and service; beer styles and culture; beer tasting and flavors; brewing ingredients and processes; and pairing beer with food. The program offers three levels of certification: Certified Beer Server, Certified Cicerone, and Master Cicerone.

To achieve the introductory level, candidates must answer a six-question multiple-choice online exam and score at least 75 percent. The test costs $69, which covers two attempts at passing (if needed). Generally, Certified Beer Servers have a working knowledge of beer storage and service issues, styles, flavors, and the fundamentals of brewing process and ingredients.

Becoming a Certified Cicerone is a considerably more involved affair. While there's no prerequisite for the Certified Beer Server Exam, applicants planning to take the Certified Cicerone test must have passed that first level. And, instead of multiple-choice, candidates must complete a written exam composed of short-answer and essay questions, as well as a tasting and demonstration element. The stakes are a bit higher, as well; the minimum acceptable score is 80 percent—at least 70 percent of the tasting component. The initial test costs $395, and that only covers the first attempt. Retaking the tasting portion requires another $100. Retaking the written costs an additional $175. And given the written and practical nature of the exam, applicants must take it in person, which are scheduled across the United States and sometimes in Canada throughout the year.

Certified Cicerone naturally ramps up the knowledge requirement. Successful candidates must have a detailed knowledge of retail beer storage and service issues, expert-level knowledge of modern beers and styles, and some familiarity with beer history and historical styles. Their palates must be trained enough to identify flaws and pinpoint off-flavors. Their familiarity with brewing processes and ingredients also must be more advanced. However, applicants aren't completely on their own. The organization provides a Certified Cicerone Syllabus that directs candidates to a range of sources to help them prepare.

The two highest levels are Advanced Cicerone and Master Cicerone. The former is actually a recent addition; it was incorporated into the program in 2016. Prior to that there was no intermediate level between Certified Cicerone and Master Cicerone. It was quite a leap between the two, as Master Cicerone is reserved for those with, as the program states, "encyclopedic knowledge" of beer and an extreme sensory acuity. The Master exam, which lasts two full days, costs $795; those needing to retake it will be charged 80 percent of that cost.

But Advanced Cicerone gives those who have passed the Certified Cicerone exam the chance to reach another level of achievement without the extensive amount of studying and preparation require to pass the Master Cicerone. The exam itself takes one day, versus the Master's two-day commitment. There also will be more opportunities for candidates to take it. While the Master exam is scheduled only once or twice a year, the Advanced test will be available at least six times a year in various cities across the US.

When Cicerone started, its sole focus was certification. It had resisted offering any formalized classes or training program, encouraging applicants to prepare through their jobs, practical experience, and/or reading many of the in-depth books on all facets of beer making, proper handling, and appreciation.

"The point was to get other organizations to create their own training programs and resources that focused on Cicerone certifications," Daniels notes. "We have seen a lot of things like that arise from individual Certified and Master Cicerones and from schools of various types."

However, despite such developments, Daniels and his team continually has fielded requests from folks to offer more training resources. As a result, Cicerone did eventually devise training of its own.

"We specifically designed it to reach people who can't attend class for whatever reason and need self-paced, part-time, and close-to-home sorts of learning," Daniels explains.

For the Certified Beer Server level, the Cicerone program offers BeerSavvy and, for those seeking the next level, there's Road to Cicerone.

"But as always, we offer these programs only as options," Daniels claims, "and no one is required to use our training programs before they take the exams."

So, outside of those specially tailored training options, home much time and effort should candidates be committing to bone up on all of the necessary concepts?

"It depends on your level of experience," Daniels adds.

Those at the basic level taking the online BeerSavvy course, they can expect that to take between five and eight hours, but additional reading is strongly encouraged.

About fifty applicants take the Certified Beer Server each day. As of the end of 2015, some 65,000 have achieved the entry level certification. Close to 3,000 have passed the much more rigorous Certified Cicerone exam. The most recent tally puts the number of Master Cicerones at ten—two of those are from overseas. As craft beer has gone global, so has interest in Cicerone.

"Having started to travel more internationally in recent years, what I've come to realize is how huge the craft beer concept is overseas now," Daniels says. "What we're starting to see now is a pull from overseas people wanting Cicerone in their home market."

Scotland's BrewDog has been a significant early international adopter with nearly forty Certified Cicerones on staff. And the exams have attracted applicants everywhere from Canada and Mexico to Australia and South Korea.

It's not only those who serve beer in bars in restaurants that are taking any of the Cicerone exams. The certification has become popular among distributors. As wholesalers have taken on more craft brands in the past decade, they've encouraged and in many cases required their sales teams and employees in other functions to get certified. It has become a significant marketing credential for many of those distributors, which are able to position themselves as educated experts, something that makes their retail customers more likely to invest in craft inventory.

And, as the world of beer is constantly in flux, the Cicerone team tweaks and updates the content of the exams every couple of years to keep things fresh and cutting edge. The program draws from a variety of well-respected sources. Cicerone uses the Brewers Association's Draft Beer Quality manual for the draft dispensing portions of the exams. Style guidelines are based on those of the Beer Judge Certification Program (BJCP).

Beer Judge Certification Program

A much older certification program came into being not for those serving beer, but for those judging it in competition. The Beer Judge Certification Program (BJCP) was founded in 1985 as a joint venture between the American Homebrewers Association and the Home, Wine, and Beer Trade Association (though now that partnership is defunct, and BJCP operates as an independent body).

Things have evolved for the organization since then, but its three stated objectives have remained pretty much consistent:

• Encourage knowledge, understanding, and appreciation of the world's diverse beer, mead, and cider styles.
• Promote, recognize, and advance beer, mead, and cider tasting, evaluation, and communication skills.
• Develop standardized tools, methods, and processes for the structured evaluation, ranking, and feedback of beer, mead, and cider.

(Mead and cider, though vastly different than beer, frequently get categorized with the more widely consumed beverage. Where beer's base is fermented barley malt, mead's is predominantly honey and cider's is predominantly apples.)

Homebrewing had just been legalized in 1978, and over the next several years, a significant number of brewing enthusiasts had started getting into the hobby. With that came a wave of new homebrew competitions at the local, regional, and national level. However there was a dearth of qualified individuals who could bring an expert's perspective to judging such contests. Current BJCP president, noted homebrewer, and author Gordon Strong paints the former landscape thusly:

"If you just kind of showed up at a beer festival or event where the general population is, what kind of beer would win if you had a people's choice award? Is that really what you want? Is the average population going to know what makes a good Vienna lager versus a pilsner and be able to recognize brewing skill and the ability to create something of a specific style? For that, people have to have sensory training to properly evaluate a beer. That was really the need [BJCP] was trying to fill."

Since its inception BJCP has administered its Beer Judge Examination to nearly 10,000 people worldwide; the organization estimates that some 5,500 are active judges in the program.

The organization has streamlined the test-taking process dramatically—to the point that there's such an intensive screening process before the practical exam that most of the people who sit down to take it pass.

Initially there was a three-hour exam consisting of ten written questions and a practical portion with four beers to judge. It eventually switched to an online qualifier that must be completed before the test-taker graduates to the 90-minute practical, which involves analyzing six beers, each for fifteen minutes.

"Before you can even get in the door to the tasting exam, you've already had to take the online [qualifier]," says Strong. "It does a good job of weeding out the unprepared."

About one-hundred-fifty locations host the BJCP exam each year. It's usually administered by a senior BJCP judge, who's required to register the exam, secure a distraction-free location, and enlist local proctors.

The six practical styles on the exam are always changing and are at the discretion of the judge administering the test. "We give them guidance and we ask them to pick from different groupings and get a range of beer styles from around the world—some from Germany, some from Belgium, the UK, the US, and different strengths."

The organization also advises that the test include both ales and lagers. And not all of the beers are going to be good. Some are going to be middling and others are going to be downright bad—on purpose. Beers with known faults are good exam beers because part of what's being tested is a prospective judge's ability to recognize those faults—and they're usually not pronounced or obvious to the layperson.

The BJCP's evolving style guidelines make up a veritable encyclopedia of beer, cider, and mead style characteristics—the voluminous text is usually the go-to document for many judging competitions, whether or not the judges are certified.

The organization updates the style guide, on average, every four or five years to keep things current. The most recent update was in 2015; it now features more than one hundred style categories. BJCP style guidelines are the most widely followed across all of brewing.

Master Brewers Association of the Americas Certification

The Master Brewers Association of the Americas (MBAA) is a venerable organization that dates back to 1887 and has the stated purpose of "promoting, advancing, and improving the professional interest of brew and malt house production and technical personnel." MBAA, like Cicerone, offers graduated levels of certification, depending on how serious about a career in beer stewardship the candidate may be. The Associate Beer Steward Certificate is geared toward front-of-the-house bartenders and wait staff, as well as beer retail personnel who want to expand their knowledge of the brews they serve. The hour-long open-book exam consists of sixty-five multiple-choice questions; candidates receive the first five chapters of the Beer Steward Handbook as a guide.

Those who desire to receive the Beer Steward Certificate proper are usually in sales and marketing roles at breweries or in managerial positions at distributorships and retail establishments and wish to maintain proper quality and freshness. This one's a seventy-five-question, multiple-choice test based on the entire Beer Steward Handbook.

Beer 101

The Brewers Association, the trade association that represents American craft brewers (and is the umbrella organization for the American Homebrewers Association) offers its own certificate in the form of Beer 101. It's an online course for anyone interested in craft beer who wants to enhance their education. The course covers the history of beer, brewing ingredients and processes, and acronym-friendly concepts like alcohol by volume (ABV), International Bitterness Units (IBU), and the Standard Reference Method (SRM) for specifying beer color. Other topics include pairing beer with food and beer styles. At the end of the course, which takes about an hour, there's a fourteen-question exam. Enrollees may review the material as often as they wish prior to taking the test, but once the online test begins, there's no cheating. The financial commitment is fairly modest—a mere $15—and if candidates don't pass it the first time, they can retake it as many times as they would like at no additional cost.

26

Kindred Categories

Craft Spirits, Cider, and Mead

One of the most visible long-term trends in the world of beverage alcohol has been the decline of US beer market. That statement sounds fairly counterintuitive, considering the fact that the past several hundred pages have been heralding the modern brewing renaissance. But there really are two beer industries. There's the macro, mass-produced industrial side, and there's the craft side. The craft side, as we've discussed, is growing in the high-teens to 20-percent range. But for most of the past decade, the overall beer market has been flat to down. What's more, beer's losses have been the other beverage categories' gains.

Industry folks like to talk about a concept called "share of stomach"—Brits tend to call it "share of throat"—usually expressed in pie charts detailing how much market share one category has versus another. In the alcohol realm, beer historically has been the dominant beverage. However, spirits and wine have been gaining.

Now, there are a few different ways to measure one category against another, but it's not always easy to get an apples-to-apples comparison. Some beverage market consultancies and research companies often express the share of stomach/throat in terms of volume; in the states, that's usually measured in gallons. The obvious problem with that is, when it comes to the volume of each type of alcohol beverage a consumer drinks, you can't get much more apples-and-oranges. A moderate, social drinker might have a pint of porter at their favorite watering hole, but if that person drank an equal quantity of whiskey in a single sitting, it's likely that he or she would wake up in the hospital after a good old-fashioned stomach pumping. The effects would not be quite so extreme after drinking a pint of wine, which is roughly equivalent to three glasses of the grape-based beverage. But after three, most people are done for the evening.

Other analysts will venture down another rabbit hole all together, trying to measure it in terms of standard drink sizes. For instance, "one drink" may be defined as a 12-ounce serving of beer, an ounce and a half of a 80-proof spirit, or a 5-ounce glass of wine. But even with those guidelines, it's hard to reach a consensus, especially when beer's ABV can vary wildly.

The most instructive method of expressing share of stomach is by revenue. It's quite eye opening to see where consumers are spending their money in the alcohol space and even more so when you look at longterm market trends.

The Distilled Spirits Council of the United States (DISCUS) has done the best job of illustrating intercategory market share shifts. Drawing from a number of data providers, DISCUS has shown that beer has lost more than eight share points in the space of a decade and a half. In 1999, beer accounted for 56 percent of all alcohol beverage dollars in the United States. That same year, spirits represented 28.2 percent and wine 15.8 percent. However, fast-forward to 2015 (the last full year for which figures are available), and the drinkable fortunes have shifted markedly in favor of spirits. Beer's share of stomach is down to 47.5 percent, wine has gained a modest 1.2 share points to hold at 17 percent, and spirits have enjoyed enjoyed a full seven point jump to reach 35.4 percent.

This is that notion of "drinking less but drinking better" at work. Consumers aren't pounding cheap beer after cheap beer; they prefer to drink more flavorful, complex beers in moderation. Those brews cost substantially more than the macros, but, since craft beer has yet to crack 15 percent of the category's overall volume, it's not enough to pull beer into solid positive-growth territory.

Where big brewers lacked the ability, until recently, to play credibly in the high end of the market, large spirits conglomerates have been able to do just that. The Diageos, Pernod Ricards, and Brown Formans of the world have extremely diversified portfolios—from high-volume, low-margin well vodkas, rums, and gins, to low-volume but high-profit single malt Scotches, small batch bourbons, and super premium vodkas and tequilas.

That's why the emergence of a craft distilling industry owes more to beer than it does to its own category. Craft brewing emerged as an alternative to industrially produced brands that essentially turned the beverage into a flavorless commodity. Craft distillers emerged, at least in part, thanks to the success of their brewing brethren. When craft beer became a bona fide phenomenon, it paved the way for similar revolutions in the other alcohol categories. The craft spirits market is the most visible of those. As of this writing, the number of small distilleries in the United States has surpassed 1,000 (according to research commissioned by the American Craft Spirits

Association), increasing tenfold since 2010. The craft distilling sector is about a decade behind craft beer in its development; its volume represents just shy of 2 percent of the overall market, but it is growing very rapidly.

Another beverage that owes a fair amount of its explosive growth to craft beer is cider. A decade ago, the market for the fermented alcohol drink was pretty quiet. The category was well developed in the United Kingdom and Ireland but had never really risen above the status of niche-within-a-niche in the United States. That started to change around 2009 when volume started to accelerate and a wave of new US players, following in the tradition of craft brewers, got into the game. Some of those were already successful craft beer producers.

Cider reached its tipping point in 2011 when the largest craft brewer in the country decided to throw its hat into the apple ring. That was when Boston Beer Company, maker of Sam Adams, created Angry Orchard. It didn't take long it to become the largest cider brand in the country, quickly passing the category's previous leader, Vermont Hard Cider Company (known for the Woodchuck line).

Angry Orchard has helped pull the reinvigorated category to high-double-digit growth for each of the past four years, making it the fastest-growing segment in all of beverage alcohol. And most agree that there wouldn't be such a cider surge without the juggernaut that is craft beer.

Cider Goes Pro

The momentum behind cider, by all accounts, seems to be a sustainable phenomenon. And on a professional level, the cider segment is starting to behave more and more like the craft beer industry. (It doesn't hurt that so many cider makers were also successful craft brewers before taking a walk through the orchard.) February 2013 saw the birth of the United States Association of Cider Makers (USACM), which is sort of the cider market's answer to the Brewers Association. The group made it official at its inaugural convention and trade show in Chicago.

In 2015 the organization unveiled the Cider Certification Program, which is not unlike its more established beer counterpart, Cicerone. (USACM originally planned to call it Sicera, after the Latin word for "strong," but it proved too similar-sounding a word to "Cicerone.") It's designed for distributors, servers, and anyone else who desires to become a trained expert on the strong apple drink. Like Cicerone, Sicera is being segmented into graduated qualification levels. The exam for Level One covers the history of the beverage, the cider making process, stylistic differences, and how to serve it. Higher levels involve sensory evaluation, keeping and serving cider, orchard basics, and federal definitions of cider, among other topics. USACM administers the exams at its annual convention.

There are some much smaller segments that are benefiting from renewed activity thanks to the interest in all things artisanal. One of those is mead, the ancient fermented-honey beverage that's moving out of the Renaissance Faire and into beer bars everywhere. It's often called "honey wine," but it doesn't share much in common with wine. There are about forty different mead variants, ranging from traditional—100 percent of its fermentable sugars come from honey—to such styles as braggot and cyser, which combine mead with elements of beer and cider, respectively. As is the case with beer, there's so much innovation happening that new substyles emerge all the time. The one prerequisite that binds all such products under the mead umbrella is that most of their fermentable base (51 percent) must be honey. Alcohol content can vary wildly, sometimes as low as 6 percent and as high as 18 percent.

Currently there are about two hundred producers of mead in the United States and that number is growing. That growth is following a trajectory similar to that of craft beer, albeit on a much smaller scale. Just as the number of brewers started to decline slightly after the turn of the millennium and then surge again a few years later, the full head count of mead makers contracted a bit during the same period before reversing a handful of years ago. After about 8,000 years, the beverage—considered one of the oldest, if not *the* oldest, fermented drink in the world—could finally be having its moment.

On an even smaller scale (if you can imagine that), the craft coattails have extended to saké, the classic Japanese alcoholic beverage. Back in 1992, Oregon's SakéOne started importing the beverage from the home islands and, five years later, decided to try its hand at producing the stuff on American soil. The company has since grown to become a respected saké brewer in its own right, holding its own against the stuff made for hundreds of years back in Japan.

Saké is another of those beverages that gets lumped in with wine, but it actually shares more in common with beer—namely the fact that it's brewed. Instead of the barley malt that beer uses as its base, the fermentable sugars in saké are derived from rice.

For most of the first decade and a half of the twenty-first century, there were fewer than ten homegrown saké brewers in the United States, and most of them were concentrated on the West Coast. However, just in the past couple of years, the number has doubled. Admittedly, it's not a huge base from which to grow, but it could be the spark of a trend. The beverage is even attracting brewers who previously worked at successful craft beer breweries, so there could be something to the fermented-rice beverage.

27

Apps, Podcasts, and Blogs

Beer in the Digital Age

It's not far-fetched to suggest that the modern, twenty-first century craft beer movement would not have reached such great heights had it not been for the Internet. The trajectory of the craft segment from the 1990s through the 2010s very closely mimics that of online world. Craft beer volume started to slow in the late '90s, just as the tech bubble was about to burst. Then, in the mid-2000s, craft growth accelerated once again, just as this social media thing started to take over. Coincidence? Yes and no. While there's no real correlation between the tech boom and the initial craft beer surge in the '90s, social media certainly has played a significant role in keeping the craft conversation going, connecting beer fans with the brewers and products they love, and fostering the sort of give-and-take relationship between brand and consumer that never really existed previously. In traditional marketing and advertising, it was pretty much a one-way discussion, with the brand owners talking at drinkers and hoping for the best. (Yes, that is admittedly an oversimplification of the branding process. Please, ad agencies, don't send any hate mail.)

Never in the history of marketing has the playing field been more level. Small brewers always have known that they'd never have access to even a small fraction of the mega brewers' marketing budgets to commit to traditional advertising. Most of the craft producers' eggs were in the word-of-mouth basket. Of course, back in the day, word-of-mouth meant actual syllables coming out of real human voice boxes. And it was a fairly localized phenomenon.

Now, if someone likes a beer, the rest of the world—and in this case "world" is not hyperbole—knows it in an instant.

The savvier brewers have learned to use this new dynamic to their advantage. It's not hard to gauge how well developed a brewery's social media program is; just look at its Twitter stats. At last count, Delaware's Dogfish Head was closing in on 300,000 followers, besting even Sierra Nevada, a brewery four times its size with which it has frequently collaborated. Of course, it's not just about followers. Dogfish Head has tweeted more than 40,000 times since it joined that social media platform in October 2008. Sierra, meanwhile, has tweeted about one-sixth of the number of times that Dogfish has since the Chico, California-based company signed on about six months after the Delaware brewery. Dogfish has a much greater Follower-to-Following (those it follows) ratio: Dogfish follows one account for every 120 accounts that follow it. Sierra follows one for every ten accounts that follow it.

But brewery does not live on Twitter alone. (Let's not forget that Sierra Nevada founder Ken Grossman is a billionaire, after all.) Instagram, Facebook, Pinterest, Yelp, and LinkedIn each plays a unique role in building a presence in the social-sphere.

But those platforms are very far from being the only games in town available to brewers and drinkers alike. Beer-themed apps and social platforms have become an industry unto themselves in recent years.

UnTappd

The most prominent app among beer geeks has been UnTappd, launched in 2010 by tech entrepreneurs Tim Mather and Greg Avola. In a little over three years, the UnTappd app has had more than one million users. Much like Yelp or Facebook users would check in to places they're currently visiting, members of the UnTappd nation check in to beers (as well as the places where they're enjoying—or not enjoying—them). And, just as they would with Yelp, they can write reviews on the spot and rate the brand on a scale of one to five bottle caps. Users also can post photos of the beers and, most importantly, connect with other drinkers and brewers anywhere around the globe. It's been an invaluable tool for brewers, as they have been able to assess the public response to a new offering. UnTappd also enables them to keep an eye on venues that serve their products. If a bar is serving an out-of-date or generally subpar pints of their beer, the brewer can alert the local distributor about that retail account; it may not be maintaining its draft lines or properly washing its glassware, or it may be generally mishandling the brands.

Pintley

If UnTappd is the Yelp of beer apps, Pintley is the Netflix—at least in the way the latter suggests movies and TV series based on your tastes and streaming history. Pintley learns drinkers' tastes based on past ratings and tasting notes, and it suggests beers that the micro-robots are sure those users will enjoy. The app also invites those beer lovers to free local events where they can taste those suggestions for real. The app launched the same year as UnTappd and was created by Boston-based entrepreneurs Tim Noetzel and Shannon Hicks.

BeerMenus

When it comes to smartphone apps, simplicity is often the greatest virtue. This is true not just in terms of smartphone apps' ease of use, but by the fact that they take the guesswork out of what it is exactly that a particular piece of tech actually does. And that, in a nutshell, is BeerMenus, an app that provides . . . well, beer menus. It tells you what's on tap and in bottles at which bars and restaurants in your immediate vicinity. It also alerts the user when favorite drinking establishments add new brews to the list. Users can follow specific beers and receive notifications when those become available nearby. Let's say you're a big fan of The Alchemist's Heady Topper, but you can never find it. (There isn't a lot of it to go around.) BeerMenus will give you real-time info on where it is so you don't have to miss it again. When New York brothers Will and Eric Stephens started the digital guide in 2008, it focused only on the city but quickly expanded nationwide. The website and app now include listings from more than 15,000 bars, restaurants, and beer shops across the United States, with updates on nearly 100,000 brews.

TapHunter

BeerMenus's most direct competitor is TapHunter, founded in San Diego in 2010 by Jeff and Melani Gordon. It offers a bit more than what types of beers your favorite watering holes are serving at a particular moment, and it also has info on wine and spirits. It gives personalized recommendations on what and where to drink based on the user's established preferences. And, like BeerMenus, it alerts users when their favorite drinks become available nearby. It's also a good tool for breweries, allowing them to spread the word about their brews and connect the libations with their target drinkers as quickly as possible. It's currently in select locations across the country but is expanding quite rapidly.

CAMRA Good Beer Guide

If you're planning a trip to the United Kingdom, do not board the plane until you've downloaded the Campaign for Real Ale's Good Beer Guide app. CAMRA still prints a fat guide annually, but the app is so much lighter and you don't have to wait a year for it to update. The app helps users find pubs throughout the UK that serve real ale on cask—and serve it well, at the right temperature, and with the appropriate level of tender, loving care. Thousands of CAMRA volunteers compile, review, and update information on more than 4,500 pubs throughout Great Britain, drilling down to details like whether a particular venue serves food (and during which hours that food is available), how many hand pumps are on the bar, which breweries' beers it typically carries, its hours of operation, and whether it's accessible for people with disabilities. Like all good apps, it's location-specific and tells you exactly how much distance separates you from a spot-on pint of bitter. (It even works in the US. It's always fun to see that your favorite Manchester pub is exactly 3,642 miles from where you're standing at this moment.)

The app is free to download, but that gets the usual a very rudimentary form of it. Much more functionality is available to those who pay the modest $6.99 annual subscription.

Beat the Brewmaster

Beat the Brewmaster turns the task of tasting and pairing beer into a game. Players find the beer they're drinking on the app or website, rate it, and then get instant feedback on how their impressions jive (or don't) with the impressions of the actual brewmaster behind that beer. The more closely their assessments align with the brewmaster's, the more points the users gain.

"It's all around sensory skills," says Chris Clarke, one of the app's creators. "To play the game, you've got to have a beer in front of you. It's visual, aroma, mouthfeel, aftertaste."

The more points users gain, the higher they climb on the leaderboard, unlocking levels Enthusiast, Pro, and Master. And they can boast about their progress by sharing their success on Facebook, Twitter, and the other usual social media suspects. It's becoming an educational tool not just for drinkers but for brewery and distributor sales reps as well. It enables them to stay sharp and speak more authoritatively about the portfolios they're hawking.

The Pioneers

BeerAdvocate

BeerAdvocate was beer-based social media before social media and smart-phones even existed. The site was founded by another Boston-based duo, brothers Jason and Todd Alstrom (Todd has since moved to Denver), way back in 1996. The site has enabled users to register and review beers, bars, and other brew-centric destinations. The number of individual beers in the BeerAdvocate database numbers well into the six figures. The number of user-contributed reviews—the Alstrom brothers also write their own takes on the brews—is well into the seven figures, somewhere around 4 million. The BeerAdvocate brand has since expanded to include a mobile app, a print magazine, and several successful Boston beer festivals throughout the year.

Ratebeer

Four years after the Alstroms posted the first BeerAdvocate review, Ratebeer came on to the scene with its own ratings-and-reviews system for beer geeks. The site has changed hands since it was initially founded by Bill Buchanan in 2000. It's now owned by executive director Joe Tucker, who runs the site from Sonoma County, California. It partnered on a third-party-developed mobile app, BeerBuddy Powered by RateBeer, which enables users to call up RateBeer scores, record and rate what they've had, and read news and discussions on user forums. The site also publishes a print compendium, The Beer Guide, based on the consensus ratings of tens of thousands of its users in its community.

Games and Other Curiosities

Beer apps don't always have to be about education and tasting notes. Sometimes they're just for fun. And they go beyond just the plethora of virtual beer pong apps on the highly saturated market (we'll leave those off).

Fiz: The Brewery Management Game

"In some games, you have to rescue the princess, slay the dragon, save the world," the little 16-bit avatar says in the trailer for Fiz. "This time, do something that really matters . . . make beer!"

To call Fiz just a game would be unfair to the innovative little mobile app. It's actually one of the most diverting primers on the process of making beer—including the nuances among different varieties of hops and malt—as well as selling it in the marketplace. It features business intelligence from retail accounts that give the player a competitive advantage over rival breweries (information that even folks doing the real-world job would covet). Getting to the next level in this game means growing your business, and that means upgrading equipment and hiring employees (from a pool of folks who bring their own unique skill sets to the job). It really stands head-and-shoulders above the other beer-game apps out there. (Again, how many beer pong apps do we need?) It truly celebrates the beverage, rather than the state of inebriation that its overconsumption can cause.

iBeer

If there were an award for Best Stupid Fun App, it would surely go to iBeer (it would narrowly defeat iFart because it gets a few extra points for being less low-brow). You're not going to learn anything, you're not going to make any friends, and you just might lose a few IQ points after playing with it for a few minutes. But it's a fantastic ice breaker in awkward social situations. It's nothing more than an interactive glass of virtual beer. The fizzy brew with generously foamy heat fills the smartphone screen and reacts to the user's movements. Tilt it toward your mouth and you can pretend-drink it. It guarantees . . . uhh . . . seconds of enjoyment!

Beer Timer

Some might say that Beer Timer borders on unnecessary, but it does serve a very important purpose, if a bit on the niche side. It tells you when the beer you've selected is going to be at optimal drinking temperature if it's currently at room temperature and you want to speed-chill it in the freezer. The user selects the size of the beer (12 ounces or 22/24 ounces), whether it's in a bottle or a can, and whether it's a pale lager, pale ale, dark lager, porter, or stout. (Yes, that selection is a little limited, but it's easy enough to extrapolate among similar styles.) It's little more than a novelty, to be sure, but at least it eliminates the possibility of forgetting about the beer(s) in the freezer and essentially ruining them (and potentially everything else in the freezer if it happens to explode).

New Beer Media

Digital technology is obviously about so much more than social media platforms and mobile apps (both useful and time-wasting); the Internet has revolutionized and democratized beer writing and broadcasting (admittedly a misnomer when we're talking about ones and zeros).

Beer blogging has become such a pervasive media genre that it now has its own quasi-professional conference every year on two continents (once in the US and once at a rotating beer destination in Europe).

And the rise of podcasting and Internet radio has given an actual, audible voice to enthusiasts and pros alike, turning hobbies into full-fledged media outlets. The advent of approachably priced audio equipment and the means to connect with an audience outside of the corporately controlled airwaves has opened up golden age of beer-related content creation.

The Heritage Radio Network is one such entity that has created an online community for the foodie set, of which craft beer is a prominent component. The network is the creation of Patrick Martins, who previously made a name for himself as the founder of Slow Food USA, a nonprofit organization that advocates a fresh, seasonal, sustainable, and healthy food supply that's available to all walks of life and promotes fair labor practices. Heritage Radio Network was built on a similar ethos. The very DIY nature of the operation is exemplified by its studio headquarters, which is inside a pair of decommissioned shipping containers—those big metal ones you see stacked up at commercial ports—in the back courtyard of trendy Bushwick, Brooklyn eatery Roberta's. Bushwick has become the center of Brooklyn's creative scene and neo-artisanal movement—it's the setting of the HBO Lena Dunham series, *Girls*—since many of the creative people living and working there were priced out of the adjacent hipster hub, Williamsburg (not that Bushwick is that much more affordable anymore).

Heritage Radio Network

Among Heritage Radio Network's beer-focused programming is "Beer Sessions Radio" (Tuesdays at 5:00 p.m. ET), which covers all facets of the craft beer world. Jimmy Carbone—owner of the popular East Village, Manhattan subterranean gastropub Jimmy's No. 43—hosts the hour-long informal discussion with notable brewers, beer writers, publicans, and other personalities from the worldwide scene, always over a few beers, of course. Carbone launched the show in 2010 with his original cohost Ray Deter, proprietor of another well-regarded East Village beer bar, dba. Sadly, a little over a year after its launch, Deter was killed in a bicycle accident in Manhattan.

Guests have ranged from *brewerati* like Garrett Oliver—brewmaster and vice president of Brooklyn Brewery (the studio's proximity to Oliver's Williamsburg base definitely has helped)—to folks involved with sister beverages like cider and saké.

Heritage is also the home of "Fuhmentaboudit," a weekly show (Mondays at 7:00 p.m. ET) hosted by writer and fermentation expert Mary Izett, author of the book *Speed Brewing* and founder of the blog MyLifeOnCraft. com, and professional brewer Chris Cuzme. (The power couple of the New York brewing scene also run the gypsy brewery Cuzett Libations.)

The Brewing Network

Where the Heritage Radio Network focuses on beer as a piece of the wider food world, the Brewing Network—if you can't already tell by its name—concentrates solely on all things beery. It also predates Heritage by about four years, having broadcast the first edition of its inaugural live program, "The Sunday Live Show," in June 2005. It was later rebranded as "The Sunday Session"—not to be confused with "Beer Sessions Radio"— and ultimately "The Session" when it moved to Mondays. It's a fairly laid-back format, combining interviews, live interaction with the listening audience and personal craft beer and home-brew-related anecdotes from the team of hosts. Topics include everything from eco-conscious brewing and experimental homebrewing to an exploration of the beer drinking scenes in such far-flung realms as Japan. It also regularly features conversations with individual luminaries in the craft brewing world.

In addition to "The Session"—which now actually broadcasts on Mondays—The Brewing Network also produces a number of regular and semi-regular shows. Among those:

- **"Brew Strong"** pairs author Jamil Zainasheff with fellow homebrewer/ author John Palmer, and the hosts answer live audience questions (along with those from expert guests) on beginner and advanced brewing techniques.
- **"The Sour Hour"** co-hosts Scott "Moscow" Moskowitz and Jay Goodwin devote each hour-plus episode to sour beers.
- **"Dr. Homebrew"** brings together "The Session co-host Jason "JP" Petros with BJCP master judges Brian Cooper and Lee Shephard to talk D-I-Y brewing.

Steal This Beer

In 2015 Augie Carton, founder of New Jersey's Carton Brewing Company, ventured into podcasting with coconspirator and fellow Jersey boy John Holl, editor of *All About Beer Magazine* and author of *The American Craft Beer Cookbook*, and producer Justin Kennedy, another accomplished freelance beer writer who also produces "Beer Sessions Radio" (it's quite an incestuous beast, this beer world). The very opinionated Garden State duo (along with special guests) dish on the week's big beer happenings across the country—and there are quite a few in an industry with some 4,000 individual companies. Carton and Holl also perform a blind tasting on a different beer each week and analyze it on the air.

Tales from the Cask

Where "Strange Brews" is firmly rooted in Chicagoland, "Tales from the Cask" has a distinctive North Carolina accent. Hosts Jennifer Balik, Tony Walldroff, and Chip Mims work at the Raleigh-based wholesaler, Mims Distributing Company. (Chip's the CEO of his family company, Balik's the brand development manager, and Walldroff's the craft and import manager.) The team kicked off the award-winning weekly podcast—it took the silver in the podcast category the same year "Strange Brews" won the gold—in 2013 and have welcomed guests ranging from Boston Beer Company's Jim Koch and Sierra Nevada's Brian Grossman to copyright attorneys talking about trademark issues to the distribution pros who clean the draft lines at bars. Working out of a renowned distributorship—*Beverage World* magazine named it Beer Distributor of the Year in 2015—gives the podcasters and enviable level of access to all facets of the beer business.

28

Kitchen Creations

Homebrewing Goes Mainstream

Homebrewing

S imply calling homebrewing a hobby does it a disservice. In the past three and a half decades or so, it has evolved to a level of sophistication that rivals some commercial operations.

The American Homebrewers Association (AHA), founded in 1978—operated as a division of the Brewers Association—now boasts a membership roster 43,000 names long. But even that number is a bit small considering how many Americans brew their own beer. At AHA's last count, there were 1.5 million people taking the brew-your-own route.

That's pretty impressive, considering the fact that homebrewing hasn't even been legal all that long. When the Twenty-first Amendment repealed Prohibition in 1933, it not only legalized the production, sale, and distribution of alcoholic beverages again, but it allowed for home wine making. However, it made no such allowances for those who might want to produce their own beer. It was quite an oversight and one that wouldn't be addressed and rectified for another forty-five years.

In 1978, then President Jimmy Carter signed H.R. 1337, a bill sponsored by Senator Alan Cranston of California, which created an exemption from taxation for beer brewed for personal or family use and effectively legalized homebrewing on a federal level. Of course, it was up to the individual states, as well, since the Twenty-first Amendment gave them authority to regulate alcohol. It took a while to get all fifty states on board. Alabama and Mississippi were the last hold outs, but both finally made homebrewing legal some eighty years after the repeal of Prohibition. When Mississippi's law took effect on July 1, 2013, it marked the first day since Prohibition that the entire country allowed homebrewing at the state level.

Much has changed since that ragtag band of hobbyists finally got to flex their creative muscles in the clear light of day after hiding for so long in the shadows. (Okay, maybe things weren't that dramatic pre-legality, but what's wrong with a little fanciful romance every now and again?)

Aside from an exponential increase in the number of individuals engaging in the hobby, there are far fewer hurdles to jump over to join in the fun. For one thing, it's a lot easier to get supplies. Most major metro areas have at least one, if not multiple, brick-and-mortar homebrew supply shops dealing in all of the necessary equipment and raw materials to make a decent beer. And those not fortunate enough to live close to such an establishment will encounter an embarrassment of riches when they Google "online homebrew shops."

"Any true barriers have been obliterated because of the availability of equipment, ingredients, and information," says Beer Judge Certification Program president Gordon Strong, who's written several books on homebrewing. "That's kind of the trifecta of easy access into the hobby. Anyone who wants to brew can brew right away and there are so many other people doing it."

The Internet hasn't just made it easier for homebrewers to find all of the necessary supplies; it's simplified the process of finding each other. Especially in less populous areas, it was largely a solitary activity. The early adopters would have to wait for national and regional homebrew conferences to meet likeminded individuals and actually talk on the telephone in the interim.

But this isn't devolving into a "Kids today have it so easy"-style rant. The reality is actually quite the contrary. For one thing, homebrewing is such a mature hobby that the game has seriously been upped.

Many supposed amateurs often are quite far from it. Much of what the upper echelons of the homebrewing subculture produce is often superior to some of the stuff that's commercially available.

Back in the day there was a lot of, "Wow, you made your own beer!" These days it's more, "Which hop varieties did you use? Did they grow in the Yakima Valley?" or "There's a pronounced astringency with this brew," and "Hmm, I'm detecting some diacetyl in this batch."

It's a much tougher crowd.

However, it's also much more supportive crowd. As daunting as it may be for a newbie to brew his or her first batch when the vast majority of DIY-ers are far more advanced and can brew circles around all who enter, there's

The American Homebrewers Association (AHA) always draws a crowd at GABF.

a massive support structure from which to draw. If the novice runs into problems early on, a solution is just a tweet, Facebook status update, or a Skype or message board post away.

Homebrewers' motivations may have shifted a bit in the past decade and a half or so. While it's always been about passion for beer and the joy of creation, in the early days some got into homebrewing because of the absence of better options available.

Some of the greatest commercial breweries in the modern era got their start when there weren't better options for its founders to drink. A classic case is Steve Hindy, cofounder of the Brooklyn Brewery. As a foreign correspondent for the Associated Press for five and a half years in the Middle East, Islamic law pretty much rendered any and all alcohol drinking options nonexistent. Some American envoys in Saudi Arabia had grown accustomed to brewing their own beer, a skill they happily shared with Hindy. When he returned to the states, he started brewing at his home in Brooklyn.

"People start looking to do things themselves when they don't have good alternatives," Strong notes.

Four thousand commercial breweries later, it goes without saying that that is hardly the case anymore. It's almost entirely about passion these days.

So, how does a complete brewing virgin make that first step into the hobby?

A better question would be, are you starting with malt extract, a partial mash, or are you jumping in with both feet and brewing with an all-grain recipe? The first option is definitely the more beginner-friendly of the options. For starters, it requires the smallest initial equipment investment. When it's in extract form, the sugars already have been pulled from the grains and they're more concentrated. Extract takes up a lot less space than whole grains and there's no need for the mechanisms to mash down those grains (which means it's less time-consuming, as well). In addition to a fermenting vessel that's impervious to oxygen—known as a carboy—all you really need for a rudimentary extract brew is a pot that's big enough—say, twenty quarts—for boiling water.

But perhaps more critical than the lower equipment outlay with extract brewing, the screw-up factor is greatly diminished as well. Since the fermentable sugars are already there, there's far less chance of error in the process of extracting them from the grain.

However, despite the lower infrastructure investment, the long-term cost of extract brewing may be greater if it's something the new brewer intends to do a lot, as extract is pricier than grain. There's also something less "hands-on" about making an all-extract beer. With all-grain, you virtually own the entire process, from mashing to bottling.

The middle-ground, of course, is the partial-grain route, which kind of gives the user the best of both worlds, combining extract with grain. It's good as a bridge. Absolute beginners might brew a few all-extract batches, transition to partial grain for a handful more, and then finally graduate to all-malt. And graduating doesn't mean brewing all-malt exclusively. A homebrewer can always go back to extract from time to time, depending on immediate needs and desires.

"It used to be people would brew extract beers for a few years before making the jump to all-grain," Strong observes. "Now I see people switch to all-grain directly."

Strong's advice: Why not brew with a more experienced hobbyist before cutting the cord? "If you haven't brewed before or haven't brewed for a while, you may not know what you want to do. That might be where a good homebrew club comes in handy. Get a flavor for that before you buy a bunch of your own stuff. It kind of helps if you don't waste a lot of money on equipment that you're going to change right away."

Brew on Premises

Anyone with any level of practical brewing experience will tell you that the most critical and labor-intensive part of the process is cleaning. Beer requires a sterile environment; otherwise its susceptible to all sorts of infections from unwelcome microorganisms that have no qualms about ruining your beer. That was one of the main draws of the brew-on-premises concepts that emerged during the '90s—originally in Canada to avoid high taxes on beer (from which brew-on-premises beer was exempt). Such establishments house all of the brewing equipment, all of the ingredients, and all of the bottles. All that a prospective brewer needs to do is show up. And it's okay if the beginner doesn't have a personal recipe in tow, as brew-on-premises establishments usually have loose-leaf binders packed with recipes based on just about any style.

And the best part, there's nothing to scrub when you're doing making the beer. It goes right into the fermenting vessels and you come back in about two weeks to bottle it; a bit longer if it's a lager.

Sounds great, right? Not so fast. The number of homebrewers and commercial breweries may have exploded in just the past decade or so, but the number of brew-on-premises businesses has not.

Much like the craft brewing movement itself, there was a wave of enthusiasm in the mid-'90s that dissipated before the end of the decade. But the momentum has yet to return for brew on premises like it has for craft beer overall. There are still a handful of new ones opening here and there, but there still aren't enough of them across the country to make it a viable option for most homebrewers (unless they want to travel and make a couple of weekends out of it). Homebrewers sans equipment have a better chance of cozying up to their local commercial brewers and seeing if they'll let them use their brewhouse (still not very likely, as they'd be hard-pressed to find brewing operations with capacity to spare).

Still, if you're fortunate enough to live within a two-hour's drive of a brew-on-premises, it's worth the trip. Staff members are usually well versed in the brewing process—they're typically seasoned homebrewers themselves—and do a lot of the handholding that novices require.

Of course, you're going to pay for the privilege, usually more for a single batch than you would for a basic homebrew kit. However, a batch will yield a good six-plus cases of beer (usually twelve 22-ounce bomber bottles per case). If you did the math, it ends up being about one-third to one-half of what you'd spend on the same quantity of a store-bought beer produced by your friendly neighborhood craft brewer. So, in purely consumer-oriented economic terms it makes good financial sense. However, it's not about the money anyway. You get to take home about seventy-two individual holiday gifts for the difficult-to-buy-for folks on your list. Stick a bow on it, and your shopping is done!

The Oscars of Homebrewing

The National Homebrew Competition, awarded at the American Homebrewers Association's annual National Homebrewers Conference, is about as big as it gets for avid homebrewers. The competition, launched in 1979, is easily the largest international beer competition awarding the efforts of brewing hobbyists. Each year judges evaluate around 8,000 beers, meads, and ciders from around the world. That's narrowed down to three winners in each of twenty-eight overall style categories. There are also a range of major non-category-specific awards, including Homebrewer of the Year, Meadmaker of the Year, Cidermaker of the Year, and Homebrew Club of the Year.

Where Pro Meets Am

It's the dream of virtually every homebrewer to go pro—and the ones who say it isn't are very likely lying. But not everyone can, of course. (There may not be a bubble now, but it doesn't take an economics prodigy to determine that the market can't sustain 1.2 million commercial breweries.) But there are plenty of fantasy-fulfilling bridges between the extremes of amateur and professional. Among those is the Great American Beer Festival's annual Pro-Am Competition.

A commercial brewery teams up with a homebrewer—the brewery must be a Brewers Association member, and the amateur must be up to date on his or her American Homebrewers Association (AHA) dues—to brew a batch based on the homebrewer's recipe. The catch is the homebrewer must already be an award-winner, having picked up a medal in a competition that's sanctioned by AHA and the Beer Judge Certification Program (BJCP).

The same panel of judges who decide the fate of the thousands of entries in the GABF's professional competition also judge the Pro-Am entries. GABF attendees get to sample the entries—usually numbering in the neighborhood of one-hundred—at the Pro-Am booth during the regular tasting sessions.

Homebrew Nation

The American Homebrewers Association offers a few stats that illustrate the state of DIY brewing in the United States.

- Two-thirds of the nation's 1.2 million homebrewers adopted the hobby in 2005 or later.
- The average age of a homebrewer is forty, with 60 percent ranging in age from thirty to forty-nine. (If it were a TV show, this would be considered a "key demographic.")
- Homebrewers aren't so obsessed with their hobby that they're impossible to live with; 78 percent of them are married or in a domestic partnership.
- They're a fairly learned bunch, as well; 69 percent have a college degree or some form of higher education
- And they've got the money to support the hobby: Nearly 60 percent have household incomes of $75,000 or more.
- Homebrewers are spread across all US time zones, though the stats understandably skew slightly toward the West, where craft brewing really got its start. Thirty-one percent of homebrewers live in the West, 23 percent live in the Midwest, 26 percent live in the South, and 17 percent live in the Northeast.
- Collectively, homebrewers produce more than 2 million barrels a year. For a little perspective on that number, it's about twice the annual output of a brewery the size of Sierra Nevada or about two-thirds of what a brewery the size of Boston Beer/Sam Adams is making a year. It's about one percent of the overall beer volume in the US.
- They also support their local economies whenever they can. Ninety-five percent of them shop in two local homebrew stores eight or nine times a year. Eighty percent also shop in three online stores five times a year.

Source: American Homebrewers Association

Epilogue
The Journey Is Just Beginning

The tagline of this book is "All That's Left to Know About the World's Most Celebrated Adult Beverage." But it's hardly "all" or even "most." There is no such thing as the definitive *work* on the subject. It's more like a definitive *library*. Entire volumes have been written on each of the chapters explored/questions answered—and even on single paragraphs within those chapters. The fact is, there's plenty left to learn about beer, and if this book has done its job, your interest is piqued and you're ready to continue the journey and learn more of what's left to know about this mesmerizingly romantic beverage that unites disparate peoples, continents, and cultures. At the very least, you'll never look at the contents of your bottle, can, or pint glass quite the same way again.

Speaking of which, cheers!

Bibliography

Acitelli, Tom. "Before the Panic Over 10 Barrel, There Was 'BudHook,'" *All About Beer*, November 7, 2014. http://allaboutbeer.com/redhook -brewery-anheuser-busch/

Acitelli, Tom. "What Price Distribution," February 13, 2013, http://www .tomacitelli.com.

Agnew, Michael. "A Brief History of Hops in Beer," A Perfect Pint, accessed May 2015, http://www.aperfectpint.net/hops.pdf.

"Altbier." German Beer Institute, accessed on August 27, 2015, http://www. germanbeerinstitute.com.

Annese, Sarah. "Shandies and Radlers," *All About Beer Magazine*, August 14, 2015.

"Back to base-ics," The Beer Files, October 9, 2012, http://www.thebeerfiles. com/back-to-base-ics/

Balik, Jennifer. Personal interview, September 26, 2015.

"Beer." Thomas Jefferson's Monticello, accessed June 2015, http://www. monticello.org.

"Beer Can History." Brewery Collectibles Club of America, accessed June 2015, http://www.bcca.com.

"Beer Cocktail: Snakebite," The Mash, August 3, 2011, http://www.brooklyn brewshop.com.

Belson, Ken. "1,386 Bottles of Beer on the Web," *New York Times*, May 14, 2008, http://nytimes.com.

Benácek, Karel. Phone interview, September 21, 2015.

Berman, Ruth. Phone interview, September 19, 2015.

Brand, William. "Thanksgiving Update: Pilgrims Stopping for Beer Is a Falsehood, Historian Bob Skilnik Says," *Inside Bay Area*, November 23, 2007, ibabuzz.com.

"Craft Brewer Defined," Brewers Association, accessed on May 31, 2015, http://www.brewersassociation.org.

"Number of Breweries," Brewers Association, accessed June 2015, http:// www.brewersassociation.org.

Calagione, Sam. *Brewing Up a Business: Adventures in Entrepreneurship from the Founder of Dogfish Head Craft Brewery*. Hoboken, NJ: John Wiley, 2005.

"Captain Beefheart Beer." Captain Beefheart Radar Station, accessed June 2015, http://www.beefheart.com,

Clarke, Chris. Personal interview. September 26, 2015.

Colby, Chris. "German Wheat Beer: II (Grains)." *Beer and Wine Journal*, September 5, 2015, http://www.beerandwinejournal.com.

Cowan, Jeremy and James Sullivan, *Craft Beer Mar Mitzvah: How It Took 13 Years, Extreme Jewish Brewing and Circus Sideshow Freaks to Make Shmaltz Brewing an International Success.* New York: Malt Shop Publishing, 2010.

Cowan, Jeremy. Personal interview. September 25, 2015.

"A Craft Beer Journey Through Chile," Cascada Expeditions, August 2, 2013, http://www.cascada.travel.

Cunningham, Benjamin. "Where a Budweiser Isn't Allowed to Be a Budweiser," *Time*, January 27, 2014, http://www.business.time.com.

Daniels, Ray. *The Brewers Association's Guide to Starting Your Own Brewery.* Boulder, Colorado: Brewers Publications, 2006.

Daniels, Ray. Personal interview. July 23, 2015.

"Dortmunder," German Beer Institute, accessed on August 26, 2015, http://www.germanbeerinstitute.com.

"Ever Wonder What the Difference Is Between Ale vs. Lager Yeast?" *Biochemistry, Molecular, Cellular & Developmental Biology*, October 22, 2014, http://www.bmcd.wordpress.com.

"Dry Hopping: Why Adding Dry Pellets Directly to the Fermenter Gets More Hope Flavour," Home Brew Manual, accessed June 2015, http://www.homebrewmanual.com.

Eckhardt, Fred. "Lager Beer vs. Ale Beer—Does It Matter?" *All About Beer Magazine*, November 1, 2008, http://www.allaboutbeer.com.

"50th Anniversary of the Aluminum Can," Miller Coors, January 22, 2009, http://www.millercoors.com.

"Finland Bans Alcohol Branded Social Media Communication in 2015," European Centre for Monitoring Alcohol Marketing, February 27, 2014, http://www.eucam.info.

Fowle, Zach. "Wals Ipe & Sao Francisco: What Makes Brazil Winners Still," *Phoenix New Times*, July 14, 2014, http://www.phoenixnewtimes.com/restaurants/wals-ipe-and-sao-francisco-what-makes-brazil-winners-still-6524901.

Furnari, Chris. "Harpoon to Boost Distribution Beyond Own Brands," Brew Bound, February 27, 2015, http://www.brewbound.com.

Gatza, Paul. Presentation, Craft Brewers Conference 2015, Portland, Oregon, April 15, 2015.

George, Anita. "10 Great Beer Cocktails," *Paste*, June 12, 2013, http://www
.pastemagazine.com.

"George Washington Entered the Whiskey Business in 1797—and It Was
Quite the Profitable Success." George Washington's Mount Vernon,
accessed June 2015, http://www.mountvernon.org.

"George Washington to William Pearce, 22 December 1793," *The Writings of
George Washington* Vol. 33: 201. http://www.mountvernon.org.

Gill, Nicholas. "Chile's New Craft," *Draft Magazine*, March 20, 2013, http://
www.draftmag.com.

Hall, Joshua. "South Korea's Craft Beer Makers Cheer New Rules, But
Worries Lurk," *The Wall Street Journal*, Dec 26, 2014, http://www.blogs.
wsj.com/korearealtime.

Hartis, Daniel. "Homebrewing Without a Home," *All About Beer Magazine*,
July 3, 2015, http://www.allaboutbeer.com.

Haynes, Brad and Luciana Bruno. "AB InBev Unit Ambev Buys Brazilian
Craft Brewer Colorado," *Reuters*, July 7, 2015. http://www.reuters.com/
article/us-ab-inbev-brazil-ambev-idUSKCN0PH1SZ20150707.

"Helles," German Beer Institute, accessed August 26, 2015, http://www
.germanbeerinstitute.com.

Hindy, Steve. *The Craft Beer Revolution: How a Band of Microbrewers Is
Transforming the World's Favorite Drink*. New York: St. Martin's Press, 2014.

Hindy, Steve. "Free Craft Beer!" *The New York Times*, March 29, 2014.

Holl, John. *The American Craft Beer Cookbook: 155 Recipes from Your Favorite
Brewpubs and Breweries*. New York: Storey Publishing, 2013.

Holl, John. "Sweden Rising: Beer Culture Booms in Scandinavian Country,"
All About Beer Magazine, November 2014.

Hsu, Tiffany. "EU Court Gives Bud Beer Name to AB InBev over Budejovicky
Budvar," *Los Angeles Times*, January 22, 2013, http://www.latimes.com.

Institute of Distilling and Brewing. Accessed June 10, 2015, http://www.ibd.
org.uk.

Jacobs, Frank. "Distilled Geography: Europe's Alcohol Belts," Big Think,
accessed on August 30, 2015, http://www.bigthink.com/strange
-maps/442-distilled-geography-europes-alcohol-belts.

Johnson, Ben. "Zwanze Day is Coming to Toronto," Ben's Beer Blog, August
27, 2013, http://www.bensbeerblog.com.

Johnson, Julie. "Fantastic Finland: Foam in the Far North," *All About Beer
Magazine*, March 1, 2002, http://www.allaboutbeer.com.

Kellerman, Aliza. "Where the Hell the Saké Bomb Came From: A Lesson in
Irony," VinePair, May 15, 2015, http://www.vinepair.com.

Lindsey, Bill. "Bottle Typing: Beer & Ale Bottles." Society for Historical Archaeology, accessed May 2015, http://www.sha.org/bottle/beer.htm.

Lord, Victoria. "The Story of American Breweries," The Ultimate History Project, accessed July 2015, http://www.ultimatehistoryproject.com.

Mastny, Steve. "Lager Yeast: What's in a Name?" BeerDownload, March 14, 2014, http://www.beerdownload.com.

Mori, Cliff. "What's the Difference Between an Ale and a Lager?" BREW-ed, Oct 28, 2013, http://www.brew-ed.com.

"Munich Malt." Homebrew Talk, accessed on July 14, 2015, http://www.homebrewtalk.com.

Mosher, Randy. *Tasting Beer: An Insider's Guide to the World's Greatest Drink.* New York: Storey Publishing, 2009.

Mueller, Angela. "Anheuser-Busch Loses Trademark Battle in Portugal." *St. Louis Business Journal,* June 30, 2014, http://www.bizjournals.com/stlouis.

Nason, Adam. "August Schell Brewing to BA in Response to 'Craft vs. Crafty:' Shame on You," BeerPulse, December 14, 2012, http://www.beerpulse.com.

Nelson, Max. *The Barbarian's Beverage: A History of Beer in Ancient Europe,* London and New York: Routledge, 2005.

Nielsen, Per Sten. Phone interview, September 2, 2015.

Ogden, Paul. "The Kings Arms Wins the CityLife Award for Best Pub," *Manchester Evening News,* January 8, 2015, http://www.manchestereveningnews.co.uk.

Ogle, Maureen. *Ambitious Brew: The Story of American Beer,* Boston: Harcourt, 2006.

Oliver, Garrett. *The Brewmaster's Table: Discovering the Pleasures of Real Beer with Real Food.* New York: Ecco Press, 2003.

Papazian, Charlie. "Beer Franchise Law Reform," *The New Brewer Magazine,* July/August 2014. http://www.brewersassociation.org/news/beer-franchise-law-reform/.

Papazian, Charlie. "BeerCity USA Poll Retires, Served Its Purpose," Examiner, March 11, 2014, http://www.examiner.com.

Rapoza, Kenneth. "In Patagonia, Argentina's Beer Biz Keeps Hopping," *Forbes,* February 21, 2015, http://www.forbes.com.

Rice, Christopher. Personal interview. June 16, 2015

Patrick, Brian. "Specialty Malt," Craft Beer Academy, March 6, 2013, http://www.craftbeeracademy.com.

"Pils." German Beer Institute, accessed on September 18, 2015, http://www.germanbeerinstitute.com.

Rousek, Leos. "InBev Buys Brewery Where Budweiser Name Began," *Wall Street Journal*, July 2 2014, http://www.wsj.com.

Rutkowski, Matthew. Personal interview, September 26, 2015.

"Say What? Says Who? Benjamin Franklin or Beer—or Not." Anchor Brewing Co., February 29, 2012, http://www.anchorbrewing.com.

Siebel Institute. Accessed June 10, 1015, http://www.siebelinstitute.org.

Soniak, Matt. "How Did Pabst Blue Ribbon Win its Blue Ribbon?" Mental Floss, April 1, 2013, http://www.mentalfloss.com.

Strong, Gordon. Phone interview, August 18, 2015.

"Summer Hoedown." Chowhound, Aug 14, 2015, http://www.chowhound.com.

Szot, Kevin. E-mail interview, September 7, 2015.

"Tenanted and Managed Pubs," This Is Money, April 18, 2008, http://www.thisismoney.co.uk

UC Davis Extension. Accessed June 10, 2015, http://www.extension.ucdavis.edu/areas-study/brewing

"U.S. Beer Weeks," The Brewers Association, accessed on September 16, 2015, http://www.craftbeer.com

Wagner, Brock. Personal interview, September 26, 2015.

Walldroff, Tony. Personal interview, September 26, 2015.

Whistler, Randy. "Specialty Grains: Caramel and Roasted Malts," *Brew Your Own*, October 1997, http://www.byo.com.

"Zwanze Day 2015 Locations." BeerAdvocate, July 29, 2015, http://www.beeradvocate.com.

Other Websites and Resources

Abbaye-rochefort.be

Anderson Valley Brewing, avbc.com

Archipelagobrewery.com

AveryBrewing.com

BeerAdvocate.com

BeerInstitute.org

BelgianFamilyBrewers.be

BellsBeer.com

Bodebrown.com.br

BostonBeer.com

Boulevard.com

Brewerkz.com

BrewersAssociation.org

BrooklynBrewery.com

BrookstonBeerBulletin.com

Brugghús.is

Budweiser.com

Budvar.cz

Cantillon.com

CartonBrewing.com

Cerveceradelpuerto.cl

CervejariaJupiter.com.br

CerverjariaLandel.com.br

CervejariaSeasons.com.br

CervezaBlest.com

Cicerone.org

CigarCityBrewing.com

CityTavern.com

CoedoBrewery.com

CraftBeer.com

Czech-Beer-Tours.eu

Delirium.be

DeschutesBrewery.com

DogfishBeer.com

DosEquis.com

Duvel.com

Einstokbeer.com

FirestoneBeer.com

FunkWerks.com

GoldenRoad.la

HarpoonBrewery.com

Heineken.com

HillFarmsteadBrewery.com

JesterKingBrewery.com

Kiuchi Brewery, Kodawari.cc

Lakefrontbrewery.com

Leffe.com

LeftHandBrewing.com

Level33.com.sg

LostAbbey.com

Mikkeller.dk

Minoh-Beer.jp

National Beer Wholesalers
    Association: NBWA.org

NewBelgium.com

NinkasiBrewing.com

Nogne-o.com

Norrebrobryghus.dk

Nyäshamns Angbryggeri, nyab.se

OdellBrewing.com

Omervanderghinste.be

Ommegang.com

Omnipollo.com

Orval.be

PabstBlueRibbon.com

PilsnerUrquell.com

RateBeer.com

ReddotBrewehouse.com.sg

Rogue.com

SaintArnold.com

Schloss-Eggenberg.at

Shmaltz.com

ShortsBrewing.com

SierraNevada.com

SintBernardus.be

SoriBrewing.com

StSixtus.be

Szot.cl

Tamamura-Honten.co.jp

TheBruery.com

Trappists.org

TrappistWestmalle.be

21stAmendmentBrewery.com

TwoRoadsBrewing.com

UintaBrewing.com

YoHoBrewing.com

Index

THE FAQ SERIES

Prices, contents, and availability subject to change without notice.